DOMESDAY ENGLAND

Lower portion of right-hand column of folio 190 of Domesday Book (same size as original). For extension and translation, see p. 372.

DOMESDAY ENGLAND

BY

H. C. DARBY

CAMBRIDGE UNIVERSITY PRESS

CAMBRIDGE

LONDON · NEW YORK · MELBOURNE

Published by the Syndics of the Cambridge University Press
The Pitt Building, Trumpington Street, Cambridge CB2 1RP
Bentley House, 200 Euston Road, London NW1 2DB
32 East 57th Street, New York, NY 10022, USA
296 Beaconsfield Parade, Middle Park, Melbourne 3206, Australia

First published 1977
Reprinted 1979

First printed in Great Britain at the
University Printing House, Cambridge.

Reprinted and bound in Great Britain by
Redwood Burn Limited
Trowbridge & Esher

Library of Congress Cataloguing in Publication Data
Darby, Henry Clifford, 1909–
Domesday England
(The Domesday geography of England)
Includes bibliographies and index.
1. Domesday book.   2. England – Historical
geography.   I. Title.   II. Series.
DA610.D23   911'.42   76–11485
ISBN 0 521 21307 X

TO E.C.D.

CONTENTS

PREFACE

Domesday Book is the most famous English public record, and it is probably the most remarkable statistical document in the history of Europe. It calls itself merely a *descriptio*, and it acquired its name in the following century because its authority seemed comparable to that of the Book by which one day all will be judged (*Revelation* 20:12). We cannot be surprised that so many scholars have felt its fascination, and have discussed again and again what it says about economic, social and legal matters. But it also tells us much about the countryside of the eleventh century, and the present volume is the seventh of a series concerned with this geographical information. As the final volume, it seeks to sum up the main features of the Domesday geography of England as a whole.

Some of the remarks that might appropriately be made here appear in Appendix 21, which consists of an informal essay entitled 'On the writing of Domesday Geography'. I would like now, however, to thank the Syndics and staff of the Cambridge University Press for their forbearance and skill. I must also thank Mr G. R. Versey who has not only drawn all the maps but who has given a very great deal of assistance at all stages of the work. The volume is inscribed to my wife, who made it possible.

H. C. DARBY

King's College,
Cambridge,
7 February 1976

LIST OF MAPS

LIST OF ABBREVIATIONS

Beds.	Bedfordshire	I.C.C.	*Inquisitio Comitatus*
Berks.	Berkshire		*Cantabrigiensis*
Bucks.	Buckinghamshire	I.E.	*Inquisitio Eliensis*
Cambs.	Cambridgeshire	Lancs.	Lancashire
Ches.	Cheshire	Leics.	Leicestershire
Corn.	Cornwall	Lincs.	Lincolnshire
D.B.	Domesday Book	L.D.B.	Little Domesday Book
Derby.	Derbyshire	Mdlx.	Middlesex
Devon	Devonshire	Norf.	Norfolk
D.G.	Domesday Gazetteer	N'hants.	Northamptonshire
D.G.E.E.	The Domesday	N.R.	North Riding of York-
	Geography of Eastern		shire
	England	Notts.	Nottinghamshire
D.G.M.E.	The Domesday	Oxon.	Oxfordshire
	Geography of Midland	Ru.	Rutland
	England	Salop.	Shropshire
D.G.N.E.	The Domesday	Som.	Somerset
	Geography of Northern	Staffs.	Staffordshire
	England	Suff.	Suffolk
D.G.S–E.E.	The Domesday	Sy.	Surrey
	Geography of	Sx.	Sussex
	South-east England	T.R.E.	*Tempore Regis Edwardi*
D.G.S–W.E.	The Domesday		(i.e. 1066)
	Geography of	T.R.V.	*Tempore Reginae*
	South-west England		*Victoriae* (i.e. 19th
Do.	Dorset		century.)
E.R.	East Riding of Yorkshire	T.R.W.	*Tempore Regis*
Ess.	Essex		*Willelmi* (i.e. 1086)
Exch. D.B.	Exchequer Domesday	Unid.	Unidentified
	Book	*V.C.H.*	The Victoria History of
Exon. D.B.	Exeter Domesday Book		the Counties of
Gloucs.	Gloucestershire		England
Hants.	Hampshire	Warw.	Warwickshire
hd	hundred	W.R.	West Riding of York-
Heref.	Herefordshire		shire
Herts.	Hertfordshire	Wilts.	Wiltshire
Hunts.	Huntingdonshire	Worcs.	Worcestershire
		Yorks.	Yorkshire

Folio references to D.B. are normally given in brackets after a place-name. References for Essex, Norfolk and Suffolk are to the L.D.B., and those in italics are to the Exon. D.B. References to the I.C.C. and I.E. are to the pages of the edition by N. E. S. A. Hamilton – *Inquisitio comitatus Cantabrigiensis...subjicitur Inquisitio Eliensis* (London, 1876).

CHAPTER I

THE DOMESDAY INQUEST

The Norman Conquest in 1066, unlike the Anglo-Saxon and Scandinavian invasions, was not a mass movement of people but the work of a small power group. Twenty years after their coming, the Normans instituted the enquiry that resulted in Domesday Book. With hindsight we can say that it came at a fortunate moment for us because it enables us to examine the economic and social foundations of the geography of England after the Anglo-Saxons and Scandinavians had firmly established themselves in their new home.

THE ANGLO-SCANDINAVIAN BACKGROUND

The Anglo-Saxons had arrived in the fifth and sixth centuries, and the Scandinavians in the eighth and ninth – Danes from the east and Norse by way of the western seas. Whatever the continuity between Roman Britain and Anglo-Scandinavian England – and it was certainly much greater than was at one time believed – the fact remains that, Cornwall apart, the villages the Normans encountered bore names that were certainly not Celtic. Where the Englishman Babba had made a 'stoc' or settlement in Wiltshire, there stood *Babestoche* in 1066 which is Baverstock today; and where the Scandinavian Bekki had made a 'by' or settlement in Lincolnshire, there stood *Bechebi* which is Bigby today. The progress of settlement must have been interrupted, time and again, by the mutual struggles of the Anglo-Saxon states, and by the campaigns of the Anglo-Danish conflict; but, even so, large stretches of countryside were colonised and transformed, and the woodland was pierced by 'dens' and 'leahs' and 'skogrs' until there were well over 13,000 vills in existence. By merely recording the names of these places, Domesday Book provides an enormous amount of information about the land and its history, but this is only a small part of what Domesday entry after entry tells us about the economy of the land and about the achievement of the two dozen or so generations of people who had lived on it since the Roman legions departed.

Their achievement was not only economic but also political. The land that William took over already possessed a highly developed territorial organisation. It was divided into shires, and these were divided into hundreds or wapentakes, and these, in turn, comprised vills. The Inquest itself, and the Book that resulted from it, was organised on the basis of the shires, or, to use the Norman word, of counties. Lancashire, it is true, did not appear under that name until towards the end of the twelfth century; the vills to the north of the Ribble were named in the folios for Yorkshire, and the southern part was described in a kind of appendix to the account of Cheshire, under the heading *Inter Ripam et Mersham*. Rutland likewise did not appear as a county until the thirteenth century. Its eastern part was in Domesday Northamptonshire, and its western part formed an anomalous unit, called *Roteland*, which was described at the end of the Nottinghamshire folios. There have also been other less important changes in the inter-county boundaries, e.g. portions of the Domesday counties of Gloucester, Warwick and Worcester were intermingled in a strange manner that reflected the scattered holdings of the bishop of Worcester.[1] Beyond Domesday England, that is beyond the Tees, the four northern counties were in the nature of border provinces, and 'it is probable that responsibility for their internal order, as for their defence, rested with the great lords of the country'.[2]

Counties were divided into smaller units called 'hundreds'. These had appeared as units of local government in the tenth century, and they provided the basis for the administration of justice and public finance.[3] In theory they were districts assessed for the purposes of taxation at 100 hides (i.e. units of assessment for tax), but there were many exceptions to this correspondence, and the assessment of different Domesday hundreds ranged from under 20 to over 150 hides. The place of the hundred was taken by the wapentake in the highly Scandinavianised counties of Derby, Leicester, Lincoln, Nottingham and *Roteland*, and in the North and West Ridings of Yorkshire, but not in the East Riding. The word is of Scandinavian origin, and 'denoted the symbolical flourishing of weapons

---

[1] C. S. Taylor, 'The origin of the Mercian shires', *Trans. Bristol and Gloucs. Archaeol. Soc.* XXI (Bristol, 1898), 32–57. Reprinted in a modified form in H. P. R. Finberg (ed.), *Gloucestershire studies* (Leicester, 1957), 17–51. See also map in *D.G.M.E.*, 2.

[2] F. M. Stenton, *Anglo-Saxon England* (Oxford, 1943), 496.

[3] O. S. Anderson, 'On the origin of the hundredal division', being pp. 209–17 of *The English hundred names: the south-eastern counties* (Lund, 1939). See also F. M. Stenton (1943), 295–8.

by which a public assembly confirmed its decisions'.[1] The earliest record of an extension of its meaning, to cover the district of an assembly, dates from 962. Its use in this sense seems to have been an innovation, 'for no divisions so named are known from Scandinavia'.[2] Functionally, the wapentake was the same as the hundred, and the terms were used interchangeably, twice in the Domesday folios for Northamptonshire (*Optongren*, 222b–227; Witchley, 219–228), and once in those for Yorkshire (*Toreshou*, 307, 373).

Other territorial units are also named in Domesday Book. Some were intermediate between those of the county and the hundred or wapentake. Thus Yorkshire was divided into three ridings (the Scandinavian word 'riding' implies a third part). There were also ridings in Lindsey, itself a third part of Lincolnshire; the other parts were those of Holland and Kesteven. Kent had 'lathes' and Sussex had 'rapes', which may have represented older divisions of those kingdoms.

Hundreds and wapentakes were composed of villages or vills, but alongside the physical reality of the vill was the institutional reality of the manor which features so prominently in the Domesday folios. Sometimes a vill coincided with a manor. Sometimes it contained two or more manors belonging to different lords. Sometimes vills themselves were components of a large manorial complex which their lord treated as one unit. Clearly, manors varied greatly in size. Important as the manor was in the social and legal organisation of the realm, the village itself was the feature prominent in the agrarian landscape.

THE MAKING OF DOMESDAY BOOK

The story of the making of the Domesday Inquest is told briefly in the Anglo-Saxon Chronicle under the year 1085. After discussion at a council held at Gloucester in mid-winter, King William sent his men into each shire to enquire in great detail about its resources and who held them; and, says the Chronicle, 'all the surveys (*gewrita*) were then brought to him'. A contemporary account by Robert Losinga, bishop of Hereford, who may have been present when the project was discussed, says that 'other investigators (*inquisitores*) followed the first; and men were sent into provinces which they did not know, and where they

---

[1] F. M. Stenton (1943), 497.
[2] O. S. Anderson, *The English hundred names* (Lund, 1934), xxi.

themselves were unknown, in order that they might be given the opportunity of checking the first description'.[1]

Interesting though these accounts are, they do not throw much light
upon the actual operation of compiling the original returns. There are,
however, other documents, besides Domesday Book, which must have
been composed from the original returns. It is true that these documents
are only fragments, but they are of supreme importance in Domesday
interpretation.[2] Among these subsidiary documents is the so-called
Exeter Domesday Book, covering Cornwall, Somerset, most of Devonshire, about one third of Dorset, and one manor in Wiltshire. F. H.
Baring, in 1912, showed that it was from this Exeter Domesday Book
that the relevant portions of the main Domesday Book were made.[3]
In the process of making it, much was omitted, e.g. details of livestock
such as sheep and swine. Obviously, any account that is nearer to
the original returns than Domesday Book itself must be of very special
interest.

Another of these subsidiary documents is the *Inquisitio Eliensis*, a
survey of the estates of the abbey of Ely in six eastern counties. It opens
with an explanatory paragraph which is usually thought to refer to the
operation of the Inquest.[4] The questions to be asked of each hundred were
as follows:

1   What is the name of the manor?
2   Who held it in the time of King Edward?
3   Who holds it now?
4   How many hides are there?
5   How many teams, in demesne and among the men?
6   How many villeins? How many cottars? How many slaves? How
      many freemen? How many sokemen?
7   How much wood? How much meadow? How much pasture? How
      many mills? How many fisheries?
8   How much has been added or taken away?
9   How much was the whole worth? How much is it worth now?
10   How much had or has each freeman or each sokeman? All this is to be

[1] W. H. Stevenson, 'A contemporary description of the Domesday Survey',
Eng. Hist. Rev. XXII (1907), 74.
[2] D. C. Douglas, 'The Domesday Survey', *History*, XXI (1936), 249–57.
[3] F. H. Baring, 'The Exeter Domesday', *Eng. Hist. Rev.*, XXVII (1912), 309–18.
See also R. Welldon I ...n, *Domesday Studies: The Liber Exoniensis* (London, 1964).
[4] N. E. S. A. Hamilton, *Inquisitio comitatus Cantabrigiensis ... subjicitur Inquisitio
Eliensis* (London, 1876), 97.

given in triplicate; that is in the time of King Edward, when King William gave it, and at the present time.

11   And whether more can be had than is had?

Whether these were the 'official instructions' for all counties, we cannot say, but they, or at any rate a similar set of questions, must also have been asked elsewhere. The *Inquisitio* tells us that the king's commissioners heard the evidence 'on the oath of the sheriff of the shire, and of the barons and of their Frenchmen, and of the whole hundred – priests, reeves and six villeins from each vill'. There was a separate jury for each hundred, consisting of eight men, whose function 'was apparently to approve and check the information variously assembled'.[1] J. H. Round showed that half the jurors were English and the other half Norman. 'Conquerors and conquered were alike bound by their common sworn verdicts.'[2] We cannot say whether the commissioners themselves attended every hundred court as Round suggested,[3] or whether, as Maitland thought, they merely held one session in the county town.[4] A number of entries make it clear that they sometimes heard conflicting evidence, and there are appendices dealing with disputes about ownership in several counties, e.g. Huntingdonshire (208), Lincolnshire (375–377b) and Yorkshire (373–374). It has been suggested 'that fiscal documents already in existence were drawn upon to help with the compilation of a partly feudal and partly fiscal enquiry'.[5] The making of the inquest may have been a far more complicated process than was at one time thought.

Whatever the exact procedure, it would seem that the commissioners conducted their operations on a geographical basis, county by county and hundred by hundred. It has been conjectured, and it is reasonable to suppose, that the counties were grouped into circuits visited by different teams of commissioners. There is no proof of this, but it is suggested by

[1] V. H. Galbraith, *The making of Domesday Book* (Oxford, 1961), 161.

[2] J. H. Round, *Feudal England* (London, 1895), 120.

[3] Ibid., 118–19.

[4] F. W. Maitland, *Domesday Book and beyond* (Cambridge, 1897), 11. See also V. H. Galbraith (1961), 155.

[5] S. P. J. Harvey, 'Domesday Book and Anglo-Norman governance', *Trans. Roy. Hist. Soc.*, 5th series, xxv (1975), 176. See also: (1) P. H. Sawyer, 'The "Original Returns" and Domesday Book', *Eng. Hist. Rev.* LXX (1955), 177–97; (2) S. P. J. Harvey, 'Domesday Book and its predecessors', *Eng. Hist. Rev.* LXXXVI (1971), 753–73.

common peculiarities among groups of counties and by differences in phraseology and in the arrangement of information. R. W. Eyton thought that there were nine circuits each marked by a similarity of language. Adolphus Ballard reduced them to seven.[2] Carl Stephenson thought that there were 'at least seven', but grouped the counties differently from Ballard (Fig. 1).[3] Within each of the seven circuits (if that is the right number), there were differences as between one county and another. We cannot believe, for example, that there were no markets in Sussex or Warwickshire, or no meadow in Shropshire, or only one church in Leicestershire. The commissioners for different circuits interpreted their remit in different ways; and within the circuits, the returns for different counties, and even for different hundreds, also display idiosyncrasies.

The word 'Domesday' does not occur in the Book itself. Richard fitz Nigel, the Treasurer of England, writing in the year 1179 or thereabouts, said: 'This book is called by the natives Domesday – that is, metaphorically speaking, the day of judgement. For as the sentence of that strict and terrible last account cannot be evaded by any skilful subterfuge, so when this book is appealed to on those matters which it contains, its sentence cannot be quashed or set aside with impunity.'[4] It may well have seemed comparable to the Book by which one day all will be judged (Revelation 20:12).

The method of the compilation of Domesday Book from the original returns has been a matter of much discussion. The older view was that the information was sent to the king's treasury at Winchester, and there summarised. But this view was challenged in 1942 by Professor V. H. Galbraith who produced a much more credible hypothesis.[5] He believed that local summaries were made for groups of counties (i.e. for the circuits); and that it was these, and not the 'original returns', which were submitted to Winchester for final assembly and editing. The Exeter Domesday Book, on this view, was the first draft of the local summary for the south-west, and it was abbreviated and edited by the Exchequer

[1] R. W. Eyton, 'Notes on Domesday', *Trans. Shropshire Archaeol. and Nat. Hist. Soc.*, I (1878), 99–118.

[2] A. Ballard, *The Domesday Inquest* (London, 1906), 12.

[3] C. Stephenson, 'Notes on the composition and interpretation of Domesday Book', *Speculum*, XXII (1947), 1–15.

[4] A. Hughes *et al.* (ed.), *Dialogus de Scaccario* (Oxford, 1902), 107–8.

[5] V. H. Galbraith, 'The making of Domesday Book', *Eng. Hist. Rev.*, LVIII (1943), 161–77. Elaborated in *The making of Domesday Book* (Oxford, 1961).

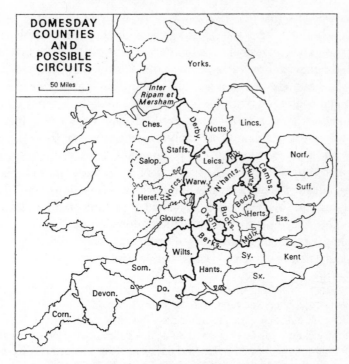

Fig. 1. Domesday counties and possible circuits.
The boundary with Wales is the western limit of named Domesday vills – see Fig. 108.
Huntingdonshire was in the northern circuit.

clerks to produce the main, or Exchequer, Domesday Book. One other local summary has survived – that for the eastern circuit; but, for one reason or another, it was never edited and converted into Exchequer form, and it became known as Little Domesday Book. The two volumes that make up Domesday Book – the Great or Exchequer Domesday and the Little Domesday – thus belong to different stages of the enquiry, and are very different from each other in format, script and scale. The length of time taken over the process of compilation, and the date of the Exchequer Domesday Book itself are also controversial matters. Some place it not long after King William's death in 1087; others place its final completion not before 1100.[1]

Whatever the stages of compilation, and however long they took,

[1] F. M. Stenton (1943), 647. D. C. Douglas, (1936), 255. See also D. C. Douglas, *The Domesday Monachorum of Christ Church Canterbury* (London, 1944), 23–41.

the fact remains that the result was very different from the original returns. The new form was more condensed, and, for example, much information about livestock was omitted. There was also a more fundamental difference. For each county, the information was rearranged under the headings of the main landholders, beginning with the king himself and continuing with the ecclesiastical lords, the bishops followed by the abbots, then with the great lay lords, and finally with the lesser landholders in descending order; only for Nottinghamshire do lay lords precede those of the church. The geographical basis of the return was thus replaced by a feudal basis. It follows that if two or more lords held land in a village, the different sets of information must be assembled from their respective folios in order to obtain a picture of the village as a whole. The village of Buckden in Huntingdonshire was held entirely by the bishop of Lincoln, and so is described in only one entry (203b) which happens to be a fairly representative one:

> In Buckden the bishop of Lincoln had 20 hides that paid geld. Land for 20 ploughteams. There, now on the demesne 5 ploughteams, and 37 villeins and 20 bordars having 14 ploughteams. There, a church and a priest and one mill yielding 30s (a year), and 84 acres of meadow. Wood for pannage one league long and one broad. In the time of King Edward (i.e. in 1066) it was worth £20 (a year), and now £16 10s.

The variety of detail in such entries as this falls into two categories. In the first place, there are those items that recur in almost every entry: hides (or other units of taxation), ploughlands, ploughteams, various categories of population, and annual values usually for 1066 and 1086 but sometimes also for an intermediate date. The second group comprises such items as the mill, meadow and wood entered for Buckden, and also, where relevant, pasture, salt-pans, fisheries, waste, vineyards and other resources. It is from these two groups of information that the geography of England in 1086, in all its regional diversity, can be reconstructed.

The repetitive uniformity of entry after entry is sometimes broken in curious and unexpected ways. Thus the account of the render of fish at Iver (149) in Buckinghamshire is elaborated to tell us that the fish was paid on Fridays for the use of the reeve of the vill (*pisces per dies veneris ad opus prepositi villae*). Or again, the only recorded inhabitant of Poston (252b) in Shropshire was a man who rendered a bundle of box on Palm Sunday (*fascis buxi in die palmarum*). The entry for the borough of

Nottingham (280) refers to a royal gift of ten acres to William Peverel for the making of an orchard (*ad faciendum pomerium*), the only mention of the word in Domesday Book. There is also a unique reference to a warren for hares (*warenna leporum*) at Gelston (347b) a few miles to the north of Grantham in Lincolnshire. Rabbits, incidentally, were unknown in Domesday England and were not introduced from France or possibly Spain until the next century. Another unusual, and unexpected, reference occurs in the account of the half-hide which Godric, the sheriff of Buckinghamshire in the time of King Edward, had given to 'Alwid the maid' on condition that she taught his daughter embroidery work (*ut illa docerat filiam ejus Aurifrifium operari*). Furthermore, in spite of the frequent record of slaves among the population, the veil is lifted only once in a reference to trade in slaves in the borough of Lewes (26) in Sussex. On a different note, the account of the resources of Wilcot (69) in Wiltshire goes out of its way to tell us of a new church, an excellent house and a good vineyard (*ecclesia nova, domus obtima et vinea bona*). Such are some of the unusual additions encountered in the regularity of the Domesday text.

THE ARTIFICIAL ASSESSMENTS

There are difficulties associated with each of the standard items in the Domesday entries. Ploughlands and annual values, for example, raise acute problems in some counties, and, what is more, the nature of the units of assessment for taxation is such that they throw no light upon the geographical realities of the time. Variations in the assessment for land tax or 'geld' might have provided most useful indications of the relative wealth of different areas, were it not for the fact that the assessment was essentially artificial in character. Its origins are very obscure, and both the tax and the machinery for its collection were already ancient when the Normans conquered England. There were four different methods of assessment; and they reflected the varying histories of different parts of the realm (Fig. 2).

In the south, in Wessex, Mercia, the southern Danelaw and Essex, the unit of assessment was the hide which comprised 4 virgates. We have no means of knowing how equitable the original assessment may have been, but by 1066 it was manifestly not so. Each county was responsible for a number of hides, and divided this among its constituent hundreds; these, in turn, apportioned their quotas among their vills and so among individual estates. The amounts were therefore imposed from above and not built up from below. It was while working on the Cambridgeshire returns that J. H. Round came across what he called 'a vast system of artificial hidation', which, moreover, he showed to be on a decimal basis.[1] Blocks of five hides or multiples thereof were assigned to individual villages. The feature is obvious when a village consisted of only one holding, but it can also be seen when the details of the various holdings in some villages are assembled together from their different folios. It is true that the assemblages for some villages do not make exact decimal totals, but these irregular assessments can often be grouped into decimal blocks covering two or more neighbouring villages. Not all counties display the five-hide system as clearly as Cambridgeshire, but whether they do or not, it is clear that villages with identical assessments had widely differing resources and populations.

In the northern Danelaw there was a different system. The unit was the Anglo-Danish carucate (*carucata terrae*) comprising 8 bovates. These carucates, like hides, were artificial in the sense that they had been imposed from above – from the county through the wapentake to the vill, but the division was duodecimal and was based on a unit of six carucates.[2] It seems likely that this system was an innovation that replaced an earlier decimal hidage characteristic of the area in the tenth century.[3] In the third place, the assessment of East Anglia was based upon groups of villages, or 'leets' (Anglo-Saxon *læth*, district), each of which contributed so many pence when the hundred in which they lay contributed 20*s*. The amounts, again, were artificial in the sense that they did not reflect geographical and economic realities.[4] Finally, in Kent the unit was the sulung, an archaic term related to the Old English word for plough; 4 yokes (*juga*) made a sulung. There is reason to believe that the incidence of these was also artificial;[5] certainly there is complete lack of correlation between the resources of a vill and its assessment in sulungs.[6]

---

[1] J. H. Round (1895), 49 *et seq.*

[2] J. H. Round (1895), 69 *et seq.*; see also F. M. Stenton in C. W. Foster and T. Longley, *The Lincolnshire Domesday and the Lindsey Survey* (Lincoln Record Soc., 1924), x–xiv.

[3] F. M. Stenton, *Types of manorial structure in the northern Danelaw* (Oxford, 1910), 87–9. See also F. M. Stenton (1943), 639–40.

[4] J .H. Round (1895), 99 *et seq.* See also: (1) C. Johnson in *V.C.H. Norfolk*, II (1906), 5–6, 204–11; (2) B. A. Lees in *V.C.H. Suffolk*, I (1911), 360–4, 412–16.

[5] J. E. A. Jolliffe, *Pre-feudal England: The Jutes* (Oxford, 1933), 43–7.

[6] *D.G.S–E.E.*, 506.

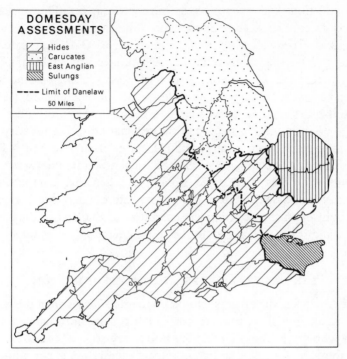

Fig. 2. Types of Domesday assessment.

The artificial nature of these systems of assessment had been greatly complicated over the years. Some individual manors, some vills, some hundreds and even some counties seem to have been exempted, to a greater or lesser degree, from paying geld.[1] We can sometimes see exemptions being made even in the Conqueror's own time. There were sweeping reductions over 1066–86 in the four adjoining counties of Berkshire, Hampshire, Surrey and Sussex, particularly on ecclesiastical estates and on those of some tenants-in-chief; but there is no clue to the reasons for these reductions.[2] Or again, six of the sixteen hundreds in Cambridgeshire show quite arbitrary reductions for which there is no explanation.[3]

[1] R. Welldon Finn, *An introduction to Domesday Book* (London, 1963), 241–65; R. S. Hoyt, *The royal demesne in English constitutional history: 1066–1272* (Cornell, 1950), 19–25.

[2] J. H. Round in P. E. Dove (ed.), *Domesday studies*, I (1888), 110–12. See also *D.G.S–E.E.*, 249–50, 300–2, 372–3, 423–4.

[3] L. F. Salzman in *V.C.H. Cambridgeshire*, I (Oxford, 1938), 341–2.

Other reductions had taken place before the Conquest. Thus it was that Somerset as compared with Dorset and Wiltshire was under-rated, and Devon and Cornwall very much under-rated.[1] To what extent the extreme under-rating of these two latter counties was, as Maitland suggested, 'perhaps as old as the subjection of West Wales', we cannot say.[2] Or, to take another example: within the county of Lincolnshire, Kesteven and Holland were much over-rated as compared with Lindsey, and 'there is no economic or geographical explanation of the severity' with which they were treated;[3] and within Lindsey itself, the North Riding came off lightly as compared with those of the South and West.[4] Much time and effort has been spent upon the fascinating complexities of Domesday assessment.[5] Great though its interest may be, it does not throw light upon the geographical condition of England in the eleventh century, and it has, therefore, not been considered in the chapters which follow.

THE UNCERTAINTIES OF THE INFORMATION

The other items in the preamble to the *Inquisitio Eliensis* are more relevant to our theme, but they, too, are not without many uncertainties. In fact anyone who works upon Domesday Book very soon comes to have two views about it. On the one hand, he can have nothing but admiration for what is the oldest 'public record' in England and probably the most remarkable statistical document in the history of Europe. The continent has no document to compare with this detailed description covering so great a stretch of territory. And the geographer, as he turns over the folios, with their details of population and of arable, woodland, meadow and other resources, cannot but be excited at the vast amount of information that passes before his eyes. There are other valuable documents that provide evidence of past geographical conditions in many areas; but, more often than not, they are fragmentary and incomplete. If they are detailed, they usually cover only a small area. If they cover a larger area, they are far from detailed. But the Inquest of 1086 was carried out with a fairly high degree of uniformity over almost the whole of England, and

[1] *D.G.S–W.E.*, 349.
[2] F. W. Maitland (1897), 467.
[3] F. M. Stenton in C. W. Foster and T. Longley (1924), x.
[4] *D.G.E.E.*, 39–40.
[5] E.g. C. Hart; (1) *The hidation of Northamptonshire* (Leicester, 1970); (2) *The hidation of Cambridgeshire* (Leicester, 1973).

the results give us today a unique opportunity of recalling some of the main features of the landscape of the eleventh century.

There is, however, another point of view. When this great wealth of data is examined more closely, perplexities and difficulties arise. Domesday Book is far from being a straightforward document. It bristles with difficulties. Many of them have been resolved as the result of the scholarship of a long line of editors and commentators, working, more particularly, from about the middle of the nineteenth century. The publication of J. H. Round's *Feudal England*, in 1895, was a great landmark in the history of Domesday scholarship. But many problems still remain, some for ever insoluble. Moreover, the Domesday clerks, as is apparent time and again, were but human; they were frequently forgetful or confused. 'No one,' wrote Round, 'who has not analysed and collated such texts for himself can realise the extreme difficulty of avoiding occasional error. The abbreviations and the *formulae* employed in these surveys are so many pitfalls for the transcriber, and the use of Roman numerals is almost fatal to accuracy.'[1] Anyone who attempts an arithmetical exercise in Roman numerals soon sees something of the difficulties that faced the clerks. Their work occasionally convicts itself of inaccurate addition, and a detailed comparison of the statistics of the Exeter and the Exchequer versions for the south-west shows how easily and frequently minor errors could arise.[2]

Then there are our own uncertainties. A casual reading of the text confronts us with obscurities, but once we begin to examine it more closely, other and more complicated problems appear. We may sometimes wonder how much has been omitted; and, in any case, 'two men not unskilled in Domesday' may well arrive at different totals because of different opinions about this or that formula.[3] Each county presents its own problems. In the light of all the uncertainties, it would be more correct to speak not of 'the Domesday geography of England', but of 'the geography of Domesday Book'. The two may not be quite the same thing, and how near the record was to reality we can never know; the gaps can never be filled; the perplexities may never be resolved. Even so, it is probably safe to assume that a picture of England based on Domesday Book, while neither complete nor accurate in all its details, does reflect

[1] J. H. Round (1895), 20.
[2] *D.G.E.E.*, 26–8; *D.G.S–W.E.*, 395–428.
[3] F. W. Maitland (1897), 407.

the main features of the geography of the eleventh century. The remark-able thing is not that there are tantalising obscurities, but that King William's men did as well as they did, considering the sheer difficulty of making a survey at a time when the central government was without the many aids we now associate with the administrative machinery of an organised state.

CHAPTER II

RURAL SETTLEMENTS

The basis of the geographical study of Domesday Book is the exact identification of place-names. Without that firm foundation all is in vain. Over 13,000 separate places are named – 13,278 in England itself, and about 140 (it is impossible to be precise) in districts now within Wales. These totals include 111 boroughs in England and one (Rhuddlan) in North Wales – see Appendix 1 (p. 336). As many as 175 places out of the grand total of 13,418 cannot be precisely located but can be assigned to particular parishes. Furthermore, 386 names out of the total (just under 3%) have not been identified, but some of these have given rise to conjecture.

Some settlements not named in Domesday Book must certainly have existed in 1086 because their names appear in pre-Domesday charters and again in documents of the twelfth and thirteenth centuries. Such, in Wiltshire, are Everleigh, Patney, Semley and Woodford.[1] The resources of such places are presumably accounted for in the statistics recorded for named places. There are also many indications in Domesday Book itself that the total of settlements in 1086 must have been far greater than the 13,400 or so named places. In the first place, the constituent vills of a large number of manors were not separately named; then, again, some adjoining places may have been described collectively under one name; and thirdly we know from contemporary and near-contemporary sources that there were yet other places about which Domesday Book is silent. Each of these three complications must now be examined.

THE INCOMPLETE RECORD OF PLACE-NAMES

Composite manors

Manors with outlying sokelands and berewicks formed a feature of northern England in the early Middle Ages. In southern England, too, there were many complex manors with dependencies and sub-tenancies that included not only *berewichae* but *appendicii*, *membrae*, *terrae* and

---

[1] J. E. B. Gover *et al.*, *The place-names of Wiltshire* (Cambridge, 1939), 329, 314, 209, 373. It must be noted however that some of these pre-Domesday charters appear only in manuscripts of the twelfth, thirteenth and even fourteenth centuries.

pertinentes. These components are sometimes described separately under the names of their respective localities, but occasionally only their names appear and their resources are included within the totals for a manor as a whole.

Frequently, however, the components are not even named, and there is no means of telling whether they were at places named in other entries or at places entirely unrecorded in Domesday Book. Thus among the Shropshire entries we hear of Ford (253b) with 14 unnamed berewicks (*cum xiiii berewichis*), and of Worthen (255b) with 13. Altogether, there were 135 unnamed berewicks in the Shropshire folios. Similar entries can be encountered elsewhere. The Hampshire manor of Chilcomb (41), for example, is described in two parts – a main portion followed by a summary account of seven unnamed subsidiary holdings; the whole included 9 churches and 213 households with 78 teams at work. We would have no clue to the identity of the subsidiary holdings but for the pre-Domesday documents which reveal that the great Chilcomb estate was scattered over eleven villages situated mainly along a twenty mile stretch of the Itchen valley (Fig. 3). All these are the subject of other entries in the Hampshire folios, with the exception of Brambridge and Tichborne; although these latter had been in existence since at least the early tenth century, they went unnamed in Domesday Book.[1]

There are entries for other manors in which some components are named and others are not. The description of Micheldever (42b) in Hampshire refers to 11 sub-tenancies of which only 4 are named; and that of Whitchurch (41), in the same county, refers to 6 of which only 2 are named. Furthermore, we hear of holdings that had been added to (*addita*) or taken away from (*ablata*) manors; some were at named places, others were not. Both addition and subtraction had taken place on, for example, the Somerset manor of Martock (*113*, 87).

The description of the land between the Ribble and the Mersey (*Inter Ripam et Mersham*) at the end of the Cheshire folios (269b–270) provides outstanding examples of compressed entries. For five of the six hundreds of the district, the entries omit the names of the dependencies of large manors which were entirely or almost entirely coincident with their respective hundreds; there were as many as 113 dependencies, but whether they were at 113 separate places we cannot say. In the same way, the description of Martinsley hundred in *Roteland*, at the end of the

[1] F. W. Maitland, *Domesday Book and beyond* (Cambridge, 1897), 496–8.

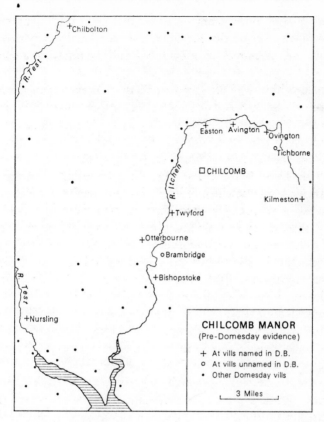

Fig. 3. The manor of Chilcomb (Hants.) according to pre-Domesday evidence.

Nottinghamshire folios (293b–294) is summarised, and a total of 19 unnamed berewicks is included within three composite manors – 7 with Hambleton, 5 with Oakham and 7 with Ridlington.

There are yet other entries which do not even tell us the number of dependencies attached to a manor, but merely refer to their existence; thus the consecutive entries for Wolstanton and Penkhull in Staffordshire (246b) speak merely of manors and their *appendicii*. Similar references to unspecified numbers of berewicks occur in the entries for Sherburn in Elmet (302b, 379) and Ulleskelf (303b, 379), both in the West Riding. A pre-Domesday account of the archbishop of York's estate of Sherburn in Elmet (dated earlier than 1069, and probably *c.* 1030) shows that its

berewicks were at not less than 20 places without Domesday names.[1] At
the other end of the realm, in Dorset, we hear of unspecified *appendicii*
belonging to Puddletown (*25*, 75) and to Wareham (*28b*, 78b), and of
unspecified *pertinentes* belonging to Portland (*26*, 75). Or again, on folio
65, unspecified numbers of *appendicii* are entered for each of four Wiltshire manors – Corsham, Melksham, Netheravon and Rushall; and there
are also other similar Wiltshire entries.[2]

Even when there is no reference to dependencies, we may strongly
suspect their existence on many manors with large totals for hides, men,
teams, mills and churches. The entry for Sonning (58), in eastern Berkshire, with 66 households and 46 teams, covered the resources of a number
of places unmentioned in Domesday Book, yet each with an Old English
name. In post-Domesday times, these were tythings of the bishop of
Salisbury's great manor of Sonning, and 'it is safe to say that they are all
covered in Domesday by the name of the manor to which they belonged'.[3]
In the same way, the large manor of Farnham (31), in Surrey, had 89
households with 43 teams; it was held by the bishop of Winchester and
was described in a single entry.[4] Or yet again, we can hardly suppose
that Pawton (*199b*, 120b), the largest of the Cornish manors, and the
only place mentioned in the hundred of that name, was the sole inhabited
settlement in the hundred, what with its 86 households and 43 teams.

Descriptions of many such large manors meet our eyes on folio after
folio of Domesday Book. They make no reference to components, but
their figures for population and teams are suspiciously large. Here are a
few more examples taken from six counties:

	Population	Teams	Value
Devonshire: Crediton (*117*, 101b)	407	185	£75
Hampshire: Chalton (44b)	104	37	£80
Kent: Hoo (8b)	158	47	£60
Middlesex: Harrow (127)	117	49	£56
Oxfordshire: Banbury (155)	107	40	£30
Wiltshire: Aldbourne (65)	150	36	£70

[1] W. H. Stevenson, 'Yorkshire surveys and other eleventh-century documents
in the York Gospels', *Eng. Hist. Rev.*, XXVII (1912), 1–25; A. J. Robertson, *Anglo-
Saxon charters* (Cambridge, 1956), 165–9.
[2] *D.G.S–W.E.*, 4n.
[3] F. M. Stenton in A. Mawer and F. M. Stenton (eds.), *Introduction to the survey
of English place-names* (Cambridge, 1934), 39. See also J. H. Round in *V.C.H.
Berkshire*, I (1906), 301.   [4] F. W. Maitland, 13–14.

Each of these manors may well have included not only dependencies hidden from our eyes, but dependencies at places not otherwise named in Domesday Book. It is very probable, for example, that the totals for Banbury included the resources of Charlbury (a pre-Domesday name) and its hamlets.[1]

Adjoining places under one name

Many Domesday place-names are represented in later times by groups of two or more adjoining names with distinguishing appellations such as Great and Little or East and West, or with some more distinctive designations often derived from the names of landholders in the twelfth and thirteenth centuries. A number of these groups may have developed as a result of colonisation by which an original village territory came to have another settlement within its limits. We cannot, however, always be sure whether the division had already taken place by 1086, and whether the Domesday name covered more than one vill; whether, say, the single name of *Fontel* (65b, 72b) in Wiltshire covered two settlements in the eleventh century as it certainly did by the fourteenth – Fonthill Bishop and Fonthill Gifford.[2] Similar doubts arise over such groups as the three Rissingtons in Gloucestershire,[3] the four Ilketshalls in Suffolk,[4] the six (at one time seven) South Elmhams also in Suffolk,[5] the seven Burnhams in Norfolk[6] and the eight Rodings in Essex.[7]

Domesday Book does occasionally reveal the fact that division had taken place by 1086, and the indication is sometimes given in a clumsy fashion as when we read of *Cocheswelle* and *alia Cocheswelle* (57b), that is Coxwell and 'the other Coxwell' in Berkshire. The distinction is occasionally more specific as these three examples show: *Bedefunt* (129, 130) and *Westbedefund* (130), that is East and West Bedfont in Middlesex; *Nortstoches* and *Sudstoches* (337b), that is North and South Stoke in Lincolnshire; and *Rollandri majore* (160b) and *parva Rollandri* (155), that is

---

[1] F. M. Stenton in *V.C.H. Oxfordshire*, I (1939), 378, 393; M. Hollings in *V.C.H. Oxfordshire*, x (1972), 135.

[2] J. E. B. Gover *et al.*, 190.   [3] Rissington: Great, Little, Wyck.

[4] Ilketshall: St Andrew, St John, St Lawrence, St Margaret.

[5] South Elmham: All Saints and St Nicholas, St Cross, St James, St Margaret, St Michael, St Peter.

[6] Burnham: Deepdale, Norton, Overy, Sutton, Thorpe, Ulph, Westgate (including the later Burnham Market).

[7] Roding: Abbess, Aythorpe, Beauchamp, Berners, High, Leaden, Margaret, White.

Great and Little Rollright in Oxfordshire. Some adjoining places bearing the same name are described under different hundred headings; thus in Suffolk, *Saham* (294, 327) in Loes hundred and *Saham* (368, 385, 405b) in Hoxne hundred have become Earl and Monk Soham respectively, and they may well have been separate places in 1086 as they were later.

We can perhaps glimpse the stages by which such division took place in a few Cambridgeshire villages. Domesday Book makes no distinction between Great and Little Wilbraham (189b, 195b, 199b); the I.C.C. (p. 15) likewise makes no distinction although it does speak of two Wilbrahams (*ii Wilburgeham*)[1]; the earliest mention of the names *Magna* and *Parva* does not appear, however, until the twelfth century.[2] In the same way Domesday Book does not distinguish between Swaffham Bulbeck and Swaffham Prior (190b, 195 *bis*, 195b, 197b, 199, 199b), but one of the documents appended to the I.E. mentions *Suuafham* and *altera Suuafham* (p. 192); what is more, the distinctive appellations of later times may also be traced back to the eleventh-century landowners – Hugo de Bolebech and the Prior of Ely, the former mentioned only in the I.C.C. (p. 12) and the I.E. (p. 102).

The mention of *alia* and *altera* in a Domesday entry does not, however, necessarily mean that there were to be two later parishes. In Essex, for example, there were three vills each with holdings distinguished by *alia* or *altera* – Fyfield (84b), Moulsham (25b) and Navestock (13), but in none of them is there any trace of two subsequent villages. Or again, in the North Riding there is mention of *Wendreslaga* and *alia Wendreslaga* (311b) and also of *in duobus Wentreslage* (381), where in later times there was only the single settlement of Wensley. We can only suppose that in these and similar entries, the *alia* or *altera* referred to another holding which never became a separate vill.

The problem of counting the total of Domesday vills becomes especially acute when groups of adjoining settlements take their respective names from the streams along which they were aligned, as they frequently do in the south-west. Thus in the Dorset folios there are 15 entries for Tarrant, and today there are 8 settlements along the river of that name. In the same way there are 10 entries for Frome and 7 later settlements; and there are 18 entries for Piddle and 11 later settlements. A

---

[1] For the subsidiary document of the I.C.C., see *D.G.E.E.*, 5.

[2] P. H. Reaney, *The place-names of Cambridgeshire and the Isle of Ely* (Cambridge, 1943), 138.

similar feature is true of other Dorset rivers. The Devonshire folios contain 14 entries for *Otri* and there are 10 later settlements along the river Otter; there are 10 entries for Clyst and 10 settlements along the river of that name. Sometimes the name of the river has changed: thus there were 9 Wiltshire entries for Deverill (the old name of the upper Wylye) and 5 adjoining places with that basic name along the river; 7 entries for Winterbourne (the present river Bourne) and 4 places; 12 entries for another Winterbourne (the present river Till) and 7 places. Clearly, in each of these groups there was very likely more than one settlement in the eleventh century, but how many we cannot say.[1]

Other unnamed places

Domesday Book sometimes convicts itself of incompleteness. For Huntingdonshire, Lincolnshire and Yorkshire, there are what amount to appendices dealing with disputes and entitled *Clamores*. That for Huntingdonshire mentions Easton (208), but we do not hear of it in the main account. That for Lincolnshire says that the soke of 'a church in (Long) Sutton' lay in the manor of Tydd (371b), but, again, there is no mention of Sutton in the Lincolnshire text itself. In the same way, Compton (373b), *Luuetotholm* (374) and Stancil (373b) are named in the Yorkshire appendix but not in the Yorkshire text. Moreover, as many as 40 additional place-names appear in the 'Summary' for Yorkshire (379–82), and another 5 in the account of the fief of William de Bruis (332b–333) which is also in the nature of an appendix. Thus while there are 1,945 place-names in the main text of the Yorkshire folios, another 48 are to be found only in the three additional sections.[2]

Furthermore, the Exeter version reveals the absence of a number of place-names from the Exchequer text – one each in Cornwall and Somerset and 11 in Devonshire.[3] What is more, the *Terrae Occupatae* for the south-west counties (corresponding to the *Clamores* elsewhere) provides an additional place-name in Cornwall and 4 in Devon. This makes 5 place-names missing from the Exeter version and a total of 18 from the Exchequer text.[4]

We also know of missing place-names from contemporary and near-contemporary sources that may have been associated with the Domesday

---

[1] *D.G.S–W.E.*, 73–6, 229–30, 8–10, 355–6.   [2] *D.G.N.E.*, 11, 94, 171.
[3] *D.G.S–W.E.*, 141, 223, 296.   [4] *D.G.S–W.E.*, 133, 224.

Inquest. Comparison with the I.C.C. and I.E. reveals the existence of settlements unnamed in the Domesday text. To the north-east of Cambridge, on the edge of the Fenland, there is the modern parish of Stow cum Quy which was once two separate villages. There is no Domesday mention of Stow, but the I.C.C. sets out the details for both under the heading *Choie et Stoua* (p. 15), thus showing the existence of Stow in the eleventh century. On the other hand, Domesday Book separately describes the adjoining villages of Hardwick (191b) and Toft (194b, 200b, 202b), but the I.C.C. includes the information for Hardwick in its account of Toft (pp. 87–8). Or again, the I.E. describes *Wicheham et Strateleie* (p. 103) together, and the hamlet of Streetly End appears on the modern map as part of the parish of West Wickham; but both Domesday Book (191a) and the I.C.C. (p. 33) speak only of *Wicheham*. Another example of Domesday silence is provided by the entry for the Huntingdonshire village of Spaldwick (204), with 60 recorded people and 29 teams at work. It so happened that Spaldwick belonged to the abbey of Ely, and the corresponding entry in the I.E. adds the fact that the description of Spaldwick also covered its berewicks of Long Stow, Easton and Barham (p. 166). All three are now separate parishes, but none of them is mentioned in the main body of the Domesday text; Easton alone is mentioned incidentally in the appendix dealing with Disputes (208).

Other revealing documents are the geld-account abstracts, or so-called Geld Rolls, for the five south-western counties. Their date has been debated – whether they belong to 1084 or to 1086; so has their relation to the original Domesday returns of 1086.[1] But whatever view one takes, they are of a date very close to that of the Inquest and they are bound up in the *Liber Exoniensis*. They give information about the fiefs within each hundred, but they rarely mention place-names. Even so, among those that they do mention are two that appear neither in the main text nor in the *Terrae Occupatae* of the Exeter Domesday Book – Woodadvent and the unidentified *Pirtochesworda*, both in Somerset. Details of these places were either omitted or lie concealed in the totals for some manor or manors.

Yet other names are revealed by two documents for Kent. One is the

---

[1] R. R. Darlington in *V.C.H. Wiltshire*, II (1955), 169–77; V. H. Galbraith, *The making of Domesday Book* (Oxford, 1961), 87–101; R. Welldon Finn, *The Domesday Inquest* (London, 1961), 138–51.

so-called 'Excerpta' or Excerpts from the White Book of St Augustine's Abbey at Canterbury. It includes information, for a number of estates, that bears a close relation to that of the original Domesday returns, and it adds five new names.[1] One of these, Margate, is a holding concealed in the Domesday totals for Chislet (12); but it is impossible to connect the other four names with any Domesday holding, anonymous or otherwise. The other document is part of the so-called Domesday Monachorum, and it surveys the manors of the archbishop and certain other landowners in Kent. Its entries, like those of the Excerpta, are closely related to the Domesday returns, and they add 14 new names including four unidentified.[2] Three of the 14 (Castweazel, *Eadruneland* and Orgarswick) cannot be connected with equivalent Domesday entries; but the information for the other 11 can be discerned among the anonymous holdings for the county.[3]

Anonymous holdings, and references to subsidiary estates which do not mention place-names, are to be found in the folios for most counties. They add an element of uncertainty because we cannot tell whether these holdings and estates were at places named in other entries or whether they were at places entirely unrecorded in Domesday Book. There were, for example, 16 such anonymous holdings in Berkshire and 26 in Surrey.[4] Chance evidence for Herefordshire enables us to identify a number of these holdings in the county. This is a transcript of the Herefordshire folios made during the reign of Henry II, most probably between 1160 and 1170. It has survived as Balliol College MS 350, and nothing like it is known for any other county. It usually repeats the names of holdings in its margins, so providing a rough index of places; and among these marginal names are 10 (including one unidentified) that do not occur in Domesday Book.[5]

---

[1] Elmstead, Little Mongeham, Margate, Ripple, Walmer. See A. Ballard (ed), *An eleventh-century inquisition of St Augustine's, Canterbury* (British Academy, London, 1920), v, xxi, 17, 22–3, 30.

[2] Brook, Castweazel, *Eadruneland*, Eyethorne, *Ezilamerth* (Stourmouth), Hunton, Loose, *Macebroc*, Orgarswick, Pett, *Sturtune*, Swarling, Thannington, *Wic*. See D. C. Douglas (ed), *The Domesday Monachorum of Christchurch, Canterbury* (Roy. Hist. Soc., London, 1944), 17, 81, 82, 83, 84, 90, 92, 95.

[3] *D.G.*, 207–8.   [4] *D.G.*, 17, 422.

[5] Aylton, Ballingham, Dewsall, Harewood, Hungerstone, Longworth, Pencombe, Underly, Upcott, *Wrmenton/Wrmoton*. See V. H. Galbraith and J. Tait, *Herefordshire Domesday, circa 1160–1170* (Pipe Roll Society, London, 1950), 57, 19, 21, 19 and 67, 6, 5, 59, 39 and 50, 32, 20 and 21.

These six sources, the I.C.C., the I.E., the Geld Rolls, the Excerpta, the Domesday Monachorum and the Herefordshire transcript, taken together, yield a total of 35 non-Domesday place-names (including 6 unidentified), 26 of which can be connected with anonymous holdings in Domesday Book itself.[1]

Far more striking than the evidence of these documents closely associated with Domesday Book is that from two, possibly three, sources somewhat later in date. One comprises the lists of churches which form the first part of the Domesday Monachorum. They were churches, mainly in the eastern half of Kent, paying various dues to the archbishop, and they include churches at 88 places unnamed in Domesday Book.[2] As the lists date from 'about the year 1100', we are safe in thinking that the settlements served by the churches must have been in existence in 1086. The second source is a somewhat similar list of dues for the diocese of Rochester. This is the *Textus Roffensis* which has been dated 'about the year 1115' but may well refer to conditions 'not later than 1089'.[3] It includes 50 places in western Kent also unnamed in Domesday Book. A third possible source is yet another list of dues that was inserted along with other eleventh-century documents in the White Book of St Augustine's Canterbury. The copy, it is true, dates from as late as 1200, but it may well have been based upon 'an original list contemporary with those of Rochester and Canterbury',[4] and it includes 25 place-names that do not appear in Domesday Book.

Bearing in mind that 15 names are common to more than one document, the additional names for Kent in the Domesday Mona-chorum (both surveys and lists), the *Textus Roffensis* and the White Book of St Augustine's (both Excerpta and list) amount to 167, of which 12 are unidentified. The total number of settlements in Kent in 1086 was therefore not the 347 of the Domesday folios but well over 500 (Fig. 4). In contemplating the remarkably large number of additional names for

---

[1] *D.G.*, 31, 185, 195, 207–8. For Geld Rolls, see p. 22 above.

[2] D. C. Douglas (1944), 3–15, 77–9; G. Ward, 'The lists of Saxon churches in the Domesday Monachorum and White Book of St Augustine's', *Archaeol. Cantiana*, XLV (1933), 60–89.

[3] G. Ward, 'The list of Saxon churches in the Textus Roffensis', *Archaeol. Cantiana*, XLIV (1932), 39–59.

[4] G. Ward (1933), 84–9. The White Book of St Augustine's Canterbury as a whole has not been edited and printed – only that portion dealing with the Excerpta. The MS is in the Public Record Office, London – E164 (27), and the list of churches is on fos. 17v–18.

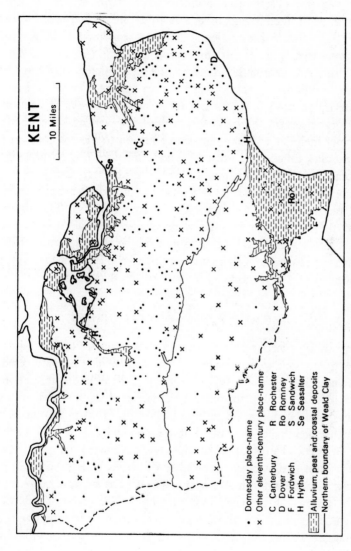

Fig. 4. Kent: Domesday and other eleventh-century place-names.

Kent, we must remember that here was a countryside of hamlets, and that here, too, was the Weald. The information relating to these numerous small settlements (yet large enough to have churches) was compressed under a more limited range of names in Domesday Book. No similar evidence is available for Sussex, but many unnamed holdings in that county were clearly small settlements in the Weald (see pp. 34–5).

Two other documents that illustrate the incompleteness of the Domesday record of names are the Lindsey Survey (1115–18) and the Leicestershire Survey (1129–30). They are not so much surveys as lists of geld liability organised on the basis of hundreds or wapentakes and of vills. The former includes 12 place-names in addition to the 492 that appear in the Domesday folios for Lindsey.[1] The latter does not cover Leicestershire completely, but deals mainly with the northern and eastern parts of the county.[2] Even so, it adds 26 names (including 2 unidentified) to the 292 place-names in the Domesday county (Fig. 5). The absence of some of these place-names (and their resources) from the Domesday record of Lindsey and Leicestershire may be the result of straightforward omission; the absence of others may be due to the fact that their resources are concealed within the totals for some of the named vills.

SIZE AND FORM OF SETTLEMENTS

In every county there were some places about which very little information was given, and we can make no estimate of their size and resources. We hear nothing, for example, of Avebury (65b) in Wiltshire beyond the fact that it had a church to which belonged 2 hides, and that its annual value was 40s. Nothing is said about Harnhill (168) in Gloucestershire beyond the fact that it was rated at 5 hides and that it had included 3 manors in 1066. On the other hand, as we have seen, many entries with abundant information cover a number of places and leave us in doubt about the size of individual settlements. Where we can be reasonably (but not always absolutely) sure that one place-name stood for one settlement, it is clear that there was much variation in size, even in the same district. The recorded populations of the dozen vills in the Cambridgeshire hundred of Wetherley ranged from 12 to 82; those of

---

[1] C. W. Foster and T. Longley, *The Lincolnshire Domesday and the Lindsey Survey* (Lincoln Record Society, 1924), xliv, 237–60.

[2] C. F. Slade, *The Leicestershire Survey* (Leicester, 1956).

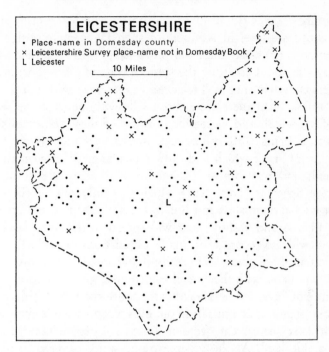

Fig. 5. Leicestershire: Domesday place-names, and Leicestershire
Survey place-names not in Domesday Book.

the fourteen vills in the adjoining hundred of Armingford ranged from
16 to 63. These Cambridgeshire vills were presumably nucleated in
character, each with one cluster of houses surrounded by arable land and
standing more or less in the centre of its territory. But, as Christopher
Taylor has shown us, even in this land of nucleated settlement we cannot
always be sure that any particular nucleated village of later time was
without a degree of dispersion in the eleventh century.[1]

Many places described in Domesday Book were very small. Thus
Westwick (201b, 202) to the north-west of Cambridge had a recorded
population of only three; Bradenham (153) in Buckinghamshire had only
two; and, to take another example, Tiddington (160b) in Oxfordshire
had only one.[2] Small named settlements were especially characteristic of
the south-west. We cannot regard as vills such Somerset settlements as

[1] C. Taylor, *The Cambridgeshire landscape* (London, 1973), 54–62.
[2] For the relation of recorded to actual population, see pp. 87–8.

Downscombe (*430*, 94) with only one bordar and half a team at about 1,000 ft above sea-level in Exmoor; or such Devonshire settlements as Willsworthy (115b) where there were but 4 slaves with a team and pasture 2 leagues by 1 at about 900 ft on the western edge of Dartmoor; or, again, such Cornish settlements as Trehawke (*257b*, 122) with but 2 bordars and one team. Then there were those vills without teams yet with no record of waste. Should we envisage some of these settlements in the south-west as being entirely pastoral – settlements such as the Cornish Trevego (*231b*, 125) which had only 1 bordar with no teams on its 3 ploughlands and but 20 acres of wood and 10 acres of pasture; or the Devonshire Speccott (*407b*, 115) which had only one villein with no teams on its 3 ploughlands and but 15 acres of meadow and 40 acres of pasture? Figs. 6 and 7 show how widespread were these places in the south-west with no record of teams or populations or both. But can we believe that all these places were really uninhabited? (see pp. 57–8).

These two maps, with their small named vills, give only a very incomplete picture of dispersed settlement in the south-west. As Maitland wrote, 'at least two types of vill must be in our eyes when we are reading Domesday Book'.[1] At one extreme were nucleated villages surrounded by their acres of arable land. At the other extreme were scattered hamlets and isolated farmsteads. Between these came a variety of intermediate types. We cannot with any certainty indicate the relative distribution of these various types in the eleventh century. It would seem, however, that over some parts of England the substantial totals in entries for composite manors and groups of places were not the only ones to cover unnamed settlements. Even the smaller totals in other entries may be deceptive in conveying an impression of single villages rather than scattered hamlets and farmsteads, thus concealing considerable variety in the pattern of settlement.

The south-western peninsula, especially that part to the west of the River Parrett, is today very largely a land of isolated farmsteads and hamlets. It may well have been so also in the eleventh century. W. G. Hoskins has suggested that the number of separate settlements, including isolated farms, in the Devonshire of 1086 was many times that of the recorded places.[2] The latter numbered 980, but Hoskins estimated the

[1] F. W. Maitland, 16.
[2] W. G. Hoskins, *Provincial England* (London, 1963), 15–52. See especially pp. 21, 33, 34, 43, 44.

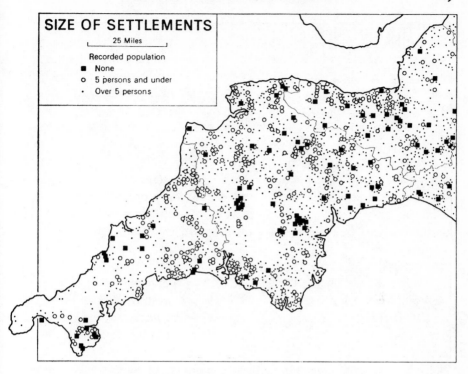

Fig. 6. Size of settlements in the south-west.

total number of separate settlements at between 9,000 and 9,500, of which up to a thousand or so were demesne farms and the remainder were occupied by villeins. This figure was obtained by apportioning the details of many Domesday manors among the isolated farms of modern parishes on the assumption that we should 'allocate every villein to a separate farmstead'. At Honeychurch (292, 106), for example, there were five ploughlands with two teams on the demesne and one with the peasantry; and the recorded population comprised 4 villeins and 4 slaves. 'Throughout all the relevant documents of Honeychurch's history, down to the tithe award of 1839–41, there are five farms in the parish.' From this it is but a step to envisage a demesne farm (on which the slaves worked) and four separate villein farmsteads. Very often, on the other hand, the number of villeins on a holding is the same as the number of ploughlands. 'In other words it looks as though when Domesday say of a Devonshire manor that "x ploughs can till it" it is really saying "there

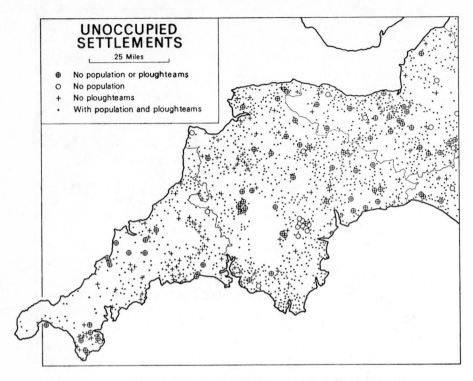

UNOCCUPIED SETTLEMENTS

| | | 25 Miles | | |

⊕   No population or ploughteams
○   No population
+   No ploughteams
·   With population and ploughteams

Fig. 7. Unoccupied settlements in the south-west.

are *x* farms on this manor in addition to the demesne farm".' But the arithmetic is not always easy. There are sometimes more villeins than ploughlands and sometimes fewer; moreover either figure often differs from the number of isolated farmsteads that appear on nineteenth-century surveys. It is clear that such interpretations involve many conjectures and assumptions, and that, as Hoskins says, 'there are many exceptions for which an explanation is not easy'. But whatever be the situation in this or that locality, we are safe in envisaging Devonshire, with its broken landscape of hill and valley, to have been a land of hamlets and dispersed settlements in the eleventh century, as it very largely is today.

Dispersed settlement was not restricted to the south-west. Today, the Ordnance Survey map shows its presence over much of Herefordshire and Shropshire, for example, and it is possible that local topographical investigation might yield evidence for dispersed settlement in earlier times. As in the south-west, the Domesday entries for counties along the Welsh border conceal the nature of the settlement. There happen to be, however, unusual entries for two settlements in the west of Herefordshire, and these may give a glimpse of conditions there in the eleventh century. Eardisley, we are told, lay in the midst of a wood. It had a fortified house, one team at work and a recorded population of only three – two slaves and a Welshman. At Ailey nearby, there was also a fortified house and a great wood for hunting but no recorded inhabitants. Portions of the relevant entries read as follows:

Eardisley (184b): *In medio cujusdam silva est posita et ibi est domus una defensabilis.*
Ailey (187): *Ibi est domus defensabilis et silva magna ad venandum.*

Appropriately enough, both names indicate a 'leah', or clearing in the wood.

Although we have to rely on the uncertainty of retrospective deduction, it seems likely that hamlets and dispersed settlements were also characteristic of parts of northern England in the eleventh century. The average recorded population of the settlements of the Pennine area of north-west Derbyshire was only about 5 or 6 apiece.[1] The Domesday entries (272–273) for the area show us manors with, in 1066, archaic renders in kind and with groups of dependent berewicks that 'are most naturally understood as a collection of scattered but dependent farmsteads playing a part accessory to the agricultural activities of the chief manor'.[2] Ashford, for example, had 12 berewicks, Bakewell had 8, Hope had 7, and there were other groups (Fig. 8). The setting for such arrangements was provided by narrow valleys with only limited strips of cultivable soil, and by upland pastures with expanses of moor and tracts of limestone. Here was a terrain 'not favourable to the development of the neat villar–manorial economy of the south of England. There is no doubt that the royal manors of north Derbyshire were largely the product of their geographical conditions'.[3]

In later times, hamlets and isolated settlements were also to be found in many districts to the south, and some at any rate had their origin in clearings in wooded areas. But the form of the Domesday entries does not

[1] *D.G.N.E.*, 305–6.
[2] F. M. Stenton, *Types of manorial structure in the northern Danelaw* (Oxford, 1910), 74.
[3] F. M. Stenton in *V.C.H. Derbyshire*, I (1905), 312.

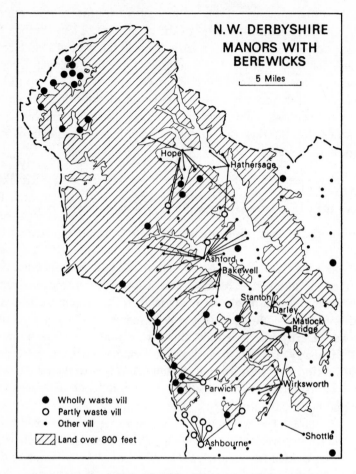

Fig. 8. North-west Derbyshire: Manors with berewicks.
The county boundary is that of 1086.

enable us to perceive whether such patterns had already come into existence by 1086; whether, for example, the wooded part of Warwickshire north of the Avon was characterised by dispersion in the eleventh century as it certainly was in later centuries. Here, an entry for Oldberrow (175b), part of Worcestershire in 1086, may hint at the circumstances of other, but unnamed, localities silently included within the descriptions of named manors. It had only 12 acres of land with one league of wood and 2 swineherds (*ii rustici porcarii*), and it appears to have been a small woodland settlement which was yet to achieve cultivation. Then again, in the wooded area of northern Buckinghamshire there was at Newport Pagnell (148b) 'woodland for 300 swine and a yield of 2*s*' together with a further payment of 4*s* from men who dwelt therein (*iiii solidi de hominibus qui manent in silva*).

There was one district in southern England where Domesday Book gives more substantial indication of the presence of small hamlets and isolated settlements; this was the Weald. Many of the minor names of the district are of a very early date, and they 'disprove, if disproof were needed, the idea that the Weald formed a trackless waste in early Saxon times'.[1] Its shades had been penetrated by herdsmen with their swine, and its resources had been organised to serve the villages around. Pre-Domesday documents show that many villages in Kent came to regard certain localities in the Weald, often some distance away, as their own particular swine-pastures or 'denes';[2] and place-names ending in 'den' are frequent in the Weald of Kent. The Domesday folios for Kent mention 52 denes together with 3 half-denes; another appears in the Surrey folios, and a third of a dene in those for Berkshire (Fig. 9). These can have been only a fraction of the total number.[3]

Amidst much obscurity we can perhaps discern three stages in the evolution of these denes. The first stage is represented by those denes mentioned, under the names of their parent centres, without any reference to people or ploughteams. We hear of 'small denes' and 'large denes', and, cutting across this division, of denes *de silva* sometimes with swine renders, and of other denes with no mention of wood but with money renders. A second stage may be reflected by those denes which had people and teams entered for them; thus attached to Peckham (7b) there were 3 denes where dwelt (*ubi manent*) 4 villeins, apparently without teams; and attached to Tinton (11) there was half a dene with a villein and 3 bordars with half a team. We are not told where the denes at these two stages were situated; we hear only of the names of their parent centres. The third stage is represented by those denes which had grown into settlements with names of their own. Tiffenden (13b) seems to have been only just emerging from being a mere swine pasture; it had 2 villeins

[1] A. Mawer *et al.*, *The place-names of Sussex* (Cambridge, 1929), xvii.

[2] N. Neilson, *The cartulary and terrier of the priory of Bilsington, Kent* (British Academy, 1928), 1–10.

[3] *D.G.S–E.E.*, 527–8.

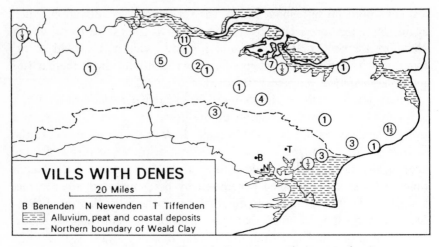

VILLS WITH DENES

20 Miles

B Benenden   N Newenden   T Tiffenden
Alluvium, peat and coastal deposits
Northern boundary of Weald Clay

Fig. 9. Domesday vills with denes in south-east England.

with half a team, but, at any rate, it appears in Domesday Book in its
own right and with its own name. Some denes had grown into fully 'adult'
villages; such were Benenden (11), the dene of Bionna's people, with 13
households, 3 teams and a church, and Newenden (4) with 29 households, 5 teams and even a market. To what extent these place-names
themselves covered hamlets or farmsteads, we cannot say.

Place-names ending in 'den' are less frequent in Sussex, but this may
reflect a local usage of words rather than the absence of swine-pastures.[1]
Such pastures were sometimes recorded in pre-Conquest Sussex charters
without necessarily being called denes; thus among those belonging to
Annington and to Washington were some with names ending in 'wic'
and 'hurst'.[2] No denes are recorded for Domesday Sussex, but the
Sussex folios certainly provide their own indications of colonisation in
the Weald. The evidence, like that for Kent, falls into three groups.

First comes that contained in the descriptions of the three Wealden
hundreds of Hawksborough, Henhurst and Shoyswell in the rape of
Hastings (18b–19b). Only six settlements are named, but there are 40
other holdings, in 25 places, entered under the names of manors that lay

---

[1] H. C. Darby, 'Place-names and the geography of the past' in A. Brown and
P. Foote, *Early English and Norse Studies* (London, 1963), 14–18.
[2] A. Mawer *et al.*, 107, 160, 226, 233; R. Lennard, *Rural England, 1086–1135*
(Oxford, 1959), 254n.

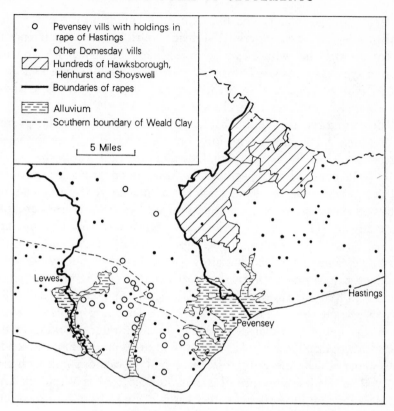

Fig. 10. Sussex: Outliers in the rape of Hastings.

outside the Weald, in the adjoining rape of Pevensey (Fig. 10). The implication is that these unnamed places were outliers colonised from parent manors.[1] Between them, by 1086, they had as many as 177 households with 123⅜ teams. The second category includes holdings which had once been connected with (*jacuit in*) manors to the south but which had acquired names of their own. They were especially characteristic of East Grinstead hundred (22b); thus Hazelden had once been part of Allington, and Fairlight part of Ditching (Fig. 11). The former means 'swine pasture where the hazels abound', and the latter implies a 'clearing in bracken'. Although having names of their own, these were still small places, and the dozen outliers in the hundred had only 37 households and

[1] L. F. Salzman, 'The rapes of Sussex', *Sussex Archaeol. Collections*, LXXII (Cambridge, 1931), 23–4; *D.G.S–E.E.*, 412–13.

13 teams between them. The third category comprises those Wealden settlements which were described in their own right without reference to parent manors, and which may be called 'adult' settlements. Such were Brambletye (22b), in East Grinstead, with 16 households and 1½ teams, and Hazelhurst (19), in Shoyswell, with 12 households, 11 teams and a church, and there were others elsewhere.

There are a few stray hints that may, or may not, fit into this picture of Wealden colonisation. The long double-hundred of Easewrithe, in Sussex, stretched from the South Downs northward across the Weald Clay to the county border; somewhere in the hundred was an unnamed holding to which one team and a mill but no people were attributed (29). It was once part of Storrington as pasture but had recently been brought into cultivation (*In Storgetune jacuit in pastura. Modo noviter est hospitata*); but whether it lay in the south near Storrington or was an outlier in the north, we cannot say. Or what are we to make of the Surrey entry for Wallington (30) not far from the border with Kent? It tells of 'wood which is in Kent' and goes on to say that Richard of Tonbridge had taken away a peasant who dwelt there (*unde abstulit rusticum qui ibi manebat*). Does this imply an isolated settlement in a clearing? Looking at the Wealden woodland as a whole, we do not know enough about the conditions under which pioneering took place, and we cannot speak with certainty. The possible sequence of events outlined for the Weald of Kent and Sussex is not inconsistent with what is likely to have happened, but when we try to penetrate the obscurity of the Domesday record we can only wonder whether we always read aright.

THE DISTRIBUTION OF SETTLEMENTS

The distribution of Domesday place-names is not necessarily that of the eleventh-century settlements themselves. Domesday entries frequently covered more than one settlement, and sometimes very many. This is certainly true for areas with nucleated villages, and it may be even more true for areas of dispersed settlement, the hamlets and isolated settlements of which are concealed under the terse totals in entry after entry. The folios for Kent do not convey the fact that it is a land of hamlets, many without Domesday names; nor do the names in Devonshire folios give any idea of the very scattered character of the habitations in the county.

On such maps as Figs. 12 and 13, we can gauge the intensity of

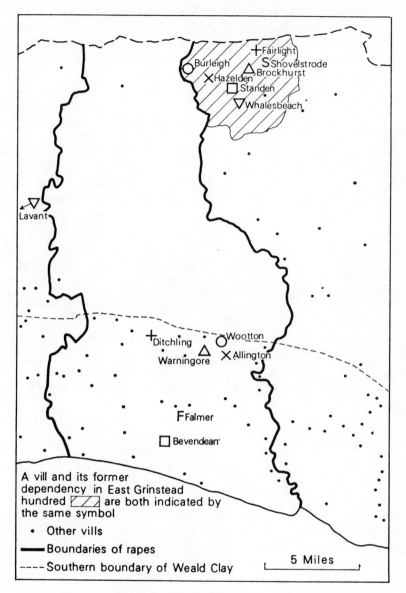

Fig. 11. Sussex: Outliers in East Grinstead hundred.

The parent manor of Shovelstode and the dependency of Falmer are not named. The total number of outliers, including unidentified holdings, amounts to twelve.

Fig. 12. Domesday place-names: West.

Fig. 13. Domesday place-names: East.

settlement over the face of the country only in a very general way. Our estimate may come near to the truth, however, for those areas over 800 ft above sea-level. The almost complete absence of place-names may mean a similar, or nearly similar, absence of inhabited sites. The Pennines and the North York Moors stand out as empty areas. The main exception to this generalisation is the presence of some vills above the 800 ft contour in the Carboniferous Limestone area of the Derbyshire Pennines; these vills were related to the water-supply yielded by the junction of the limestone itself with various igneous rocks intruded into it. Such, for example, at about 1,000 ft were Blackwell and Priestcliffe, two berewicks of Ashford (272b). This district may have been the scene of lead-mining from the veins of metalliferous ores within the limestone. To the north, in the West Riding, the main chain of the Pennines is broken by the Aire Gap, where the land falls below 800 ft; here, the settlements of the upper Aire valley continued westward to meet those of the Ribble, thus breaking the barrier of the Pennine moorlands.

In the south-west peninsula there are other elevated areas devoid of names. Chief among them is the large granitic mass of Dartmoor, much of which lies over 1,200 ft above sea-level. Its central portion was completely without Domesday names, and its western portion largely so; a few western settlements, however, were at high altitudes, e.g. Willsworthy (115b), at about 900 ft, where there were 4 slaves and a team. The eastern margin of Dartmoor, on the other hand, is broken by the valleys of the Dart, the Bovey, the Teign and their tributaries, and a few names were to be found up to, and even above, the 1,000 ft contour; such was Natsworthy (113b) at 1,200 ft with a recorded population of 5, with 2 teams and with even a little meadow and underwood. Considerable tracts of the grit and shale upland of Exmoor were also over 1,000 ft. Its peaty soils provided little inducement to settlement, but a number of place-names were to be found in the valleys that break its surface. At above 1,200 ft in Devon was Radworthy (415, 111) with 4 recorded people and 1¼ teams and also with pasture and a little meadow and wood; and at about the same height was Lank Combe (337, 114) with a solitary villein who had no team. Across the border, in Somerset, in the sheltered valley of the Exe was Almsworthy (430, 94), at about 1,000 ft, with 17 recorded people and 4 teams and with pasture and, again, some meadow and wood. Among the smaller areas above 800 ft in the south-west were Bodmin Moor, the Quantock Hills and the Blackdown Hills, all without recorded names. This was true also of the upland areas along the Welsh border in Shropshire and Herefordshire.

When we turn south-eastwards from the uplands to the English lowland, the emptiness of the peat portion of the Fenland stands out in contrast to the belt of names on the silt lands between Lincolnshire and Norfolk. The Breckland in Norfolk and Suffolk is empty, so is the sandstone area of western Nottinghamshire and also much of the chalk country, among other districts. Many place-names in the plain at the head of the Humber are of post-Domesday record, so are many in the soke of Peterborough. But, as we look at these empty areas in general, we must remember, for example, the compressed nature of those Lancashire entries which covered many places, and also the fact that the lack of names in the Weald does less than justice to its scattered pioneer communities.

The considerations that entered into the siting and distribution of the lowland settlements were varied. They reflected not only social habits but also many different physical circumstances – the width of a valley, the extent of a gravel patch, the line of a road, and other geological and topographical details capable of almost infinite variation. Had we the full information behind the place-names, it would need to be discussed in detail, locality by locality, bearing in mind that the over-riding need in the selection of a site was for water. Although we are without this information we can, at any rate, examine some characteristic sites of nucleated villages that bear Domesday names.

One very familiar type of site is at the foot of a scarp with porous rocks above and impervious ones below. Here, water is available in the form of springs or wells, and the result is a series of 'scarp-foot' or 'spring-line' villages. There are several lines of such villages in Lincolnshire. One, for example, extends for some 25 miles south-eastwards from South Ferriby on the Humber, through a score of villages, to Sixhills. Among other lines of villages in Lincolnshire are two that run north and south of the city of Lincoln, on either side of the dry belt of Oolitic Limestone. Elsewhere, other examples often mentioned are those at the base of the scarplands around the Weald. It was these that William Topley discussed in a classic memoir published as long ago as 1875. He noted 'the continuous line of villages lying under the steep slope of the South Downs; generally on the Upper Greensand terrace, but sometimes at the base of the Chalk. This is the case all through Sussex and Hants.'[1]

[1] W. Topley, *The geology of the Weald* (Mem. Geol. Survey, London, 1875), 396.

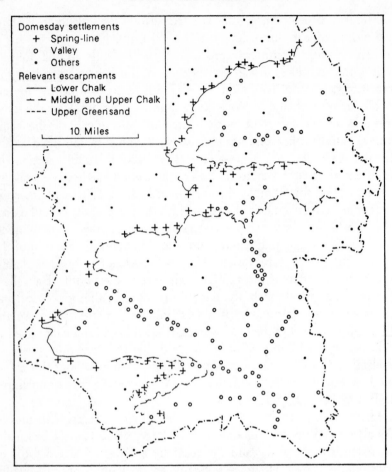

Fig. 14. Wiltshire: Types of settlements.

Among these was Selborne, the home of Gilbert White, who wrote of 'a fine perennial spring little influenced by drought or wet seasons'.[1] The line of springs continues through Kent, though sometimes complicated by the varying disposition of the outcrops.[2] Then again, the scarplands of Wiltshire provide as good an example as any of spring-line villages (Fig. 14).

[1] Gilbert White, *The natural history of Selborne* (Everyman's Library, London), 6. First published in 1789.
[2] S. W. Wooldridge, *The Weald* (London, 1953), 202–3.

These are straightforward linear arrangements. A more complicated example of spring-line sites is provided by those villages in Northampton-shire that are situated on the line of contact between the Northampton Sands and the Upper Lias Clay (Fig. 15); they do not lie along a simple line because the outcrop of Northampton Sands is very broken, and the contact with the clay is very sinuous.[1] The dictum of Vidal de la Blache comes to mind: 'It may be stated as a general principle that human establishments preferably select lines of contact between different geological formations.'[2] Water supply was not the only advantage of such contact-sites; another advantage was the variety of soil which such a site ensured. The different formations on either hand provided not only arable but the meadow, wood and pasture that are noted so often in Domesday entry after entry. Thus was secured the need of the early village community to be as self-sufficient as possible.

Another characteristic site was in a river valley, and such sites are to be found everywhere in England – along the Ouse in Bedfordshire, along the Trent in Nottinghamshire and along many another river as may be seen from the maps in the *Domesday Gazetteer*. The strings of villages that mark the valleys of the chalk country in Wiltshire stand out with the clarity of a diagram (Fig. 14). The gravel terraces along the Ebble, the Nadder, the Wylye, the Bourne and the Salisbury Avon support nucle-ated villages set at about a mile apart, sometimes less, so producing a contrast with the bare sweep of the down above. The exact position of such a village depends on the liability of the valley to flooding. A cluster of houses is usually situated at some distance from the river itself, if not on a gravel terrace then at some little way above the flood plain. Such sites, with their territories stretching up the valley sides, also ensured a variety of land use possibilities, what with meadow, arable, pasture and maybe wood.

These two types of site – contact and valley – are far from exhausting all the variations to be found in the siting of English villages. Attention has been drawn, for example, to the 'dry point' villages that are found on the Cheshire plain, villages such as Tarvin (263) and Waverton (267b) situated on 'knolls of Sandstone which rise above the Boulder-clay'.[3]

---

[1] S. H. Beaver, *Northamptonshire* (London, 1943), 364–8; this is pt 58 of L. D. Stamp (ed), *The Land of Britain*.

[2] P. Vidal de la Blache, *Principles of human geography* (London, 1926), 285.

[3] Lord Avebury, *The scenery of England* (London, 1902), 485.

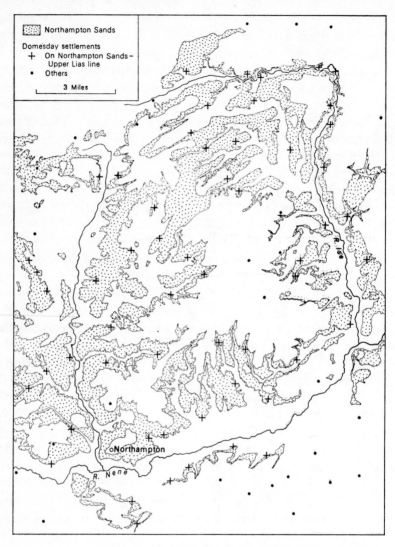

Fig. 15. Central Northamptonshire: Spring-line settlements.

Or again, the clue to the siting of villages in eastern Leicestershire lies in the water-bearing sand and gravel patches that are to be found amidst the Boulder Clay and that support such villages as Misterton (236) and Mowsley (235b, 236).[1]

DOMESDAY VILLAGES LATER DESERTED

It was F. W. Maitland who wrote in 1897 that 'a place mentioned in Domesday Book will probably be recognized as a vill in the thirteenth, a civil parish in the nineteenth century'.[2] This is certainly so in some counties such as Cambridgeshire, where the vills of 1086 are almost all represented by the civil parishes of modern times. But Maitland would not make the same generalisation today. C. W. Foster in 1920–4 noted nearly 70 Domesday vills, in Lincolnshire, which had failed to survive.[3] Since then, the work of M. W. Beresford and others has shown the existence of over 2,000 deserted villages in England; not all of these are named in Domesday Book, but many of them are.[4]

They became extinct at various times and for a variety of reasons. Some do not appear to have been very viable in 1086, and no reference to them appears in the taxation lists of the late thirteenth and early fourteenth centuries. It is true that a number of these may not have vanished but may have become too small to be separately counted, and so were silently included in other taxation units.[5] Although the exact locations of a number of them are in doubt, their localities can sometimes be assigned to modern parishes.[6] The names of others, on the other hand, remain completely unidentified, although it is always possible that further work will enable them to be located. It was usually but not always the smallest vills that were the first to disappear. In Northamptonshire, for example, the smallest vill in 1086 was Hothorpe (222); it had but one sokeman and half a team in 1086 but was still

[1] R. M. Auty, *Leicestershire* (London, 1943), 260; this is pt 57 of L. D. Stamp (ed), *The Land of Britain*; W. G. Hoskins, 'The Anglian and Scandinavian settlement of Leicestershire', *Trans. Leics. Archaeol. Soc.* XVII (1934–35), 125.

[2] F. W. Maitland, 12.

[3] C. W. Foster, *Final concords of the county of Lincoln* (Lincoln Record Society, 1920), l–lxv; C. W. Foster and T. Longley (1924), xlvii–lxxii.

[4] M. W. Beresford, *The lost villages of England* (London, 1954); M. W. Beresford and J. G. Hurst (eds.), *Deserted medieval villages* (London, 1971), 3–226.

[5] K. J. Allison, 'The lost villages of Norfolk', *Norfolk Archaeology*, XXI (1955), 123.   [6] *D.G.*, 1.

surviving in 1350.[1] Interestingly enough, some villages said to be waste in 1086 were soon reoccupied to continue throughout later ages.[2]

The reasons for the early depopulation of many villages are obscure, and may never be known, but we can say that some were deliberately destroyed. The Cistercian Order first arrived in England in 1128, and the development of the countryside came to owe much to it; but there was also a debit side to Cistercian activities. Their rule enjoined seclusion from the world, and many of their houses were founded in the remoteness of the North and of Wales. Other houses achieved seclusion by depopulating their neighbourhoods.[3] In 1147, Bruerne Abbey, in Oxfordshire, depopulated the settlement of *Draitone* (158) where, in 1086, there had been 23 households with 11 teams.[4] In 1150, Combe Abbey in Warwickshire depopulated *Smitham* (239b) which in 1086 had 47 households with 14 teams; the name survives today in Smite Bank, Smite Hall and Smeeton Lane in the parish of Combe Fields.[5] Or again, in 1180 Garendon Abbey emptied the village of *Dislea* (230b *bis*), in Leicestershire, where there had been, in 1086, 33 households with 8 teams; its site was later marked by Dishley Grange so famous in the agricultural history of the eighteenth century.[6] These few examples far from exhaust the record of Cistercian depopulation. When the territories of the abbey passed back into lay hands in 1536 there was no question of recreating the settlements destroyed several centuries earlier.

Many villages were enfeebled by the Black Death of 1349 but, although mortality was high, there is little evidence of the complete disappearance of villages. Two Domesday villages certainly seem to have vanished entirely – Middle Carlton (354b, 362) in Lincolnshire and Tusmore (157b) in Oxfordshire; so did a few others not named in Domesday

[1] K. J. Allison *et al.*, *The deserted villages of Northamptonshire* (Leicester, 1966), 41; M. W. Beresford and J. G. Hurst (1971), 25.

[2] T. A. M. Bishop: (1) 'Assarting and the growth of open fields', *Econ. Hist. Rev.*, VI (1935), 13; (2) 'The distribution of manorial demesne in the Vale of York', *Eng. Hist. Rev.*, XLIX (1934), 386.

[3] R. A. Donkin, 'Settlement and depopulation on Cistercian estates during the twelfth and thirteenth centuries, especially in Yorkshire', *Bull. Inst. Hist. Research*, XXXIII (1960), 146–9; H. N. Colvin, 'Deserted villages and the archaeologist', *Archaeol. News Letter*, IV (1951–3), 129–31; D. Knowles, *The monastic order in England, 943–1216* (2nd edn, Cambridge, 1963), 350–1.

[4] K. J. Allison *et al.*, *The deserted villages of Oxfordshire* (Leicester, 1965), 37.

[5] M. W. Beresford, 'The deserted villages of Warwickshire', *Trans. Birmingham Archaeol. Soc.*, LXVI (1950), 95–6.

[6] M. W. Beresford (1954), 153; R. A. McKinley in *V.C.H. Leicestershire*, II (1954), 5.

Book.[1] But the main effect of the Black Death was to weaken villages, and subsequent pestilences and the general economic contraction between 1350 and 1450 brought further decline. Enfeebled villages situated on marginal lands were especially vulnerable.[2] The deserted and all-but-deserted villages of Norfolk were mostly on the light and sandy marginal soils in the west of the county.[3] *Estretona* (257b) is now represented by Testerton House and a ruined church in the parish of Pudding Norton; and *Toimere* (230b) by Toombers Wood in Shouldham Thorpe. *Suatinga* or Swathing (121b *bis*) has left no mark on the map, and now forms part of the parishes of Cranworth and Letton. Norfolk deserves its reputation as a land of solitary ruined churches. Something similar also took place on the light soils of the Lincolnshire Wolds where amalgamation of parishes became frequent. West Wykeham (364), for example, was joined with Ludford Magna (351, 354, 356b, 364) in 1397 because, so we are told, its population had been reduced by divers pestilences.[4] It was for the same reason that, in 1450, Fordington (349) was joined with Ulceby (355b, 364), and Beesby (347b *bis*) with Hawerby (347b).[5] There was also depopulation on the light soils of the Yorkshire Wolds, at Cottam (303, 382), at Towthorpe (301, 307, 382), and at 20 or so other villages.[6] And when, in the eighteenth century, agricultural improvement came to these light soils in Norfolk, Lincoln, the East Riding and elsewhere, it did not bring with it a revival of these ancient centres of village life.

Even in areas with better soils, desertion and amalgamation took place, mostly for local reasons unknown to us. Thunderley (76b) and Wimbish (69b) on the chalky Boulder Clay of north-west Essex were once distinct villages, but in 1425 the vicarage of Thunderley was united with that of Wimbish, and 'as to the church of Thunderley', wrote the eighteenth-century historian of Essex, 'the place where it stood is now part of a field'. Thunderley has therefore disappeared as a village, leaving Thunderley Hall to testify to its former existence.[7]

[1] M. W. Beresford (1954), 158–60.
[2] J. Saltmarsh, 'Plague and economic decline in England in the later Middle Ages', *Cambridge Hist. Jour.*, VII (1941), 23–41.
[3] K. J. Allison (1955), 138.
[4] C. W. Foster and T. Longley, lxxi–lxxii.
[5] M. W. Beresford (1954), 171.
[6] M. W. Beresford and J. K. S. St Joseph, *Medieval England: an aerial survey* (Cambridge, 1958), 117–18; M. W. Beresford, 'The lost villages of Yorkshire, Part II', *Yorks. Archaeol. Jour.*, XXXVIII (1952), 44–70.
[7] P. Morant, *History and antiquities of the county of Essex*, II (London, 1768), 338.

Easily the most important cause of the desertion of villages came later in time. This was the depopulation following upon enclosure and the conversion of arable to pasture between about 1450 and 1520. That was the fate, to take but one example, of Ingarsby (230, 232b), in Leicestershire. In 1086 it had 7 teams at work and a recorded population of 31, which may imply a total population of about 150. It had become greatly enfeebled by 1352 when the greater part of it came into the possession of Leicester Abbey; the abbey acquired the whole lordship by 1458, and in 1469 the village fields were enclosed and nearly all converted to pasture. Enclosure was followed by complete desertion, and today its site is marked by banks and ditches, and the line of the main street by 'ancient twisted thorn trees'.[1] Out of the 292 Domesday vills of Leicestershire as many as 39 were deserted and are now marked only by mounds and other irregularities on the surface of the ground.[2] Only 8 of the 39 sites are in the western half of the county; the richer pastures of the east and south took the heavier toll.[3] Similar events took place in other midland counties. Not only Leicestershire but Warwickshire, Northamptonshire, Nottinghamshire and also the northern parts of Oxfordshire and Buckinghamshire were the classic areas of the desertion that followed upon enclosure for pasture.

Still later in time, and particularly in the eighteenth century, another cause of the disappearance of villages was the making of landscape parks when villages were sometimes removed to make way for mansions or to secure uninterrupted views across landscapes.[4] Occasionally, removal was followed by the building of a new village nearby as at Harewood (301, 379) in the West Riding, and at Nuneham Courtenay (159) in Oxfordshire, both in the 1770s. But frequently this did not take place, as when the park at Castle Howard in the North Riding was made out of the fields of Henderskelfe (314, 380b) about 1710. This was also the fate of Ickworth (357b) in Suffolk shortly after 1800. Sometimes the landscape

---

[1] W. G. Hoskins, 'The deserted villages of Leicestershire', *Trans. Leics. Archaeol. Soc.*, XXII (1944–45), 247; reprinted with additions in W. G. Hoskins, *Essays in Leicestershire history* (Liverpool, 1950), 78.

[2] Deserted Medieval Village Research Group, 'Provisional list of deserted medieval villages in Leicestershire', *Trans. Leics. Archaeol. and Hist. Soc.*, XXXIX (1963–4), 24–33. See *D.G.M.E.*, 320.

[3] *D.G.M.E.*, 320.

[4] M. W. Beresford (1954), 139–41; M. W. Beresford and J. G. Hurst (1971), 27, 54–6.

gardener but completed the work of an earlier encloser as when Capability Brown laid out the grounds of Compton Verney (239b, 241b) in Warwickshire in the 1760s. As Professor Beresford has said, 'Many a lost village stands in the shadow of the Great House'.[1]

As a result of these varied changes, the names of many Domesday vills are represented today only by those of hamlets or individual farms and houses or by topographical features such as fields or woods. In Bedfordshire, for example, as many as 32 out of a total of 145 Domesday names (i.e. over 20%) fall into this category (Fig. 16). Here are some examples. *Salchow* (213) is now the hamlet of Salph End in the parish of Renhold; and *Calnestorne* (213b) or *Chauelestorne* (212, 215) is that of Chawston in Roxton. *Polehangre* (137b) is represented by Polehanger Farm in Meppershall; *Putenhow* (212b *ter*) by Putnoe Farm and Putnoe Wood in Goldington; and *Cainow* (218) or *Chainehou* (214) by Cainhoe Farm and Cainhoepark Wood in Clophill. *Segenhou* (216) survives as Segenhoe Manor in Ridgmont; *Holma* (213b) or *Holme* (212, 214b, 215b, 217, 217b, 218b) as the hamlet of Holme in Biggleswade, and *Stratone* (211b, 215b, 217, 217b) as Stratton Farm and Stratton Park in the same parish. *Chenemondewicke* (210b) survived until 1804 in Kinwick Field in Sandy. The name of *Subberie* (216), or Sudbury, is no longer to be found in Eaton Socon, nor that of *Elvendone* (216b), or Elvedon, in Pertenhall.[2] To these must be added two unidentified names – *Cudessane* (211b, 214) and *Hanefelde* (211b, 218b). On the other hand, 19 of the 133 parishes on the modern map of Bedfordshire are not mentioned in Domedsay Book, i.e. 14%. Their names do not appear until the twelfth or thirteenth centuries. Whether or not any of these missing names refer to estates that were in fact in existence in 1086, we cannot say, but it is clear that some at any rate refer to settlements which were founded at a later date.

Fig. 16 shows that the sites of some deserted or shrunken Domesday villages lie within parishes that are not themselves named in Domesday Book. Occasionally, more than one Domesday name is to be found in a non-Domesday parish. Thus the earliest record of Ault Hucknall in Derbyshire was not until 1291, but the parish of that name includes the sites of five Domesday settlements, all now represented by hamlets or

---

[1] M. W. Beresford (1954), 29.
[2] A. Mawer and F. M. Stenton, *The place-names of Bedfordshire and Huntingdonshire* (Cambridge, 1926), *passim*.

BEDFORDSHIRE

- • Parishes named in Domesday Book
- + Other Domesday place-names
- ▨ Parishes not named in Domesday Book

Elvedon
Shirdon
Hinwick
Sudbury
Radwell
Channell's End
Wyboston
Chawston
Salph End
Putnoe
Chalton
Kinwick
Beeston
Harrowden
Wilshamstead
Cotton End
Stratton
Holme
Millow
Shelton
Broom
Stanford
Cainhoe
Segenhoe
Polehanger
Priestley
Pegsdon
Nares
Gladley
Biscot
Sewell
Barwythe

5 Miles

Fig. 16. Bedfordshire: Domesday place-names and modern parishes.

houses.[1] Another noteworthy example is the parish of Stone in Stafford-shire (first named in 1187) with as many as eight Domesday names.[2] It is clear that there have been many changes in the village geography of England, and that a list of Domesday place-names is very different from a list of present-day parishes. The total number of modern parishes not mentioned in the whole area covered by Domesday Book amounts to just over 2,300.

One other set of changes must be mentioned, the result not of human but of natural agency. Along the coast of the East Riding as many as 16 Domesday vills have disappeared under the sea at various times, though only three have left no trace; the others survive at least in name.[3] Thus the modern settlement of Kilnsea perpetuates the name of the Domesday manor of *Chilnesse* (323b, 382) which in 1086 had 27 households with 8 teams. To the south, along the Humber estuary, Tharlesthorpe (302, 382) was inundated and abandoned in 1393. There are no lost villages along the Lincolnshire coast, but there is reference to damage in the account of a holding at Wrangle (367b): there was land for one team, but it was waste on account of the action of the sea (*Wastum est propter fluxum maris*). There has also been erosion along the Norfolk coast. Cromer (not named in Domesday Book) was first mentioned in 1262, and it came to replace Shipden (185, 194b, 216) which the sea overwhelmed in the fourteenth and fifteenth centuries. Whimpwell (220, 220b) also disappeared, but it is remembered by the hamlet of Whimpwell Green in Happisburgh. Por-tions of other parishes, e.g. Overstrand (268) and Eccles (220b, 272b), likewise now lie beneath the sea. There were similar losses along the Suffolk coast but only two places have entirely disappeared – Newton (284b) in Lothingland, and the Domesday borough of Dunwich (311b). The encroachment, which was to prove the undoing of the old town, had already begun by 1086; the record is terse but eloquent enough: 'Then 2 carucates of land, now one. The sea carried away the other' (*mare abstulit alia*).

---

[1] *D.G.N.E.*, 286; K. Cameron, *The place-names of Derbyshire*, II (Cambridge, 1959), 268–70.
[2] *D.G.M.E.*, 174.
[3] *D.G.*, map 57; *D.G.N.E.*, 174.

VILLAGE CHURCHES

It would seem that by 1086 the village church was a familiar feature of the countryside, but the Domesday enumeration of churches is very uneven. Different decisions about their recording were made not only as between one circuit and another but as between different counties within the same circuit. Thus churches are mentioned for 352 out of the 639 vills of Suffolk but for merely 17 out of the 444 vills in the adjoining county of Essex, and for only two of the 342 vills of Staffordshire. Fig. 17 shows how great was the variation. Huntingdonshire and Suffolk were the only counties with churches mentioned for over 50% of their vills, and there were only six other counties where the proportion was over 25%.

If proof were wanted that many churches went unrecorded, it would not be difficult to find. The two churches mentioned for Horsey Pignes and Kilmersdon in the Exeter folios for Somerset (*477*, 198b) do not appear in the corresponding Exchequer entries (98b, 91b). Then again, for seven places in Norfolk the Ely Inquest records churches not mentioned in the Domesday text,[1] and there is also non-Domesday evidence for churches at several places in Wiltshire.[2] But the outstanding example comes from Kent. Here, Domesday Book records churches for 147 places, but associated documents dealing with the payment of ecclesiastical dues record churches at over 400 places, including many places not even mentioned in the Domesday text.[3] Furthermore, some Domesday place-names imply the existence of churches even if they are not mentioned, e.g. *Jacobescherche* or St James's Church in Devonshire (*487*, 118b), *Sudcerea* or Southchurch in Essex (8b), and *Witcerce* or Whitchurch in Hampshire (41).

The mention of a church is frequently accompanied for some counties by a reference to a priest. Thus the usual formula for Huntingdonshire is *Ibi est ecclesia et presbyter*; so it frequently is for Derbyshire and Yorkshire. Just occasionally, the absence of a priest is specifically noted as at Houghton in Huntingdonshire (204b, *Ibi ecclesia non presbyter*) or at Easington in the North Riding (305, *Ecclesia sine presbytero*). On the

---

[1] *D.G.E.E.*, 138.
[2] R. R. Darlington in *V.C.H. Wiltshire*, II (1955), 32–3.
[3] G. Ward (1933), 89; D. C. Douglas, 15. See also p. 24 above.

other hand, there are counties for which a reference to a church is never, or only rarely, followed by mention of a priest. Thus no priests are recorded for the 62 vills with churches in Surrey; and they only occasionally appear in connection with the churches of Norfolk and Suffolk. There are yet other counties for which the reverse is true; churches are rarely mentioned, but priests (without churches) appear quite often, e.g. for the counties of Leicester, Northampton and Warwick (Fig. 17); and here we may suppose that priests implied village churches. The number of churches recorded in Domesday Book is 2,061 at 1,796 places. If to the latter we add those places with priests but no churches, the total becomes 2,287 places – out of a grand total of 13,400 or so places named in Domesday Book as a whole – see Appendix 4 (p. 346).

Village churches were owned just as other resources of a manor. When founded and endowed, often by laymen, they were of profit because they brought in revenue from the glebe, from tithes and from such dues as marriage and burial fees or, as was said in the entry for Mottisfont (42) in Hampshire, from the customary payments of the living and the dead (*omnes consuetudines . . . vivorum et mortuorum*). The owner of a church was therefore entitled to a rent from the incumbent; this was sometimes stated separately, e.g. the church at Droxford (41b) in Hampshire paid 20s (*ecclesia de xx s*); but other churches, as was explicitly said in the account of the lands of William de Warenne in Norfolk (159b, 172), were valued with their manors (*omnes ecclesiae . . . appreciatae sunt cum maneriis*).[1]

One result of such ownership is that we often hear of fractions of churches. They may have originated from the foundation of a church, not by one of the great men of the realm but by groups of villagers. Or they may have resulted from the partition of an estate. The latter seems to be indicated by the third of a mill as well as the third of a church at Linwood (365) in Lincolnshire, and by the quarter of a mill and quarter of a church at Taverham (158) in Norfolk. Sometimes it is possible to put the fractions together in a satisfactory manner; thus at Wantisden in Suffolk there was half a church (306b) and two quarters (307, 344), but such neat addition is not usually possible, and this makes exact enumeration difficult. An extreme example of division was Threekingham (341b, 365b, 370), in Lincolnshire, with two churches, St Mary and St Peter;

[1] For other examples, see R. Welldon Finn, *Domesday studies: the eastern counties* (London, 1967), 175.

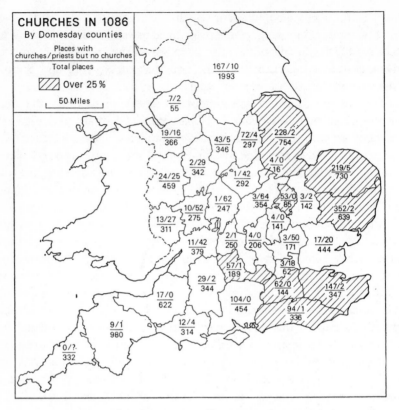

Fig. 17. Churches in 1086 (by Domesday counties).

the following fractions are recorded for the former: $\frac{1}{6} + \frac{1}{3} + \frac{1}{6}$; and these for the latter: $\frac{1}{12} + \frac{1}{6} + \frac{1}{12}$. Nothing is said of the remaining one third of St Mary's or of the remaining two thirds of St Peter's.[1] We even hear of half a church and half a priest at Laythorpe (357) in Lincolnshire and of 'half-priests' at Langley (196) in Norfolk and at Middleton (400) in Suffolk, which seems to imply obligations partly to one lord and partly to another. Further indication of the division of a church and its land is provided by the occasional statement in the Suffolk folios to the effect that 'others shared in it' e.g. *plures ibi participantur* at Kenton (326) and *plures habent partem* at Burgh (400b). Fractions are most frequent for Norfolk, Suffolk and Lincolnshire where freemen were numerous and

---

[1] F. M. Stenton in C. W. Foster and T. Longley, xxi–xxii.

where traces of partible inheritance can be found. Beyond these three counties there are only occasional instances of the divided ownership of churches.[1]

Standing in contrast to entries with only a fraction of a church each, there are other entries which attribute two or more churches or priests to a manor.[2] It is reasonable to suppose that such manors often included more than one settlement; thus the Hampshire manor of Penton (43b, 44b) had two churches, and it is represented today by Penton Grafton and Penton Mewsey. Or again, the Domesday churches of South Elmham (356, 380), in Suffolk add up to 6⅓, and in later times there were seven adjoining parishes with this name in common, now six because two have been united (see p. 19). On the other hand, some manors with two or more churches seem always to have been single villages, e.g. Dummer (45b, 49b) in Hampshire and Shimpling (415b, 430b) in Suffolk, and it is possible that in each of these vills the same church was recorded twice in connection with both holdings.

The assumption made in the preamble to the Ely Inquest that every village could furnish a priest can be accepted only with reserve for England as a whole (see p. 5 above). It is certainly true, however, that some entries refer specifically to the church or priest of a vill. Thus a number of entries for Thedwastre hundred in Suffolk (361b–362) speak of the village church (ecclesia villae) e.g. at Bradfield; and the phrase occasionally occurs for other places, e.g. for the Hertfordshire vill of Welwyn (142b) and the Shropshire vill of Baschurch (253). A variant is 'the church of the manor', e.g. at Aldbourne (65) in Wiltshire. Analogous to these are the entries for 'the priest of the vill' at Farndon in Cheshire (257) and at Fulletby (349b) in Lincolnshire and at other places, or 'the priest of the manor' at Potterne (66) in Wiltshire and at Hinton Martell (76) in Dorset. But these references must not lead us to suppose that England was everywhere divided into parishes with vills each with its own church and priest. Now and again there are glimpses of an older system by which a central collegiate minster with its group of clergy served a number of villages around.[3] Relics of this older system may be seen in the 8 canons who before 1066 had served (serviebant) the church

---

[1] E.g. *D.G.E.E.*, 346 (Hunts.); *D.G.M.E.*, 209 (Staffs.); *D.G.S-E.E.*, 135 (Mdlx.), 272 (Berks.); *D.G.N.E.*, 74, 153 (Yorks.), 271 (Notts.), 321 (Derby.); 373 (Ches.); *D.G.S-W.E.*, 49 (Wilts.).

[2] E.g. *D.G.S-E.E.*, 348–9.

[3] R. Lennard, *Rural England: 1086–1135* (Oxford, 1959), 300–2, 396–404.

of Morville with its 18 berewicks in Shropshire (253), or in the 12 canons of the church of Bromfield (252b) in the same county. Then in 1086 there were 12 canons in Stoke St Nectan in Devonshire (*456*, 117), and groups of canons in at least five different places in Cornwall (*205b–207*, 121). We also sometimes hear of minor churches, e.g. at Dartford (2b) in Kent, with its three *ecclesiolae* as well as a church. The church at Mottisfont (42) in Hampshire had six *capellae* at named places, and a priest and his curate seems to be implied by *presbyter cum diacono* at Market Bosworth (233) in Leicestershire. One curiosity is found in the entry for Wissett (293) in Suffolk: *In hac ecclesia sunt xii monachi et sub hac i capella.*

The terseness of the entries is occasionally broken to provide some unusual information. Thus there is the remarkable sentence in the joint entry for Offenham, Littleton and Bretforton (Worcs., 175b) which reads: *Ibi sunt boves ad i carucam sed petram trahunt ad ecclesiam.* There is one reference to a wooden church (*ecclesia lignea*) at Old Byland (320b) in the North Riding. There was a new church (*ecclesia nova*) at Wilcot (69) Wiltshire, and a new and beautiful church (*nova et pulchra ecclesia*) at Bermondsey (30) in Surrey. What is more, we read in the Wiltshire folios that the church at Netheravon (65) was ruined, roofless and on the point of collapse (*Ipsa vero vasta est et ita discooperta ut pene corruat*); and the very next entry says that the church at Collingbourne Ducis was also ruined and decayed (*vasta est et dissipata*). The growth of daughter churches or chapels is illustrated by an incident on the Suffolk manor of Thorney (281b). Here, four brothers, who were freemen, had built a chapel on land near the cemetery of the mother church because it could not contain the whole 'parish' (*quod non poterat capere totam parochiam*). The entry goes on to record the arrangement about burial fees between church and chapel. Not far away, in the same hundred of Stow, were Combs and Stowmarket, two miles or so apart. Some rearrangement had obviously taken place because we are told that the 'parishioners' (*parrochiani*) of the church of Stow had been transferred to that of Combs (291b).

CHAPTER III

POPULATION

The Domesday folios present a wealth of detail about population, which constitutes one of the standard items of information that appear in entry after entry. Even so, the picture that emerges is only a very imperfect one. There is no record for the area now covered by the four northern counties of Cumberland, Westmorland, Northumberland and Durham, and the account of what is now the county of Lancaster is meagre in content and unsatisfactory in form. For the rest of England, the information, though abundant, raises many problems. Some of the obscurities or omissions are possibly the result of clerical errors, but there are many that cannot be explained in this way.

THE IMPERFECT STATISTICS

A striking example of the imperfection of the Domesday record is provided by the reference to Avebury in Wiltshire (65b). It was rated at 2 hides and was worth 20s a year, and had a church, but nowhere do we find any mention of those who worshipped in the church or of the land they tilled. In the same way there is no reference to those who may have attended the churches at Kilmersdon in Somerset (*198b*, 91b), at Whitchurch Canonicorum in Dorset (*28*, 78b) and at places in other counties.

Quite a number of entries record teams and other resources but no people. Thus there were teams, meadow, underwood and 2 mills at Stainby (Lincs., 358), but there is no mention of those who worked in the village. There is likewise no reference to those who ploughed with the teams at Rimswell (Yorks., 324), Todber (Do., *47*, 82), Weethley (Warw., 239), and at many other places. A possible explanation of some of these omissions may be given by an entry for Almeley (Heref., 182b); neither teams nor people are entered for it, but we are told that 'the men of another vill work in this vill' (*Alterius villae homines laborant in hac villa*). This entry raises other problems because we know from another source that the other unnamed vill was Upcott, now a hamlet in Almeley parish, but Upcott is nowhere mentioned in Domesday Book.[1] We may

---

[1] V. H. Galbraith and J. Tait, *Herefordshire Domesday, circa 1160–1170* (Pipe Roll Soc., London, 1950), 32, 92; *D.G.M.E.*, 73.

also ask who worked the team at Harding in Wiltshire (74b) unless it was men from Richard Sturmy's other holdings in the neighbouring villages of Burbage, Grafton and Shalbourne. Where, as for Laverton in the West Riding, one entry records teams but no population (330b) while the other records population but no teams (330), it is tempting to think that perhaps the former may have been cultivated by the latter; the two holdings were held by different sub-tenants but under the same tenant-in-chief; but it is equally possible that the absence of recorded population on the former holding is simply the result of accidental omission.

A number of entries are not specific. At Besford (Worcs., 174b), William the priest 'with his men' (cum suis hominibus) had 1½ teams, but there is no mention of the number of men. Likewise at Ashley (Cambs., 199b) we read that 'the villeins' had 2 teams, but we are not told how many villeins there were. Or, to take another example, there were unspecified numbers of men (homines) in Herefordshire at Bromyard (182b), Hopley's Green (184b), Ledbury (182) and Lyonshall (184b), and an unspecified number of bordars at Cradley (182), while at Eastnor (182) there were '2 bordars with certain others' (cum aliquibus aliis). Or yet again, we hear of a render of 4s from an unspecified number of men who lived in the wood (qui manent in silva) at Newport Pagnell in Buckinghamshire (148b). Many entries for Norfolk and Suffolk conclude by saying Alii ibi tenent or Plures ibi tenent. This has sometimes been taken to imply additional uncounted men; but, more probably, it refers to holdings at the same place described under other fiefs but included within one given assessment.[1]

Another element of uncertainty is that some Domesday figures may be inaccurate. For Duxford, in Cambridgeshire, where the Domesday text enters '2 villeins with 6 bordars' (196), the I.C.C. reads '2½ bordars and 5 villeins' (p. 41). Comparison of Domesday Book with the Exeter version also reveals differences, usually small in amount; thus the 3 Domesday cottars at Radstock appear as 4 in the Exeter text (Som., *146b*, 88) and there are many similar examples.[2] Occasionally the difference is appreciable, e.g. 16 Domesday villeins at Werrington were entered by the Exeter scribe as 116 (Devon, *98*, 101). Sometimes the Domesday text appears to convict itself of inaccuracy. The account of five sokelands in Lincolnshire gives a summary for each group of villages and then sets out the details for each village, but the figures in the summaries do not

---

[1] D.G.E.E., 115, 171.   [2] D.G.S–W.E., 396–426.

always agree with the totals of those in the separate entries, and the differences are occasionally substantial.[1]

At times, the Domesday scribe was conscious of the imperfection of his work. An entry for Tadlow in Cambridgeshire (200) refers to an unspecified number of villeins, but in the margin of the folio the scribe wrote a note to remind himself to look into the matter: *rq qot. vill.*, i.e. *require quot villani*; the answer was never entered in the Domesday text, but the I.C.C. version gives it as 2½ villeins (p. 52). An entry for Overton in Wiltshire (65b) also leaves a space for the number of villeins, and the letters *rq* are to be found in the margin in red ink. In an entry for Leckhampstead (Bucks., 149b) the scribe again left a space for the number of villeins to be inserted, but this, too, was never done. There is likewise a blank for the number of coscets in an entry for Tollard Royal (Wilts., 71b); and the entry for Morden in Dorset (83b) has a blank for the numbers of villeins and teams which the Exeter text does not supply (*56*). No information at all appears for one of the two holdings at Woodchester (Gloucs., 164), and the entry tells us that no one came to give an account of it to the king's commissioners and that none of its people were present at the making of the description (*De quo manerio nemo Legatis regis reddidit rationem, nec aliquis eorum venit ad hanc descriptionem*). Something similar happened at Hankham (Sx., 22) where there was land for one team, and we are told *Inde nullum responsum*. Another entry that confesses to lack of knowledge is that which deals with the 62 vills associated with (*jacet ad*) Preston in Lancashire (301b); a few people lived in 16 of these, but how many was not known, and the rest were waste – *Ex his, xvi a paucis incoluntur, sed quot sint habitantes ignoratur. Reliqua sunt wasta.*

More general questions are raised by the absence of slaves from the Ely estates in Huntingdonshire, and by that of *censarii* from the Burton estates in Derbyshire and Staffordshire, and also by the fact that many more churches than priests are entered for some counties (see pp. 53 and 346). The enumeration is also defective in other ways. We hear of many monastic houses and cathedrals, but only rarely of monks and nuns and canons. Thus the vill of Spalding in Lincolnshire (351b) is said to be a berewick of Crowland, but of Crowland itself we are told nothing, neither of the settlement nor of its monks; and yet Crowland Abbey was large enough to hold property in Lincolnshire, Cambridgeshire and a number of other counties. Another example is that of Battle Abbey in

[1] *D.G.E.E.*, 26–8.

Sussex, founded by William in gratitude for his victory, on the spot where Harold fell. By 1086 its possessions stretched over more than one county, but again we are told nothing of its brethren. This absence of information is true of abbeys in general, and there were many of them. Moreover, associated with the great abbeys there must have been many servants and retainers, but only for the abbey of Bury St Edmunds in Suffolk (372) are we given an account of those 'who daily wait upon the Saint, the abbot and the brethren' (see p. 309). In the same way, the households of the king and of the great barons of the realm must have employed considerable numbers of people who went unrecorded. There were also the garrisons of the castles, many built soon after the Conquest.

Furthermore, the incomplete and unsystematic nature of the statistics for the boroughs makes it impossible to estimate their populations. The descriptions of many boroughs mention burgesses, but even when these are enumerated, we can never be sure that the totals are complete, and, in any case, it would seem that burgesses comprised only one element in the population of a town (see p. 293). Moreover, there are no accounts of what were certainly the two largest cities in the realm – London and Winchester. The description of London should have been entered on folio 126 which was left blank and which precedes the survey of Middlesex. Both for it and for Winchester there are only a few scattered and incidental references that tell us little.

While the fact of many omissions is obvious enough, another possibility is not so clear. Was there any duplication? It has been suggested that some freemen and sokemen may have been entered more than once because they held small quantities of land at different places under different lords, particularly in Norfolk and Suffolk. For the hundred of Colneis in Suffolk, Ballard counted 315 references to only 122 different names, and he noted that a certain Blakeman, for example, held land in five different places. But Ballard did not give sufficient weight to the fact that some names were very common; the name Blakeman, for example, is found not only in Suffolk but in many other counties. On balance, it would seem that the number of freemen and sokemen with more than one tenement apiece was very small. In this connection it may be relevant to note that half-freemen and half-sokemen occasionally appear in the entries for some counties, and that at Bredfield in Suffolk (318) there was even a quarter of a freeman – which seem to suggest an attempt to distinguish those who held under more than one lord. There must always remain an element of doubt about the possibility of some duplication of freemen and sokemen but it does not seem to be statistically very appreciable.[1]

CATEGORIES OF PEOPLE

As we have seen, the preamble to the *Inquisitio Eliensis* sets out the questions that were asked by at least one group of commissioners: *Quot villani, quot cot* (*cothcethle* in one MS), *quot servi, quot liberi homines, quot sochemanni* (see p. 4). It is a logical order in that the people closely associated with the demesne come first – villeins, cottars and slaves; then follow the free peasantry – freemen and sokemen. But the categories mentioned in Domesday Book itself are more numerous, and they include a variety of other people. Broadly speaking, the rural population recorded in entry after entry falls into three main groups. First come freemen and sokemen; then come villeins together with bordars, cottars and coscets; and lastly there are slaves. These three groups account for about 98% of the total recorded rural population – see table on p. 63, and Appendix 2 (p. 337). The remainder includes a variety of smaller categories, often restricted to one or more circuits or even to a single county; elsewhere some of them might well have been included within one or other of the larger categories. The numbers within each category and each Domesday county are summarised in Appendix 3 (pp. 338–45). To these must be added yet another category – that of burgesses and other inhabitants of towns; but the record of these is particularly incomplete (see pp. 306–7). There has been much discussion about the differences between various categories and about their legal status and economic condition. Our primary concern is not so much with these distinctions as with numbers and their distribution.

Freemen and sokemen

Commentator after commentator has drawn attention to the fact that the distinction between freemen and sokemen was not a clear one.[2] In this connection it is interesting to note that in the manor of Methwold in

---

[1] A. Ballard, *The Domesday Inquest* (London, 1906), 144; R. Lennard, 'The economic position of the Domesday sokemen', *Econ. Jour.* LVII (1947), 193–5; B. Dodwell, 'The free peasantry of East Anglia in Domesday', *Trans. Norfolk and Norwich Archaeol. Soc.*, XXVII (1939), 159; R. Welldon Finn, *Domesday studies: the eastern counties* (London, 1967), 198–9; *D.G.E.E.*, 114–15, 170–1.

[2] E.g. F. W. Maitland, *Domesday Book and beyond* (Cambridge, 1897), 66–8.

Norfolk, the Little Domesday Book records 4 freemen (136b) where the I.E. enters 4 sokemen (p. 138), but this may have been a slip of the pen. The distinction was certainly not based on size of holding which varied considerably within each group and which was sometimes very small.[1] The relative frequency of the two groups as between one Domesday county and another shows some curious features (Fig. 18). The free peasantry of Lincolnshire and Nottinghamshire consisted entirely of sokemen; that of Northamptonshire and Leicestershire almost entirely. In Essex there were more sokemen than freemen. In Norfolk the numbers were roughly equal, but in Suffolk there were nine times as many freemen as sokemen. Some counties with small numbers of sokemen had no freemen, and vice versa.

The sokemen were to be found entirely in the east and north of the realm, and the bulk of the free peasantry as a whole were also in these areas (Figs. 19 and 20). Some scholars have believed that they, and in particular the sokemen, were the descendants of 'the rank and file of the Scandinavian armies' which had settled in the ninth century.[2] But this belief in an intensive Scandinavian colonisation of much of the north and east of England has not gone without criticism, and it has been held that some of the differences between the Danish districts and the rest of England were of pre-Danish origin.[3] While there may be much in these arguments, especially in relation to East Anglia, the indications of Scandinavian influence upon place-names, law, language and administrative division have made it difficult for other scholars to believe that an intensive colonisation did not take place.[4] The Danish armies themselves may well have been small in size, but behind them, and protected by them, considerable immigration may have taken place. One can only conclude that the Scandinavian settlement may have been a much more complicated process than was at one time thought.

Whatever be the truth, one thing is certain: the free peasantry were less

[1] *D.G.E.E.*, 114, 170; R. Lennard (1947), 190–2.

[2] F. M. Stenton, 'The free peasantry of the northern Danelaw', *Bulletin de la Société Royale des Lettres de Lund, 1925–26* (Lund, 1926), 79; B. Dodwell, 153.

[3] H. W. C. Davis, 'East Anglia and the Danelaw', *Trans. Roy. Hist. Soc.*, 5th series, V (1955), 23–39; P. H. Sawyer, 'The density of the Danish settlement in England', *Univ. of Birmingham Hist. Jour.*, VI (1958), 1–17; P. H. Sawyer, *The age of the Vikings* (London, 1962), 145–67.

[4] H. R. Loyn, *Anglo-Saxon England and the Norman Conquest* (London, 1962), 55; K. Cameron, *Scandinavian settlement in the territory of the five boroughs: The place-name evidence* (University of Nottingham, 1965), 10–11.

Recorded population in 1086 (in thousands)

Freemen	13.6	
Sokemen	23.3	36.9
Villeins	109.2	
Bordars	81.8	
Cottars	5.2	
Coscets	1.7	197.9
Slaves	28.2	28.2
Others		
Priests	1.0	
Coliberts	0.8	
Oxmen	0.8	
Men (*homines*)	0.6	
Swineherds	0.6	
Radmen	0.5	
Miscellaneous	1.5	5.8
Total		269.0

(The arithmetical total of the figures is slightly less than the total here because the figures
have been rounded to a single decimal place - see pp. 338-45.)

numerous than they had been in pre-Norman times. In Cambridgeshire, the number of sokemen had fallen from nearly 900 in 1066 to 177 in 1086; the decrease in Bedfordshire was from about 700 to 90, and in Hertfordshire from some 250 to 43. The smaller number of sokemen in Buckinghamshire, Middlesex and Surrey had disappeared either entirely or nearly so.[1] Freemen had disappeared in the same way.[2] Thus at Benfleet (Essex), described on first folio of the Little Domesday Book, a freeman with half a hide had become one of the villeins (*effectus est unus de villanis*). The brief account of Abberton (46b) also in Essex contains the significant line: 'Then 1 freeman, now 1 bordar.' Or, again, a cry of complaint comes through the terse statistics for Marsh Gibbon (Bucks., 148b); the manor there had been held by Ailric in 1066, but in 1086 he occupied it, 'at feorm' of a Norman lord, in heaviness and misery (*graviter et miserabiliter*).

[1] *D.G.E.E.*, 290; *D.G.S-E.E.*, 24, 67, 156-7, 115, 382.
[2] F. W. Maitland, 63-5.

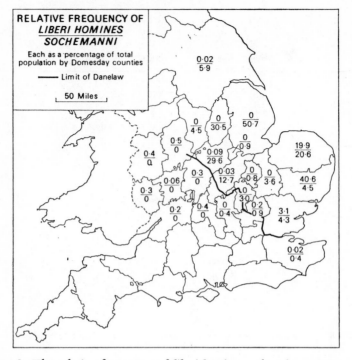

Fig. 18. The relative frequency of *liberi homines* and *sochemanni* in 1086
(by Domesday counties).

Villeins

Villeins constituted the largest single category, and amounted to over
one-third of the total recorded rural population. They accounted for
over one half in a large number of counties (Fig. 21). They included men
of varying substance and obligation, and their holdings were often larger
than those of freemen and sokemen.[1] Half-villeins, like half-sokemen,
are occasionally entered, and, presumably, they implied either half-
villein tenements or those whose land and services were divided between
two estates. At Alverstoke and at Milbrook in Hampshire (41b) there
were villeins who held directly from the bishop of Winchester, not through
an under-tenant. Both entries say: *Villani tenuerunt et tenent*, and the
latter adds: *Non est ibi aula*. Moreover, for Lessland in the Isle of

[1] R. Lennard, 'The economic position of the Domesday villani', *Econ. Jour.*,
LVI (1946), 244–64; F. W. Maitland, 106–7.

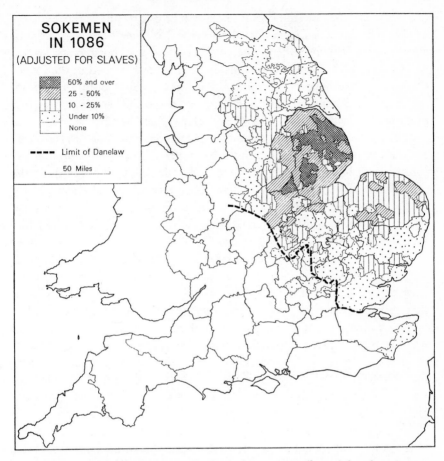

Fig. 19. The distribution of sokemen in 1086 (adjusted for slaves).

On this map, slaves have been regarded as individuals and not as heads of households—
see pp. 73–4 and 88.

Wight (39b) we encounter the most unusual statement that 4 villeins held
2½ teams in demesne (*in dominio*) where once 5 freemen had held of the
king. Or, again, at the unidentified *Madescame* in Devon (*404*, 110b)
the only recorded inhabitant was one villein who, the Exeter text adds,
tenet totam terram in dominio. Villeins are sometimes said to render sums
of money, particularly in Devon and Kent, e.g. at Stonehouse (Devon,
113b) and Buckland (Kent, 10b), but the sums were mostly below 10s.
Four villeins at Wraxall (Do., *52*, 83b) who paid £3 did so, the Exeter

text adds, *de gablo*; and the Exeter text also tells us that one of the 7 villeins at Alford in Somerset (*277b*, 92b) rendered 8 blooms of iron (*reddit viii blumas ferri*). Villeins either alone, or on holdings with bordars and slaves, were able to rent manors, and sums *ad firmam* are recorded in the Exeter entries for Bluehayes (*398*) and Lympstone (*460*), both in Devon. Holdings *ad firmam* are also encountered in the Exchequer text at, for example, Willesden (Mdlx., 127b) and Oare (Kent, 10).[1]

Indications of local arrangements come from Hidcote Bartrim (Gloucs., 166) where the widows of 4 villeins lately deceased (*iiii villanorum nuper defunctorum*) had a team between them. Another curiosity appears in the entry for Barford (Norf., 145) where there were said to be 6 free villeins (*vi liberes villani*). On two occasions the Exeter text uses *rusticus* instead of the Domesday *villanus* – in entries for Long Bredy (*37b*, 78) and Uploders (*58*, 83b), both in Dorset.

In entry after entry, villeins appear in association with ploughteams, but only rarely do we hear of them at work in the field. One of these occasions is in the entry for Leominster (Heref., 180) where the villeins had to plough and sow with their own wheat-seed 125 acres of their lord's land; another is in that for Much Marcle (Heref., 179b) where they likewise ploughed and sowed 80 acres of wheat and 71 of oats. Somewhat similar references are to be found in consecutive entries for Bricklehampton, Defford and Eckington in Worcestershire (174b). References to the other activities of villeins are also rare. At Tidenham (Gloucs., 164) there were fisheries belonging to the villeins, and at *Udeford* and Ruyton (Salop., 257b) there were fisheries in *censu villanorum*. At Rothley (Leics., 130) distinction was drawn between the wood of the demesne and that of the villeins (*silva villanorum*). At Pagham (Sx., 16b) each villein rendered one pig for every six that grazed upon the herbage (*de herbagio*), and at Leominster (Heref., 180) each villein rendered one out of every 10 for pannage (*de pasnagio*).

Occasionally there were villeins who did no ploughing (*non arantes*), recorded, for example, in consecutive entries for Addlethorpe and Friskney (Lincs., 370b). Likewise at Hambleton (Yorks., 315b) there were 6 villeins, one bordar and one sokeman without teams (*sed carucas non habent*), but again we are given no indication of how they were employed. Few though they are, such entries serve to remind us of the multifarious

---

[1] R. S. Hoyt, 'Farm of the manor and community of the vill in Domesday Book', *Speculum*, XXX (1955), 147–69.

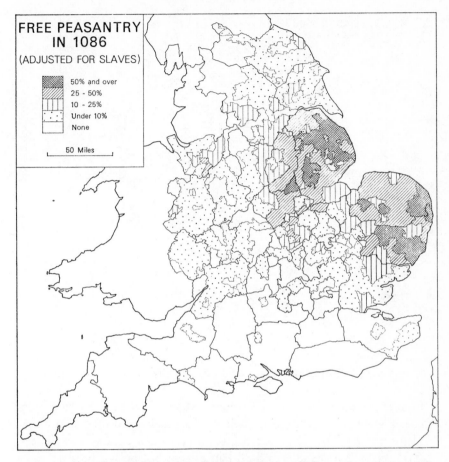

FREE PEASANTRY IN 1086
(ADJUSTED FOR SLAVES)

50% and over
25 - 50%
10 - 25%
Under 10%
None

50 Miles

Fig. 20. The distribution of the free peasantry, including sokemen, in 1086 (adjusted for slaves).

On this map, slaves have been regarded as individuals and not as heads of households – see pp. 73–4 and 88.

activities concealed behind the bare numbers of villeins and teams in entry after entry. Quite a number of entries record villeins but no teams, e.g. those for Aiderton (72b) and Stanley (72) in Wiltshire, and it is difficult to gauge their significance. Some such entries may be no more than the result of omission; thus no Domesday teams are entered for the men of Snailwell (Cambs., 199) but both the I.C.C. (p. 3) and the I.E. (p. 101) supply the missing figure for *carucae villanorum*. The word

Fig. 21. The distribution of villeins in 1086 (by Domesday counties).

villani is sometimes used in the Exeter text, and in the I.C.C., in a broad generic sense; we read of teams held by the villeins and then discover no villeins among the enumerated peasantry. Thus at Lannear (Corn., *235b*) the *villani* are said to hold half a team but only 2 bordars and 6 slaves appear in the subsequent enumeration; this form is much too frequent to be due to scribal error. A similar use of the term *villani* sometimes occurs in Domesday Book itself, e.g. in an entry for Stepney (Mdlx., 127*b*) where there were only 14 bordars, and at Dean (Beds., 210) where there were only 8 bordars and 2 slaves. Clearly the word *villani* was used in various senses, sometimes specific, sometimes generic. When used even in a specific sense, it seems to have covered a wide variety of people.

Bordars, cottars and coscets

Below the villeins in the economic scale came bordars and cottars. The Middlesex folios are unusually detailed in that they indicate a difference between bordars with some land and cottars either with no land or with only very small amounts, sometimes with only what were described as gardens (*horti*) e.g. at Fulham (127b) and Westminster (128); both these bordars and cottars occasionally paid small money renders.[1] Elsewhere, the information is less detailed, but for some counties bordars and cottars appear together in the same entry, as for Middlesex, and this fact also implies a distinction between them. On the other hand, this distinction is very obscure and has given rise to much discussion. It seems that in some places the two terms may have been interchangeable. Thus Domesday bordars at Wratworth (Cambs., 200) are called cottars in the I.C.C. (p. 80). Furthermore, also in Cambridgeshire, the Domesday bordars at Soham (190b) and Snailwell (199b) appear as cottars in the I.E. (p. 101), while the Domesday cottars at Whaddon (191) appear as bordars (p. 107). What is more, the 'breviate', or abstract, of the estates of the abbey of Ely in the I.E. never mentions the cottars of Cambridgeshire and Hertfordshire, but includes them in the total for bordars (pp. 168–73). In the same way the I.E. Summaries for these two counties make no reference to cottars (p. 122). Another example comes from the southwest where 9 bordars and 2 cottars at Moreton (Som., 98) are entered in the Exeter folios as 11 bordars (*453b*).

There are also other indications of the similarity of the two groups. In four Berkshire hundreds cottars not bordars are recorded, but in another seventeen hundreds the reverse is true. In Surrey, Sussex and Kent there is also a high degree of mutual exclusion. Or again, in Cambridgeshire no cottars are recorded for a block of six hundreds in the south-east of the county. In Buckinghamshire, the only 10 cottars were on the estate of the church of Buckingham itself (143). The term 'bordar' does not appear in the preamble to the I.E., and is encountered only infrequently both before and after the Domesday Inquest, yet bordars formed a substantial proportion of the Domesday population of every county (Fig. 22). No cottars appear for 19 counties, but in Cambridgeshire, Hertfordshire and Middlesex, on the other hand, they were particularly

---

[1] R. Lennard, 'The economic position of the bordars and cottars of Domesday Book', *Econ. Jour.*, LXI (1951), 342–71.

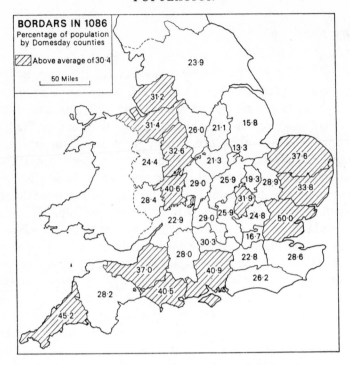

Fig. 22. The distribution of bordars in 1086 (by Domesday counties).

numerous (Fig. 23). It would seem that, in some counties, the difference was one of nomenclature and that the category of bordars often included that of cottars. In Maitland's words: 'We cannot tell how the English jurors would have expressed the distinction between *bordarii* and *cotarii*, for while the *cot* is English, the *borde* is French'.[1] A variant phrase in Worcestershire uses *cotmanni* instead of *cotarii* – at Cofton Hackett (177b) and Northfield (177). Then, again, there were 16 *coteri* at Tanshelf, now within Pontefract (Yorks., 316b); presumably they were cottars, and they were the only ones mentioned in the Yorkshire folios. For Stokesay in Shropshire (260b) there is a solitary reference to 9 female cottars (*ix feminae cotarii*).

A further complication is the mention of another category – that of coscets (or *cosce*ʒ), about 80% of whom appear in the Wiltshire folios (Fig. 24). Here, as elsewhere, they are sometimes entered alongside cottars

---

[1] F. W. Maitland, 39.

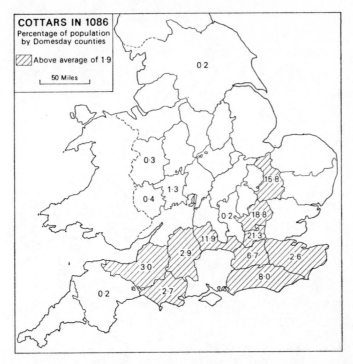

COTTARS IN 1086
Percentage of population
by Domesday counties

▨ Above average of 1·9

50 Miles

0·2

0·3

0·4 1·3

15·8

0·2 18·8

21·3

11·9

2·9 6·7 2·6

3·0 8·0

0·2 2·7

Fig. 23. The distribution of cottars in 1086 (by Domesday counties).

as for Bromham (65), and sometimes alongside bordars as for Pewsey (67b). On the other hand, what both the Domesday and the Exeter texts call bordars are described as *coceti* in the Bath Abbey document which is allied to the Domesday Inquest.[1] What is more, the Domesday bordars, cottars and coscets on the fief of Glastonbury Abbey are all totalled as bordars in the Exeter Summaries (*527–528*).[2] We can only sum up the evidence, or lack of it, by saying that, while in some counties it was possible to distinguish between the three groups, in other counties the differences were thought to be so slight as not to matter. They may have been, in part, the result merely of varying vocabulary. In any case we may not be far wrong in thinking of all three groups as constituting a general class of cottagers.

[1] R. Lennard, 'A neglected Domesday satellite', *Eng. Hist. Rev.*, LVIII (1943), 37.
[2] *D.G.S–W.E.*, 2, 68, 71, 137.

Fig. 24. The number of coscets in 1086 (by Domesday counties).

Slaves

At the lowest end of the economic scale came the *servi*, or slaves, often translated as serfs. They numbered just over 10% of the recorded population. They normally had no share in the teams of a village but worked on the lord's demesne. Only rarely do we hear of slaves with, apparently, their own teams; thus at Boasley in Devon (*288*, 105b) there were 1½ teams on the demesne, and the only recorded population was 7 slaves with one team (*vii servi cum i caruca*). Or, again, at Buckfast (*183*, 104) in the same county we read of 10 slaves who had 2 teams (*qui habent ii carucas*); and for Moortown in Somerset (*429b*, 94) the Exeter text says that 6 slaves held a virgate (*vi servi qui tenent i virgatam*). At Ipswich in Suffolk (393) we even hear of a burgess who was a slave. Whatever be the implications of these unusual entries, the account of the borough of Lewes (Sx., 26) contains a grim reminder of the general status of slaves for it tells us that the toll paid on the sale of a man was 4*d*.

The Little Domesday Book gives information for 1066 as well as for 1086, and sometimes also for an intermediate date, and so we are able to discern a reduction in the number of slaves in Norfolk, Suffolk and Essex. The entry for Somerton (Norf., 146b) is characteristic: *Tunc vi servi, post et modo ii.* The slaves on some holdings had completely disappeared, e.g. under Theydon (Ess., 47b) we read: *Tunc iiii servi, modo nullus.* One Domesday entry alone, that for Hailes in Gloucestershire (167b) refers specifically to the freeing of slaves: *Ibi erant xii servi quos Willelmus liberos fecit.* From other sources we know that the grant of freedom was sometimes an act of piety, but it was more generally the result of the changing economy of the time. A lord came to rely less and less on the work of slaves whom he had to maintain, and more and more on that of peasants who had teams of their own but who also contributed labour to the demesne. In the generations after 1086 slavery disappeared as part of a process by which both slaves and other peasantry merged into a condition of serfdom.[1]

The statistics for slaves raise two major difficulties. The first is that very few are entered for Derbyshire, Lancashire and Nottinghamshire, and none for Huntingdonshire, Lincolnshire, Yorkshire and *Roteland.* We might therefore conclude that slavery had ceased to exist in these latter counties. But an I.E. Summary (p. 162) shows the presence of slaves on the Huntingdonshire estates of the abbey of Ely. On four manors they numbered just over 10% of the recorded population, and this percentage, incidentally, is about the same as that for the slaves of the adjacent counties of Cambridge and Northampton.[2] This immediately suggests the possibility of unrecorded slaves on the other fiefs in Huntingdonshire. The suspicion is strengthened by the fact that the 24 slaves recorded for Nottingham-shire are restricted to three out of the thirty or so fiefs in the county, and that of the 20 slaves recorded for Derbyshire, 13 are entered for a single fief out of seventeen or so.[3] Might not the other fiefs of these two counties have had unrecorded slaves? Can we be sure that there were no slaves even in Lincolnshire and Yorkshire?

The second difficulty about the record of slaves arises from the fact

[1] R. Lennard, *Rural England, 1086–1135* (Oxford, 1959), 389.
[2] *D.G.E.E.*, 330–1.
[3] *D.G.N.E.*, 252–3, 299.

that they may have been entered as individuals and not as heads of house-holds, as for the other categories of population. Vinogradoff hesitated to think that this was so.[1] Maitland also considered this 'difficult question', and thought that we could not be sure 'that the enumeration of the *servi* is always governed by one consistent principle'.[2] A possible indica-tion that the figures refer to individuals is that a number of entries give a combined figure for male and female slaves (*inter servos et ancillas*), e.g. for Haselor (Warw., 244) or for Stanton Lacy (Salop., 260b). The formula is found relatively frequently for the counties of Gloucester, Hereford and Shropshire, and also occasionally for Cheshire, Kent and Warwickshire. A similar formula, *inter bordarios et villanos*, is also found for some counties, but *ancillae* are never linked with any category other than *servi*.

These doubts about the number of slaves affect not only any estimate of total population but also any attempt to indicate its varying density over the country. They also enter into any estimate of the importance of slavery in the realm as a whole – whether it affected some 10% of the working population or only some much lower figure such as $2\frac{1}{2}$%. In a like way they enter into any picture of the varying incidence of slavery through-out different parts of the realm. In view of this difficulty two maps show-ing the distribution of slaves have been prepared. Fig. 25 is based on the actual numbers recorded in the Domesday entries. In constructing Fig. 26, on the other hand, these have been adjusted on the assumption that the slaves were recorded as individuals and that the average size of the Domesday household was 4.5 (not 4.0 as in earlier volumes of this series).[3] At first sight the two maps appear very different, but they both show the same general pattern – the frequency of slaves towards the west as com-pared with that of the free peasantry towards the east.

Priests

Just over one thousand priests appear among the recorded population of the Domesday entries, but the total number in Domesday England must have been much more than this. In the first place, the figure does not include those non-resident priests who were tenants-in-chief or under-tenants, and the decision whether or not to include them is not always easy.[4]

[1] P. Vinogradoff, *English society in the eleventh century* (Oxford, 1908), 463–4.
[2] F. W. Maitland, 17, 34.   [3] For the Domesday household, see p. 87.
[4] See, for example, *D.G.S–E.E.*, 435, and *D.G.N.E.*, 250–1, 299.

Then, in the second place, it would appear that the commissioners acted upon a different basis in different counties. For some counties (e.g. in the northern circuit), the usual formula is: *Ibi est presbyter et ecclesia,* with variants. For other counties such as those of Leicester, Northampton and Warwick, priests are usually entered without any mention of churches. Both formulae appear in yet other counties such as Cheshire, Shropshire and Worcestershire. The sum of the priests in these two types of entry can only provide a minimum total, minimum because there are counties that record churches but no priests. Thus none are entered for the 62 vills with churches in Surrey, and there are also churches with no recorded priests in other counties, e.g. in Norfolk and Suffolk and in Sussex (Fig. 17). In such entries it is possible that the priest was silently included within some other rural category such as the *villani.* Moreover, apart from the village clergy there were those of monasteries and cathedrals about whom we hear so little. The relative numbers of places with churches and recorded priests, as between one Domesday county and another, is set out in Appendix 4 (p. 346 below).

There is much that is obscure about the economic and social position of the village clergy, but it is clear that they varied greatly in standing and wealth.[1] Some churches were without land (*sine terra*) as at Calthorpe (218) and Fulmodeston (168b) in Norfolk. The glebe attached to others ranged from a few acres to over two ploughlands. Some village churches held as much land as many manors, e.g. at Aldbourne (65) in Wiltshire and at Shrivenham (57b) in Berkshire, rated respectively at 2 and no less than 5 hides; but it is often doubtful whether such entries refer to parochial glebe or to personal property.[2] Taken as a whole, the evidence suggests that 'the village priest was usually reckoned to be a member of the peasant community',[3] and he was very frequently enumerated with the peasantry. Thus the description of a holding at Harbury (241b) in Warwickshire runs: *Ibi sunt xxv villani cum presbytero habent iii carucas.* Or again, the entry for Clifton upon Teme (176b), in Worcestershire, lists villeins, bordars and oxmen, and then adds: *Inter omnes cum presbytero habent vi carucas.* Occasional entries provide glimpses of married clergy, e.g. in the account of the city of Lincoln (336) and of Blofield (194b) in Norfolk; and we know from other sources that the ban of 1076 upon clerical marriage was proving difficult to enforce.[4]

[1] R. Lennard (1959), 327.   [2] Ibid., 314.
[3] Ibid., 329.   [4] F. M. Stenton (1943), 668.

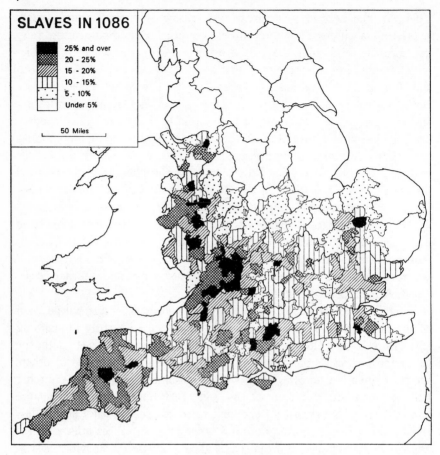

Fig. 25. The distribution of slaves in 1086.

Coliberts

Coliberts were in some way intermediate between slaves and the rest of the peasantry.[1] They were to be found only in the shires of Wessex and western Mercia, and over 50% of them were in the two counties of Wiltshire and Somerset (Fig. 27); they were entered mostly for royal manors and for those of the larger monastic houses. They sometimes held teams as at Barton (Gloucs., 163) and Barton Stacey (Hants., 38b); and

[1] F. W. Maitland, 36–7; P. Vinogradoff, 468–9.

Fig. 26. The distribution of slaves in 1086 (adjusted for slaves).
On this map, slaves have been regarded as individuals and not as heads of households –
see pp. 73–4 and 88.

we occasionally hear of their money renders as at King's Clere (Hants., 39) and Pucklechurch (Gloucs., 165), and of their renders of wheat, barley, sheep and lambs as at Eardisland (Heref., 179b). At Eckington (Worcs., 174b) six rendered 11*s* 2*d*, and ploughed and sowed 12 acres with their own seed.

With coliberts must be grouped the 65 *buri* or *bures* that are entered for six counties. Coliberts and *buri* never occur together in the same entry, and on three occasions they seem to be equated. In the entry for Nether

Fig. 27. The numbers of coliberts and *buri* in 1086 (by Domesday counties).

Wallop (Hants., 38b), *vel Bures* is interlined above *coliberti*; in that for Powick (Worcs., 174b), *coliberti* is interlined above *buri*; and in that for Cosham (Hants., 38), we read of *viii bures i coliberti* which may suggest that the clerk had it in mind to write *viii bures id est coliberti*.

Oxmen

Oxmen or *bovarii* were almost entirely restricted to four counties along or near the Welsh border, and some 50% were to be found in the single county of Shropshire (Fig. 28). Their status has provoked much discussion. Round thought that *bovarius* was virtually an alternative term for *servus*.[1] Certainly in the entry for Huntington (Salop., 256b) *bovarii* is interlined above *servi*, and that most were unfree may be indicated by the mention of *bovarii liberi*; there was, for example, one such

---

[1] J. H. Round in *V.C.H. Worcestershire*, I (1901), 274–5. But see the discussion by J. Tait in *V.C.H. Shropshire*, I (1908), 302–3.

BOVARII IN 1086
Numbers in each
Domesday county
Bovarii liberi in brackets
—— Circuit boundary
50 Miles

Fig. 28. The number of *bovarii* (oxmen) in 1086 (by Domesday counties).

The *bovarii liberi* are additional to the *bovarii*.

at Upton Cresset (Salop., 255), and a total of eleven at Monkland (183), Leinthall and Covenhope (183b) in Herefordshire. But Tait saw difficulties in accepting Round's view, one being the occurrence of both *bovarii* and *servi* in the same entry, e.g. in those for Grafton (Worcs., 172), Orleton (Heref., 183b) and Weaverham (Ches., 263b).[1] It is difficult to be certain of the shade of difference between the two terms.

Men (*homines*)

Some people were described merely as men (*homines*). They were generally distributed in small numbers among the counties except that Hereford and Norfolk each had well over a hundred (Fig. 29). Sometimes their teams are specified, as for Swinford (Leics., 234): *Ibi ii homines ejus*

[1] J. Tait, *The Domesday Survey of Cheshire* (Chetham Soc., Manchester, 1916), 67–9.

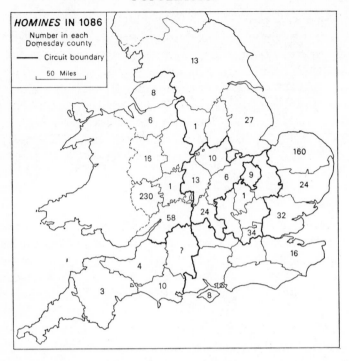

Fig. 29. The number of *homines* in 1086 (by Domesday counties).
The query refers to an unspecified number in Wiltshire – at Lavington (73).

habent ii carucas. Sometimes they rendered money as at St Pancras
(Mdlx., 128): *xxiiii homines qui reddunt xxx solidos per annum*; at other
times we hear merely of their presence as at Thorpe Langton (Leics.,
232): *Ibi sunt ii homines.* At West Wykeham in Lincolnshire (364), there
were 10 men who did not plough: *x homines non arantes.* Outside the
city of Oxford, at Holywell (158), there were 23 men with gardens
(*homines hortulos habentes*), and on the lands of St Martin of Dover (Kent,
2), there were not only 6 men with teams but 8 men dwelling with the
mills (*sub illis molinis manent viii homines*). Then again, in Archenfield
(Heref., 181) the king had 96 men who held 73 teams 'with their men'.

On one of the Herefordshire folios (184b) we hear of unspecified
numbers of men at Hopley's Green and at Lyonshall who paid money
for their tenancies (*pro suis hospitiis*); and at Letton (near Clifford),
described on the same folio, there were 7 *hospites* who also rendered
money. Three Shropshire entries also mention *hospites* rendering

money – one at Hatton (259), 4 at Colemere (259) and 2 at Leaton (259b). There were also another 3 at Hampton in Cheshire (264) who had nothing (*nil habentes*). The term *hospites* was common in France but unusual in England, and it seems to have denoted colonists whom a lord invited to settle on his land.[1] It may be significant that all seven places were not far from the Welsh border (Fig. 30). We cannot say to what extent the equivalents of the various *homines* in these and other counties were included in one or other of the specific categories of population. Quite frequently, where the I.C.C. says *carucae villanis*, the I.E. says *carucae hominibus* or *carucae ad homines*.[2]

Swineherds

There are several surprising features about the Domesday references to swineherds (*porcarii*). Two-thirds of the total number are recorded for Devonshire alone (Fig. 31). Moreover, while the Exeter text for Devonshire refers to 370 swineherds in 67 entries, the Exchequer text omits 69 of these in 23 entries. In the same way, the Exeter text for Somerset refers to 84 swineherds in 14 entries, but the Exchequer text omits 27 of these in 6 entries.[3] Renders in swine or money are frequently stated and are sometimes considerable; thus the 17 swineherds at Taunton (87, *173b*) paid as much as £7 10s. Both in Devon and Somerset, some manors with swineherds had only a few swine or even none entered for them. Thus at Kenton (Devon, *94b*), 4 swineherds rendered 20s, but we hear only of sheep, goats and *animalia* in the list of demesne stock; and at Cutcombe (Som., *357b*) 6 swineherds rendered 31 swine but only 3 swine appear in the list of stock.

Swineherds were occasionally entered in substantial groups. The 87 for Wiltshire were on only 4 manors: 22 on the abbess of Shaftesbury's manor of Bradford on Avon (67b), and the rest on three royal manors, 23 at Chippenham (64b), 13 at Warminster (64b) and 29 at Westbury (65). Some swineherds had teams; thus at Forthampton (180b), in Gloucestershire, 4 had one team and rendered 35 pigs, and at Hanley Castle (180b), in Worcestershire, there were 6 who had 4 teams and rendered 60 pigs.

Clearly, the references to swineherds are the result of idiosyncrasies in the returns for some western counties, and especially for Devonshire. There must have been many others in the rest of England but we can

---

[1] F. W. Maitland, 60; P. Vinogradoff, 231–2.
[2] *D.G.E.E.*, 286.   [3] *D.G.S–W.E.*, 419–20, 402–3.

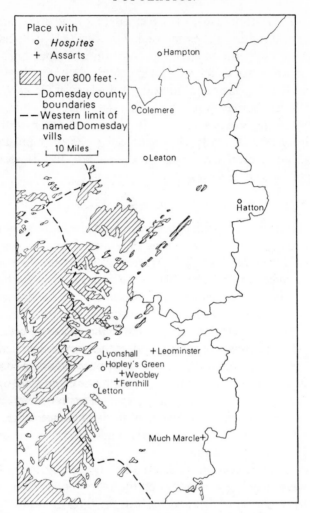

Fig. 30. Places with *hospites* and assarts along the Welsh border
(by Domesday counties).

only suppose they were concealed in the record of other peasantry such as
villeins. The Exeter entry for Tetcott refers to one villein and one swineherd who appear in the Exchequer version as 2 villeins (*319*, 108b), but
this may be due to nothing more than a slip of the pen. The entry for
Oldberrow (Worcs., 175b) speaks of 2 *rustici porcarii*. Far away from the
western manors there was a swineherd at Coggeshall in Essex (26b), on a

Fig. 31. The number of swineherds in 1086 (by Domesday counties).

holding with wood for 500 swine but with only 15 swine on the demesne. Another Essex swineherd is entered for Writtle (5b) in 1066, but he had been made forester of the king's wood.

Radmen

Radmen (*radmans, radmanni* or *radchenistres*) were to be found almost entirely in the counties along the Welsh border, especially in Cheshire, Gloucestershire and Shropshire (Fig. 32). Their name was derived from their 'riding services', that is, their duty to act as escorts or messengers for their lords.[1] They were also required to perform other services. On the Deerhurst estates (Gloucs., 166), in 1066, they had to plough, harrow, mow and reap; and on the Tewkesbury estates (Gloucs., 163) they had also ploughed and harrowed *ad curiam domini*. Those at Powick (Worcs., 174b) had rendered mowing services in the meadows of their lord and

---

[1] P. Vinogradoff, 69–71; J. Tait, 64–5; J. H. Round, (1901), 250–1; L. H. Nelson, *The Normans in South Wales, 1070–1171* (University of Texas, Austin, 1966), 44–51.

had done 'whatever is commanded them'. Moreover, at a number of places we hear that they were unable to leave the manor to which they belonged – at Mapledurham (Hants., 38), Marden (Heref., 179b) and Westbury on Trym (Gloucs., 164b). The lord himself at Martley (Heref., 180b) had separated 2 radmen and their land from the manor. Yet they were in a sense freemen, and are specifically described as such in the entry for Deerhurst (Gloucs., 166) where we read: *Radchenistres id est liberi homines*; they are likewise described as freemen in the account of the Berkeley estates (Gloucs., 163).

A few other entries provide further details about their activities. At Ditton Priors (Salop., 260b), 3 radmen had 2½ ploughlands with the same number of teams. At Meole Brace (Salop., 260b) there was a radman with half a team. On an unnamed manor in *Tornelaus* hundred in Herefordshire (187) there were 3 radmen with 3 teams, and they rendered service to their lord (*serviunt domino*). At Feckenham (Heref., 180b) a radman held a croft and had one team (*tenet . . . unam croftam et habet i carucam*). At Dormington (Heref., 183), on the other hand, there was a radman with land but without a team (*cum terra sine caruca*).[1] On the Leominster manors (Heref., 180), the radmen rendered 14s 4d and 3 sesters of honey. Only one radman is entered for Berkshire, and he was at Goosey (59) where he had his own team (*cum sua caruca*). It is possible that radmen were also to be found in other counties but that they were concealed under such descriptions as *servientes* and freemen.

Miscellaneous inhabitants

The remaining recorded population comprised a great variety of people who seem to be mentioned quite sporadically. Some are described in terms of their occupations – bee-keepers, fishermen, foresters, iron-workers, millers, potters, salt-workers, shepherds and others. An unusual category is that of *cervisarii* who are mentioned twice – in the entry for Bury St Edmunds in Suffolk (372), and in that for the Cornish manor of Helston (*100b*, 120) where there were 40 of them. The word has been variously rendered as ale-brewers or as tenants who paid their dues in ale.[2] Some people are described in terms of their nationality – English, Flemings, French and Welsh. Quite separate from these are the

---

[1] That the unnamed Domesday holding was at Dormington we know from the Herefordshire transcript – V. H. Galbraith and J. Tait, 32, 92. See p. 23 above.

[2] *D.G.S–W.E.*, 321.

Fig. 32. The number of radmen in 1086 (by Domesday counties).

occupational designations sometimes attached to the names of land-holders not included in our count. Such were Grimbold the goldsmith at Manningford (74) and Gunduin the keeper of the granaries at White-cliff (74b), both in Wiltshire. The burgesses and townsmen are considered separately below (see pp. 289 *et seq.*); and in the unusual account of Bury St Edmunds (372) we hear, for example, of bakers, tailors, shoemakers, cooks and porters, all of whom must have had fellow-workers of a like sort elsewhere.

Yet other people appear under such designations as *alodarii*, *vavassores*, *censores* (or *censarii*) and *gablatores*. The first two terms describe types of tenure, the others indicate rent-payers. There were only seven Domesday *gablatores*, all on one holding at Cheddar (*90*, 86) in Somerset. The majority of the *censarii* were to be found in the counties of the northern circuit (see p. 340); the 18 with 5 teams at Duckmanton (277) in Derbyshire were the sole recorded inhabitants of the vill. No *censarii* are entered for the estates of Burton Abbey in Derbyshire and Staffordshire,

4-2

yet surveys from 1114 and about 1126 show them to be numerous within a generation or so of 1086.[1] F. H. Baring thought that they had been omitted by the Domesday scribe, and this view has found support from P. H. Sawyer and J. F. R. Walmsley.[2] If true, this raises problems of credibility comparable with those raised by the missing slaves in Huntingdonshire (see p. 73). Others have taken a different view, and we are left with the possibility of increased cultivation and new settlers since 1086.[3] It is certainly true that in 1114 and 1126 or so, some estates were being farmed at between two and five times their Domesday annual values.[4] On this view we must envisage a prodigious effort of cultivation. Either hypothesis raises difficulties.

Appendix 3 (pp. 338–45) shows how uneven was the incidence of the miscellaneous population as between one Domesday county and another. Moreover, there must have been in England as a whole more than 92 fishermen or 64 smiths or 10 shepherds or 10 iron-workers or 6 millers or a single carpenter. We cannot say why these particular individuals were recorded in this sporadic fashion. The infrequent mention of craftsmen such as carpenters, plasterers and potters is surprising, and we can only suppose that they were entered either by chance, or under some other category (e.g. *villani*), or when the clerks thought it necessary to do so. For the majority of manors it would seem that men were described not in terms of their occupations but under one or other of the principal categories of the Inquest. In spite of the classification in the preamble to the I.E. we do not find anything like complete uniformity among the Domesday entries.

Finally, there is the occasional, and again sporadic, mention of women. As many as 706 *ancillae* are recorded. Nearly 80% of them appear in the folios for Gloucestershire, Herefordshire, Worcestershire and Shropshire. The majority of counties had only a few each or none at all (Fig. 33). There are also other references to women such as dairymaids, female

---

[1] J. H. Round, 'The Burton Abbey surveys', *Collections for a history of Staffordshire*, New series, IX (1906), 271–89; C. G. O. Bridgeman, 'The Burton Abbey twelfth-century surveys', ibid., 1916 (1918), 209–300.

[2] F. H. Baring, 'Domesday Book and the Burton Cartulary', *Eng. Hist. Rev.*, XI (1896), 98–102; P. H. Sawyer, 'The wealth of England in the eleventh century', *Trans. Roy. Hist. Soc.* 5th series, XV (1965), 154; J. F. R. Walmsley, 'The "censarii" of Burton Abbey and the Domesday population', *North Staffs. Jour. of Field Studies*, VIII (1968), 73–80.

[3] F. W. Maitland, 363n; P. Vinogradoff, 462–3; C. G. O. Bridgeman, 268.

[4] C. F. Slade, *V.C.H. Staffordshire*, IV (1958), 21–2.

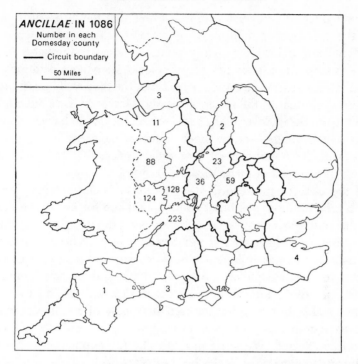

Fig. 33. The number of *ancillae* in 1086 (by Domesday counties).

cottars, nuns, widows and wives. At Barfreston in Kent (9b), for example, there was one poor woman (*una paupercula mulier*) who rendered 3½*d*, and who has thus gained immortality.

TOTAL POPULATION

The details that recur in entry after entry do not provide us with the total populations of manors and villages, and we are left to suppose that each recorded man was the head of a household. We are thus faced with the difficult question of the size of the Domesday household. There is no certain information, but Maitland 'for the sake of argument' suggested five as a multiplier that might enable us to calculate the total from the recorded population.[1] Others have generally accepted this figure as 'a reasonable guess'.[2] J. C. Russell, however, believed that the multiplier should be no more than 3.5, a figure that many historians have thought

[1] F. W. Maitland, 437.   [2] E.g. H. R. Loyn, 337.

too low.[1] J. Krause, in particular, has argued that the 'attempt to under-
mine the evidence of multipliers of 4.5 and 5.0 has not succeeded'.[2]
Later medieval evidence certainly points to such multipliers, and the
figure for 1086 is not likely to have been less.[3] Many considerations enter
into an estimate of such a figure. The size of the medieval household was
not necessarily that of the medieval family. Moreover if we attempted to
penetrate into the dark recesses of conjecture, we should have to consider,
among other things, and without much reliable evidence, the age-
structure of the population of Domesday times; life was short, many
children were born but many died.

On the basis of the recorded population, a multiplier of 4.0 would
imply a total rural population of about 1.1 million for England excluding
the four northern counties; a multiplier of 5.0 would give about 1.3
million. But, as we have seen, slaves may have been recorded not as heads
of households but as individuals; and in that case a multiplier of 4.0
would give a total population of just under a million, and a multiplier
of 5.0 would give a population of a little over 1.2 millon. This calculation
does not make allowance for the fact that many of the thousand or so
priests were unmarried; but even if this were so, the figures would not be
appreciably affected. We must also add that the population recorded in
the Domesday entries for Wales has been excluded.

But our arithmetic cannot stop at this point. What of the missing
population which, as we have seen, may have been quite appreciable?
We cannot say how appreciable, but we can guess that it was something of
the order of not less than 5%, and possibly more. Then again our totals
have not included tenants-in-chief and under-tenants. A list of the former
is given at the beginning of the folios for each county, but we must
allow for ecclesiastical tenants, and for the fact that many tenants held
in more than one county, and that some lesser tenants-in-chief appear
also as under-tenants in other counties; the last group included the
'taini regis', the 'servientes regis' and the 'ministri regis' of such counties
as Berkshire (56, 63b), Hampshire (38, 49b–50b), Surrey (30, 36b) and

---

[1] E.g. J. Z. Titow, *English rural society, 1200–1350* (London, 1969), 67–9, 89.
[2] J. Krause, 'The medieval household: large or small?' *Econ. Hist. Rev.*, 2nd
series, IX (1956–7), 420–32.
[3] H. E. Hallam, 'Some thirteenth-century censuses', *Econ. Hist. Rev.*, 2nd series,
X (1957–8), 340–1; H. E. Hallam, 'Population density in medieval Fenland', *Econ.
Hist. Rev.*, 2nd series, XIV (1961–2), 71–80; J. C. Russell, 'Demographic limitations of
the Spalding serf lists', *Econ. Hist. Rev.*, 2nd series, XV (1962–3), 138–44.

The population of England in 1086

The table excludes the population of those districts now in Wales – see Appendix 3 (pp. 338–45). The incomplete Domesday figures for Lancashire have been replaced by an estimate.

Counting slaves as heads of households

	Multiplier of 4.0	Multiplier of 4.5	Multiplier of 5.0
Recorded in entries	1,073,116	1,207,256	1,341,395
5% addition for omissions	53,656	60,363	67,070
1,100 tenants-in-chief	4,400	4,950	5,500
6,000 under-tenants	24,000	27,000	30,000
Burgesses etc.	120,000	120,000	120,000
	1,275,172	1,419,569	1,563,965
? 1,800 for Lancashire	7,200	8,100	9,000
Four northern counties, say	25,000	25,000	25,000
	1,307,372	1,452,669	1,597,965

Counting slaves as individuals

	Multiplier of 4.0	Multiplier of 4.5	Multiplier of 5.0
Recorded in entries	988,684	1,108,752	1,228,820
5% addition for omissions	49,434	55,438	61,441
1,100 tenants-in-chief	4,400	4,950	5,500
6,000 under-tenants	24,000	27,000	30,000
Burgesses etc.	120,000	120,000	120,000
	1,186,518	1,316,140	1,445,761
? 1,800 for Lancashire	7,200	8,100	9,000
Four northern counties, say	25,000	25,000	25,000
	1,218,718	1,349,240	1,479,761

Wiltshire (64b, 74b). Ellis put the total of tenants-in-chief at 1,400, but a more selective count might reduce the figure to about 1,100.[1] When we consider under-tenants we are on even more doubtful ground. Ellis counted 7,871, but it is likely that this figure is an overestimate in view of the frequent repetition of some names; a more conservative total of 6,000 might be more realistic. We must also take into account the figures for towns, the uncertainties of which are discussed in Chapter 10. A possible urban total (not recorded) population might be about 120,000. Finally, the entries for what is now Lancashire are very unsatisfactory. It is conceivable that the figures may imply a possible 'recorded population'

[1] Henry Ellis, *A general introduction to Domesday Book*, ii (London, 1833), 511.

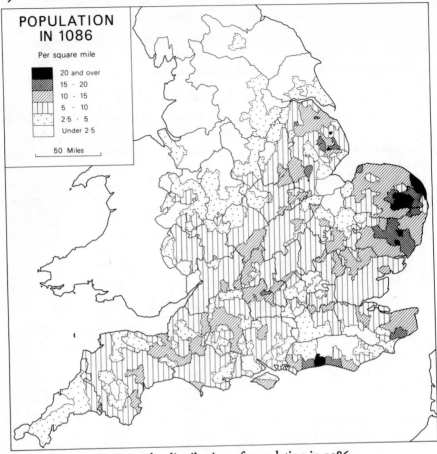

**POPULATION
IN 1086**

Per square mile

20 and over
15 - 20
10 - 15
5 - 10
2·5 - 5
Under 2·5

50 Miles

Fig. 34. The distribution of population in 1086.

of about 1,800.[1] In order to complete the picture for the area included in the later kingdom of England, an hypothetical total must be added for the four northern counties; this is based on analogy with conditions in Cheshire, Lancashire and Yorkshire.

The figures for these various groups are assembled on p. 89. Different sets of figures are set out depending upon whether or not one counts slaves as heads of households or as individuals, and also on whether one adopts a multiplier of 4.0, 4.5 or 5.0. The estimates range from just over 1.2 million to just under 1.6 million. It might seem hardly worthwhile to

[1] *D.G.N.E.*, 407.

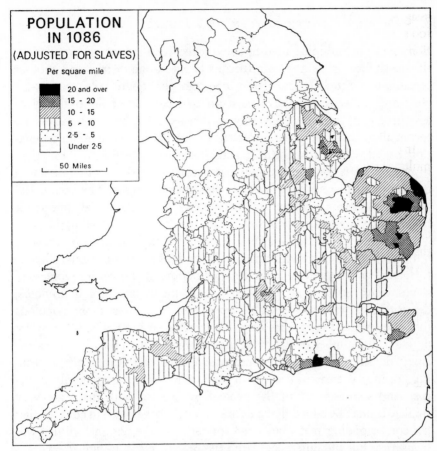

**POPULATION
IN 1086**
(ADJUSTED FOR SLAVES)

Per square mile

20 and over
15 - 20
10 - 15
5 - 10
2·5 - 5
Under 2·5

50 Miles

Fig. 35. The distribution of population in 1086 (adjusted for slaves).

On this map, slaves have been regarded as individuals and not as heads of households –
see pp. 73–4 and 88.

attempt such arithmetic in view of so many imponderables; the figure of
5% for omissions may be too low; the total for the four northern counties
may be too small; and the figures for the towns are very uncertain. But
we must not under-value our material. The results show that there can
hardly have been less than one million people in England in 1086, and
that there may well have been substantially more. An estimate around
1.5 million may be not far from the truth. Merely to be able to say this
for such a remote date is in itself an indication of the value of Domesday
Book as a source of information.

DISTRIBUTION OF POPULATION

Whatever the multiplier used to convert recorded into actual population, the possibility of making comparisons between one district and another remains unaffected. In calculating densities per square mile, tenants-in-chief and under-tenants have been omitted because of the difficulty of assigning them, with any certainty, to density units; but the numbers are too small to affect the general patterns of distribution. The urban population has also been disregarded; and, therefore, in estimating the areas of density units, one square mile has been deducted for London, and a quarter of a square mile for each of the other boroughs. The boundaries between the various density units inevitably have an artificial appearance because they are based upon those of nineteenth-century civil parishes.

In looking at Fig. 34, one should remember that the densities must be multiplied by some factor, perhaps 4.5 or 5.0 in order to obtain figures for actual as opposed to recorded population. If, however, Domesday slaves were recorded as individuals, and not as heads of households, density units with slaves would appear to have been more populous than they were. Fig. 35 has been constructed to meet this difficulty by dividing the number of slaves by the arbitrary figure of 4.5 before calculating densities of population per square mile. The result differs from Fig. 34 in that areas of low density are more extended, especially in the west and south-west, but the general patterns of both maps are very similar. It must be added that a figure of only 4.0 was used in constructing the corresponding maps 'adjusted for serfs' in the regional volumes of this series; but the differences from the present maps are not great.

Another way of presenting the information is to show not specific densities but variations from the median of 6.2 per square mile for England as a whole, excluding Lancashire and the four northern counties. The more general view that results may be more suited to the uncertainty of the data. Fig. 36 attempts to indicate (and incidentally to emphasise) those areas with densities markedly above and those with densities markedly below the median. Between these two groups, the unshaded areas are those characterised, within broad limits, by more or less average densities.

The outstanding fact that emerges from all three maps is the great contrast between the territory on either side of a line joining the estuaries of the Humber and the Severn. Nowhere to the north is a density of 10.0

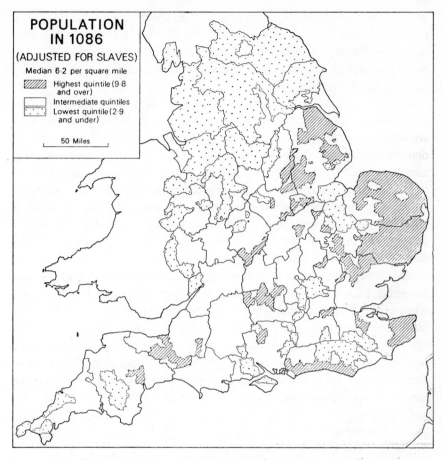

POPULATION IN 1086
(ADJUSTED FOR SLAVES)

Median 6·2 per square mile

Highest quintile (9·8 and over)

Intermediate quintiles

Lowest quintile (2·9 and under)

50 Miles

Fig. 36. The distribution of population in 1086 (by quintiles, and adjusted for slaves).

On this map, slaves have been regarded as individuals and not as heads of household – see pp. 73–4 and 88.

per square mile reached on Figs. 34 or 35; over much of the area, the density is below 5.0, and even below 2.5. The explanation lies partly in the great extent of land over 800 ft above sea-level, and partly in the fact that so much of the area had been deliberately wasted by marching armies (see chapter 8). A reference to 62 vills north of the Ribble (301b) is indicative of conditions generally: ' Of these, 16 are inhabited by a few people, but it is not known how many the inhabitants may be. The rest

are waste.' Along its southern margin the continuous expanse of low
density extended into what was to become Sherwood Forest in Nottinghamshire, Charnwood Forest in Leicestershire and the Forest of Arden
in Warwickshire; none of these forests are specifically mentioned by
name in the Domesday folios.

To the south of the Humber–Severn line, most areas have densities
above the median of 6.2. East Anglia stands out on Figs. 34 and 35 with
densities of over 10 recorded people, and in some districts with over 15
and even over 20; these last may well imply actual densities of from
about 70 up to nearly 100 or so per square mile. Concentrations of
people in eastern Kent, along the coastal lowlands of Sussex, and in the
southern part of the Lincolnshire Wolds, are also notable. But districts
with low densities were also to be found locally south of the Humber–
Severn line in areas with poor soils – coarse sands and gravels, marsh
and high-lying moorland. Some were considerable – the Fenland and the
nearby Breckland, the Weald, the Bagshot Sands area of Surrey and the
adjoining parts of Berkshire, Buckinghamshire and Hampshire, the New
Forest, the Dorset heathlands, the Somerset Levels and, to the south-
west, Exmoor, Dartmoor and the Cornish peninsula. Other areas with
low densities were more limited in extent and included the ill-drained
northern portion of the Isle of Wight and many districts that were to
appear later as royal forests such as Wychwood in Oxfordshire, and the
forests of Wiltshire – Savernake, Chute, Clarendon, Melchet, Grovely
and Selwood.

CHAPTER IV

ARABLE LAND

From numerous hints in late Anglo-Saxon documents we may suppose that the arable, or much of it at any rate, was arranged in open-field strips. There is, however, only a solitary Domesday entry that seems to refer to scattered strips – that for Garsington in Oxfordshire (156b) which reads: 'There 1 hide of inland which never paid geld, lying scattered (*particulatim*) among the king's land.' For possible variations in field arrangements from district to district in 1086, we have to conjecture from later evidence. But although Domesday Book gives us no information about these matters, it does enable us, in a broad way, to perceive the relative distribution of arable over the face of the countryside.

Entry after entry for most counties states: (a) the amount of land for which there were teams (*terra n carucis*), and (b) the number of teams (*carucae*) actually at work. The first statement sounds very straightforward but only seemingly so because its implications are far from clear. The second statement also sounds straightforward, and it may well be so, but it is also not without difficulties and uncertainties. We must therefore consider both these statements before examining the distribution of arable land; and, of course, we can only exclude any possible tillage by the spade or some kind of digging stick.

PLOUGHLANDS

At first sight the statement that there is land for so many teams or so many oxen sounds simple. Domesday Book is apparently telling us that the cultivable land of a holding was such that it could be tilled by that number of teams or oxen, and this implication is occasionally strengthened by the use of the term 'arable land' instead of 'land' e.g. three times on folio 351 for Lincolnshire. But the formula is not as obvious as it seems to be, and it has provoked much discussion. Attention has sometimes been drawn to the fact that an enquiry about *terra carucis* was not among the questions in the preamble to the Ely Inquest; Maitland even spoke of 'apparently unasked for information'.[1] But we need not make too much

[1] F. W. Maitland, *Domesday Book and beyond* (Cambridge, 1897), 420.

of this because it could be argued that the question was implied by the general enquiry with which the preamble ended – *si potest plus haberi quam habeatur*.[1]

In trying to grapple with the problems posed by the information, it seems reasonable to approach them by way of the various circuits of the Domesday commissioners, and to examine the differences in the information both between and within each circuit before venturing upon some general conclusions (Fig. 37).

1. *The south-east circuit*

Five counties in the south-east form a block in which the statement about ploughlands normally runs: *terra est n carucis* with occasional variants such as *terra ad n carucas*. But a remarkable fact is that in a large number of entries the words *terra est* are followed by blank spaces which were never filled in. Furthermore, many other entries mention teams but not ploughlands. This was so, for example, for the large manor of Milton Regis (Kent, 2b) where there were as many as 173 teams at work, and also for the lands of the canons of St Martin of Dover (1b, 2). Taken together, about 20% of the total number of places in the five counties are without information for ploughlands. Clearly, the clerks in these five counties either found difficulty in estimating the *terra carucis* or were in doubt about its meaning. All five counties formed the first circuit described in Domesday Book. Blanks and omissions are especially characteristic of Kent, the opening county. Could the absence of information be the result of experiment as the work was begun? We can only conjecture.

In entries that record both teams and ploughlands, the former are sometimes the same as the latter, sometimes less and sometimes more (Figs. 38 and 39). When they are more, attention is occasionally drawn to the excess by the word *tamen*;[2] thus the entry for Preston Candover (Hants., 49b) runs: *Terra est dimidia caruca et tamen in dominio est i caruca.* Some figures such as 120, 100, 60, 50 or 40 seem to be estimates or approximations, but, on the other hand, many figures sound real enough, e.g. $1\frac{1}{2}$, 26 or 56.

---

[1] V. H. Galbraith, *The making of the Domesday Book* (Oxford, 1961), 74n. See p. 5 above.

[2] E.g. Ashford (Kent, 13); Milford (Hants., 53b); Preston Candover (Hants., 49b); an anonymous holding in Wantage hundred (Berks., 58).

Omission of ploughlands for Domesday counties of the south-east

Entries which mention neither ploughlands nor teams are excluded.

			Terra est blank		Total places with omission
Kent	92	⎫	84	⎫	110
Sussex	17		15		61
Surrey	20	⎬ entries for	17	⎬ places	30
Hampshire	16		16		59
Berkshire	20	⎭	19	⎭	32
Total	165	entries for	151	places	292

One brief entry for Rooting in Kent (12) does not mention plough-lands but says instead that there had been, and still was, one team on the demesne: *Ibi fuit et est una caruca in dominio.* This formula, unusual for

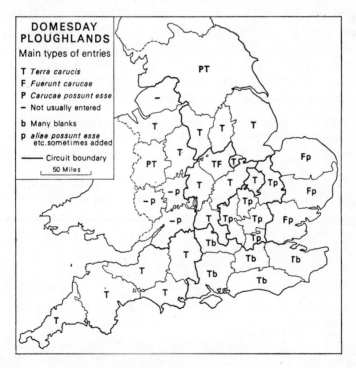

Fig. 37. Domesday ploughlands: Main types of entries (by Domeday counties).

these counties, is also to be found in some entries relating to land which had been taken into the New Forest, but amongst these we also find *terra est n carucis* or *terra n carucis*; thus of the five entries relating to the unidentified *Truham* or *Trucham* (51–51b), two give *fuit*, two *est* and one merely *terra carucis*. It would be reasonable to suppose that all five entries were providing the same kind of information. But on the basis of these few examples we cannot venture to assert that in this circuit *terra carucis* implied the teams of some date earlier than 1086.

2. The south-west circuit

For the five south-western counties the Exchequer formula is normally *terra n carucis* which in the Exeter version is rendered as *hanc terram possunt arare n carucae*, with variants such as *potest arari cum n carucis*. Very occasionally the Exeter formula, or something like it, appears in the Exchequer text,[1] and the converse is also true.[2] The phrase *terra est* is sometimes followed by a blank space which was never filled in, twice each in Dorset, Somerset and Wiltshire,[3] and there are also 33 entries which mention teams but not ploughlands.

The wording of some Exchequer entries seems to suggest that the clerk thought there should be as many teams as ploughlands. At any rate this is what may be inferred from entries such as these:

Cann Orchard (Corn., 124): *Terra ii carucis quae ibi sunt.*
Highworth (Wilts., 65b): *Terra est ii carucis. Has habet ibi presbyter.*
Kenn (Devon, 106b): *Terra est xxv carucis et totidem ibi sunt.*

When there was an excess of teams on a holding, attention is sometimes drawn to the excess by the use of the word *tamen* as in the entry for Frome (Do., 84b): *Terra est ii carucis. Tamen sunt ibi iii carucae.*[4] There are eight such entries for Dorset, fifteen for Devon and six for Somerset.[5]

A deficiency of teams was more usual than an excess (Figs. 38 and 39), and one of the outstanding facts about the Domesday south-west is the frequency with which the number of ploughlands exceeds that of teams.

---

[1] E.g. Charminster (Do., 75b); North Newnton (Wilts., 67b); Sturminster Newton (Do., 77b).

[2] E.g. Banwell (Som., *157*).

[3] Cheselbourne (Do., 78b) and Nettlecombe (Do., *38*, 78); Lilstock (Som., *478b*, 98b) and Stawley (Som., *373b*, 97); Biddestone (Wilts., 71) and Tockenham (Wilts., 71b).   [4] I.e. Frome Billet and Frome Whitfield.

[5] *D.G.S–W.E.*, 87, 241, 157.

The large number of these apparently 'understocked' settlements, particularly in Cornwall and Devon, is very striking, and yet these areas had not been devastated as had the northern counties of the realm. We are immediately faced with the possibility that this feature was the result of some form of infield–outfield agriculture whereby small numbers of teams, in successive years, ploughed various parts of large tracts of territory.[1] Certainly, in later times, the agrarian arrangements of the south-west were very different from those over most of the rest of England.

The figures for ploughlands often look suspiciously as if they were estimates rather than precise quantities. Such are those for North Molton (Devon, 100b) with 100 for 47 teams, Bruton (Som., 86b) with 50 for 21 teams, and Roseworthy (Corn., 120) with 30 for 13 teams. The frequency of such round numbers is so great as to suggest that they may have had an 'arbitrary character'.[2] Against this, many figures appear to be real enough, e.g. 7, 18 or 28, but some of these latter figures make us suspect that the number of ploughlands had been obtained by adding up the existing teams. Thus Crediton (Devon, 101b) had 185 ploughlands and the same number of teams, and Ramsbury (Wilts., 66) had 54 of each. We can perhaps see this happening in the remarkable entry for Long Bredy (Do., *37b*, 78); the Exeter text does not give the number of *carucae possunt*, but the Exchequer version says that there was land for 9 teams, a figure obtained presumably by adding the 3 + 5 + 1 teams of the Exeter text.

The entry for the Cornish vill of Ludgvan is also unusual. At the foot of folio *260*, the Exeter scribe wrote *hanc possunt arare xv carucae* but when he turned over the page he repeated himself, giving the same details about ownership and hidage and then going on to say *hanc possunt arare xxx carucae*. The Exchequer scribe was unable to decide which figure was correct and so he wrote *terra xv carucis vel xxx carucis* (122b). We may wonder what exigencies lay behind many other entries.

3. *The Bedford–Middlesex circuit*

The statement about ploughlands is fairly uniform throughout another group of five counties – Bedford, Buckingham, Cambridge, Hertford and Middlesex; and the usual phrase is *terra est n carucis* with minor variants. Only rarely is the information not given; there is for example a

[1] F. W. Maitland, 425.
[2] J. H. Round in *V.C.H. Somerset*, 1 (1906), 388.

blank after *terra est* in the account of a small estate at Beachendon (Bucks., 144b). The idea that there should be as many teams as ploughlands may be suggested by such variations as the following:

Aldenham (Herts., 136): *Terra est i carucae sed deest caruca.*
Dean (Beds., 211b): *Terra est iii carucis et ibi sunt.*
Greenford (Mdlx., 130b): *Terra est dimidiae carucae sed non est ibi modo.*
Stanford (Beds., 218b): *Terra est dimidio bovi et ibi est semibos.*
Wymington (Beds., 218b): *Terra est i carucae sed non est ibi.*

A feature of the circuit is that when the number of teams is smaller than that of ploughlands (Fig. 38), there is usually a statement to the effect that additional teams could be employed as in the following example:

Shipton (Bucks., 151): *Terra est vii carucis. In dominio iii hidae et ibi sunt ii carucae et aliae ii possunt esse. Ibi iiii villani cum i bordario habent ii carucas et tercia potest fieri.*

Occasionally the scribe omitted to point out the possibility of additional teams; thus at Ware (Herts., 138b) there were 38 ploughlands but only 29½ teams and 3 possible demesne teams are mentioned; nothing is said about the additional 5½ teams needed to make the equation correct. Some of these omissions can be made good for Cambridgeshire. The Domesday account of Cottenham (191b) tells of 8 ploughlands and of only 7 teams, but the I.E. version (p. 114) supplies the missing information and speaks of *aliaque potest fieri*. The I.C.C. likewise supplies the figures missing from the Domesday entries for Fulbourn (201b, p. 25) and Kirtling (202, p. 11).

A few holdings had an excess of teams (Fig. 39); Wyboston (Beds., 212), for example, had 5 ploughlands but 6 teams. Sometimes, it was the total of actual and possible teams that was in excess; Milton Keynes (Bucks., 153) had 10 ploughlands and 10½ teams but there could also be another half team (*dimidia potest fieri*). That some of these perplexities may be due to scribal errors is shown by a number of Cambridgeshire entries in which the I.C.C. corrects, or seems to correct, the Domesday figures. The Domesday entry for Woodditton (189b) speaks of 16 ploughlands, with 2 teams on the demesne, 3 with the peasants and another 13 that could be added (*xiii carucae possunt fieri*), but the I.C.C. (p. 10) correctly reads 11 instead of 13. Some arithmetical inconsistencies may be the result not of error but of arrangements unknown to us. There is a reference to one complication in the account of Bennington (Herts., 141) where there were 11 ploughlands with 11 teams and 2 possible teams, but the discrepancy is explained in the preceding entry for Box where there were 2 ploughlands but no teams because it was worked by teams from Bennington – *Haec terra jacet et appreciatur in Belintone et colitur propriis carucis*. Such complications are exceptional. Generally speaking, the entries for the circuit as a whole are straightforward, and they are unusual in that they account arithmetically for any deficiency of teams on a holding.

4. *The western circuit*

Ploughlands are not generally entered for the three counties of Gloucester, Hereford and Worcester, but occasional references to them appear here and there in an isolated fashion. For Hambrook (Gloucs., 165), where there were 4 teams at work, the phrase *terra est v carucis* is interlined above the entry. This formula also occurs for two Worcestershire holdings, both waste and both described on folio 177, though in different fiefs.[1] For Herefordshire, the formula is found for as many as 24 holdings (7% of the total), 9 of which were waste.[2] Here, the entry for Clifford (183) seems to imply agrarian reality for it reads: *Ibi habet Radulfus terra ad iii carucas sed non est nisi i caruca*; so does the entry for Weobley (184b): *terra ad i carucam de Essar*ʒ.

More frequent is an indication of possible additional teams by the use of such phrases as *possent fieri, possent esse, adhuc possent fieri* and *plus possent esse*. They occur in only two Gloucestershire entries which follow one another on the same folio,[3] but in 53 Herefordshire entries (15% of the total), and 38 Worcestershire entries (16% of the total); they are rare in the first part of the description of Worcestershire (172–176) but become more frequent in the latter part (176b–177b). There are also some curiosities. The account of a number of the holdings of the church of Worcester (174) tells us that no further teams could be added: *In omnibus his maneriis non possunt esse plus carucae quam dictum est*. One

---

[1] Stildon and Bellingdon (117).

[2] *Wapleford* (179b); Burlingjobb, Old Radnor (181); Brampton Abbotts, Almeley (182b); Bartestree, Bowley, Sutton, Clifford (183); Pilleth *et al.* (183b); Upleadon, Hopley's Green, Weobley, Fernhill, *Pletune* (184b); Wormsley, Sawbury, Grendon Bishop (185); Bradley *et al.*, Titley (186b); Ailey, Lincumbe (187); Wickton, *Curdeslege* (187b).

[3] Alderton and Naunton (165b).

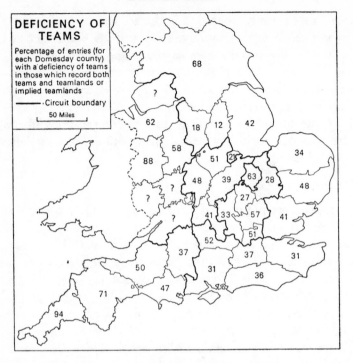

DEFICIENCY OF TEAMS

Percentage of entries (for each Domesday county) with a deficiency of teams in those which record both teams and teamlands or implied teamlands

——— Circuit boundary

50 Miles

Fig. 38. Deficiency of teams over ploughlands or implied ploughlands (by Domesday counties).

The Lancashire record is imperfect. For the other three queries, see p. 101.

Herefordshire entry, that for Preston on Wye (181b), says that the villeins had more teams than arable land: *Villani plus habent carucas quam arabilem terram*. At Mansell (Heref., 182b) there was a team on the demesne together with an idle team (*alia ociosa*).

The Gloucestershire entry for Tewkesbury (163) refers to teams in the past tense, possibly for 1066. Three Herefordshire entries also refer to conditions before 1086. One relates to the large manor of Leominster (180) where 260 teams had been reduced to 230 by 1086. Another, that for Wellington (187), refers to former (*antea*) teams as well as to those of 1086, and concludes that there had once been more: *Plus erant ibi carucae quae nunc sunt*. Thirdly, the account of Rotherwas (186b), where 4 teams were at work, ends with the unusual statement: *Ibi fuerunt x villani cum xiii carucis*. Could this have been a substitute for *terra carucis*?

There is also another variant. In assessing the potential arable of some

Fig. 39. Excess of teams over ploughlands or implied ploughlands
(by Domesday counties).

The Lancashire record is imperfect. For the other three queries, see p. 101.

holdings in Herefordshire, an arbitrary ratio of 2 ploughlands per hide
seems to have been assumed. Thus the eleven waste manors 'on the
marches of Wales' had a total assessment of 18 hides with land for 36
teams (186b). Similarly, the summary for the valley of *Stradelie* speaks
of 56 hides which 112 teams could plough (187). Traces of a similar
relationship are found elsewhere in the county, e.g. at Almeley (182b)
and Grendon Bishop (185) each with 4 hides and 8 ploughlands, but
it is impossible to say whether these are significant or the result of chance.

In contrast to the entries for these three counties, those for Cheshire
and Staffordshire are characterised by the general use of *terra carucis*. A
deficiency of teams is far more frequent than an excess (Figs. 38 and 39).
In one entry for Cheshire and in five for Staffordshire, *terra est* is followed
by a blank space. In one of the Staffordshire entries (Cotwalton, 248),
the words *est terra* have been deleted, and in another (Warslow, 248) an

'r' (= *require*) appears in the margin.[1] There are also a number of entries
which mention teams but not ploughlands.[2] The Cheshire folios include
an entry for Allington and two other places now in Denbighshire (266b);
we hear of two teams, and then come across a unique phrase for Cheshire:
Ibi iiii carucae plus possent esse. The Staffordshire entries are a little more
irregular. It would seem that the compilers could only speculate about the
ploughlands on six waste holdings (246b); the entries for Sheen, Stans-
hope, Farley, Endon and Rudyard each record *terra i caruca* but insert
vel ii (or 2) above; the sixth entry, that for Wootton under Weaver,
similarly has *vel iii* written above *terra ii carucis*. Then there are three
Staffordshire entries which state teams both for 1066 and 1086, but with
the complication that two of the entries also state a differing number of
ploughlands:

	Hidae	Terra carucis	Carucae T.R.E.	Carucae T.R.W.
Burton upon Trent (248b)	½	—	12	4
Weston under Lizard				
et al. (250b)	4	6	11	5
Wolverhampton (247b)	1	3	8	19

Another Staffordshire curiosity is the statement for Syerscote (249) that
there could be teams (*Ibi possent esse carucae*) followed by an enumeration
of 3½ ploughs.

The entries for Shropshire are unusual in that, for the most part, they
employ two different formulae, but there are complications as the
analysis in Appendix 5 (p. 347) shows. The earlier folios (252–257)
normally state the number of teams at work and then go on to say that
more could be employed; the phrases are *possent esse, plus possent esse* or
adhuc possent esse, with minor variants; where such a statement does not
occur we can only infer that the arable was fully cultivated. The later
folios (257–260), on the other hand, are characterised by *terra est n carucis.*
The transition from one formula to the other on folio 257 does not
correspond with a change of hundred or of ownership but comes in the
middle of Earl Roger's fief. Nor is the transition sharp because the two
formulae are intermingled in the left-hand column of folio 257. Moreover,
a number of *terra carucis* entries are to be found in the earlier part – for

[1] Trafford (263); Drayton (246); Chartley (246b); Eccleshall (247); Cotwalton
(248); Warslow (248). For Cotwalton and Warslow, see C. F. Slade in *V.C.H.
Staffordshire,* IV (1958), 47n.   [2] *D.G.M.E.,* 182; *D.G.N.E.,* 340–1.

example on folio 252 and in ten consecutive entries on folios 254b–255. Conversely, two entries on folio 257b are of the *possent esse* variety. It would seem as if the two formulae were interchangeable; certainly both are very frequently accompanied by a deficiency of teams (Figs. 38 and 39). Finally, three Shropshire entries refer to former teams – for an unnamed holding in Overs hundred (252), for Clunbury (258) and specifically in T.R.E. for Onibury (252).

5. The midland circuit

The ploughland formula in the majority of entries for the four counties of the midland circuit is simply *terra est n carucis* or *terra n carucis*. The phrase *terra est* is occasionally followed by a blank space – in seven entries for the fief of Robert Dispensator in Leicestershire (234b), in five entries for Warwickshire, four of them for royal manors (238, 238b), and in three entries for Northamptonshire (219b, 220b), two of them for royal manors. There are also many holdings for which teams but not ploughlands are entered. These include seven out of the nine royal manors of Oxfordshire (154b), and thirteen out of the fourteen of the royal manors of Leicestershire (230–230b), together with other holdings both in these two counties and in Northamptonshire and Warwickshire.

In the entries which mention both teams and ploughlands, a deficiency is more frequent than an excess in each county (Figs. 38 and 39). The wording of some entries seems to suggest that it was natural for a ploughland to carry a team. At any rate, this is what may be inferred from such entries as these:

Aston (Warw., 243): *In dominio est terra vi carucis, sed carucae non ibi sunt.*
Geddington (N'hants., 222): *Terra est ii carucis. Ipsae ibi sunt cum v sochemanni et iiii bordarii.*
Littlethorpe (Leics., 231b): *Terra est ii carucis. Has habent ibi ii villani cum bordariis.*

When there was an excess of teams on a holding, our attention is sometimes drawn to this by the use of the word *tamen*, as in the entry for Wolfhamcote (Warw., 241): *Terra est ii carucis et tamen sunt ibi iii carucae.* There are seven such entries in the account of the Warwickshire fief of Turchil (241–241b) and an eighth on folio 242b. There are also four similar entries for the Northamptonshire fief of Robert de Buci (225–225b), and another three for places elsewhere in the county.[1] Furthermore, the word is also

---

[1] Elton (222), now in Hunts.; Casterton (229), now in Rutland; East Farndon (229).

found for two entries in Leicestershire, and for another two in Oxfordshire.[1]

The Warwickshire entries are relatively straightforward, but some of those for Oxfordshire raise many difficulties. Does that for Duns Tew (156) link ploughlands with assessment: *Ibi sunt iii hidae et dimidiae. Terra est totidem carucis?* Or is this due merely to a chance similarity of numbers? Three Oxfordshire entries on folio 154b tell us not of ploughlands but of the number of teams at work in 1066 – on royal holdings at Bampton, at Benson and at Bloxham and Adderbury. Then again, three consecutive entries for Banbury, Cropredy and Eynsham (155), while not as clear, also tell us how many teams had once existed – at all three when the bishop of Lincoln received them, and at Banbury for 1066 as well. Moreover, the entry for Waterstock (155b), also in the bishop's fief, reads *Terra est v carucis*, but in the margin there is added *Ibi fuerunt v carucae T.R.E.* There is also a short unnamed entry following that for Cadwell (157) which does not mention ploughlands but says *Ibi fuit i caruca.* Furthermore, most Oxfordshire entries follow the pattern: *Terra est m carucis . . . Nunc in dominio est n carucae*; and *nunc* seems to imply a contrast between 1086 and some earlier date. The word *nunc* is never found in the Northamptonshire entries, only twice in those for Warwickshire,[2] and four times in the *terra carucis* entries for Leicestershire.[3] In the *carucae fuerunt* entries for the last county (see p. 109), the contrast in time is obvious, but it is very doubtful whether we can go on to assume that to the clerk *terra carucis* and past teams were one and the same.

Although using the same formula, the ploughlands of Northamptonshire seem to have been quite different from those of Oxfordshire and Warwickshire. Both Round and Baring showed that these Northamptonshire ploughlands referred not to existing arable land but to an older assessment, heavier than the current rating in hides; and Hart has carried the discussion further by a detailed analysis of the entries.[4] In the south-

---

[1] Cadeby (Leics., 232b); Husbands Bosworth (Leics., 235); Northbrook (Oxon., 159); Brize Norton (Oxon., 169b). [2] Hill, Newbold Comyn (239).
[3] Newbold Verdon (233), Peatling Parva, Barkby, Eastwell (236b).
[4] J. H. Round, 'The hidation of Northamptonshire', *Eng. Hist. Rev.*, xv (1900), 78–86; F. H. Baring, 'The hidation of Northamptonshire', *Eng. Hist. Rev.*, xvii (1902), 76–83; F. H. Baring, 'The pre-Domesday hidation of Northamptonshire', *Eng. Hist. Rev.*, xvii (1902), 470–9; C. Hart, *The hidation of Northamptonshire* (Leicester, 1970). See also F. W. Maitland, 473.

western hundreds of the county, the ratio of hides to ploughlands is usually 2:5 (Fig. 40). 'When a vill is assessed at four "hides" and as containing ten ploughlands, the combination really means that its assessment has been reduced from ten units to four.'[1] The reassessment may have taken place in more than one stage at various times before the Norman Conquest. The artificial nature of this 2:5 ratio is best seen when the assessment is given in terms of complicated fractions as in the following examples:

	Hides	Ploughlands
Evenley (226b)	$1\frac{3}{8}$	4
Grafton Regis (224)	$\frac{4}{5}$	2
Syresham (223b)	$\frac{1}{4}$	$1\frac{1}{4}$

Over the rest of the southern half of the county, the ratio of hides to ploughlands is usually 1:2, and the implication is that here also the ploughlands represent an obsolete assessment, except that the reduction was only 50%.

In the northern half of the county no such regular ratios are dominant, but there are clear signs of a duodecimal element in the ploughland figures. This Danish system was most obviously developed in Nassaborough hundred (the soke of Peterborough), and it would seem that the ploughlands here, too, were artificial in character. For four holdings in this hundred we are given not only ploughlands but teams T.R.E. for two successive entries on folio 221 and for another two in close proximity on folio 221b, all in the fief of Peterborough Abbey:

Glinton (221): *In hac cum appendiciis T.R.E. fuerunt xxx carucae. Terra est xii carucis* (8 teams *T.R.W.*).

Werrington (221): *Ibi cum appendiciis fuerunt xxx carucae T.R.E. Terra est xii carucis* (24 teams *T.R.W.*).

Wittering (221b): *Terra est xvi carucis. T.R.E. fuerunt ibi xxx* (15 teams *T.R.W.*).

Southorpe (221b): *Terra est xvi carucis. T.R.E. fuerunt xii* (10 teams *T.R.W.*).

It is clear that there is much that is artificial about these figures and that these ploughlands were something quite different from teams T.R.E. Traces of a duodecimal system can also be observed for Witchley hundred (the southern part of the later shire of Rutland). Here, as in the

[1] J. H. Round, *V.C.H. Northamptonshire*, I (London, 1902), 264.

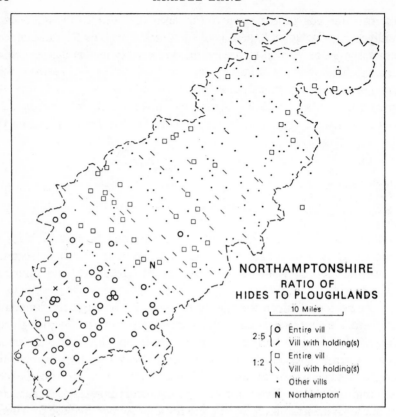

Fig. 40. Northamptonshire: Ratio of hides to ploughlands in the
Domesday county.

The symbols outside the county boundary refer to places with holdings partly in
Northamptonshire and partly in Bedfordshire or Huntingdonshire.

rest of Domesday Northamptonshire, are indications of an artificial
and fiscal system.[1]

Finally, among the Northamptonshire entries, are two quite different
from the rest, for Adstone in the south-west and for Burton Latimer in
the middle of the county:

Adstone (222b): One virgate. *Ibi dimidia caruca potest esse.*
Burton Latimer (226b): 8½ hides. *Ibi T.R.E. fuerunt xiiii carucae.*

---

[1] F. M. Stenton in *V.C.H. Rutland*, I (London, 1908), 126.

It is difficult to imagine how these, like the four in Nassaborough hundred, came to appear amongst the regular Northamptonshire entries. They resemble some of the varied formulae encountered for Leicestershire.

Four different types of entry are encountered in the Leicestershire folios, as the following examples show:

(a) Sharnford (231): *Una caruca potest esse.*
(b) Old Dalby (235): *Terra est xii carucis.*
(c) Coston (233): *T.R.E. erant ibi x carucae.*
(d) Cranoe (236b): *Ibi iii carucae fuerunt.*

The first is rare but each of the other three is frequent. The distribution of the four formulae, folio by folio and fief by fief, is set out in Appendix 6 (pp. 348–9), and it shows a high degree of correspondence between formula and fief. Different fiefs apparently made their returns in different ways. It follows that two or more of the different formulae occur for separate holdings in the same vill, e.g. at Kilworth (234, 235, 237) and Sproxton (235, 236b). The entry for Aylestone (231b) contains two formulae. It says *Ibi fuerunt xiiii carucae* and then closes by adding: *Saxi tenuit et Leuuinus de eo terra vi carucis*; but it is doubtful whether we can equate the figures or assume that the lesser was included within the greater. As the analysis in Appendix 6 shows, some fiefs employed more than one formula, and J. S. Moore has explained this in two ways: either by assuming that some tenants-in-chief made returns for their demesne manors separately from their under-tenants who made their own returns, or by assuming that 'each manorial bailiff supplied such details for each individual manor as he was able or inclined'.[1] One further point should be noted. The formula found for a fief in Leicestershire does not necessarily appear for the same fief in other counties. Thus the fief of Henry de Ferrers uses the T.R.E. formula for Leicestershire but *terra carucis* for the other three counties of the circuit.

From the mutual exclusion of the four types it might seem that all are giving the same information, and that all denote land fit for ploughing in 1086 by virtue of past cultivation or present condition. But before being tempted towards such a conclusion we must note that an artificial element has been discerned in the figures. Stenton showed that in many entries the ratio of carucates to ploughlands was 2:1 or 3:2 or 1:1. He suggested

[1] J. S. Moore, 'The Domesday teamland in Leicestershire', *Eng. Hist. Rev.*, LXXVIII (1963), 700.

that 'it is quite possible in view of the heavy rating of Leicestershire as a whole that the jurors in the Domesday Inquest may have been allowed to express the agricultural possibilities of their vills and manors in figures which bore a conscious reference to the carucates of assessment in each case'. The entries can therefore be construed as a suggestion for a reduction of assessment.[1] On this assumption, although not a fiscal unit comparable with that of Northamptonshire, the Leicestershire ploughland may have been conventional. The table below gives an analysis of the entries with the various ratios for each formula:

The Leicestershire Carucate
Numbers of entries with different ratios of carucates to ploughlands or to teams *fuerunt* or *potest esse* in the Domesday county.

	2:1	3:2	1:1	Fewer carucates
(a) *Potest esse*	—	—	2	—
(b) *Terra est n carucis*	19	25	28	23
(c) *T.R.E. fuerunt n carucae*	3	3	19	29
(d) *Ibi fuerunt n carucae*	3	9	15	16

In considering the figures one must remember that some of the examples (especially those with a ratio of 1:1) may be no more than the result of chance coincidence. Even so, it is clear that the postulated reductions form a marked feature only of the *terra carucis* entries, and it may be that these are telling us something quite different from entries with the other three formulae.

6. The northern circuit

The formulae encountered in the Yorkshire folios, with minor variations, fall into two groups:

(a) *Ubi possunt esse n carucae* or *Quam n carucae possunt arare.*
(b) *Terra est n carucis* or *Terra ad n carucis.*

There are also some entries, particularly those for waste holdings, which make no reference to ploughlands. The earlier folios (299–325) are characterised by the *possunt esse* formula, but examples of *terra carucis* are also to be found here, especially for waste holdings. The later folios (325–332) employ only the *terra carucis* formula with but one exception – for the sokeland of Nunnington on folio 325b. The distribution of formulae

---

[1] F. M. Stenton in *V.C.H. Leicestershire*, I (London, 1907), 286.

is shown in Appendix 7 (pp. 350–51). That both formulae could mean the same thing is suggested by a comparison of several duplicate entries. A combined entry for Chellow and four other places on folio 318 says *vi carucae possunt ibi esse*, but a repetition of this at the end of the folio (which has been cancelled in the MS.) reads: *Terra est vi carucis*. Or again, one entry for Darton on folio 301 says *Terra ad dimidiam carucam*, while its duplicate on folio 316b says *dimidia caruca potest ibi esse*. These, and a number of other entries like them, seem to indicate that *terra carucis* means what it says in agricultural terms. So do a number of entries which refer to ploughlands that were said to be tilled or not tilled. They include the following:

Loftus Hill (330b): *Terra ad ii carucas. Ipsi* (i.e. *iii taini*) *adhuc habent et colunt eam.*

Winksley (330): *Terra ad ii carucas. Ipse* (i.e. Gospatric) *habet nunc sed non colit.*

Another possibility, however, is suggested by the fact that the number of ploughlands is often duodecimal in character – 3, 6, 9, 12 or 24. The idea of artificiality is also encouraged by the ratios of 2:1 or 1:1 that are frequently encountered between carucates and ploughlands. In some entries, the phraseology itself can be taken as implying a relationship, as in the entry for Egton (305): *ad geldum iii carucatae et totidem carucae possunt esse*, or, more strikingly, in that for Hessay (329): *ii carucatae terrae et ii bovatae ad geldum. Terra est ad totidem carucas.* But, on the other hand, there are many non-duodecimal numbers and also very different ratios in individual entries, and there seems, on the face of it, no reason to doubt that the ploughlands of such entries represent agricultural reality.

One other point must be mentioned. Very many *terra carucis* entries refer to waste holdings where no land had been ploughed for 15 years or more. Faced with this, the Yorkshire jurors, according to Maitland, found a basis for estimating the arable in terms of the assessment: 'This estate is rated to the geld at two carucates; the assessment seems tolerably fair; so they say that two teams would plough the land. Or again, this estate is rated to the geld at four carucates; but its assessment is certainly too high, so let it be set down for two teamlands.'[1] This sounds plausible, but it is entirely speculation. Many other waste holdings have no record of ploughlands.

[1] F. W. Maitland, 426.

Two entries, unique in the Yorkshire folios, give not only ploughlands of the 'possunt arare' formula but also former teams. Both describe
royal holdings and they occur near one another on the same folio (299):

> Northallerton: *In Aluertone sunt ad geldum xliiii carucatae terrae quas xxx
> carucae possunt arare. Hanc tenuit Eduinus comes pro uno manerio T.R.E.
> et habebat lxvi villanos cum xxxv carucis ... Modo est in manu regis et
> wasta est.*
>
> Falsgrave sokelands: *Inter totum sunt ad geldum quater xx et iiii carucatae
> quas possunt arare xlii carucae. In his fuerunt c et viii sochemanni cum xlvi
> carucae. Modo sunt vii sochemanni et xv villani et xiiii bordarii habentes vii
> carucas et dimidiam. Caetera sunt wasta.*

These astonishing entries seem to show that some 'ploughlands' in
Yorkshire at any rate were quite different from former teams, and there is a
suspicion of artificiality about the 42 ploughlands for the 84 carucates
of the Falsgrave sokelands.

The formula for Huntingdonshire is consistently *terra carucis*, but the
I.E. has variants of this – usually *ad arandum carucae* or *carucae possunt
arare terram istam*. There are very few omissions. It has been suggested
that these ploughlands do not measure arable land, but 'preserve a
record of the taxation imposed by Danish earls soon after the settlement
of 877', on a duodecimal basis.[1] This may well be so, but, on the other
hand, many figures are not duodecimal, nor do they combine into
duodecimal groups. Furthermore, the number of teams is frequently
prefaced by *Ibi nunc* or *Ibi modo* which may possibly imply a contrast
between the teams of 1086 and those of some earlier date as indicated
by ploughlands.

The Nottinghamshire formula is also consistently *terra carucis*, with
occasional omissions and with a blank space after *terra* in the entry for
the waste holding of Eastwood (287b). The figures for ploughlands are
frequently duodecimal, much more so than those for the carucates themselves, and it has been suggested that these ploughlands represent 'fragments of an obsolete system of assessment' which was heavier than the
current assessment in carucates.[2] This may be true, but the duodecimal
element is apparent in only 106 out of 457 entries that record ploughlands.[3]

---

[1] C. Hart, 'The hidation of Huntingdonshire', *Proc. Camb. Antiq. Soc.*, LXI
(1968), 55–66.
[2] F. M. Stenton, *V.C.H. Nottinghamshire*, I (1906), 213.
[3] *D.G.N.E.*, 247.

It is true that there were many holdings with one or two ploughlands, and that some of these might be grouped to form duodecimal units. Unfortunately we cannot produce satisfactory figures for the vills themselves because of the frequency of composite entries in the Nottinghamshire folios. Very many entries show an excess of teams which suggests a conventional element in the ploughland figures (Fig. 39).

After Nottinghamshire in the Domesday text comes a section on *Roteland* (293b–294) which comprised two of the three hundreds of the later county of Rutland; and in these two hundreds the duodecimal system is clear.[1] Incidentally, a prefatory summary to the *Roteland* section speaks of *carucae esse possunt* while the entries for the individual holdings themselves record *terra carucis*.

Derbyshire is another county for which the formula is consistently *terra carucis*, with occasional omissions and with blank spaces after *terra* in the entry for Mapperley (273) and in two successive entries for Breaston and Riley (278). The figures do not show a marked duodecimal element, but they are of interest for another reason. The ploughlands number the same as carucates in 117 of 228 entries that record both, i.e. 51%; and the similarity sometimes involves fractions in a striking manner. Chaddesden (275), for example, was rated at 4½ carucates and ¾ bovate, and we are told *terra totidem carucis* which involves two thirds of an ox, but it may be that the Domesday clerk 'merely wished to say that the rateable value of the land corresponded well enough with its agricultural possibilities'.[2] Could it be that for Derbyshire as for some other counties of the northern circuit, there was a conventional element in the record of ploughlands? Entries with an excess of teams are certainly very frequent (Fig. 39). On the other hand, here, as for Huntingdonshire, the number of teams is frequently prefaced by *Ibi nunc* which may imply a contrast with some earlier date for the ploughlands.

The Lincolnshire formula is also consistently *terra carucis* or sometimes *terra arabilis ad carucas*. There are occasional omissions, and *terra* is followed by a blank space in six entries.[3] The number of ploughlands is the same as that of carucates in 520 entries out of 1,441 that record both, i.e. 36%; the figures usually speak for themselves, but we often hear of

[1] F. M. Stenton (1908), 122–4. See also *D.G.M.E.*, 368–71.
[2] F. M. Stenton in *V.C.H. Derbyshire*, I (1905), 317. See also *D.G.N.E.*, 293–4.
[3] Binbrook (366b), Cumberworth (364), Dunston (362), Nocton (362), Somercotes (364), Spalding (368).

totidem ad carucas.[1] What is more, the coincidence is sometimes apparent for each of a number of holdings making up a vill.[2] This is so, for example, in the five entries for Burgh le Marsh where the total amounts to 11 carucates 7 bovates and the same number of ploughlands and oxen (348b, 355, 360 *ter*). On 253 holdings (i.e. 18%) the number of plough-lands is exactly double that of carucates; thus at Minting (351) there were 7 carucates and 5½ bovates, and this is followed by the statement *terra arabilis duplex*; and for Rothwell (365), with '13½ bovates and ½ bovate', the phrase is *terra dupliciter ad arandum*. It may be, as for other counties of the northern circuit, that such figures give a general and not an exact indication of the arable; and that we are being told, in effect, that the assessment was just about right in relation to the arable or that it was only about one half, or maybe one third, of what it should be.[3] But we must not exaggerate the conventional element. Many other Lincolnshire entries seem to be giving us 'a genuine estimate of the existing arable'.[4]

7. The eastern circuit

The folios for the three counties of the Little Domesday Book make no reference to *terra carucis*. It is true that for Norfolk and Suffolk the entries usually begin with a statement of *car' terrae* (i.e. carucates), but the phrase *ad geldum* is not added as in the entries for the carucated counties, and the information about geld is given in quite another way which is peculiar to the two counties. In view, therefore, of this second statement about geld we might for a moment suppose that the East Anglian *car' terrae* were the equivalent of the ploughlands of other counties. They were, however, divided into acres not bovates, and Mait-land came to the conclusion that they referred to the apportionment of geld among the various landholders of a vill as opposed to the other statement of liability for a vill as a whole.[5] Vinogradoff likewise thought that they were concerned with assessment, and that they referred either to 'a former fiscal arrangement displaced by a new mode of distribution', or that 'they still had some significance for purposes of assessment in

[1] There is a detailed analysis of the carucate–ploughland figures for Lincolnshire in P. Vinogradoff, *English society in the eleventh century* (Oxford, 1908), 510–34.
[2] F. M. Stenton in C. W. Foster and T. Longley (eds.), *The Lincolnshire Domesday and the Lindsey survey* (Lincoln Record Society, 1924), xv–xix.
[3] F. W. Maitland, 426.
[4] F. M. Stenton in C. W. Foster and T. Longley (eds.), xix.
[5] F. W. Maitland, 429–31.

regard to one or other kind of service'.[1] A number of other commentators have also believed that they referred to assessment rather than to agrarian reality.[2] Others, however, have taken the contrary view that they were nothing other than the equivalent of the ploughlands found elsewhere.[3] In the latter case, we are then faced with the fact that in entry after entry teams outnumber ploughlands to a degree found nowhere else in England, and this is reflected in the totals for the two Domesday counties:

	Car' terrae	Carucae
Norfolk	2,423	5,006
Suffolk	2,411	4,480

Such differences hardly support the idea that car' terrae reflected agrarian reality. They probably relate to assessment, but whichever view we take, the fog that surrounds the phrase is not lessened. Essex stands in a different category for it is assessed in a straightforward fashion in hides.

There is another complication. The Little Domesday Book is unusual in that it gives, for all three counties, information about teams at three dates, 1066, 'afterwards' and 1086. The entries are, however, somewhat irregular, and it is not always possible, with any certainty, to make comparisons between the three dates or between 1066 and 1086.[4] When the teams of 1086 were fewer than in times past we are sometimes told that further teams could be employed. The phrases used are possent esse, possent restaurari, possent fieri and once for Staverton (Suff., 325) possent refieri. They occur in 25 entries for Suffolk, in 27 for Essex and in 100 for Norfolk; they are also to be found in the I.E. These additional teams do not always bring the 1086 totals up to those of 1066, and there was often a deficiency (Fig. 38). On the other hand, there were potentially excess teams on some holdings (Fig. 39). Thus the entry for Gusford (Suff., 431) reads: Tunc ii carucae hominum, modo i et iii carucae possent restaurari. Similar extra teams are noted in entries for Norfolk and Essex. It is always possible that such entries were due to scribal errors; but if

[1] P. Vinogradoff, 145, 199n.

[2] E.g. D. C. Douglas, The social structure of medieval East Anglia (Oxford, 1927), 4; R. Welldon Finn, Domesday studies: the eastern counties (London, 1967), 109.

[3] C. Johnson in V.C.H. Norfolk, II (1906), 7–8; J. E. A. Jolliffe, 'A survey of fiscal tenements', Econ. Hist. Rev., 1st ser., VI (1936), 136.

[4] R. Welldon Finn; (1) Domesday studies: the eastern counties (London, 1967), 183–5, 192–4, 201–2; (2) The Norman Conquest and its effects on the economy: 1066–1086 (London, 1971), 242–6.

they were not, it would seem that we are being told of teams in 1066 and in 1086, and then of potential arable beyond the arable of either date. These entries make us pause in any attempt to equate teams T.R.E. with *terra carucis*. There are three unusual entries which include the *terra carucis* formula. That for Blythburgh (Suff., 282) runs: *tunc i caruca dominio. Terra v carucis in dominio sed Rogerus recepit iii boves et modo sunt similiter. Semper xxi carucae hominum.* That for Bayfield (Norf., 112) runs *terre ii carucis.* The third, for an unnamed holding in Lexden hundred (Ess., 99), reads: *terra ad ii boves.* We may well wonder what form the entries of the Little Domesday Book would have taken had they been incorporated into the Exchequer Domesday Book itself.

What was the ploughland?

There is much to make us believe that, for some counties at any rate, the phrase *terra carucis* means what it says. The Exeter version of this certainly seems clear enough – '*n* ploughs can till this land'. So do the occasional duplicate versions in the Yorkshire folios where *terra carucis* seems but another way of referring to land that so many ploughs could till. The impression is reinforced by the arithmetic of the entries for the Bedford–Middlesex circuit; these bring teams at work into relation with *terra carucis* by referring to possible additional teams and so accounting for any deficiency in 1086. We also hear of further possible teams in occasional entries for four counties of the western circuit,[1] but these entries do not mention *terra carucis* although, presumably, we could arrive at this figure by addition. The officials of the south-east circuit seem to have had difficulty in assembling the information, judging from the blank spaces in many entries and the lack of information in others. There are also blank spaces in entries for some other counties but we perhaps should not attach too much importance to these latter because of their sporadic character. Lack of information may reflect idiosyncrasy in the returns of some fiefs, and so explain, for example, why the account of Robert Dispensator's fief in Leicestershire has seven defective entries (234b) (see Appendix 6, pp. 348–9).

It is possible that on occasions we are given estimates or approximations. Figures such as 100, 60, 50 or 40 ploughlands on the royal holdings in Somerset (86–87b) arouse suspicion.[2] There are very many similar

---

[1] Gloucestershire, Herefordshire, Shropshire and Worcestershire. See pp. 101 and 104 above.   [2] J. H. Round in *V.C.H. Somerset*, I (1906), 388.

examples and it is difficult to know what importance to attach to them. Certainly, other figures sound precise enough but even some of these are not above suspicion, and, on occasions, we may wonder whether the number of ploughlands has been obtained simply by adding up the teams. That this may be more than conjecture may be indicated by the remarkable entry for Long Bredy in Dorset *(37b,* 78) where we see the Exchequer clerk adding together the teams of the Exeter text and calling them ploughlands.[1]

Artificiality of another sort may be suspected in some Danelaw counties with their complicated history of reductions in assessment. When in many Lincolnshire entries the record of assessment is followed by the statement *terra arabilis duplex* we can only doubt whether we are being told of agrarian reality. And, again, the figures for Northamptonshire have provoked a great deal of discussion which seems to indicate that *terra carucis* here represented an obsolete assessment. Moreover, the duodecimal figures for some other Danish counties also suggest conventional figures rather than agrarian facts.[2]

An artificial or conventional element also seems indicated by the frequent excess (sometimes great excess) of teams over ploughlands (Fig. 39). A deficiency of teams is easy to explain in terms of wasting, afforestation, murrain or other local vicissitude, and we are occasionally told of such hazards.[3] But it is not easy to explain the fact that teams outnumbered ploughlands on so many holdings. Our attention is sometimes drawn to this by the word *tamen* which implies that things are not what one might expect them to be. Various attempts have been made to explain this surprising feature of excess. In some places it is possible that it was the result of a large free element in the population; that is to say, as Maitland wrote, were these lands with excess to come into 'the hands of lords who held large and compact estates, the number of plough-teams would be reduced';[4] a fully-fledged manorial regime would have been more efficient. But in Lincolnshire, for example, the districts with the highest percentages of sokemen had no excess of teams, and the reverse was also true.[5] Stenton suggested that the excess was sometimes due to the creation of new demesne. Thus Sibsey (Lincs., 351) contained 6 plough-

---

[1] *D.G.S–W.E.,* 427. See p. 99 above.
[2] For the counties of Huntingdon, Northampton Nottingham and York.
[3] *D.G.E.E.,* 221; *D.G.M.E.,* 204, 302; *D.G.S–E.E.,* 521.
[4] F. W. Maitland, 428.   [5] *D.G.E.E.,* 41.

lands, but 7 teams, one in demesne and 6 among the men of the village; 'the lord's team appears here very plainly as an innovation' on the existing arable.[1] Individual examples of excess may be thus explained, but no general explanation emerges from the Lincolnshire evidence. Welldon Finn put forward another possible explanation: 'It is obvious that over and over again, in complex manors, we are given the teamlands both of the lord's demesne and of the *terra villanorum*, but not those of the sub-tenancies.' At Crondall in Hampshire (41), for example, there were 29 ploughlands and the same number of teams held by lord and villeins on the main holding, but there were also $17\frac{1}{2}$ teams on the sub-tenancies for which no ploughlands were entered.[2] There are many examples of such complex manors.

The entries for three counties are of particular interest because in each county two or more formulae regularly occur. It is conceivable that *terra carucis* is interchangeable in Shropshire with the *plus possent esse* formula, and in Yorkshire with *possunt esse carucae* or *carucae possunt arare*. The four formulae of Leicestershire, on the other hand, show a high degree of correspondence with fiefs which may have employed different methods of making returns; and to suppose that these are interchangeable is much more doubtful. Some refer to *terra carucis* and some to former teams, and it is possible that they may be telling us quite different things.

One of the tantalising features about the record of ploughlands is the sudden appearance of uncharacteristic formulae among the regular entries for a county. Amidst the folios for Kent we suddenly encounter not the phrase *terra carucis* but, instead, the sentence: *Ibi fuit et est una caruca* in the entry for Rooting (12). Likewise among the *terra carucis* of Northamptonshire we come across not only *Ibi T.R.E. fuerunt xiiii carucae* for Burton Latimer (226b) but *Ibi dimidia caruca potest esse* for Adstone (222b); and among the *terrae carucis* of Cheshire there abruptly appears, in the entry for Allington and two other places (266b), the phrase *Ibi iiii carucae plus possent esse*, a formula common for some other counties of the western circuit. Oxfordshire is another county characterised by the *terra carucis* formula but, replacing it, we hear eight times of

---

[1] F. M. Stenton in C. W. Foster and T. Longley (eds.), xix.
[2] R. Welldon Finn, 'The teamland of the Domesday Inquest', *Eng. Hist. Rev.*, LXXXIII (1968), 99; R. Welldon Finn, *The Domesday Inquest and the making of Domesday Book* (London, 1961), 127–30.

teams at some date earlier than 1086, some of which refer specifically to T.R.E. Gloucestershire, on the other hand, is a county with no record of ploughlands, yet *Terra est v carucis* appears suddenly interlined in the entry for Hambrook (165); and the formula *adhuc possent esse* appears in two consecutive entries for Alderton and Naunton (165b), and teams possibly for 1066 appear in that for Tewkesbury (163). Herefordshire is another county without regular mention of *terra carucis* but the phrase occurs for 24 holdings (7% of the total) in different fiefs and the phrase *plus possent esse*, or something like it, for another 53 holdings (15% of the total) also scattered among different fiefs. Moreover, three mysterious Herefordshire entries refer to ploughs for some date before 1086 (see p. 102). Then again, amidst the two regular formulae for Shropshire, there are also three references to teams earlier than 1086, one specifically for T.R.E. (see p. 105).

Why should the references to past teams emerge now and again, seemingly in substitution for *terra carucis*? Maitland believed that *terra carucis* and teams T.R.E. meant 'much the same thing'.[1] On the face of it, this might seem to be possible. The preamble to the I.E. certainly included a question about teams T.R.E., and they are regularly entered in the Little Domesday Book. They also constitute one of the regular formulae for Leicestershire, although an analysis of the figures raises doubts about their equivalence with *terra carucis*. The addition of *nunc* or *modo* to the teams at work in 1086 in some entries for the counties of Derby, Huntingdon, Leicester, Oxford, Warwick and occasionally for Sussex, also seems to imply a contrast with past conditions that may be indicated by *terra carucis*. But, as Vinogradoff pointed out, when the number of ploughlands exceeds that of teams, the T.R.E. value of an estate is often less (and sometimes much less) than the T.R.W. value; the converse is also true.[2] In Derbyshire, for example, there were often more teams than ploughlands, and yet a heavy decline in value; the phenomenon can be seen in entry after entry. These facts alone do not make it easy to believe that *terra carucis* in these entries refers to 1066. Moreover, Maitland asserted that on no occasion do *terra carucis* and teams T.R.E. occur together in the same entry,[3] but this is not so. There are a few entries in which both appear – once for Oxfordshire, once for Leicestershire, twice each for Staffordshire and Yorkshire, and four times

[1] F. W. Maitland, 423.   [2] P. Vinogradoff, 159.   [3] F. W. Maitland, 421.

for Northamptonshire.[1] To these must be added the astonishing appearance of *Terra v carucis*, *terre ii carucis* and *terra ad ii boves* in three entries in the Little Domesday Book – for Blythburgh in Suffolk (282), for Bayfield in Norfolk (112) and for an unnamed holding in Lexden hundred in Essex (99). Moreover, in the Oxfordshire entry for Waterstock (155b) the phrase *Ibi fuerunt v carucae T.R.E.* appears in the margin, and the number of teams is the same as that of the *terra carucis* in the entry itself.

This array of evidence is very bewildering. Miss S. P. J. Harvey has suggested that 'the varying and regional nature of the ploughland is explicable if we regard it as a new fiscal assessment which took the best basis it could, given the regional character of agriculture and of local administration.'[2] Whether we accept this interesting view or not, it would seem that, in the attempt to provide information about the available land, no uniform approach was adopted throughout the whole of the realm. Nor need this surprise us when we see in what varied ways such resources as wood and meadow were recorded. This variety, together with the occasional uncharacteristic formula for a county, is all the more intelligible now that it seems that not only were hundreds important in the making of the survey but also returns from individual fiefs and even manors.[3] Attempts to provide information differed between one circuit and another, between one county and another within each circuit, between one fief and another within each county, and even between one estate and another within each fief. We can never know what processes of thought lay behind the decisions of the bailiffs of different fiefs, of the local juries within each hundred and county, and of the commissioners within each circuit. It may be that their uncertainty about what should be returned, and how it should be returned, was as great as our uncertainty about what they did return. One thing seems clear. We cannot use the ploughland figures to provide a consistent picture of the available arable land throughout all England in 1086.

[1] Waterstock (Oxon., 155b); Aylestone (Leics., 231b); Weston under Lizard *et al.* (Staffs., 250b), Wolverhampton (Staffs., 247b); Northallerton (Yorks., 299), Falsgrave sokelands (Yorks., 299); Glinton (N'hants., 221), Werrington (N'hants., 221), Wittering (N'hants., 221b), Southorpe (N'hants., 221b).

[2] S. P. J. Harvey, 'Domesday Book and Anglo-Norman governance', *Trans. Roy. Hist. Soc.*, 5th ser., xxv (1975), 187.

[3] V. H. Galbraith, (1961), 166–7; R. Welldon Finn (1961), 78–88.

PLOUGHTEAMS

Imperfect entries

Domesday entries usually distinguish between the teams on the demesne and those held by the peasantry, but in some entries no distinction is made, especially for small manors, and at other times it is not clear. Furthermore, occasional entries seem to be defective, and there are also a few gaps where figures for teams were never inserted. The Exchequer description of West Lydford (Som., 99) merely says *Ibi sunt vii carucae*, but the Exeter version (*493*) tells of 3 teams in demesne and 4 with the peasantry. Detailed comparison of Exeter and Exchequer entries also reveals many small differences between the number of teams given in each version.[1] The I.C.C. and the I.E. also show many divergencies from the Exchequer text. Thus the Exchequer account of Snailwell (Cambs., 199) mentions teams in demesne yet omits any reference to those of the peasantry, but both the I.C.C. (p. 3) and the I.E. (p. 101) supply the missing details, i.e. 8 teams 'with the villeins'. In a number of entries the I.C.C. supplies not additional information but what is apparently a more correct version. For one of the Ely holdings at Meldreth, for example, the Exchequer text enters 3 teams with the peasants (191) but the I.C.C. (p. 66) enters 5 teams which seems to be correct; at any rate that figure is what the I.E. (p. 108) also gives, and it makes the total number of teams equal to that of ploughlands. On other occasions it is the Exchequer text that supplements or corrects the I.C.C., e.g. at Isleham where the I.C.C. omits the demesne teams (199, p. 8) and at Silverley where the I.C.C. omits the men's teams (199b, p. 9). Such omissions and mistakes illustrate the margin of error that must always be remembered when dealing with Domesday statistics.

For other counties there are also many entries which tell of ploughlands and of people as well as of such resources as wood and meadow but which mention only demesne teams or only peasant teams or neither. Such is the account of Cottisford (N'hants., 224b) in which we are told of 3 demesne teams and of a fourth that was possible (*posset esse*), but nothing of the teams of the 10 villeins and 5 bordars on the holding. Such lack of any reference to teams is a marked feature of the entries for the five south-western counties (Fig. 7).[2] Was this the result of error?

---

[1] *D.G.S–W.E.*, 397–426. [2] *D.G.S–W.E.*, 22, 88, 160, 245, 316.

Or did the clerks sometimes ignore the presence of small numbers of oxen? Or were these settlements mainly pastoral in spite of the plough-lands entered for them? Or did oxen from other settlements till these lands?

A few entries refer specifically to the absence of teams. The plough-land at Aldenham (Herts., 136) was said to be without a team (*sed deest caruca*). The three ploughlands on a holding at Bengeo (Herts., 140b) had no teams apart from that on the demesne (*Ibi non sunt carucae nisi dominica caruca*). At Ospringe (Kent, 10), on the other hand, the men had 9 teams but none were said to be on the demesne (*In dominio non sunt carucae*). Or, again, there were 2 demesne teams at Shipton (Gloucs., 167b) but the men were without a team (*sine caruca*). Occasional York-shire entries, such as that for Oulston (330) refer to men who did not till (*sed non arant*). It would be possible to explain such entries by assuming that the men were otherwise employed as at Ower (Do., *44b*, 78) where the recorded population comprised only 13 salt-workers, and for which the Exeter version says *nulla caruca est nec arare potest*. It is, however, more difficult to understand those entries which mention teams but no men who might have ploughed with them, such as the entries for the Sussex vills of Hurst (20), Moustone (27b) and Offington (28b), each with a team at work. Then there were those vills which seem to have possessed teams beyond the capacity of their inhabitants. Surely one team was too much for the solitary villein at Goosebradon (Som., *491b*, 98b), or the solitary cottar at Moulham (Do., 85), to manage without help.

The absence of recorded teams was sometimes due to the fact that estates were tilled by teams from neighbouring manors – at any rate that is what a few entries explicitly tell us. Eudo the Steward worked his demesne at Barley in Hertfordshire with teams from the nearby vill of Newsells; and in the same county Peter de Valonges also worked his demesne at Box with teams from neighbouring Bennington. Similarly, an unnamed holding in Newchurch hundred in Kent was valued with land at Tinton because it was tilled by the demesne teams of the latter. Likewise, at Uffington in Lincolnshire, the Countess Judith had no stock but ploughed her land with teams belonging to Belmesthorpe just across the boundary in Rutland. Or again, at Almeley in Herefordshire there were 8 ploughlands, and the annual value of the holding was 37s 8d; we hear of no teams or men but are told that men from another vill worked here. The entries relating to these five examples are as follows:

Barley (Herts., 139): *Terra est iii carucis. In dominio i hida et dimidia et xx acrae et (Eudo) laborat cum propriis carucis de Nuesselle. Ibi iiii villani habent i carucam.*

Box (Herts., 141): *Haec terra jacet et appreciatur in Belintone et colitur cum propriis carucis.*

Newchurch hd (Kent, 13): *Haec terra appreciatur in Titentone quia illuc arata est cum dominicis carucis.*

Uffington (Lincs., 366b): *Judita comitissa hanc terram habet. In ea nil pecunie (sic) habet sed colit eam in belmestorp M.*

Almeley (Heref., 182b): *Terra est viii carucis. Alterius villae homines laborant in hac villa, et reddunt xxxvii solidos et viii denarios.*

These, and a few others like them, are unusual entries but some such arrangements may lie behind the perplexities of other entries to which the terse language of Domesday Book gives no clue. At Harding (74b) in Wiltshire, for example, we hear of land for one team which was there in demesne (*quae ibi est in dominio*). Who, we may ask, could have worked this team unless perhaps it was men from Richard Sturmy's other holdings in the nearby villages of Burbage, Grafton and Shalbourne (74b)?

There are also a number of other unusual entries. At Brattleby (340b) in Lincolnshire, for example, the bishop of Durham had land for 6 oxen, and we are told that 'Colswen has it of him and tills it' (*et colit eam*), but there is no mention of the teams with which Colswen worked. There were also no teams on the land for 12 oxen at Fotherby (354) in the same county, but it was tilled by Fulk (*Fulk homo Willelmi habet eam et colit*). Could he have done so with teams from his holdings in the adjoining villages of Elkington and Little Grimsby (354)? Or again at North Stoke (360b), also in Lincolnshire, there was land for one team but all we hear is that the rent-payers ploughing there rendered 7s (*ibi arantes censores vii solidos reddunt*); there is no mention of their number nor of their teams.[1] Another unusual piece of information occurs in a composite entry for Offenham, Littleton and Bretforton (Worcs., 175b) which tells of oxen that did not plough but drew stone to the church – *Ibi sunt boves ad i carucam sed petram trahunt ad ecclesiam*. We hear even of half an ox at Stanford (218b), in Bedfordshire, presumably an ox shared with another man – *Terra est dimidio bovi et ibi est semibos*.[2] On the demesne at Mansell (182b), in Herefordshire, there was a team and another idle

---

[1] For other Lincolnshire examples see *D.G.E.E.*, 45–6.
[2] F. W. Maitland, 142; but see J. H. Round in *V.C.H. Bedfordshire*, 1 (1904), 264n.

team (*In dominio est una caruca et alia ociosa*).[1] This selection serves to illustrate the variety occasionally encountered among the recurring regular statements about teams. To them must be added three entries that tell of the conversion of pasture into arable. For Bourne (9), in Kent, we hear of men from elsewhere who had ploughed up 6 acres of pasture: *Pastura unde araverunt extranei homines vi acras terrae*. The second entry tells of the conversion to arable of an unnamed holding belonging to Storrington (29) in Sussex; *In Storgetune jacuit in pastura. Modo noviter est hospitata*. The third entry records the conversion of land at Swyre (80b) in Dorset: *Prius erat pascualis, modo seminabilis*. On the other hand, we hear of arable apparently turned into pasture at Thetford (118b) in Norfolk: *ii carucae remanent in pastura*.

The record of teams for 1086 reflects but a transitory situation caught in the cross-section of Domesday Book. Occasionally the number of teams had increased but usually they had remained the same or had decreased, and in the latter case we are sometimes told of teams that could be restored. The men of the unidentified *Eruestuna* (409), in Suffolk, once had 3 teams among them but in 1086 they scarcely had one (*modo vix habent i carucam*). Only rarely is there any explanation of the decrease. Two unusual entries in the Essex folios say that the men's teams at Witham (1) had been reduced from 18 to 7, and that those of the men of Hatfield Broad Oak (2) had been reduced from 40 to 31½, and each entry tells us that the loss had taken place through the death of the beasts (*per mortem bestiarum*). To murrain must be added the hazards of farming in general, and there were also other causes of devastation; thus the ploughland at Wrangle (367b), on the coast of Lincolnshire, was waste on account of the action of the sea (*propter fluxum maris*). Human agency, too, was important. The inclusion of land within royal forest often led to the disappearance of teams; the 8 ploughlands at *Haswic* (247b), in Staffordshire, were waste because of the king's forest (*Modo est wasta propter forestam regis*). Along the Welsh border, raiding and reprisal resulted in devastated holdings, although many of these had recovered to carry teams by 1086 (Fig. 87).[2] The greatest human agent of destruction was deliberate harrying by the armies of the king, although only once is this specifically mentioned when we hear of a wasted ploughland

---

[1] For the identification of Mansell, see V. H. Galbraith and J. Tait, *Herefordshire Domesday, circa 1160–1170* (Pipe Roll Soc., London, 1950), 28, 90–1.

[2] *D.G.M.E.*, 97–9, 145–9.

per exercitum regis at Harbury (239) in Warwickshire. But the many empty settlements without teams in 1086 bear eloquent testimony to the devastation that had taken place in the northern counties of the realm.

The size of the team

Comparison of the Domesday text with that of the I.C.C. points to the fact that the Domesday ploughteam was composed of 8 oxen, and this has been the opinion of most scholars.[1] Thus the Domesday entry for Babraham (Cambs., 202) speaks of 4 oxen where the I.C.C. entry speaks of half a team (p. 37); and the Domesday half-team at Over (Cambs., 201) appears in the I.C.C. as 4 oxen (p. 92). Moreover, in the Lincolnshire text, for example, we are frequently told that there was 'land for *n* teams and *n* oxen', and it was this feature that Maitland had in mind when he wrote: 'the theory of a variable *caruca* would in our eyes reduce to an absurdity the practice of stating the capacity of land in terms of the teams and the oxen that can plough it'.[2] Moreover, the arithmetic involved in the duodecimal assessment of many Lincolnshire and other villages seems to indicate that 1 carucate comprised 8 bovates, and the number of entries that link assessment and ploughlands do so on the assumption that 1 team comprised 8 oxen.

This view, it must be emphasised, does not conflict with the fact that the teams to be seen in the field may have varied in size. Indeed, it is most unlikely that a uniform team of 8 oxen was at work on all the different soils throughout the length and breadth of England – on heavy clayland and chalk alike.[3] Faced with variation in the size of working teams, the Domesday clerks found it convenient to reckon at the rate of 8 oxen to a team, otherwise, argued Maitland, the inquest would have resulted 'in a collection of unknown quantities'.[4] Instead of saying that 27 sokemen had 38 oxen at North Thoresby and Autby (Lincs., 342b), they said that '27 sokemen had 5 teams less 2 oxen'; alternatively they might have said '4 teams and 6 oxen'. For Beckering (Lincs., 339b), they did say that 4 sokemen had '1 team and 6 ploughing oxen'.

The same equivalent of 4 oxen and half a team is also found when the Exeter text is compared with that of Domesday Book, e.g. in entries for

[1] E.g. J. H. Round, *Feudal England* (London, 1895), 35–6; F. W. Maitland, 142; P. Vinogradoff, 154.
[2] F. W. Maitland, 414.
[3] H. G. Richardson, 'The medieval ploughteam', *History*, XXVI (1942), 287–96.
[4] F. W. Maitland, 417.

Bickham (Devon, *420b*, 113), Eastrip (Som., *493b*, 99) and St Buryan (Corn., *207*, 121). The equivalent is also apparent in such entries as that for Treveniel (*234b*, 123) where the single team of the Domesday entry (124) appears as 6 oxen + 2 oxen in the Exeter version (*244b*). There are, however, a number of discrepancies, a selection of which are given in the table below. Such anomalies led Lennard to believe that the accepted equation of 8 oxen to 1 team was not always true in the south-west, particularly in Cornwall and Devon and possibly in Somerset, but not in Dorset and Wiltshire, the other two counties of the circuit.[1] He argued that the Domesday team was variable in size and

Comparison of some Exeter and Exchequer ploughteam figures

	Exeter	*Exchequer*
Blachford (Devon, *327*, 109b)	2 teams +6 oxen	3 teams
Cheriton (Som., *364b*, 96b)	3 oxen	½ team
Draynes (Corn., *231*, 124b)	1 ox +4 oxen	¼ team
Littleton (Som., *433b*, 94)	2½ teams +2 oxen	3 teams
Tilleslow (Devon, *317b*, 108b)	1 team +3 oxen	1½ teams
Trenant in Fowey (Corn., *252b*, 124)	7 oxen	1 team

comprised maybe 4, 6, 7, 8 or even 10 or 12 oxen. He also pointed to the fact that the Exchequer text 'often ignores odd oxen and odd pairs of oxen which are recorded' in the Exeter version.[2] Finberg, in reply, suggested that this fact in itself, this 'contempt for small fractions', is sufficient to explain the anomalies. 'One or two beasts more or less', he wrote, 'were not allowed to interfere with the standard reckoning. It was only the threes and sixes that gave any difficulty ... If a man had three oxen, was that near enough to half a team to justify his being assessed at half? If six or seven, could he be safely charged with a whole team? The clerks of the Exchequer answered these questions sometimes affirmatively, sometimes negatively; the really significant fact in the whole business is their hesitation. They never hesitated when they had to deal with groups of four or eight.'[3] In the light of Finberg's discussion, the balance of probability must incline to the traditional belief in a uniform team of 8 oxen.

[1] R. Lennard: (1) 'Domesday plough-teams: the south-western evidence', *Eng. Hist. Rev.*, LX (1945), 217–33; (2) 'The composition of the Domesday caruca', *Eng. Hist. Rev.*, LXXXI (1966), 770–5.   [2] R. Lennard (1966), 773–4.

[3] H. P. R. Finberg, 'The Domesday plough-team', *Eng. Hist. Rev.*, LXVI (1951), 67–71.

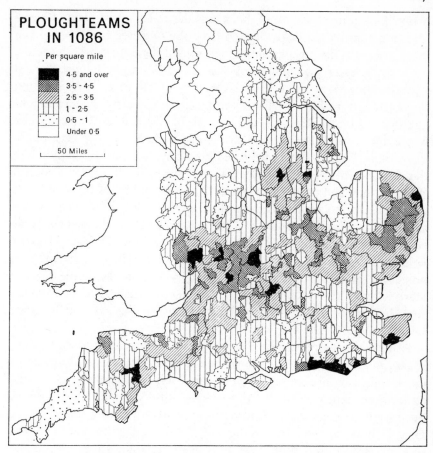

Fig. 41. The distribution of ploughteams in 1086.

The distribution of arable

On Fig. 41, variations in the distribution of ploughteams reflect, to a great extent, the nature of the soil and terrain. The areas with most arable land, those with say over 3.5 teams per square mile, were usually the areas where, in the context of the time, soils were most favourable, where there were loams and valley gravels and medium clays derived from chalky Boulder Clay. These arable areas included the coastal plain of Sussex with its alluvial valleys, much of the eastern part of East Anglia and the upper valley of the Cam in south Cambridgeshire and north-west

Essex. A prominent feature of the map is the arable of the plain of Herefordshire with its red marls derived from the Old Red Sandstone. Even more striking is the great extent of highly arable land that stretched across the boundaries of the counties of Worcester, Warwick, Gloucester and Oxford. Here were tracts of soil very favourable to early agriculture: the north Oxfordshire 'Redland' with soils coloured by the ferruginous marlstone of the Middle Lias, and the Vale of Evesham in Worcestershire where the Lower Lias Clays are covered by various drift deposits. But in this striking district some of the less kind clays were also heavily under the plough, on the fairly densely settled claylands of Feldon in south Warwickshire and on the varying soils, heavy to light, of the Cotswolds in north Gloucestershire and north-west Oxfordshire, broken by the valleys of the Evenlode and the Windrush. Some badly drained claylands elsewhere also carried much arable: such were the Jurassic Clays of Huntingdonshire and of other localities in the Midlands. There were also a number of well-tilled areas in the south-west – on the fertile Keuper Marls between the Quantocks and the Somerset marshes, on the Permian Red Marls of the Exe basin in south Devon, and on the Taw and Torridge lowland of north Devon.

At the other extreme were districts with less than about one team per square mile. These included areas of heavy, ill-drained and intractable clays and also those areas of very light soil unrewarding before the agricultural improvements of the seventeenth and eighteenth centuries. Such were the Bagshot Sands district of north-west Surrey and adjoining areas in Berkshire and Hampshire, and the other Bagshot Sands district in south-east Dorset. With these must be grouped the sands, gravels and clays of the New Forest, the sands of the Breckland, the sands and clays of the Weald, and bordering the Weald on the west, the light soils of the Lower Greensand outcrop. Other infertile areas were the Chilterns where the chalk is overlain by difficult Clay-with-flints soil in eastern Hertfordshire and southern Buckinghamshire, and the nearby Burnham Plateau with its sterile soils derived from spreads of glacial gravels. In addition to these tracts of soil too heavy or too light, there were such poor districts as the Fenland, the Somerset Marshes, the Mendips, Exmoor, Dartmoor and remote Cornwall. Then there were also the royal forests not always named in Domesday Book. They were usually on poor soils and included small forests such as those of eastern Wiltshire and large forests such as Sherwood in Nottinghamshire. To these less favoured districts must be added much of the northern counties of Domesday England – Yorkshire, Cheshire and large tracts of Derbyshire and Staffordshire. There are only a few hints of these uplands and their utilisation for pasture: the *morae* at Crooksby (311) and at Otley (303b) and the *vacaria* or cattle farm at Denby (317) near Penistone, all three places in the Pennines; 'the pasture of the moors' at Molland (101) near Exmoor; that at Sherford (109b) to the south of Dartmoor; and those woods and moors in North Wales (269) which could not be ploughed (*nec potest arari*). There were also *morae* at Edge (264) in the poor countryside of the south Cheshire upland. But the lack of teams in many of these areas was the result not only of their inhospitable terrain but also, and very largely in places, to deliberate wasting by the armies of the king (see p. 251).

We must not expect to find too close a correlation between the highly arable areas and the most favourable terrains; history as well as soil entered into the utilisation of the land, and we must never forget the imperfections of our evidence. Even so, the contrast between the north and north-west and the rest of England is clear enough. So are the striking contrasts within some counties – between east and west Norfolk, between north and south Warwickshire, between north and south Hertfordshire, between east and west Leicestershire, and more obviously between north and south Cambridgeshire. Some of these general contrasts also appear on Fig. 42 which shows the areas markedly above and markedly below the median of 2.1 teams per square mile for Domesday England as a whole. Lancashire has been excluded from the calculation because of the imperfect nature of its record, but it was clearly in the lowest quintile and has been so shown.

Figs. 41 and 42 show the variations in the arable over the face of the countryside, but they do not tell us how much of the surface was tilled. Seebohm attempted an estimate of the total arable acreage on the basis of the amount of land that might have been held by each freeman, sokeman, villein, bordar and cottar, to which he added an allowance for land held in demesne. His result was that 'about five million acres were under the plough'; this was 'from one-third to one-half' of the arable in the same counties of England at the time that he wrote, i.e. 1879. He came to the conclusion that the arable acreage 'was thus really very large'.[1]

Maitland attempted another estimate for twelve counties on the assump-

[1] F. Seebohm, *The English village community* (Cambridge, 1883), 101–3.

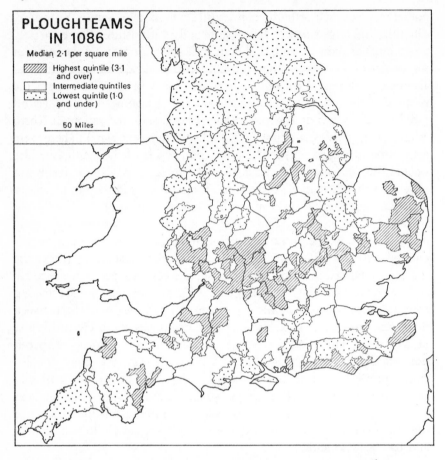

**PLOUGHTEAMS
IN 1086**

Median 2·1 per square mile

▨ Highest quintile (3·1 and over)

☐ Intermediate quintiles

☐ Lowest quintile (1·0 and under)

50 Miles

Fig. 42. The distribution of ploughteams in 1086 (by quintiles).

tion that the average ploughland contained 'about 120 acres'.[1] In this way he compared his hypothetical arable of 1086 with that of the Agricultural Returns for 1895. The result, as he said, was startling enough: 'We are required to believe that in many counties, even in Sussex where the forest still filled a large space, there were more acres ploughed T.R.W. than are ploughed T.R.V., while in some cases the number has been reduced by one half during the intervening centuries'.[2] Such a comparison

[1] F. W. Maitland, 435. The twelve counties were Sussex, Surrey, Berkshire, Dorset, Somerset, Devon, Buckingham, Oxford, Gloucester, Bedford, Northampton and Lincoln.

[2] F. W. Maitland, 436.

can be made only with great reservations. We must remember how very different were the circumstances of the two periods. By 1895, the area available for agriculture had been reduced by the immense spread of towns and industry and, moreover, the arable of the time included large areas of rotation grass. But even if we reject Maitland's calculation entirely, it still opens an interesting vista of speculation.

Maitland's ideas were further developed by Lennard. He based his calculations not on ploughlands but on teams, and he adopted the more conservative estimate of 'only 100 acres per plough'.[1] He also extended the comparison to the whole of Domesday England with the exception of: (1) Lancashire because of its imperfect record, (2) Yorkshire, Derbyshire, Cheshire, Staffordshire and Shropshire because of their abnormal devastated character, and (3) Middlesex because of the growth of London. In the remaining 28 counties he counted 71,785 teams at work, which thus imply a total of 7.2 million acres of arable in 1086 as compared with 7.7 million acres in the Agricultural Returns for 1914; on Maitland's assumption of 120 acres to the plough, the 1086 total would be 8.6 million acres. Titow, while recognising the 'highly hypothetical' nature of such estimates, thought, as had Maitland and Lennard, that they certainly showed that 'the area under the plough in 1086 was already very extensive'.[2]

Whether or not we accept the fact that the total arable of 1086 was near to that of 1900 or so, we must recognise that its distribution was very different. The main arable acreage of 1900 was precisely in those very districts where great enterprises of improvement had taken place in the years after 1600. The draining of the Fenland and of other marshy areas, and the reclamation of the light soils of western Norfolk, of Lincolnshire and of other counties had produced areas that were pre-eminently those of arable farming in 1900. Moreover, the laying down to grass of the clay soils of the Midlands and elsewhere had contributed further to changes in the relative distribution of arable over the face of the realm. In the light of these changes, and as a complement to the over-all estimates, Fig. 43 has been compiled as a further exercise in speculation. It is based upon a team of 100 acres and covers the whole of Domesday England except for Lancashire. Lennard was at pains to point out that in 1086 'the proportion of the land' which was under the plough varied

[1] R. Lennard, *Rural England, 1086–1135* (Oxford, 1959), 393.
[2] J. Z. Titow, *English rural society, 1200–1350* (London, 1969), 71–2.

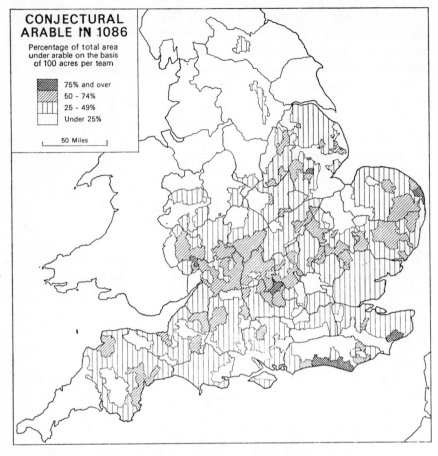

Fig. 43. Conjectural arable in 1086.

less from one district to another than it does under modern conditions of agricultural specialisation and urban development'.[1] One could certainly argue that the semi-subsistence farming of the eleventh century made this likely. But Lennard's conclusion was based on county totals and not on those of the 715 small units which form the basis of Fig. 43; these certainly show considerable variation, even if one excludes the inhospitable areas below 25% With all their uncertainties, the variations do, at any rate, provide an incentive to yet further speculation. It is possible that Lennard's estimate of 100 acres per team is too high and that

[1] R. Lennard (1959), 5.

Fig. 43 exaggerates the extent of the arable, but even so it must have been considerable.

There remains to be considered the ratio between ploughteams and recorded population. Excluding slaves, the number of recorded people per team is just under 3.0 for Domesday England apart from Lancashire. If slaves be included, and their number adjusted so as to count them as heads of households, the figure becomes very slightly over 3.0. Either way, the figure to the nearest decimal place is 3.0. But when, as in Figs. 44 and 45, we consider the variations of this population–team ratio over the face of the realm, we can discern marked regional differences. At one extreme, holdings in Norfolk and Lincolnshire (particularly in Lindsey) were small; so were they over much of Suffolk. At the other extreme, holdings in Gloucestershire, Herefordshire and Worcestershire must have been large. Could it be that Lincolnshire and Norfolk were overpopulated and that many of their inhabitants, even if free, were poor owing to the intense sub-division of their holdings? Were large numbers in these districts 'maintaining themselves as independent members of society on resources which can have been little more than adequate for bare subsistence?'[1] Or could it be that these relatively large numbers of men per team were helping to maintain themselves by other activities such as sheep-farming? And what of the fairly large numbers per team in parts of Cornwall, Dorset, Hampshire, Kent, Middlesex and other counties? Were they, too, dependent upon activities other than tillage for a livelihood? On this, as on so many other matters, Domesday Book does not enlighten us.

Lennard approached the problem in a different way.[2] His enquiry was directed not to broad geographical distributions but to the relative economic position of villeins, sokemen, bordars and cottars as measured by 'the number of ploughing oxen which a man possessed'. For this he was able to use only those entries which give 'details about the ploughs for the members of one class only'.[3] His sample was thus unevenly distributed between class and class, and between county and county;

[1] F. M. Stenton (1943), 510.
[2] R. Lennard: (1) 'The economic position of the Domesday villani', *Econ. Jour.*, LVI (1946), 244–64; (2) 'The economic position of the Domesday sokemen', *Econ. Jour.*, LVII (1947), 179–95; 'The economic position of the bordars and cottars of Domesday Book', *Econ. Jour.*, LXI (1951), 342–71.
[3] R. Lennard (1946), 245–6. See also R. Lennard (1947), 186 and R. Lennard (1951), 365–6.

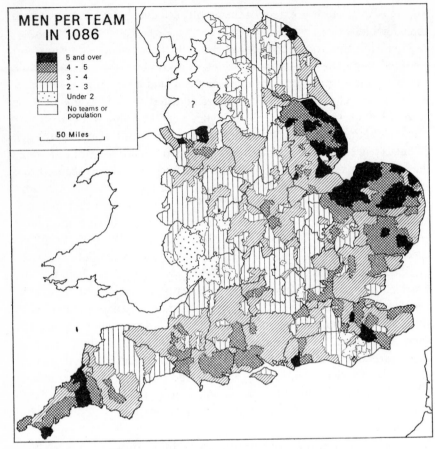

MEN PER TEAM
IN 1086

5 and over
4 - 5
3 - 4
2 - 3
Under 2
No teams or
population

50 Miles

Fig. 44. Recorded men per team in 1086.

he omitted Cornwall and Middlesex because of the very small sample
available in each. Within each class the number of oxen varied as between
one man and another, but in each class there was 'a remarkable regional
difference' between the small holdings 'in the counties on the east coast
south of the Humber' and the especially large holdings 'in Herefordshire,
Gloucestershire and Worcestershire'.[1] Thus for the different classes of
population as well as for the total population, differences in the size of
holdings were a marked feature of the agrarian geography of Domesday
England.

[1] R. Lennard (1959), 356.

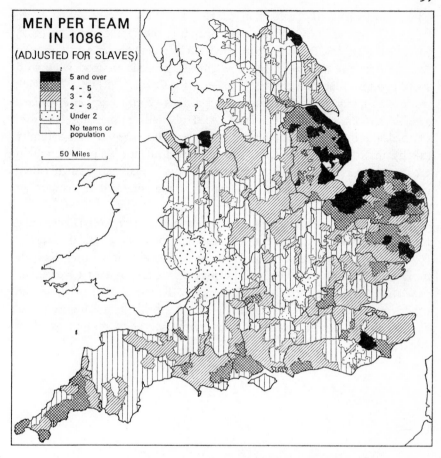

**MEN PER TEAM
IN 1086**
(ADJUSTED FOR SLAVES)

5 and over
4 - 5
3 - 4
2 - 3
Under 2
No teams or
population

50 Miles

Fig. 45. Recorded men per team in 1086 (adjusted for slaves).

GARDENS AND ORCHARDS

To complete the record of cultivation as provided by Domesday Book, we must note the occasional references to gardens (*horti, orti, hortuli*). They are sometimes said to belong to cottars who occasionally rendered money for them. Thus, in Middlesex, there were 8 cottars with their gardens at Fulham (127b) and there were 41 cottars at Westminster (128) who paid annually 40s for their gardens (*pro ortis suis*). The incompleteness of the record may be illustrated from Cambridgeshire. The Domesday text refers to gardens at only two places in the county –

Clopton (200b) and Cottenham (201b), but they appear much more frequently in the I.C.C. Where, for example, the Domesday text (202) enters 5 cottars for Trumpington, the I.C.C. (p. 51) enters 5 cottars with their gardens (*de suis ortis*). In a few entries, gardens are associated with social groups other than cottars. The entry for Coton (238) near Warwick records as many as 100 bordars with gardens (*Extra burgum c bordarii cum hortulis suis reddunt l solidos*). At Holywell (158b), not far from Oxford, there were 23 men with gardens (*hortulos habentes*). At Saundby (281b), in Nottinghamshire, a villein rendered salt for his garden, and at Gosberton (344b), in Lincolnshire, there was a sokeman with his own garden (*de suo orto*). Other entries record the presence of gardens without giving any detail.

The references to orchards are even fewer. One (*virgultum*) is entered for Exeter itself (*222b*, 140b), and another for a place called Orchard (*61b*, 84) which still survives as the name of a locality in Church Knowle in Dorset. Finally, we hear of the making of an orchard (*x acrae ad faciendum pomerium*) at Nottingham (280). The sum total of these and other references does not constitute a survey of this form of agricultural activity in the eleventh century, but merely serves to remind us of its existence.

CHAPTER V

GRASSLAND, MARSH AND LIVESTOCK

Meadow and pasture were important elements in village economy in an age when root crops and the so-called artificial grasses were not available. The distinction between them was clear. Meadow was land bordering a stream liable to flood, producing hay, and afterwards used for grazing. Pasture was land available for grazing all the year round. The two varieties of grassland were used to supplement grazing upon the arable fields in their fallow years. Meadow, in particular, was of great value, and thirteenth-century evidence shows that an acre of meadow was frequently two or three times as valuable as an acre of the best arable.[1] Domesday Book records meadow for by far the great majority of villages, except that none appears in the Shropshire folios and none for what is now Lancashire. Pasture, on the other hand, is entered irregularly and not at all for some counties.

MEADOW

Variety of entries

For one circuit, that comprising the five counties of Bedford, Buckingham, Cambridge, Hertford and Middlesex, meadow is for the most part recorded in terms of the teams or the oxen which it could support (Fig. 46). The usual formula is *pratum n carucis* or *pratum n bobus*. The amount is usually equal to or less than the number of ploughlands on a holding; this means that it is sometimes in excess of the number of teams actually at work. Very occasionally it is in excess of the number of ploughlands themselves e.g. at Cainhoe (Beds., 214) where there were 6 ploughlands, 4 teams at work and yet meadow enough to support 8 teams. Sometimes the meadow not only supported teams but also yielded a profit, usually expressed in money which is occasionally said to be for the hay. The following entries indicate the variety of phrasing:

Aylesbury (Bucks., 143): *Pratum viii carucis et de remanenti xx solidi.*
Cheshunt (Herts., 137): *Pratum xxiii carucis et ad dominicos equos.*
Ebury (Mdlx., 129b): *Pratum viii carucis et de feno lx solidi.*

[1] E. Lipson, *An economic history of England*, I (London, 5th edn, 1929), 70.

Edmonton (Mdlx., 129b): *Pratum xxvi carucis et xxv solidi de super plus.*

Shingay (Cambs., 193): *Pratum vi carucis et de reddita prati ii solidi.*

Stiuicesworde (Herts., 139b): *Pratum i carucae et dimidiae et ad dominicum opus.*

Sutton (Beds., 218b): *pratum ii carucis et xii denarii.*

Wooburn (Bucks., 144): *pratum vi carucis et ad equos.*

Wycombe (Bucks., 149): *pratum iii carucis et ad equos de curia et carucis villanorum.*

Wyrardisbury (Bucks., 149b): *pratum v carucis et fenum ad animalia curiae.*

The meadow on a number of Cambridgeshire holdings, particularly in the south-east of the county, was recorded in terms of acres, and, occasionally, ploughteams and acres appear for different holdings in the same village. There were also a few holdings for which meadow was measured differently in Domesday Book and in the I.C.C., and for one of them there is also an I.E. entry:

	D.B.	I.C.C.	I.E.
Westley Waterless (1)	2 oxen (190b)	2 acres (p. 19)	2 acres (p. 104)
Westley Waterless (2)	2 acres (202)	2 oxen (p. 19)	—
Burrough Green	4 acres (195b)	4 oxen (p. 20)	—

This equation of 1 ox = 1 acre breaks down in an entry for Carlton nearby; the Domesday text says 2 acres (202) but the I.C.C. says 1 team (p. 20). As this allows only ¼ acre for an ox, it was probably a mistake.[1] It is also possible that the substitution of 'acres' for 'oxen' in the other entries may have been due to slips of the pen. On the basis of later evidence, G. H. Fowler suggested that 3 acres of meadow was needed to support one ox, but this may be argued, and no attempt has been made to convert teams into acres on Figs. 47–9.[2]

There are also a few other unusual entries. At Stetchworth (Cambs., 190b) the abbot of Ely had half a hide of meadow in demesne; and we also hear of another half hide of meadow at Aldbury (Herts., 136b), but *hidae* here may well be a slip for *carucae*.[3] Another unusual entry is that for Orwell Bury (Herts., 141b) where we are simply told *Pratum nil.*

Outside the Bedford–Middlesex circuit, meadow was normally recorded in acres, and the formula runs *n acrae prati*. Amounts vary from

[1] L. F. Salzman in *V.C.H. Cambridgeshire*, 1 (1938), 344.

[2] G. H. Fowler, *Bedfordshire in 1086: an analysis and synthesis of Domesday Book* (Beds., Hist. Rec. Soc., Aspley Guise, 1922), 61–2, 106–7; *D.G.S–E.E.*, 36.

[3] J. H. Round in *V.C.H. Hertfordshire*, 1 (1902), 318n.

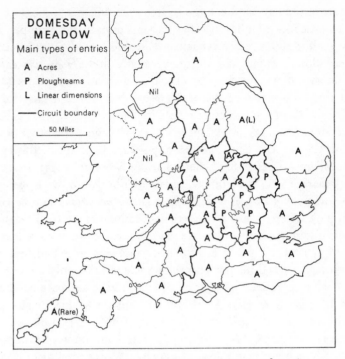

Fig. 46. Domesday meadow: Main types of entries
(by Domesday counties).

In Lincolnshire, entries with linear dimensions form a very small
proportion of the total number.

half an acre to many hundred acres; the round numbers in some entries
suggest that they were estimates e.g. 60, 100 or 350, but the detailed
figures in other entries seem to indicate actual amounts e.g. 14, 73 or
121½. We certainly cannot assume that these were the statute acres of
later times, and it would be wise to regard them merely as indicating
relative amounts as between one locality and another.

Occasionally we hear not of acres but of linear dimensions – in leagues
or perches or, more usually, furlongs; thus the entry for Aldbourne
(Wilts., 65) reads: *Pratum i leuua longum et v quarentenis latum*. A few
entries record but one dimension, e g. that for a holding at Wolverton
(Warw., 242b) where only *i quarentina prati* is entered. Four entries for
Wiltshire use the arpent, a measure usually reserved for estimating the
extent of vineyard; there was one such entry on folio 73 and three on the

upper part of the left-hand column of folio 74b where an arpent of wood is also recorded. A number of other variants appear, for example, in the Gloucestershire folios, variants such as *aliquantum prati, parvum prati* and just *prata* alone.[1] Here, too, we unexpectedly find *Ibi pratum sufficiens carucis* in an entry covering Haresfield and two other places (162b); next to this comes the entry for Harescombe with 2 teams and with *prata carucis*. Then again at Macclesfield in Cheshire (263b), at Inkberrow in Worcestershire (173), at Maund Bryan (185b) and a few other places in Herefordshire we also encounter *pratum bobus*; a variant of this appears for Bodenham (Heref., 184) where 8 teams were at work: *Pratum est tantum bobus.* Two Yorkshire entries describe meadow as being *per loca* on some sokelands of Whitby (305), and *per aliqua loca* at Hutton Magna (309). There is also a Gloucestershire joint entry for Foxcote and six other holdings which runs: *In quibusdam locis pratum et silva sed non multa* (165). At Dartford in Kent (2b) certain resources had been withdrawn from the royal manor, and these included not only *unum pratum* but as much as pertained to 10 acres of land (*adhuc tantum prati quantum pertinet ad x acras terrae*). At Houghton and Awbridge in Hampshire (45), with 18 acres of meadow between them, there was a dispute about one corner of meadow (*angulum prati*). There are only very occasional blank spaces such as that for Abbots Lench in Worcestershire (173) where *pratum* is followed by a space which was never filled in.

This meadow, like that measured in terms of ploughteams, sometimes yielded a profit, usually expressed in money, occasionally said to come from the hay. The following entries show the variety of phrasing:

Cogges (Oxon., 156): *De feno x solidi. Pratum xi quarentenis longum et ii quarentenis latum.*
Fawsley (N'hants., 219b): *De prato ii solidi exeunt.*
Grafton (Oxon., 157): *Ibi lxiii acrae prati et reddunt x solidos.*
Kempsford (Gloucs., 169): *de pratis ix librae praeter pasturam boum et de ovilii cxx pensas caseorum.*
Lechlade (Gloucs., 169): *De pratis vii librae et vii solidi praeter fenum boum.*
Stretford (Heref., 186): *pratum reddit iii solidos.*
Thornbury (Gloucs., 163b): *unum pratum de xl solidos.*

Twelve acres of meadow at Melcombe in Dorset (75b) had been leased out (*praestitae fuerunt*); and another 8 acres at Canterbury (Kent, 2)

[1] *D.G.M.E.*, 33–4.

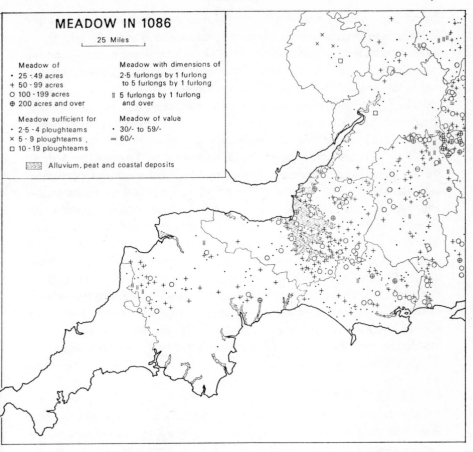

MEADOW IN 1086

25 Miles

Meadow of
- 25 - 49 acres
+ 50 - 99 acres
O 100 - 199 acres
⊕ 200 acres and over

Meadow with dimensions of
2·5 furlongs by 1 furlong
to 5 furlongs by 1 furlong
‖ 5 furlongs by 1 furlong
and over

Meadow sufficient for
- 2·5 - 4 ploughteams
× 5 - 9 ploughteams
□ 10 - 19 ploughteams

Meadow of value
- 30/- to 59/-
= 60/-

Alluvium, peat and coastal deposits

Fig. 47. The distribution of meadow in 1086 in south-west England.

Note that vills with small quantities are not plotted.

returned 15s as rent (*modo reddunt de censu xv solidos*). At Watchingwell in the Isle of Wight (52b) an unspecified amount of meadow was said to be in the park (*pratum est in parco*). Another peculiarity in the Hampshire folios is that a number of New Forest entries tell us that the whole of a manor 'except the meadow' had been taken into the forest. Why this meadow should have been thus excluded from the Forest is difficult to explain.[1]

For the purpose of estimating its size, meadow is sometimes linked with

[1] *D.G.S–E.E.*, 331, 338.

marsh (*inter pratum et maresc*) as in three Essex entries,[1] or with pasture (*inter pratum et pasturam* or *de pratis et pascuis*) as in entries for Oxfordshire, Warwickshire and Wiltshire.[2] The Wiltshire entry for Edington (74b) is unusual in that it tells of meadow and pasture appropriate for one hide – *tantum prati et pasturae quantum convenit i hidae*. Also strange are the few Lincolnshire entries that record carucates and bovates of meadow.[3] Another unusual entry is that for Stockton on the Forest (Yorks., 298) where there was *nec pratum nec silva*.

For six Worcestershire holdings, all belonging to Westminster Abbey, we are given some very unusual information about services connected with the mowing of the meadows. They are described on folios 174b–175 and the relevant phrase in each refers to conditions in 1066. At Eckington, for example, the two English tenants 'used to mow in the meadows of their lord for one day as a customary service' (*secabant in pratis domini sui pro consuetudinem unam diem*). There is also another unusual item of information in the entry for Botolph Bridge in Huntingdonshire (203b) where we are told that on this and other manors the weir of the abbot of Thorney was doing harm to 300 acres of meadow (*necat exclusa abbatis de Torni ccc acras prati*). This presumably refers to some interference along the Nene; and there were certainly several villages held by the abbot in the Nene valley.

Distribution of meadow

Like the maps of woodland, Figs. 47–50 have the inherent defect that it is impossible to reduce ploughteams and acres, to say nothing of the various miscellaneous entries, to a common denominator (see pp. 190–1). The number of acres needed to feed an eleventh-century team is very uncertain and may well have varied from place to place. Moreover, we do not know the size of a Domesday acre which may also have varied. All that the maps can do is to indicate the relative distribution of meadow in a general way, and, even so, we cannot be sure that symbols for acres and teams convey a correct visual impression as between the one and the other. Very little meadow was entered for Cornwall which may reflect geographical conditions, and none at all for Shropshire and for what is now Lancashire which must indicate local idiosyncrasies in the

[1] *D.G.E.E.*, 239.
[2] *D.G.S–E.E.*, 217; *D.G.M.E.*, 300; *D.G.S–W.E.*, 40.
[3] *D.G.E.E.*, 62.

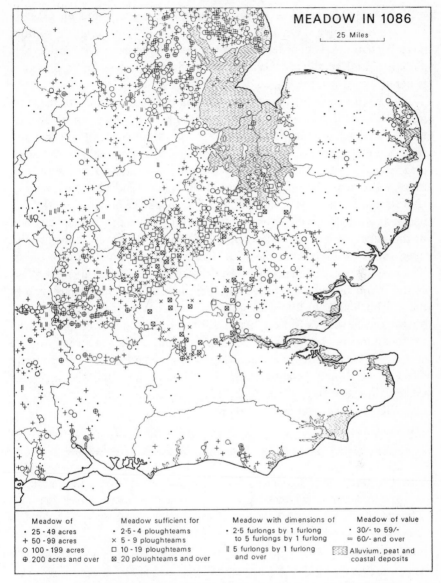

Fig. 48. The distribution of meadow in 1086 in east and south-east England.

Note that vills with small quantities are not plotted.

record. Apart from these three counties, there was some meadow in almost every village. On Figs. 47–9 only the vills with larger quantities have been plotted in order to emphasise those areas with considerable amounts. Fig. 50 shows only very large quantities in order to present a generalised picture for England as a whole.

One of the main features of the maps is the large amount of meadow in the lowland that stretches below the Chalk escarpment from Wiltshire north-eastwards to the Fenland. Here, a close network of streams and their tributaries cross the clays, and there were few villages without meadow throughout the district. Substantial amounts of 100 acres and more were to be found along the Thames itself and along its various tributaries. To the south, the valley of the Ock, in northern Berkshire, had many villages with over 200, and even over 300, acres apiece; and in the valley of the Kennet (also in Berkshire) there were villages with over 100 acres each, and one with over 200 acres. To the north of the Thames, substantial quantities were likewise to be found in the valleys of the Windrush, the Evenlode and the Cherwell in Oxfordshire, and in that of the Thame in Buckinghamshire. Large amounts were also characteristic of the valleys of the Ouse, the Ouzel and the Ivel in the counties of Buckingham, Bedford and Huntingdon, and along the streams of the adjoining parts of western Cambridgeshire. Some hint of the economy of these well-watered claylands may be given by three unusual entries for villages in the valley of the Ock. They record dues of cheese and, for two villages, they also mention dairies:

> Buckland (58b): 220 acres of meadow and a dairy farm yielding 10 weys of cheese worth 32s 4d (*Wica de x pensis caseorum valentes xxxii solidos et iiii denarios*).
> Shellingford (59b): 104 acres of meadow and 12s 6d from other meadows and from customary dues of cheese (*de consuetudinibus caseorum*) £4 16s 8d.
> Sparsholt (57b): 12 acres of meadow and one dairy yielding 6 weys of cheese (*unam vacariam de vi pensis caseorum*).

Thus we may see the early emergence of the Vale of White Horse as a dairying district; and a dispute about dues of cheese, some thirty years after the Inquest, enables us to trace further the local production of cheese.[1]

Lines of villages with substantial amounts of meadow stood out along

---

[1] J. H. Round in *V.C.H. Berkshire*, I (1906), 305–6.

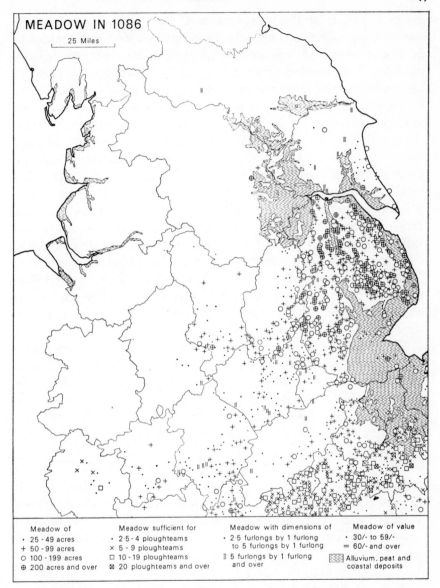

Fig. 49. The distribution of meadow in 1086 in central and northern England.

Note that vills with small quantities are not plotted.

the lower Thames and its tributaries, the Colne and the Lea. There were also sizable amounts in some villages along the Chiltern tributaries of the Colne, such as the Misbourne, the Chess and the Gade in Buckinghamshire and west Hertfordshire; but it was more widely distributed in eastern Hertfordshire, drained by the upper Lea and its associated streams. To the east, in north Essex, amounts of over 100 acres were entered for many villages along the rivers that flow across the Boulder Clay upland – along the Stour, the Essex Colne, the Pant, the Chelmer and others; all this was in contrast to the practically meadowless countryside of the rest of Essex. The southern tributaries of the lower Thames were also bordered by villages with small amounts – along such streams as the Wey and the Wandle in Surrey, and the Darent, the Medway and the Great and Little Stour in Kent. In the south of Kent, most of the villages in and around Romney Marsh were either without meadow or had only small amounts; the main exception was Aldington (4), situated on the upland bordering the Marsh, with as much as 170 acres; but it does not necessarily follow that these were in the Marsh itself. It is difficult to see where the 140 acres entered under Folkestone (9b) could have been, because there is no large stream in the neighbourhood.

The rivers of the chalk country to the south of the Thames basin often flow along flat alluvial flood plains, and here there were fair, and often considerable, amounts of meadow. Cutting through the South Downs and the Sussex coastal plain are the valleys of the Little Ouse, the Adur and the Arun. Further west are the Hampshire rivers of the Itchen, the Test and the Avon, and, beyond them are the Dorset Stour, Piddle and Frome – all stand out on the maps of meadow; their villages sometimes had over 100 and more acres apiece. Inland, in Wiltshire, there were lines of villages with meadow along the valleys that break the chalk plateau, the valleys of the Wylye, the Nadder, the Ebble, the Bourne and the upper Avon; there were considerable amounts (sometimes over 100 acres and more) along the headwaters of the last-named stream, in the Vale of Pewsey.

In the south-west, the villages of lowland Somerset were particularly well endowed with meadow, and amounts of 100 acres and more were entered for a large number of vills – for many around the Levels, especially along the northern coastal belt; for many on the Lias Clay plain to the south, drained by the upper courses of the Brue, the Cam, the Cary, the Parrett and the Isle; and for many to the north of the Mendips, in the

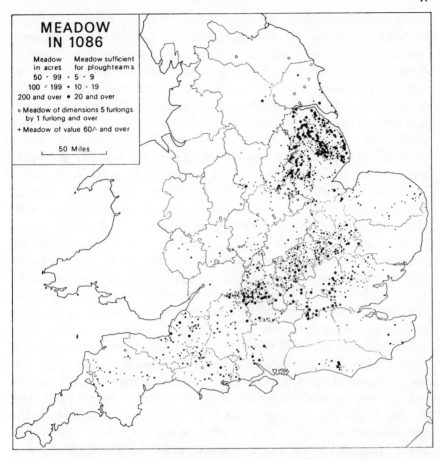

**MEADOW
IN 1086**

Meadow in acres	Meadow sufficient for ploughteams
50 - 99	· 5 - 9
100 - 199	• 10 - 19
200 and over	● 20 and over

o Meadow of dimensions 5 furlongs
 by 1 furlong and over

+ Meadow of value 60/- and over

50 Miles

Fig. 50. The distribution of meadow in 1086 (generalised).

Based on Figs. 47–9 with the omission of the lowest category of each type of entry.

area of the Chew and other tributaries of the Bristol Avon. The valleys of Devonshire were less well endowed, but, even so, amounts of 50 acres and over were to be found in the south-east, along the Axe, the Otter, the Clyst, the Culm and the Exe. In the north-west, similar amounts bordered the tributaries of the upper Torridge and the Thrushel. Further west still, meadow was entered for only 13% of the settlements of Cornwall, and the amounts were very small, usually only one or two acres apiece.

A surprising feature of the west Midlands was the scarcity of meadow

6

along the Severn; amounts of over 50 acres were only rarely to be found in the villages of the Vale of Gloucester and the plain of Hereford. Larger amounts, rising occasionally to 100 acres, bordered the Avon in south Worcestershire and south Warwickshire. A total of 160 acres was returned for Pershore on the Avon (Worcs., 174b, 175) and its seven berewicks. At one of these, Wadborough, was a hide of land where there had been a monks' dairy farm (*in qua fuit vaccaria monachorum*) in 1066, a reference to the estates of Pershore Abbey. To the north, the villages of Staffordshire, with its network of small streams, frequently had some meadow, but the amounts were small. So were they in Cheshire.

In many northern parts of the realm, villages with meadow were not only frequent, but amounts of meadow were substantial. This was so along the Trent and its tributaries in southern Derbyshire, eastern Nottinghamshire and northern Leicestershire where villages with 100 acres were not unusual. Meadow was frequently entered for the settlements on the damp lowland of Holderness, but the amounts were only rarely above 100 acres. One feature of the north was the very considerable amount of meadow recorded for Lincolnshire – on the coastal claylands of Lindsey, along the streams of the southern Wolds, in the Ancholme valley and over much of Kesteven. Quantities of over 400 acres were frequent. It is difficult to see why so many Lincolnshire villages had such large amounts of meadow as measured in numbers of acres. Many Norfolk villages were as well placed for meadow as those of the Lincolnshire Wolds. Might the explanation lie in a difference of size between the Lincolnshire and East Anglian 'acre'? Or did the men of Lincolnshire use the term meadow in a more extensive sense than was customary elsewhere? Or do the Domesday figures after all represent the facts in a straightforward way?

Substantial quantities of meadow in Norfolk were relatively infrequent and were mostly limited to villages in and bordering the Fenland in the west, and in and around the Broadland in the east. In Suffolk, while most villages had some meadow, as in Norfolk, few had over 50 acres each.

PASTURE

Variety of entries

Pasture was irregularly entered not only as between one circuit and another but as between counties within the same circuit and as between places within the same county. It is not recorded at all for some counties, and only occasionally for others (Fig. 51); yet an enquiry about pasture is one of the questions set out in the preamble to the I.E. It is reasonable to regard the complete, or almost complete, lack of pasture entries for a county as the result of some idiosyncrasy in the making or editing of the returns, the kind of idiosyncrasy in which Domesday Book abounds. But what of those counties for which pasture is recorded for as many as a half or three quarters of their villages? Are we to assume that the remaining villages in these counties had no pasture beyond the arable field that was taking its turn in fallow? It is true that there is record of such manors in the early thirteenth century, but that is 150 years later.[1] Or are we to assume that such villages had pasture but no more than was required for their stock, and that therefore it was not a source of income? Both answers may be correct, although to what varying degree we cannot say.

For three counties, all in the same circuit, we hear quite regularly of *pastura ad pecuniam villae* – for those of Cambridge, Hertford and Middlesex. Taking the three counties together, pasture is entered for some 63% of their villages. There are occasional discrepancies between the Domesday text and the I.C.C.; thus one of the Domesday entries for Duxford (196b) makes no reference to the pasture that appears in the corresponding entry in the I.C.C. (p. 42). The phrase does appear, but only very rarely, for the other two counties of the circuit, those of Bedford and Buckingham, and not at all for the other counties of the realm.[2]

The phrase pasture for sheep (*pastura n ovibus*), on the other hand, is a feature of the Essex folios, and is entered for 26% of the villages of the county (see p. 157). There are also references to pasture for sheep at two places near the north Norfolk coast and at three places in Broadland.[3]

---

[1] F. W. Maitland, *Domesday Book and beyond* (Cambridge, 1897), 446.

[2] *D.G.S–E.E.*, 36–7, 172.

[3] Houghton St Giles (113), Wells next the Sea (192, 271); Haddiscoe (181b, 182, 190), Herringby (273), Wheatacre (250). For *maresc lx ovibus* in Broadland, see p. 159.

On the analogy of the similar formula in the Essex folios, these may reflect the presence of nearby coastal marsh. So may the similar entries for four places along the north coast of Kent, although one of these speaks only of *pastura animalibus*.[1] Another north Kent entry, that for Higham (9), says that the pasture was in Essex – *in Exesse pastura cc ovibus*. Yet another north Kent entry refers to a total render of $56\frac{1}{2}$ weys of cheese (*pensae caseorum*) from the manor of Milton Regis (14b) which, as was likely for Essex, may have been made from ewes' milk. Pasture for sheep is also entered for Langford (215b) in Bedfordshire and for Porton (69b) in Wiltshire. Finally, we hear sporadically of pasture for horses, e.g. at Kintbury (57b) in Berkshire.

For the whole of one circuit, that of the south-west (see p. 154), and for Oxfordshire in the midland circuit, pasture is generally entered in terms either of linear dimensions or of acres; such measurements likewise appear for a few scattered places elsewhere in other counties. The Oxfordshire pasture is recorded for 105 of its 250 vills; there are a few miscellaneous entries, but dimensions are used for 48 places and acres for another 53. For two places, each comprising holdings in different fiefs, both dimensions and acres appear – for Black Bourton (160, 161 *bis*) and Shipton on Cherwell (156, 224b).[2] It is possible that small amounts could not be expressed conveniently in terms of dimensions and so were entered in acres. There are minor variations in the formula for dimensions but that for Fulbrook (Oxon., 158b) is representative: *Pastura x quarentenis longa et iii quarentenis lata*. Occasionally, the figures are more precise and employ perches, as in the entry for Stoke Talmage (Oxon., 159). As for wood, the exact significance of these linear dimensions is far from clear. The number of acres in the Oxfordshire entries ranges from a mere 2 acres at Berrick Salome (159b) to as many as 200 at Lyneham (156b). Round numbers such as 40, 60 or 100 acres may suggest estimates but, on the other hand, detailed figures such as $9\frac{1}{2}$, 24 or 156 give the impression of being actual amounts. We cannot convert either linear dimensions or Domesday acres into modern acreages (see pp. 190–1).

The pasture of a number of villages scattered through various counties yielded a render, sometimes in money or in ploughshares or in iron for the ploughs. At Hatfield Broad Oak, in Essex, there was the curious render of 9 wethers to the manor and the service of ploughing 41 acres.

[1] Birling (7b), Cliffe (9), Farningham (6), Wickhambreux (9).
[2] *D.G.S–E.E.*, 220.

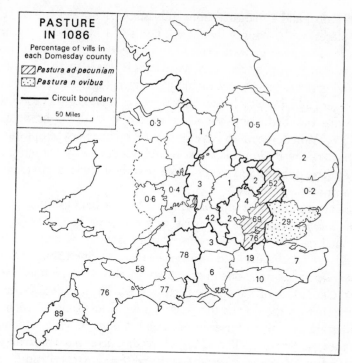

Fig. 51. Domesday pasture in 1086: Frequency of record
(by Domesday counties).

The following entries illustrate the variety that is encountered:

Kempston (Beds., 217): *de pastura ii solidi.*
Abington (Cambs., 199b): *De pastura vi soci.*
Wing (Bucks., 146): *De pastura ferra ad v carucas.*
Hatfield Broad Oak (Ess., 2): *Pastura quae reddit ix multones in manerio et xli acrae de aratura.*

At Breckles (Norf., 110b) there was a dispute over a certain customary due in pasture (*quaedam consuetudo in pastura*); and at Fodderstone (Norf., 274) six freemen rendered a due because they could not do without their pasture (*quia non possunt carere sua pastura*).

Sometimes we hear not of *pastura* but of *herbagium*, and there were not only money renders *de herbagio* but also swine renders. Some entries for Surrey and Sussex mention a ratio between the render and the number of swine pastured. This was 1 in 7 at five places in Sussex; one of these was

Pagham (16b), and a marginal note adds *Similiter per totum Sudsex*; but at two places in the county there were ratios of 1 in 6 and 1 in 3, that is unless the *vi* and the *iii* were errors for *vii*. At two places in Surrey the ratio was 1 in 7, but for another two places it was 1 in 10.[1] Renders of wood and grass swine are occasionally grouped together as in the entry for Abinger (Sy., 36) which reads: *De herbagio et pasnagio xl porci*, and it may be that the distinction was not always easy to draw. At Somborne (Hants., 39b) there seems to have been a difference between pasture and herbage for we read: *Pascua de xvii solidis et x denarii de herbagio*; and at Pevensey (Sx., 20b) 7s 3d was due from pasture in 1066, and 15s 4d from herbage in 1086.

There are a number of unusual entries. At Corsham (Wilts., 65) there was *una hida pasturae*; and belonging to Angmering in Sussex (29) there was a small pasture (*parva pastura*). On one holding at Stepney (Mdlx., 127b) we are specifically told *Pastura non est*. At Spettisbury (Do., 82) there were two pastures, one of which lay by the water (*et alio loco super aquam*). Could one of these have been in the alluvial valley of the Stour and the other on the downs that stand above the village? Two separate quantities are also given for each of three holdings in Wiltshire; and for one of these, at Stratford Tony (69), we read: *ii acrae pastura juxta flumen et alia pastura i leuua longa et vi quarentenis lata.*[2] At Molland (Devon., 95, 101), near Exmoor we are told of a render of animals from the pasture of the moors (*pascua morarum*), and to the west at Mullacott (Devon., 469, 117) there was land lying uncultivated as pasture (*terra iacet vastata ad pasturam*). Tracts of pasture were occasionally called by specific names. At Somborne (Hants., 39b) there was dispute about a pasture called Down (*pascua quae vocant dunam*); and at one of the Worthys (42b), also in Hampshire, there was a pasture called Moor (*pascua quae vocant moram*). At Yatton (*159b*, 89b), in Somerset, there was a pasture called Wemberham, and the Exeter text runs: *i pascua quae vocatur Weimoram*. A number of entries group pasture with some other feature. At West Ashby (Lincs., 339) there were '500 acres of meadow and pasture'; at Guiting (Gloucs., 167b) 40 hens were rendered from 'the wood and pasture'; and at Colchester (Ess., 107) there were 240 acres of pasture and scrub (*inter pasturam et fructetam*). With this may be grouped the only reference to heath in Domesday Book. It occurs in

---

[1] *D.G.S–E.E.*, 391, 451, 597. See pp. 177–8 below.

[2] *D.G.S–W.E.*, 45.

the entry for Boveridge (77b) in Dorset between the statement about pasture and that about wood: *Bruaria ii leuuis longa et lata*. Boveridge is situated near Cranborne, just outside the main area of heathland in Dorset. Finally, we hear, on three occasions, of pasture that had been converted into arable (see p. 124 above). On another occasion we hear of arable apparently turned into pasture at Thetford (118b) in Norfolk: *ii carucae remanent in pastura*.

There are only occasional glimpses of the arrangements under which pasture was utilised. Entries for twelve places in Devonshire refer to common pasture and this was sometimes measured in acres; the pastures entered for Benton and for Haxton (*117b*, 101b) were each said to lie in the neighbouring manor of Bratton Fleming (*communa pascua Bratonae*).[1] Two Somerset entries also reveal what seems to have been an arrangement for intercommoning between Hardington and Hemington, neighbouring villages that belonged to different fiefs. Here are the Exchequer entries:

Hardington (*147*, 88b): *In hoc manerio est una hida pertinens ad Hamintone. Balduuinus tenet et habet communem pasturam huic manerio.*
Hemington (*315*, 93): *De hac terra i hida est in communi pastura in Hardintone.*

There is also the famous reference to the pasture of the Suffolk hundred of Colneis which was common to all the men of the hundred (339b): *In Hundret de Colenes est quaedam pastura communis omnibus hominibus de hundret.* Furthermore the main entry for Oxford (154) records that the burgesses had common pasture outside the city wall: *Omnes burgenses Oxenford habent communiter extra murum pasturam reddentem vi solidos et viii denarios.* There was also common pasture at Cambridge (189) which Picot the Sheriff had taken away from the burgesses.

The irregular record makes it impossible to reconstruct the distribution of pasture over the country as a whole. In the counties of Cambridge, Hertford and Middlesex, for which pasture was entered frequently, its distribution was fairly general; and it is also difficult to perceive any consistent geographical basis for the distribution of pasture in Oxfordshire, another county for which entries are relatively frequent. One circuit alone and one county alone stand out as being of especial interest, the south-west circuit because of the consistent record of pasture throughout the whole area, and the county of Essex because of the regular appear-

[1] *D.G.S–W.E.*, 268.

ance of the formula 'pasture for sheep'. These two areas are therefore considered in some detail.

Pasture in the south-west circuit

Apart from a few unusual entries, the pasture of the south-west was recorded in one of two ways – in linear dimensions and in acres. It is normally called *pascua* in the Exeter text and *pastura* in the Exchequer version. Presumably, the smaller amounts were usually measured in acres, but it is impossible to equate the two measurements and so reduce them to a common denominator. On Fig. 52 amounts of one league by one league and more, and of 200 acres and over, have been distinguished from the smaller amounts in an attempt to emphasise the main features of the distribution. This is not meant to imply an equation of these two amounts, and we certainly cannot say whether the relative visual impression conveyed by the two sets of symbols is correct.

As for wood, some entries give only one dimension e.g. *una leuua pasturae* (see pp. 179–80). Collation with the Exeter version shows that this formula was occasionally used when length and breadth were the same, as may be seen in these three Devonshire entries, one of which (that for King's Nympton) is unique:

Clawton
  Exch. D.B. (108b): *una leuua pasturae.*
  Exon. D.B. (*318b*): *i leuga pascuae in longitudine et latitudine.*
Holne
  Exch. D.B. (111): *i leuua pasturae.*
  Exon. D.B. (*367b*): *i leuga pascuae inter longitudinem et latitudinem.*
King's Nympton
  Exch. D.B. (101): *una leuua pasturae in longitudine et latitudine.*
  Exon. D.B. (*98*): *i leuga pascuae ab omni parte.*

Sometimes, one set of measurements is found in a linked entry covering a number of widely separated places. This seems to imply, although not necessarily, some process of addition whereby the dimensions of separate tracts of pasture were consolidated into one sum. On Fig. 52 such measurements have been plotted for the first-named settlement only, and the other places in the entry have each been indicated by the symbol for 'miscellaneous', that is unless they had pasture on other holdings. The amount of pasture entered for a large manor may likewise have been at separate places. The largest amount entered under a single name is the

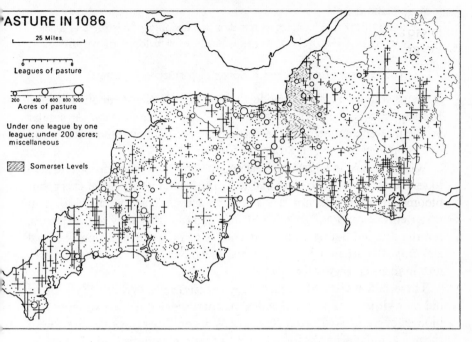

Fig. 52. The distribution of pasture in 1086 in the south-west circuit.
The county boundaries are those of 1086.

7 leagues by 7 for Melksham in Wiltshire (65). The Exeter text for two
Dorset entries gives separate quantities for manorial components that
are combined into single amounts in the Exchequer text; but the possibility of seeing what lies behind the formula '*m* leagues by *n* leagues' is
doomed to disappointment as may be seen in the entries below. The
figures for wood and meadow are also given in order to make clear the
division into two halves:

Frome
 Exch. D.B. (81b): 9 acres of wood; 20 acres of meadow; pasture 17 furlongs
 by 17 furlongs.
 Exon. D.B. (*48b*): (a) 4½ acres of wood; 10 acres of meadow; pasture 8½
 furlongs by 8½ furlongs.
 (b) 4½ acres of wood; 10 acres of meadow; pasture 8½ furlongs by 8½
 furlongs.

West Stafford

Exch. D.B. (83b): 24 acres of meadow; 16 furlongs of pasture and 8 acres.

Exon. D.B. (*55b*): (a) 12 acres of meadow; 8 furlongs of pasture and 4 acres.

(b) 12 acres of meadow; 8 furlongs of pasture and 4 acres.

It seems impossible to reconcile the acreage seemingly implied by the Exchequer total with the sum of the Exeter components. A similar problem is encountered in the Exchequer and Exeter figures for wood in a combined holding in Somerset (see pp. 180–1).

When pasture is measured in acres, the amounts range from one acre to 550 and even to 1,000 acres in one Cornish and one Somerset entry, but the great majority do not rise above 50 acres.[1] The round numbers in many entries (e.g. 30, 40 or 100) may indicate that they are estimates, but the detailed figures in other entries (e.g. 13, 31 or 53) suggest actual amounts. No attempt has been made to convert these Domesday acres into modern acreages (see p. 139).

There is a variety of miscellaneous entries. We occasionally hear of hides or virgates of pasture.[2] A few pastures yielded renders of money or blooms of iron.[3] At Porton (69b), in Wiltshire, there was pasture for 50 sheep – a unique entry for the south-western counties. At Exford in Somerset, (*359b*, 95b) half a ploughland lay in pasture (*iacet in pastura*). Part of Mullacott, in Devon, (*469*, 117) lay uncultivated as pasture (*alia terra iacet vastata ad pasturam*). At Swyre (80b), in Dorset, on the other hand, some pasture had been cultivated – *Prius erat pascualis, modo seminabilis*. Finally, as we have seen, twelve Devonshire entries refer to 'common pasture' and two Somerset entries show us what seems to have been an arrangement for intercommoning between villages.

One of the outstanding features of Fig. 52 is the large amount of pasture associated with the chalklands of Dorset as compared with those of Wiltshire. In Dorset, too, villages around the heathland had substantial amounts entered for them. In Somerset and Devonshire, large amounts of pasture appear in entries for complex manors close to upland areas that were unsuitable for tillage. This is true of the Mendips, the Quantocks, Exmoor and, to a lesser extent, of Dartmoor. Near Bodmin Moor, in Cornwall, there were even larger amounts. It is clear, however, that large amounts of pasture were not limited to settlements close to uplands. They were also to be found on the lower-lying lands of Somerset

[1] *D.G.S–W.E.*, 332, 183–4.   [2] *D.G.S–W.E.*, 266.   [3] *D.G.S–W.E.*, 184.

and Devon, and especially on those of Cornwall. The landscape of the south-west was characterised by its pastoral character, and nowhere was this more true than in Cornwall.

'Pasture for sheep' in Essex

Entries referring generally to pasture occur for fourteen fairly widely scattered places in Essex; the pasture occasionally yielded a money render and was sometimes measured in acres.[1] But in addition to these entries there were also many references to pasture for sheep (*pastura n ovibus*). They relate to as many as 114 places (i.e. 26%) and constitute a peculiar feature of the Essex folios. The number of sheep varied from under 20 up to 1,300 at Southminster (10); a unique entry for Wigborough (18) records 'pasture for sheep rendering 16*d*'.

When plotted on a map the villages with pasture for sheep are seen to lie in a belt parallel with the coast (Fig. 53), and J. H. Round showed that this Domesday pasture lay on the famous Essex marshes. The large area of coastal alluvium that appears on the modern geological map indicates how extensive these marshes must have been. It is clear from later evidence that the production of cheese from ewes' milk was an important Essex activity, and in the seventeenth century the coastal hundreds were famous for their 'huge cheeses'.[2] This activity must have been of long standing; the numerous 'wics' that enter into the names of small places along the coast testify to the primitive dairies of the marshes, and corroborative evidence is not wanting.[3]

One interesting feature of these pasture entries is that they are not restricted to coastal parishes. Numerous nearby inland places are also recorded as having pasture for sheep. 'A glance at the ordnance map,' wrote Round, 'will suggest the explanation of the curious fact that these manors enjoyed feed in the marsh, though themselves inland. Canvey Island affords the clue.'[4] The parish of Canvey was created in 1881, and before then the island was a mosaic of detached portions of other parishes situated up to 8 or 10 miles away on the nearby mainland (Fig. 54). The intermixed system of Canvey could also be found elsewhere along the Essex coast. To the north, the island of Foulness, though now a separate

---

[1] *D.G.E.E.*, 244–5.
[2] J. H. Round in *V.C.H. Essex*, I (1903), 368–74.
[3] P. H. Reaney, *The place-names of Essex* (Cambridge, 1935), 569 and 594.
[4] J. H. Round (1903), 369.

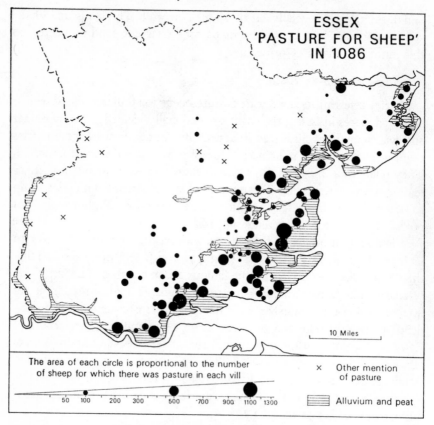

Fig. 53. Essex: 'Pasture for sheep' in 1086.

The county boundary is that of 1086.

parish, was formerly divided among six mainland parishes. The nearby island of Wallasea was likewise divided among five parishes; the detached portions were bounded by the ditches that separate individual marshes one from another. All these arrangements were relics of a system under which a number of parishes had rights in a common pasture. At a later date there were similar groups of intercommoning parishes in the Fen-land and elsewhere.[1] As we have seen, there is mention in the Suffolk folios of a certain pasture common to all the men of the hundred of Colneis (339b) close to the Essex border. The Essex folios do not make such explicit statements about Canvey, Foulness and Wallasea; but the

[1] N. Neilson, *A terrier of Fleet, Lincolnshire* (British Academy, 1920).

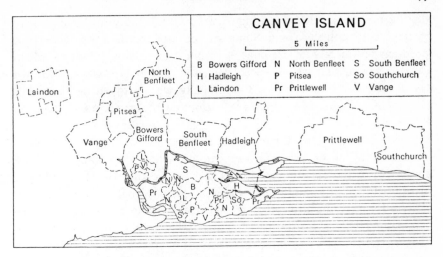

Fig. 54. Parish boundaries in and around Canvey Island
in Essex before 1881.

Domesday evidence, taken in conjunction with that of nineteenth-
century maps, shows that something of the older economy can be discerned beneath the changes of later times.

MARSH

It would seem as if, in some places, grassland merged into marshland,
and as if the distinction between them was not always a sharp one. The
'pasture for sheep' of the Essex folios lay along the marshy coastal flats,
and a few Essex entries measure meadow and marsh together; thus at
Parndon (78b) there were 45 acres of both jointly (*inter pratum et maresc*).
The marsh at Heckingham (205), in Norfolk was specifically said to be
for sheep – *maresc lx ovibus*. The circumstances and character of marshland must have varied a great deal from place to place. It not only provided pasture but could supply eels as in the Cambridgeshire Fens and
also rushes as at Wilburton (192) in the same area.[1] It could also supply
turves from the *toruelande* recorded for three places along the Lincolnshire coast – Grainsby (347), North Thoresby and Autby (342b).
Sometimes its yield is stated not in kind but as a money render, but at
Wedmore (*159b*), in Somerset, we are told (but only in the Exeter text)

[1] *D.G.E.E.*, 304–7.

that the marshes rendered nothing (*nichil reddunt*). Many entries, especially those for Lincolnshire and Somerset, do not mention its renders or products but merely its size in acres or linear dimensions; but at Marham (212b), in Norfolk, we are specifically told that its size was not known (*in Maresc nescit mensuram*). Occasionally we are given no detail but hear merely of *maresc* or *morae*. The various entries are set out in Appendix 8 (pp. 352–3).

Apart from the general mention of Romney Marsh (13), the references to marshland fall broadly into two groups. One group comprises those for places in the eastern counties (Fig. 55). To the Isle of Axholme is attributed the large amount of 10 leagues by 3 (369b). Most of the other entries for Lincolnshire refer to three localities on the margins of the Fenland. There is no means of telling whether the *morae* of Morton (Lincs., 350) referred to the Trent marshes or to the moors of the sandy upland nearby. To the south, especially in the Fenland of Cambridge-shire, eel renders were usual. There are a few references to scattered places with marsh in Norfolk and Essex; some of those in Essex were inland at Canfield (35), Parndon (78b) and Tilty (56b). The second group of references comprise those of Somerset (Fig. 56). They speak not of *maresc* but of *morae*, and give not renders but measurements, in acres or linear dimensions; the entry for Seavington (*265b*, 91b) speaks of 25 acres of marsh and meadow (*morae et prati*). In addition to these two groups there are a few other references. One is to a pasture called Moor (*pascua quae vocant moram*) in an entry for one of the Worthys (42b) near Winchester in Hampshire; but whether this refers to marsh in the Itchen valley or to downland pasture, we cannot say. Another is to 26 acres of moor (*morae*) at Eaton (158b) in Oxfordshire; this may refer to marsh in the Cherwell valley or to Otmoor nearby. Other references to *morae* elsewhere obviously refer to upland moors (see p. 129).

Clearly, the sum of these references gives a very incomplete picture of the marshland of England in the eleventh century. We can only infer the existence of many other marshy areas from the distribution of peat and alluvium on the geological map – of such marshes as those of the Humber lowlands, of the Ancholme valley, of the peaty areas of north Shropshire, to say nothing of the marshy tracts along many a river valley and many a stretch of coast.

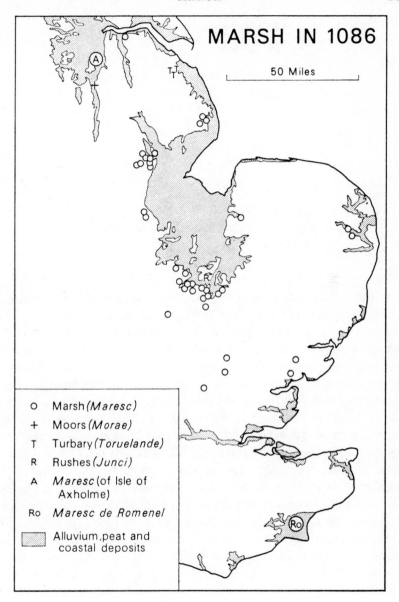

Fig. 55. Eastern England: Marsh in 1086.

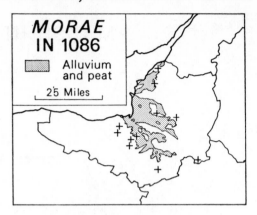

Fig. 56. Somerset: *Morae* in 1086.

LIVESTOCK

There is no reference in the Ely preamble to livestock other than plough-teams, but the Anglo-Saxon chronicler, under the year 1085, complained that every ox, cow and pig was noted in the survey. This detailed infor-mation was omitted during the process of compilation which transformed the original returns into the Domesday Book we know. It appears, however, in the two intermediate circuit summaries that have survived – the Little Domesday Book and the Exeter Domesday Book, although the coverage in the latter is incomplete. We may suppose that it also formed part of the other circuit summaries because it is found in the I.C.C. for Cambridgeshire and in the I.E. which includes a few Hertford-shire manors, and also a few in Huntingdonshire, belonging to yet another circuit. The livestock thus recorded was not the total on a holding but only that on the demesne, and this is sometimes explicitly stated, e.g. in entries for Barstable (22b) in Essex and for Wilton (162) in Norfolk. Demesne stock can have been only a fraction of the total stock in a village. A number of entries for holdings with demesne land make no reference to livestock e.g. those for Bradney (*353b*) and for Sutton Bingham (*444*) in Somerset. Conversely, stock is occasionally entered for holdings without recorded demesne, e.g. for East Myne (*360*) in the same county. Some figures are round numbers that may indicate estimates, but, on the other hand, the many instances of detailed figures suggest exactness, e.g. the 103 sheep at Hurpston (*60b*) and the 1,037 at Cranborne (29), both in Dorset. Some of the difficulties presented by the information may be illustrated by an entry for Hempnall (249) in Norfolk. After giving particulars about stock and other matters, the entry goes on to say: 'Besides all this the manor renders (*reddit*) 6 cows and 20 swine and 20 rams'; but neither cows nor rams are mentioned in the enumeration of stock that appears in the earlier part of the entry.

The totals of livestock from the Little Domesday Book and the Exeter Domesday Book, and from the I.C.C. (for southern Cambridgeshire) and the I.E. (for northern Cambridgeshire) are assembled on p. 164. Their main interest, perhaps, lies in their indication of the relative numbers of different kinds of stock. Sheep were by far the most numerous, and they must have played an important part in the economy of the time. Some flocks numbered many hundreds, rising to over 1,000. It is true that the high figures for large complex manors may be deceptive in the sense that they covered separate unnamed places, e.g. the 1,600 sheep entered for Puddletown (25) in Dorset. Entries for Norfolk and Suffolk make frequent reference to fold-soke (*soca faldae*); a man's sheep had to lie in his lord's fold and so manure it – 'the demand for manure has played a large part in the history of the human race'.[1] Six men at Hellington (203b) in Norfolk owed fold-soke, yet no sheep were recorded there; presumably they were not on the demesne of a manor and so escaped record. Many other examples of *soca faldae* in the Norfolk and Suffolk folios reflect the particular agrarian arrangements that are seen, from later evidence, to characterise East Anglia.

Goats were less numerous but were still important. The record is often of *caprae* which supplied milk. In Somerset they do not appear to have been entered at all for some hundreds, e.g. those of Pitminster and Taunton, which may point to idiosyncrasy in the returns for these hundreds. Swine, too, were important but the number on the demesne of a holding was rarely the same as the number its woodland could support; occasionally it was more, and swine were sometimes recorded for holdings without any record of wood; there were, for example, 55 swine on the demesne at Stansfield (390b, 396) in Suffolk, but no wood is entered for the village. *Animalia* presumably included the non-ploughing oxen. Curiously enough cows are seldom specifically mentioned, and frequently there was only one per manor. Yet they must have been kept in considerable numbers for breeding the oxen of the teams which formed

[1] F. W. Maitland, 76.

Livestock in 1086 by Domesday counties

The interest of these figures lies in the relative numbers of the different kinds of stock, and not in total numbers. They do not give complete totals even for demesne stock. The Exeter text omits nearly 5% of places in Devonshire and over 60% of places in Dorset. In the same way, the I.C.C. and the I.E. together omit 10% of places in Cambridgeshire. *Hercerarius* was a beast used for harrowing.

	Norfolk	Suffolk	Essex	Cambridge	Dorset	Somerset	Devon	Cornwall
Sheep	46,176	37,817	47,013	20,512	22,025	46,868	50,024	13,059
Wethers	—	—	—	—	297	948	155	240
Swine	8,082	9,789	13,323	4,591	1,501	6,980	3,694	513
Goats	3,015	4,348	3,642	225	800	4,482	7,246	926
Cows	23	9	160	2	59	123	23	55
Calves	—	—	77	—	—	—	—	—
Oxen	—	—	—	—	9	—	—	—
Bull	—	—	—	—	—	—	—	1
Animalia	2,102	3,052	3,808	958	521	4,343	7,341	1,092
Horses	50	127	3	—	123	—	159	21
Rounceys	767	527	793	170	13	448	1	12
Mares	56	—	21	11	12	35	155	352
Wild mares	—	—	—	24	—	318	—	58
Forest mares	139	114	—	—	12	38	162	—
Foals	25	—	103	7	—	—	—	—
Hercerarius	—	—	—	1	—	—	—	—
Mules	1	—	1	1	—	—	—	—
Donkeys	2	2	26	24	1	3	2	—
Foals	—	—	—	2	—	—	—	—

the mainstay of the economic life of the countryside. And there must have been more than one bull. Horses are mentioned in a variety of ways. Rounceys (*runcini*) were probably pack horses. Mares were described variously as *equae silvestres, silvaticae* or *indomitae*. Finally, we may well have expected to hear of a larger number of mules and donkeys.

Some of the figures in the Little Domesday Book refer to a date earlier than 1086 – to 1066 or to an intermediate date or to both. But the form of many entries is so obscure that it is often impossible to make a comparison between conditions in 1086 and in the earlier years. When a comparison is possible, the changes are sometimes appreciable. At Appleton (173b, 256), in Norfolk, the number of sheep had dropped from 163 to 16, while at Harpley (161b) nearby, it had risen from 180 to 308. At Hanningfield (25), in Essex, the number had increased from 117 to as many as 810. At Easton Bavents (444b), in Suffolk, the demesne livestock (86 beasts in all) had disappeared and the entry merely says 'now nothing'. There is no clue to the cause of these and similar changes elsewhere; and we can only conjecture whether they were due to the policy of a land-owner, to the ravages of murrain and mortality or to changes in the composition of holdings.

We can explore the figures further by looking at Fig. 57. In spite of its many imperfections, it may serve to give some hint about the considerations involved in the distribution of sheep in the eastern counties. There were some sheep in most villages and smaller flocks have been disregarded on Fig. 57 so as to emphasise the districts with large numbers. Comparison with Fig. 62 shows that there were fewest sheep where there was most wood. They were, on the other hand, most numerous in two kinds of countryside. In the first place, there were many associated with the marshes of Norfolk and Essex; thus the demesne sheep of West Walton (160, 213) in Norfolk Fenland amounted to 2,100, and those of Brancaster (215b) along the coast to 600; those of Halvergate (128b) in Norfolk Broadland, to 960; and those of Southminster (10), along the Essex coast, to 1,300. In view of their incomplete nature, it is not sur-prising that the statistics for Essex cannot be related to the information about 'pasture for sheep' (see p. 157 above). Thus there were 42 sheep on the demesne at Langdon (42), but sufficient pasture for 100. Conversely there were 500 sheep on the demesne at Corringham (12), but pasture for only 400; presumably many sheep grazed at places other than on the coastal marshes. The second kind of countryside where sheep were

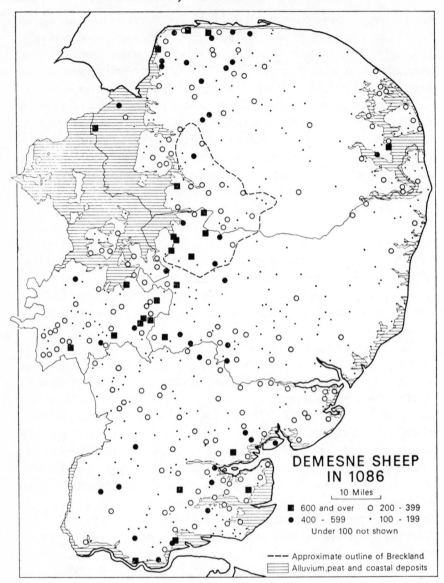

DEMESNE SHEEP
IN 1086

|_____ 10 Miles _____|

■ 600 and over   ○ 200 - 399
● 400 - 599   · 100 - 199
Under 100 not shown

- - - Approximate outline of Breckland
▤ Alluvium,peat and coastal deposits

Fig. 57. Eastern England: Demesne sheep in 1086.
Note that vills with less than 100 demesne sheep are not plotted.

numerous was that of the dry sandy lands of western Norfolk and Suffolk, especially in the district later to be known as Breckland. As many as 1,029 were entered for Mildenhall (263, 288b), and there were flocks of 750 and over at a number of places nearby; some of these may have grazed on the adjacent fenland. The I.C.C. enables us to extend the map to the west, and substantial flocks were entered for some of the villages of southern Cambridgeshire, e.g. the 767 at West Wratting (pp. 23–4), and the 765 at Weston Colville (pp. 21–2). They grazed presumably not with the swine on the wooded claylands but on the open chalk belt that stretched from Royston to Newmarket. Furthermore, the I.E. enables us to extend the map into northern Cambridgeshire by providing figures for the sheep of villages in the Isle of Ely, together with those for three villages in the upland hundred of Northstow not covered by the I.C.C. It is true that the I.E. may date from a few years later than Domesday Book,[1] but when it provides figures for the same holdings as the Little Domesday Book or the I.C.C., they differ, if at all, by only small amounts. The inference from their distribution on Fig. 57 is that the southern Fenland was not a great sheep-rearing area in 1086.

Large demesne flocks were not as frequent in the south-western peninsula (Figs. 58–9). The Cranborne flock of 1,037 (29) and the flock of 826 at Ashmore (29b) and the other large flocks in Dorset were most likely downland sheep; and their distribution shows a close correlation with the chalk outcrop. In the north-east of Somerset, on the Mendips and elsewhere there were also large flocks, e.g. the 800 at Chewton Mendip (114b), and the 700 at Keynsham (113b); some may have grazed on the marshland below. Westwards in Devon there were relatively few substantial flocks and still less in Cornwall.

Although livestock (apart from ploughteams and, in some counties, woodland swine) are not enumerated in the Exchequer text, there are a number of incidental references to them. It seems that the Exchequer clerks failed to omit them when describing an unnamed Hertfordshire holding belonging to Eudo Dapifer (139), with 68 *animalia*, 350 sheep, 150 swine, 50 goats and a mare. Duplicate entries for Abington (190, 199b) in Cambridgeshire also mention 380 sheep. At Eynesbury (206b) in Huntingdonshire, we hear of a sheep-fold (*ovile*) for 662 sheep, and of another at Kempsford (169), in Gloucestershire, which rendered 120 weys of cheese, presumably made from ewes' milk. At Bloxham and

[1] V. H. Galbraith, *The making of Domesday Book* (Oxford, 1961), 140–1.

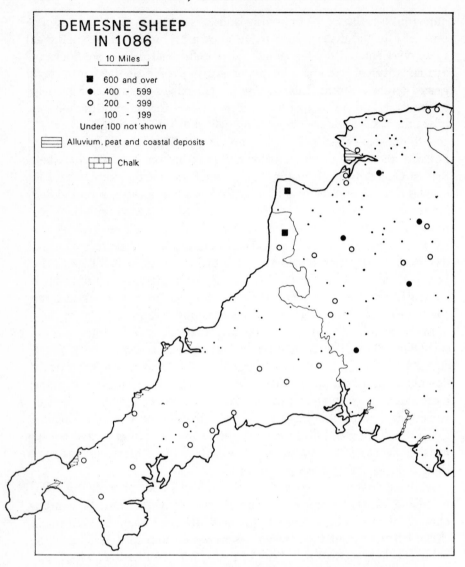

DEMESNE SHEEP IN 1086

⌞ 10 Miles ⌟

■ 600 and over
● 400 - 599
○ 200 - 399
· 100 - 199
Under 100 not shown

▤ Alluvium, peat and coastal deposits

▦ Chalk

Fig. 58. South-west England (West): Demesne sheep in 1086.

Note that vills with less than 100 demesne sheep are not plotted.

Adderbury (154b) in north Oxfordshire there was a render of 40s from wool and cheese (*De lana et caseis*). At Sutton (354b), in Lincolnshire, Gilbert de Gand had a flock of sheep (*grex ovium*), and at Stallingborough

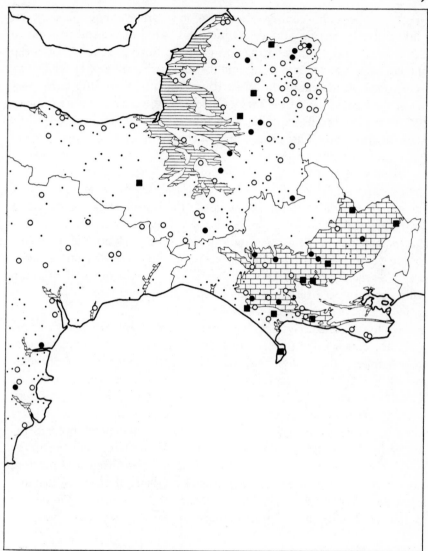

Fig. 59. South-west England (East): Demesne sheep in 1086.
For key see Fig. 58.

Note that vills with less than 100 demesne sheep are not plotted.

(340), in the same county, there was a shearing house (*lanina*). At Cirencester (162b), in Gloucestershire, the 'wool of the sheep' went to the queen; so did that at Kingston (30b) in Surrey. Renders of sheep and lambs, moreover, appear in a number of entries.[1] The entry for Denby (317), near Penistone in the West Riding, mentions a cattle farm (*vacaria*); there must have been many others in those parts. The description of Lewes (26), in Sussex, tells of trade in horses, but we hear very little of them elsewhere. There was a man in charge of the king's forest mares (*silvaticae equae*) in the Surrey hundred of Kingston (36); there were 4 cart-horses (*afri*) at Bishop's Cleeve (165) in Gloucestershire; there was a render of horses from Fulbourn (190) in Cambridgeshire; and provender for horses is mentioned for five places in the Lincolnshire wapentake of Loveden (347b) which may reflect some idiosyncrasy in the return for the wapentake.[2] Among other indications of livestock are the references to dairy farms in northern Berkshire.[3] One entry alone mentions shepherds (*berquarii*); there were 10 at Patcham (26) to the north of Brighton which constitutes a reminder that sheep-rearing must already have been an important occupation on the South Downs.

Such limited and unsystematic references cannot give any picture of the pastoral element in English farming. In the absence of evidence, we can, for example, only assume that in the eleventh century the Cotswolds formed a district of sheepwalks. We realise what Domesday Book does not tell us when we read in an early twelfth-century survey of the English lands of the Abbaye aux Dames at Caen that there was a flock of 1,012 sheep at Avening and another of 467 at Minchinhampton, both in the southern Cotswolds. In the same way a Glastonbury Abbey survey from about the same period reveals flocks of 700 sheep at Idmiston, 1,000 at Monkton Deverill and 2,500 at Damerham, all in the Wiltshire–Hampshire chalklands.[4] Valuable as they are, the unconnected Domesday fragments of information form no substitute for a systematic survey.

[1] *D.G.M.E.*, 106.   [2] *D.G.E.E.*, 85.
[3] *D.G.S–E.E.*, 280, 556. See p. 144 above.
[4] R. Lennard, *Rural England, 1086–1135* (Oxford, 1959), 264.

CHAPTER VI

WOODLAND AND FOREST

One of the outstanding facts about the landscape of eleventh-century England was its wooded aspect. The Anglo-Saxons and Scandinavians, it is true, had pierced the woodland, and broken it everywhere with their 'dens' and 'leahs' and 'skogrs'; but, even so, almost every page of Domesday Book shows that a great deal of wood still remained in 1086. One of the questions included in the preamble to the Ely Inquest was *quantum silvae* – 'how much wood?' Broadly speaking, the answers to this question fell into one of five categories. Sometimes they said that there was enough wood to support a given number of swine, for the swine fed upon acorns and beechmast. A variant of this was a statement not of total swine but of annual renders of swine in return for pannage. A third type of answer gave the length and breadth of wood in terms of leagues, furlongs and, sometimes, perches. A fourth type stated the size of a wood in terms of acres. The fifth category of answers was a miscellaneous one that included a number of variants and idiosyncrasies occasionally encountered in the text, e.g. wood for fuel or for the repair of houses.

Normally, each county was characterised by one of the four main types of entry, but this predominant type was accompanied by a number of miscellaneous entries. Thus the wood of most Norfolk villages was recorded in terms of swine totals, but there was a number of holdings in the county for which acres of wood were entered. Or, again, the wood of Lincolnshire was usually recorded in acres, but on some holdings it was measured in terms of length and breadth. Only where the miscellaneous entries were appreciable in number has the fact been indicated in Fig. 60. The variations between groups of counties reflect the circuits of the Domesday commissioners, but the difference between the counties of Lincoln and York, for example, shows that there were limits to the degree of uniformity that could be secured within each circuit.

In addition to woodland there were forests about which Domesday Book says relatively little. Pre-Domesday kings had set aside districts for hunting, and forest wardens had been maintained by Edward the Confessor. These royal activities greatly increased after the Norman

Conquest, and forest law safeguarded the king's hunting over large areas. Within the royal forests no animals could be taken without express permission, and the right of cutting wood was severely restricted and subject to dues and fines. Forest and woodland were thus not synonymous terms, for the forested areas included land that was not wooded, and they sometimes covered whole counties. The subjects of the king also hunted – in deer parks and in woodland generally, as is shown by a variety of scattered evidence.

WOODLAND

Swine totals

In the three counties of the eastern circuit, surveyed in the Little Domesday Book, the normal formula is 'wood for *n* swine' – *silva ad n porcos, silva de n porcis* or merely *silva n porcis*. This, in the form *silva n porcis*, was also the formula for the five counties of the adjoining Bedford–Middlesex circuit. The number of swine thus recorded ranges from a few (one, two or three) up to many hundreds and even occasionally up to 2,000 and over. As many as 2,200 swine are entered for one holding and 182 for another holding at Waltham Holy Cross in Essex (15b). The round figures of some entries may indicate that they are estimates rather than precise amounts; but the very detailed figures for other entries suggest exactness, e.g. 32, 49 or 262. For Hevingham (*Strincham*) in Norfolk (196b) we even hear of wood for 18⅔ swine (*silva de xviii porcis et ii partibus alterius*).[1] It does not necessarily follow that any of these figures indicated the actual number of swine grazing in a wood; they may have been used merely as units of measurement. Conversely, swine were often entered for places with no record of wood; thus they frequently appear in entries for the Breckland hundred of Lackford in Suffolk, yet it had no recorded wood.

It is impossible to convert these swine totals into modern acreages with any degree of certainty. G. H. Fowler did so for Bedfordshire on the basis of 2½ statute acres of wood for each pig; and he then expressed these acreages as percentages of the total areas of the modern parishes. He was, however, careful to point out the 'difficulties and dangers' of the method, and it certainly raises many problems.[2] In the first place, the

[1] *D.G.E.E.*, 125.
[2] G. H. Fowler, *Bedfordshire in 1086: an analysis and synthesis of Domesday Book* (Beds. Hist. Rec. Soc., Aspley Guise, 1922), 62–3.

medieval pig must have been a very different animal, with a different appetite, from that of today. Then again, the feeding capacity of woods varied from place to place, so that any general equation is impossible. Furthermore, it is certain that the areas of many parishes have changed since the eleventh century. Fowler's maps constitute an interesting experiment in mapping, but in view of the uncertainties involved, it would seem best to plot swine totals, as conventional units, directly on to a map.

While swine formed the normal unit of measurement for the eight counties of these two circuits, there are, in each county, exceptional entries that indicate the presence of wood in other ways. The Norfolk hundred of Clackclose included a number of places (belonging to different tenants-in-chief) with wood measured in acres; and there are similar entries for the other counties. We also occasionally hear of hides of wood; thus there were 4 hides of wood at Tilbury in Essex (42), itself assessed at only 2 hides, and at Wheatley (43) in the same county there was half a hide of wasted wood (*silva vastata*). Among other variants we may note the entry for Gislingham in Suffolk (322) where a certain Lewin held the 'fourth part of a wood', but there is no mention of the other three parts, that is unless they comprised the wood for a total of 43 swine also to be found there.

Renders in money or in kind (rams, oats or iron for the ploughs) appear among the entries for the Bedford–Middlesex circuit – for 17 entries in Bedfordshire, for 16 each in Buckinghamshire and Middlesex, for 8 in Hertfordshire, and for one in Cambridgeshire.[1] Here are some representative examples:

Bledlow (Bucks., 146): *Silva mille porcis et de redditis silvae ferra carucis sufficienter.*

Buckland (Herts., 134b): *Pastura ad pecuniam. Silva xl porcis. De pastura et silva x solidi.*

Gransden (Cambs., 191b): *Silva ad lx porcos et de consuetudine silvae ii solidi.*

Hendon (Mdlx., 128b): *Silva mille porcis et x solidi.*

Segenhoe (Beds., 216): *Silva ccc porcis et de consuetudine silvae x arietes per annum.*

The entry for Newport Pagnell (Bucks., 148b) is unusual in that it records wood for 300 swine and a yield of 2s, and then goes on to mention a further yield of 4s from the men who dwelt in the wood (*et adhuc iiii solidi de hominibus qui manent in silva*).

[1] *D.G.S–E.E.*, 31, 166, 122–3, 77; *D.G.E.E.*, 298.

Another formula encountered for the three counties of Cambridge, Hertford and, occasionally, Middlesex, speaks of wood 'for making fences' or 'for the houses' or, in one entry, for fuel. Here are some representative entries:

Clopton (Cambs., 197b): *Nemus ad sepes reficiendas.*
St Paul's Walden (Herts., 135b): *Nemus ad sepes et domos.*
Stepney (Mdlx., 130b): *Nemus ad sepes.*
Toft (Cambs., 202b): *Nemus ad sepes et ad focum.*

An unusual variant occurs in an entry for Graveley (Herts., 140b) which tells of underwood for fencing (*Rispalia ad sepes*). In Hertfordshire, such phrases occur, mingled with swine entries, for the northern half of the county. In Cambridgeshire they constitute the only type of entry for 29 villages with wood in the south-west.[1] The almost invariable use of the word *nemus* instead of *silva* suggests either some local idiosyncrasy in phrasing or a difference in the character of the wood. The latter might be implied by the entry for Offley (Herts., 132b) which runs: *Silva ccx porcis. Nemus ad sepes.* On the other hand, where the Domesday folios for Cambridgeshire enter *nemus*, the I.C.C. enters *silva*, e.g. for Arrington (193b, p. 77), Wendy (194, p. 58) and elsewhere. There are also other differences; thus in one entry for Orwell, the Domesday text reads *nemus ad sepes claudendas* (198b) where the I.C.C. reads *silva ad sepes reficiendas* (p. 78). Comparison of the two texts also shows that the I.C.C. occasionally supplies what Domesday Book leaves out, e.g. in an entry for Harlton (196, p. 74) where the I.C.C. alone refers to *silva ad sepes reficiendas*. Occasionally, the wood on separate holdings at the same place is entered differently, e.g. swine totals, acres and hides appear for the Essex village of Wickford (23 *ter*, 42b *bis*, 43 *bis*).

The variety and number of these miscellaneous phrases show some idiosyncrasies as between one county and another, but do not alter the fact that the wood entries of these two circuits are overwhelmingly of the 'swine total' variety. They also show that as within circuits so within counties (and even within hundreds and fiefs), there were limits to the degree of uniformity that could be achieved.

[1] *D.G.E.E.*, 298.

Swine renders

The wood of the five counties of the south-eastern circuit was normally recorded in terms of annual renders in return for the right of pannage. The precise form of the entry varies and its meaning is not always made explicit. The range of expression is shown by the following six entries:

Mereworth (Kent, 14): *tantum silvae unde exeunt lx porci de pasnagio.*
Mortlake (Sy., 306): *De silva lv porci de pasnagio.*
Windsor (Berks., 56): *Silva de cl porcis de pasnagio.*
Singleton (Sx., 226): *de silva cl porci.*
Crawley (Hants., 40): *Silva de xv porcis.*
Wouldham (Kent, 5b): *Silva xx porcis.*

The first is an example of an unusually explicit entry. The last three occur very frequently, as if the scribe did not think it worth while to write out the statement in full each time. There are also other variations. At Wrotham (3) in Kent a render was due when the wood bore mast (*Silva quando fructificatur quingentis porcis*). Several holdings in Hampshire had useless wood (*silva inutilis*) or wood without pannage (*silva sine pasnagio*);[1] the greater part of the wood at Sunwood (Hants., 44b) may also have been useless because it had been blown down by the wind: *Silva de iiii porcis. Maxima pars ejus vento corruit.* The wood at the unidentified *Cildresham* in Kent (10) rendered nothing (*Silva est sed nil reddit*); that at Canterbury seems to have borne no mast because it is described as *silva infructuosa* (2), and it is called *minute silve* in the Excerpta.[2]

The renders thus recorded ranged from only one pig to several hundred and even to 500, but it must be remembered that the larger amounts were on manors that may have included more than one settlement. The round figures of many entries suggest that they were estimates, e.g. 20, 50 and 100; but, on the other hand there were many detailed figures that seem to indicate exactness, e.g. 3, 13 and 133. We hear even of 1½ pigs from Donnington in Sussex (17b), of 6½ from Bourne in Kent (9) and of 150½ from Farnham in Surrey (31).

What was the relation of these renders to total numbers of swine? It is impossible to give a satisfactory answer to this question. The only Domesday entry that clearly states a ratio comes from another circuit,

[1] *D.G.S–E.E.*, 321.
[2] A. Ballard (ed.) *An eleventh-century inquisition of St Augustine's*, Canterbury (British Academy, London, 1920), 7.

Domesday woodland: characteristic formulae

Eastern circuit

Swine totals; acres very rare. Reduction in wood 1066–86 for at least 112 places out of 1,813. No underwood.

Bedford–Middlesex circuit

Swine totals. *Silva ad sepes* occasional in Mdlx., and frequent in north Herts. and especially in west Cambs. Occasional renders of money or kind. No underwood.

South-east circuit

Swine renders (usually *de pasnagio*). Occasional *silva ad clausuram* (but not for Sy.). Occasional money renders. *Denae*: 53 and three halves in Kent, one in Sy, one-third in Berks. *Silva in foresta* in Hants. and very rarely in Berks. Underwood only in Kent, and very rare.

Western circuit

Linear dimensions, occasionally single especially for Salop. and Worcs. Acres rare. Renders rare. *Silva pastilis* occasionally in Staffs., mostly in Offlow hd. Many miscellaneous entries for Heref. Underwood rare. Salop unusual in two ways: (1) two thirds entries in swine (usually *n porcis incrassandis*); (2) one third in single linear dimensions, and in leagues only.

Midland circuit

Linear dimensions, single in a few entries. Occasional acres, but not for Warw. Occasional renders in money or kind (sometimes *cum oneratur*). Underwood very rare.

Northern circuit

Linear dimensions usually with *silva pastilis*. Acres rare. Occasional *per loca*. Some underwood. Lincs. unusual in two ways: (1) normally in acres; rare linear dimensions; (2) underwood frequent.

South-west circuit

Linear dimensions, *silva* in Exch. D.B., *nemus* in Exon D.B. Occasional single dimensions for Devon and Do. Acres frequent and outnumber dimensions in Devon and Corn. Underwood frequent for Som. and Devon.

Fig. 60. Domesday woodland: Main types of entries
(by Domesday counties).

from Leominster (180) in Herefordshire, where we are told that each villein having ten pigs gave one for pannage (*Quisque villanus habens x porcos dat unum porcum de pasnagio*). But in the folios relating to the south-eastern circuit – the very area for which swine renders were characteristically entered – we find no such explicit statement. On the other hand, swine were also rendered for pasturage (*pro pastura* or *de herbagio*) and there are some entries for Surrey and Sussex which give ratios for these renders of grass swine. In Surrey it was 1 in 7 at two places and 1 in 10 at another two. In Sussex it was 1 in 7 at five places, 1 in 6 at one place, and 1 in 3 at another; but it is possible that the *vi* and the *iii* of the latter entries are mistakes for *vii*.[1] One of the Sussex entries with a ratio of 1 in 7 is that for Pagham (16b) and a marginal note adds: *Similiter per totum Sudsex.* It is tempting to assume that a similar ratio applied to mast swine. W. H. Legge thought this unlikely in view of the

[1] *D.G.S–E.E.*, 391–2, 451, 597. See pp. 151–2 above.

entry for Ferring (16b) in Sussex, which might be taken to imply that wood and grass renders were evaluated differently: *silva iiii porcis et pro herbagio unus porcus de vii.*[1] On the other hand, similar methods of reckoning seem to be indicated by the fact that a number of entries for Kent, Surrey and Sussex link renders of mast swine and grass swine in single totals; thus from Barkham (22b) in Sussex there came *de silva et herbagio ix porci.* Even if we assume a constant ratio of 1 in 7, we are still far away from the possibility of converting these totals into modern acreages.

The folios for the circuit contain a variety of miscellaneous hints that throw light upon the utilisation of the woodland. Some entries (but not for Surrey) refer to wood for fencing (*silva ad clausuram*), and on the Hampshire manor of Broughton with East Dean and Nether Wallop (38b) there had formerly been timber for house-building – *silva ad faciendas domos*; other entries mention a money render, either alone or in addition to that for swine. We hear of denes or swine pastures and of denes *de silva*, frequently for Kent and once each for Berkshire and Surrey (see p. 33). The Hampshire folios, on the other hand, refer to wood which had been taken into the forest (*silva est in foresta*), and this occasionally rendered honey as well as swine. Underwood (*silva minuta*) appears in three entries for Kent; and *silva* is replaced by *nemus* in a few Hampshire entries and by *lucus* in one for Berkshire.[2] Finally, there are a few entries that refer to wood in very general terms and speak only of *silva, parva silva* or *parva silvula.*

Linear dimensions

Taking the four remaining circuits as a whole, the dominant method of indicating woodland was in terms of its length and breadth, although there were some striking differences of expression as between some counties and others. The units of measurement were the league, the furlong and, occasionally, the perch. The length of each of these units is open to doubt. The twelfth-century Register of Battle Abbey suggests that a league comprised 12 furlongs and that a furlong comprised 40 perches.[3] This would make a league the equivalent of 1½ miles, and this has been adopted in the construction of our maps of woodland. When the quantities are in furlongs, the number is usually less than twelve but higher

[1] W. H. Legge, in *V.C.H. Sussex*, II (1907), 293. [2] *D.G.S–E.E.*, 525, 322, 263.
[3] See H. Ellis, *A general introduction to Domesday Book*, II (London, 1833), 159–60.

figures are occasionally encountered e.g. the wood 16 by 13 furlongs at Halberton (*110b*, 101b) in Devonshire, and that as much as 40 by 20 furlongs at Ashill in Somerset (*268b*, 92). J. H. Round maintained that a league comprised only four furlongs for the reason that the Worcestershire folios never mention a figure greater than three furlongs below the league.[1] This is not so because three Worcestershire folios each mention four furlongs – for Bellington (177), Croome d'Abitot (173), Grafton Flyford (175), and the entry for the last-named speaks of wood half a league by 4 furlongs. Whatever be the truth, we must remember that the whole question of measurement in medieval England is extremely obscure, and may well be complicated by local usage. Our knowledge of the measures characterising different districts is far too slight to allow us to speak with confidence on these matters.

In any case, the exact significance of the formula *m* leagues by *n* leagues is not clear. Is it giving us the extreme diameters of irregularly shaped woods, or is it making an estimate of mean diameters, or is it attempting to convey some other notion? It is impossible to tell, and we certainly cannot assume that a definite geometrical figure was in the minds of those who supplied the information. Nor can we hope to convert these measurements into modern acreages by some arithmetical process. All we can safely do is to regard the dimensions as conventional units, and to plot them diagrammatically as intersecting straight lines. The resulting map will give us some idea of the relative distribution of wood over the face of the countryside, but we cannot tell how the outlines of individual stretches of wood should be filled in.

Some linear entries, especially those for Shropshire and to a less extent for Worcestershire, give only one dimension – *n leuuae silvae*. Collation of Exchequer entries with those of the Exeter text show that this formula was occasionally used when length and breadth were the same, as may be seen from the examples below. Here, as is usual, the Exchequer *silva* appears as *nemus* in the Exeter text:

Clawton (Devonshire)
> Exch. D.B. (108b): *una leuua silva.*
> Exon. D.B. (*318b*): *una leuga nemoris in longitudine et latitudine.*

Hurpston (Dorset)
> Exch. D.B. (84): *i quarentena silvae.*

[1] *V.C.H. Worcestershire,* I (1901), 271–2. See also J. H. Round in *V.C.H. Northamptonshire,* I (1902), 279–81.

Exon. D.B. (*60b*): *i quadragenaria nemoris in longitudine et tantundem in latitudine.*

In the absence of alternative Exeter versions, such entries have been plotted as single lines on our maps of wood, in order to indicate their frequency.

Whatever they imply, it looks as if these linear dimensions often represented a total of separate tracts of woodland. In the first place, the phrase *per loca*, which is found in a number of entries, seems to imply a scattered distribution. Thus for Bulcote (288b) in Nottinghamshire, we hear of *Silva pastilis per loca* 1 league by 8 furlongs, and it does seem as if the dimensions of a number of tracts of wood had been consolidated into one set of measurements. In the second place, a single set of measurements is often found in a composite entry covering a number of widely separated places; thus the wood of Ashford and its twelve berewicks (272b) in Derbyshire is said to be two leagues by two. Another example of addition is provided by the large amounts of wood that appear in the abbreviated descriptions of some Lancashire hundreds; the wood of the 15 manors of the hundred of Newton (269b) is said to be 10 leagues by 6 leagues and 2 furlongs broad. The amount of wood entered for a large manor may also have been at separate places; the wood 6 leagues by 4 on the Wiltshire manor of Amesbury *cum appendiciis suis* (64b) very likely represented the total of separate amounts. For Bedwyn (64b) in the same county the dimensions of two woods were specifically compacted into one set of measurements; *Duae silvae habentes ii leuuas longitudine et unam leuuam latitudine.*

It is easier to suggest the possibility of addition than to see what process of arithmetic was involved. The Exeter text sometimes gives separate quantities for manorial components that are combined into single amounts in the Exchequer version. With one exception, the amounts involved are in acres, so that only simple addition is involved. The exception is the Somerset entry for Hornblotton, Alhampton and Lamyatt where wood is measured in linear dimensions. Here are the details:

Exch. D.B. (90b): All three holdings: Wood 9 furlongs by $1\frac{1}{2}$ furlongs.
Exon. D.B. (*169b-170*).
Hornblotton: Wood 4 furlongs by 1 furlong.
Alhampton: Wood 5 acres.
Lamyatt: Wood 3 furlongs by $\frac{1}{2}$ furlong.

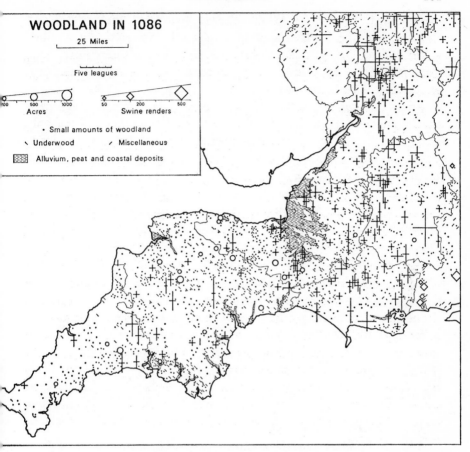

WOODLAND IN 1086

25 Miles

Five leagues

Acres

Swine renders

• Small amounts of woodland

⟍ Underwood   ⟋ Miscellaneous

▨ Alluvium, peat and coastal deposits

Fig. 61. The distribution of woodland in 1086 in south-west England.

'Small amounts of woodland' include quantities under one league by one league,
below 200 acres and less than 50 swine renders.

It seems impossible to reconcile the sum of the Exeter components with
the Exchequer total, and this impossibility defeats any attempt to discover
a clue to the arithmetic that lay behind the ubiquitous formula '*m* furlongs
by *n* furlongs'. The only other discrepancy in the entry is 12 Exchequer
bordars for 13 in the Exeter text; the totals for teams, meadow, pasture,
villeins, slaves and coscets are correct. A similar problem is encountered
in the Exchequer and the Exeter figures for pasture on two manors in
Dorset (see pp. 155-6).

Measurement in acres rarely appears for three of the four circuits characterised by linear dimensions, except for Lincolnshire and Northamptonshire. But it is important in the south-western circuit, so much so that both for Devon and for Cornwall entries with acres are more frequent than those with dimensions; and, it must be said, the incidence of neither is associated with particular fiefs or hundreds. This general frequency of acres may reflect a peculiarity in the returns for the circuit as a whole, and especially for Devon and Cornwall. On the other hand, it is conceivable that only smaller amounts of wood were measured in acres and that their frequency reflects the lack of wood in the south-west. The amounts range from half an acre up to several hundred and up to 500 acres for Winkleigh (*109*, 101b) in Devonshire. The detailed figures in many entries (e.g. 1½, 13 or 31) suggest an attempt at precision, but we cannot try to convert these Domesday 'acres' into those of the present day (see p. 139). A few entries appear to use acres as linear measurements and to combine furlongs and acres in a curious manner, as may be seen from the following examples:

> Calne (Wilts., 64b): *Silva ii quarentenis longa et una quarentena et xxiiii acris lata.*
> Ottery et al. (Devon, *419*, 113): *xx acrae silvae in longitudine et latitudine.*
> Witchampton (Do., 79b): *Silva una quarentena longa et viii acris lata.*

R. W. Eyton explained these as references to 'lineal' acres comprising 4 perches,[1] but on our maps they have been indicated under the category of 'miscellaneous'. A very unusual measure, normally used in connection with Domesday vineyards, was that of the arpent; at Grafton (74b) in Wiltshire there were *ii arpenz silvae.*

A relatively small number of entries mention underwood. The Exchequer phrase is *silva minuta*, with variants of *silva parva* and *silva modica*; and the usual Exeter equivalent is *nemusculus*. Underwood, like wood, is measured sometimes in linear dimensions and sometimes in acres. A very unusual entry for Hambleton (293) in Rutland speaks of underwood three leagues by 1½ as being fertile in places (*Silva minuta fertilis per loca*).

For all four circuits there is a variety of miscellaneous entries. We hear, for example, of a hide and of a virgate of wood, of renders of honey, venison and money from woods, of places with very little wood (*paululum silvae*) and of woods that were without pannage (*non pastilis*) or unfruitful (*infructuosae*). A unique entry for Ketton (219), in Northamptonshire,

---

[1] R. W. Eyton, *A key to Domesday . . . an analysis and digest of the Dorset survey* (London and Dorchester, 1878), 25–7.

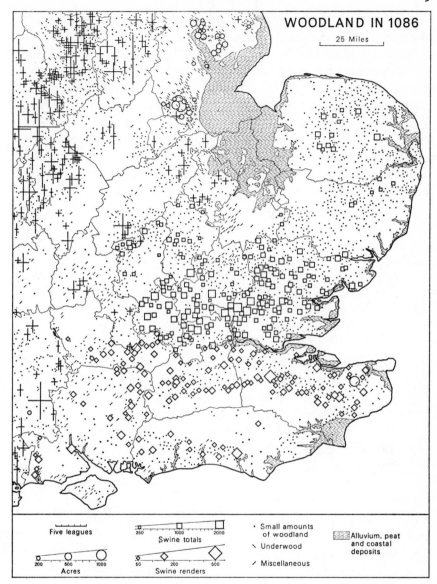

WOODLAND IN 1086

25 Miles

Five leagues	Swine totals	• Small amounts of woodland	Alluvium, peat and coastal deposits
Acres	Swine renders	＼ Underwood	
		／ Miscellaneous	

Fig. 62. The distribution of woodland in 1086 in east and south-east England.

'Small amounts of woodland' include quantities under one league by one league, below 200 acres, less than 350 swine and less than 50 swine renders.

refers to 16 acres of poor wood (*Silvae vilis xvi acrae*). There are occasional entries with *silva pastilis* in Staffordshire, most of them in Offlow hundred.[1] A few entries in the counties of Northampton, Oxford and Warwick (all in the Midland circuit), record money renders from wood when it bore mast (*cum oneratur*);[2] a number of such entries also record measurements, e.g. that for Claverdon (Warw., 240) runs: *Silva i leuua longa et dimidia lata. Valet x solidos cum oneratur.* The folios for Herefordshire have many miscellaneous entries, including the very unusual reference to pannage dues of one pig in seven on the manor of Leominster (180). Here are a few other examples of the way in which the laconic entries are very occasionally expanded in the folios for all four circuits:

> Malvern (Worcs., 173): Wood ½ league by 4 furlongs placed in the forest, but the bishop retained its pannage and timber for fuel and the repair of houses (*Pasnagium vero et ignem et domorum emendationem*).
>
> Old Hexthorpe (Yorks., 307b): *Silva per loca pastilis, per loca inutilis.*
>
> Pembridge (Heref., 186): Wood for 160 swine if it bore mast (*Silva ibi erat ad clx porcos si fructificasset*).
>
> Washern (Wilts., 68): In the wood of Melchet, pasture for 80 swine and 80 cartloads of timber and wood for the houses and fences (*In silva Milchete pastura quater xx porcis et quater xx caretedes lignorum et ad domos et ad sepes*).

With these miscellaneous entries must be counted the various references to hunting in woods and to the presence of *haia* or enclosures for catching deer.

The entries for Shropshire are unusually eccentric. In the first place, only about one third are of the linear variety, and these almost invariably give only one dimension which is always a number of leagues; furlongs or perches never appear. In the second place, the remaining entries use the unusual formula *Silva n porcis incrassandis* with minor variants; the number of swine ranges from 6 to 600, and the round figures of most entries (e.g. 20, 60 or 200) suggest that they are estimates. *Haiae*, for catching deer, are mentioned in connexion with both formulae. The few miscellaneous references include one mention of underwood (*silva modica*) at Eaton Constantine (254b) and of a small tract of wood (*Ibi parva landa silvae*) at Morton and *Aitone* (254b).

[1] *D.G.M.E.*, 198.   [2] *D.G.M.E.*, 294, 406; *D.G.S–E.E.*, 212.

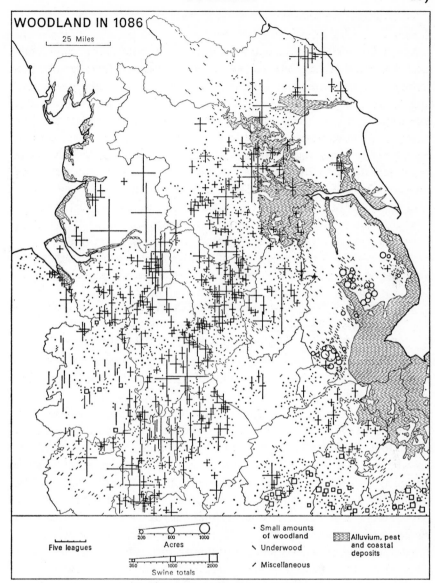

WOODLAND IN 1086

25 Miles

Five leagues

200 — 500 — 1000
Acres

350 — 1000 — 2000
Swine totals

· Small amounts
  of woodland
\ Underwood
/ Miscellaneous

Alluvium, peat
and coastal
deposits

Fig. 63. The distribution of woodland in 1086 in central and
northern England.

'Small amounts of woodland' include quantities under one league by one league,
below 200 acres and less than 350 swine.

Measurement in acres

As we have seen, the wood of a number of counties is sometimes measured in acres, especially for Devon and Cornwall. For the northern counties, on the other hand, acres are only rarely encountered – with one striking exception. Lincolnshire differs from the rest of the northern circuit in that by far the greater part of its wood is measured in acres and not in terms of linear dimensions. It is true that the Lincolnshire formula begins with the customary northern phrase *silva pastilis* with only occasional references to *silva* alone, but there the resemblance ceases. The amounts of wood range from one acre to 1,130 acres at Corby (344b, 371). Amounts of over 100 acres are common, unlike those of the south-western counties, and this may mean that large as well as small quantities were measured in acres and not by linear dimensions. The detail of many entries (e.g. 3, 63 or 117) suggests that they were precise figures rather than estimates. No attempt can be made to translate these Domesday 'acres' into those of the present day, because of the doubts associated with the size of the acre and the prevalence of 'customary acres'. The phrase *per loca* is sometimes added, and this may imply a scattered distribution; there are a few entries common to the folios for Lincolnshire and *Roteland* in which *per loca* is omitted from the Lincolnshire versions.[1]

Of subsidiary importance in Lincolnshire is the linear type of entry, the problem of which has already been discussed. Six such entries appear in close juxtaposition for villages in the wapentake of Axholme belonging to the fief of Geoffrey de Wirce (369). There are also a number in the fief of Countess Judith (366b–367), and a few others in scattered villages elsewhere. Sometimes, the wood on two or more holdings in the same village is recorded differently, one in acres and another in dimensions. Occasionally, as at Irnham (363) both formulae appear in the same entry: *Silva pastilis i leuua longa et x quarentenis lata. Extra hanc adhuc cc acrae silvae pastilis per loca.*

Another way in which the description of Lincolnshire differs from that of the rest of the northern circuit is in its very frequent mention of underwood (*silva minuta*). Like wood itself this is recorded mostly in acres but occasionally in linear dimensions. An entry for Swinderby (367) takes a unique form: the wood 8 furlongs by 5 was partly for pannage and partly underwood (*medietas pascuae alia medietas minutae silvae*). The small

[1] *D.G.M.E.*, 360

number of miscellaneous entries includes references to bovates of wood at Bleasby (352) and to money renders from wood at Langtoft (346b) and Tydd St Mary (338).

Miscellaneous entries

The predominant type of wood entry for a county is usually accompanied by a number of scattered miscellaneous entries that appear unexpectedly as we proceed from folio to folio. A reference to, say, swine or acres thus suddenly presents itself with no apparent logic or method. Why, for example, should we hear about cartloads of timber and about wood for fences and houses twice on folio 68 amid the entries for Wiltshire? Or why, to our surprise, should we come across the item of '12 oak trees' in the entry for Laughern (172b) in Worcestershire? Or, again, why should the measurements of an oak wood be given just once in the whole of Domesday Book – in an entry for Shipley (239) in Warwickshire: *una quarentena quercuum in longitudine et latitudine?* The miscellaneous references to wood exhibit the greatest variety, and speak not only of *silva, nemus, silva minuta,* and *nemusculus,* but occasionally of *broca* (brushwood), *grava* (grove), *lucus* (grove) and *spinetum* (spinney). Individual species of trees are only rarely named, and the following list of references is complete:

Alder grove (*alnetum*): Ashleigh (Devon, *317*, 108b); Buckwell (Kent, 10b); Burslem (Staffs., 249); Dartford (Kent, 2b); Loxhore (Devon, 106b); Spalding (Lincs., 351b); Stanton St Bernard (Wilts., 67b).
Ash grove (*fraxinetum*): Lamport (Northants., 226b).
Oak trees (*quercus*): Burton Bradstock (Do., *25*, 75); Laughern (Worcs., 172b); Shipley (Warw., 239).
Thorns (*runcetum*): Chilmark (Wilts., 67b).
Willow bed (*salictum*): Chilwell (Notts., 289b); Toton (Notts., 287b).

Only occasionally are specific woods named, and this list is likewise complete:

1. *Tercia pars silvae quae vocatur cetum* (Chute) in Collingbourne Ducis (Wilts., 65).
2. *Silva de fangeham* (Fakenham) in Colkirk (Norf., 197b).
3. *Boscus de Havocumbe* (Hawcombe) in Burton Bradstock (Do., *27*, 75).
4. *Silva totius Vicecomitatis Hereswode vocata* (later Leicester Forest) in Leicester (Leics., 230).

5. *Silva Milcheti* (Melchet) in South Newton and in Washern (Wilts., 68).
6. *Silva ... vocatur Schieteshaga* in Hempnall (Norf., 248b).
7. *Silva nomine Triveline* (Treville) in Kingstone (Heref., 179b).

The twelfth-century cartulary of the priory of Bath includes a document which may belong to an early stage of the Domesday Inquest; it describes seven Somerset manors and occasionally renders *nemusculus* as *pascua*, but whether the difference was more than verbal we cannot say.[1]

For one county, the group of *ad sepes* and *ad domos* entries call for special comment. They characterised 29 villages that lay close together on the western claylands of Cambridgeshire, and they stood in contrast to the swine entries of the eastern claylands (Fig. 62). The difference in the method of recording was certainly not due to the absence of swine in the west, for we know from the parallel record of the I.C.C. that there were many swine in the western hundreds. Can we conclude that the woodland of this area was not dense enough to provide pannage for them, although it was sufficient for the miscellaneous needs of the inhabitants? In this district there were only a few villages with small amounts of 'wood for swine'.

Clearing the wood

Domesday Book, being essentially a cross-section, tells us little about the process of clearing, but there are a few entries that show what was happening at a number of places. The contrast between 1066 and 1086 in the Little Domesday Book makes plain that wood had been cut down in at least 112 of the 1,813 recorded places in Norfolk, Suffolk and Essex.[2] Thus for Blickling (196b), in Norfolk, we read: *Tunc silva cc porcis, modo c.* We are given no indication of the purpose of this clearing, and we might naturally suppose it was for agriculture. Reginald Lennard, however, showed that the reduction in wood was not accompanied by an expansion of the arable. Many of the holdings from which wood had disappeared did not have, as one might expect, a greater number of teams in 1086 than in 1066, but a smaller number. Thus at Leiston (311b), in Suffolk, the swine which the wood could support had dropped from 500 to 200, but the number of teams showed no corresponding increase; on the contrary they had decreased from 17 to 10½. Only occasionally was there an increase of teams on a holding where wood had been reduced. The

[1] R. Lennard, 'A neglected Domesday satellite', *Eng. Hist. Rev.*, LVIII (1943), 32–41.
[2] *D.G.E.E.*, 126–8, 180–2, 234–7.

evidence would seem to point not to clearing for cultivation but to wasting, and three Essex entries specifically tell us that this was so; wasted wood (*silva vastata*) is entered for Bowers Gifford (86, 98), Fanton (14) and Wheatley (43). 'The tall trees,' wrote Lennard, 'had gone and with them the acorns and beech mast on which the pigs of the peasantry fed. But the tree stumps, one suspects, remained and they must have been a serious obstacle to cultivation, while thickets of scrub must have taken the place of the standing timber.'[1]

Some clearing, however, did lead to cultivation. That is what the circumstantial evidence of the Kentish denes indicates; so does the circumstantial evidence for the Sussex Weald (see pp. 33–6). It is also certain that clearings for cultivation were already known as 'assarts', a word derived from the French *essarter* meaning to grub up or clear the land of bushes and trees. Hereford is the only county for which the Domesday entries mention them (Fig. 30). The four unique entries are as follows:

> Fernhill (184b): Wood there half a league long and 4 furlongs broad, and assart land for 1 plough renders 54*d* (*et terra ad i carucam de Essarʒ reddit liiii denarios*).
>
> Leominster (180): Of the land reclaimed from the wood, the profits are 17*s* 4*d* (*De exartis silvae exeunt xvii solidi et iiii denarii*).
>
> Much Marcle (179b): In the same manor are 58 acres of land reclaimed from the wood, and the reeve and 2 other men hold several acres of this same land (*In eodem manerio sunt lviii acrae terrae projecte de silva, et prepositus et alii ii homines tenent plures acras de ipsa terra*). In this entry *essarʒ* is interlined above *projecte*.
>
> Weobley (184b): The wood is half a league long and 4 furlongs broad. A park is there and assart land for one plough renders 11*s* 9*d* (*et terra ad i carucam de Essarʒ reddit xi solidos et ix denarios*).

There is every reason to believe that what was happening in Herefordshire was also happening in other counties.

Industry also took its toll. Iron works must have consumed a great quantity of wood, but we are told nothing of this. For the salt industry, on the other hand, there are four Worcestershire entries that mention fuel and cartloads of wood for the salt-pans of Droitwich (*caretedes lignorum ad salinas de Wich*) at Bromsgrove (172), Fladbury (172b), Martin Hussingtree (174b) and Northwick and Tibberton (173b). The

---

[1] R. Lennard, 'The destruction of woodland in the eastern counties under William the Conqueror', *Econ. Hist. Rev.*, XV (1945), 36–43.

entry for Martin Hussingtree is a puzzling one because it records no wood. The holding belonged to Westminster Abbey and, apparently, had no demesne land; the carting service may therefore have been required from the villeins in lieu of other labour, and the wood itself may have come from one of the abbey's demesne manors nearby.[1] Two Herefordshire entries link wood and salt at Droitwich, though not as clearly – for Leominster (108) and Much Marcle (179b). There is no similar evidence for the salt works of Cheshire, but we must suppose that considerable quantities of timber were also used there; Cheshire was certainly well supplied with wood.

Clearing was, however, not an uninterrupted process. Land devastated by raiding, or by the march of armies, soon became overgrown with thicket and wood if allowed to remain unattended. This had certainly happened in north-west Herefordshire. There, Osbern fitz Richard held eleven waste vills with land for 36 ploughs (186b), and we are told that on these devastated lands there had grown up woods in which he hunted (*In his wastis terris excreverunt silvae in quibus isdem Osbernus venationem exercet*). These lands were lying waste in 1066, and so it is likely that they had been sacked in the 1050s when Gruffydd ap Llewellyn raided Hereford.[2] If this were so, the trees would thus be some thirty years old by the time of the Inquest. The entry for Harewood (187) in Clifford, also tells of conversion into wood: *Haec terra in silvam est tota redacta. Wasta fuit et nil reddit.*

Distribution of woodland

When we attempt to plot the Domesday information for wood on a map, we are faced with a variety of difficulties. In the first place, we cannot convert the totals of swine into modern acreages with any degree of certainty. Then again, swine renders introduce another difficulty because of the uncertainty about the ratio of renders to totals. In the third place, the linear formula raises misgivings because of doubts about the size of the units of measurements, and not least because of the obscurity of the formula itself. Fourthly, the 'acre' formula cannot be construed to imply modern statute acres. Finally, most of the miscellaneous entries are very vague.

As well as the problems associated with each method of recording wood,

[1] R. Lennard, *Rural England, 1086–1135* (Oxford, 1959), 247n.
[2] J. H. Round in *V.C.H. Herefordshire*, 1 (1908), 264–5.

an overwhelming difficulty is presented by the fact that we cannot reduce them to a common denominator. Even if, for example, we make the symbol for a render of 50 swine the same as that for a total of 350, we can hazard no answer to the wider question of what acreages of wood these figures imply. The relation of both acres and swine to linear dimensions raises further difficulties. It is true that we are given occasional glimpses of possible relationships between swine and linear dimensions, but there is no foundation for a constant and reliable relationship. Here are examples of entries that connect the two methods of recording:

Ashby de la Zouch (Leics., 233): 1 league by 4 furlongs for (*ad*) 100 swine.
Coughton (Warw., 241b): 6 furlongs by 4 furlongs; feed for 50 swine (*Pascua l porcis*).
Crowle (Worcs., 176b): ½ league for (*ad*) 100 swine.
Leighton (now in Montgomeryshire, 255b): 2 leagues; feed for 200 swine (*sufficit cc porcos incrassandis*).
Worthen (Salop., 255b): 2 leagues in which are 2 hays; feed for 200 swine (*cc porcos incrassandis sufficit*).

Even if it were possible to derive an equation from these entries we could not be sure that it could be applied to the whole of England.

In the compilation of Figs 61–4, an attempt has been made to secure some degree of equivalence between the different formulae. It can only be subjective; the equivalence has been attempted by comparing areas likely to have had similar amounts of wood. We cannot be sure, however, that the visual impression as between one set of symbols and another correctly represents reality. Linear dimensions in a composite entry have been plotted for the first named place only, and the other places have each been indicated by a subordinate symbol to show the possible presence of wood there. Furthermore, it must be remembered that wood was recorded in connection with settlement sites, and may have been physically situated at some distance away. This raises particular problems for the Wealden counties where portions of woodland in the Weald were attached to villages around. These wood symbols therefore represent not the location of the wood on the ground but that of parent estates to which renders were paid. Many of the symbols should therefore be 'spread out' by eye over the adjacent Weald. Even so, with all their uncertainties the maps still tell us much about the character of the eleventh-century countryside.

Fig. 64 gives a generalised picture for England as a whole. This tries to meet the 'overwhelming difficulty' by showing the different formulae under one symbol, again subjectively. Only the larger quantities of wood have been indicated in order to emphasise those areas with considerable amounts of wood. One wooded area that stands out is the Weald. Even so, its denes testify to the presence of groups of swineherds within the wood itself; and unnamed holdings in the Sussex Weald show that it, too, was being pierced by the coloniser. Some of these outliers were already developing into small agricultural settlements by 1086 (see pp. 33–6). Comparable in extent with the Weald was the belt of wood that extended from the claylands of Essex westward to those of Middlesex and so into the Chiltern country of Hertfordshire and south Buckinghamshire, and even beyond into eastern Berkshire. Unlike the Weald, however, this was a landscape with many fully developed agricultural villages.

To the north and west, separate but still substantial areas of wood still remained on the claylands of the counties of Norfolk, Suffolk, Lincoln, Bedford, Huntingdon, Northampton, north Buckingham and in the Wychwood area of Oxfordshire. But another broad and fairly continuous belt of wood was not encountered until the Arden district of Warwickshire was approached. This formed part of a large wooded area, broken with villages it is true, reaching from the Severn basin into that of the Trent. Northward, this continued on either side of the Pennines; on the west into Cheshire, and on the east into Derbyshire, Nottinghamshire and the West Riding.

In the south-west there was relatively less wood. If we traced the outlines of wooded areas in detail, we should find them either on areas of fairly heavy clay e.g. on the Lias Clay plain of Somerset and the Jurassic clay vale of north-west Wiltshire, or on those areas later to be known as 'forests' e.g. Grovely and Savernake. The Domesday text refers not to Melchet Forest but to *Silva Milcheti* (68) and not to Chute Forest but to *silva vocatur cetum* (65). Many other forests named in Domesday Book had very little wood entered for them. Such was the Forest of Dean and the New Forest itself to which a special section is devoted in the Hampshire folios.

Even when allowance is made for unrecorded wood that may have been placed *in foresta* and so usually beyond our ken, we are still left with a suspicion that yet other wood may have gone unmentioned. Can it be that the wood entries for manors surrounding the Weald account for all the wood that may have been there? A few stray hints strengthen the

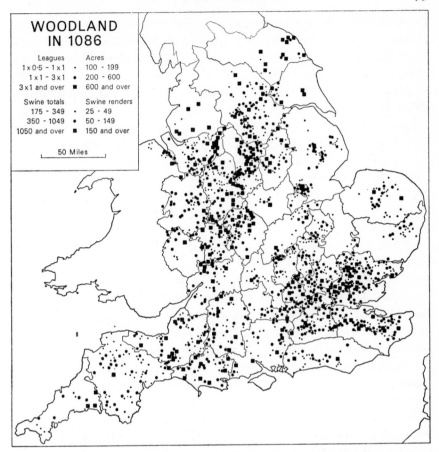

WOODLAND IN 1086

Leagues	Acres
1 x 0·5 - 1 x 1	100 - 199
1 x 1 - 3 x 1	200 - 600
3 x 1 and over	600 and over

Swine totals	Swine renders
175 - 349	25 - 49
350 - 1049	50 - 149
1050 and over	150 and over

50 Miles

Fig. 64. The distribution of woodland in 1086 (generalised).

Note that vills with small quantities are not plotted.

suspicion that there may have been more. The entry for Wallington (30) in Surrey near the border with Kent refers to *Silva quae est in Chent,* but no amount is specified. The same entry goes on to say that Richard of Tonbridge held one virgate with a wood from which he took away a peasant who dwelt there (*cum silva unde abstulit rusticum qui ibi manebat*), and again we hear nothing more of the wood. A different kind of hint comes from the Lincolnshire folios which conclude with an appendix on disputes. This mentions 20 acres of wood at Hanby (375) but the main survey (351b *bis*) does not refer to wood there and says very little about the place. There is another dispute about 'the fourth part of a wood' at Reepham (376b) but the main entries for Reepham mention only under-wood (345b, 356b, 364b). Quite possibly, these disputed items are in addition to what the main survey records. But in that case, are items left out of the main survey for those counties without appendices dealing with disputes?

F. H. Baring thought that the absence of recorded wood from Cottes-loe hundred in Buckinghamshire might be 'due to mistake in the original return' to the hundred jury. He was struck by the same doubt for Surrey: 'there must surely have been woodland at Ashtead in Copthorn which still has a large and wooded common', and we might add that this is oak-wood on heavy London Clay. Then, again, he noted the absence of wood from the lowland of northern Berkshire, and attributed it 'to omission in the returns'.[1] F. W. Morgan, on the other hand, thought that the lack of wood here was the result of clearing, and that 'the rich clays were proving agriculturally attractive'; this may well have been true because the densities of teams and population were relatively high.[2] But, even so, there is evidence that some wood, at any rate, in this area went unrecorded. Several charters of the eleventh and twelfth centuries in the Abingdon Chronicle refer to the woods of Cumnor and Bagley in the extreme north, within the great bend of the Thames,[3] but there is no reference to wood in the entry for Cumnor (58b), nor is there any Domesday reference to Bagley Wood which later in time was extra-parochial. It is impossible to come to any general conclusion from such hints. The I.C.C. mentions wood at the Cambridgeshire villages of Harlton (p. 74) and Tadlow (p. 52); that none appears in the corresponding Domesday entries (196, 200) may be due to nothing more than clerical errors. We can never know how imperfect the record was.

[1] F. H. Baring, *Domesday tables for the counties of Surrey, Berkshire, Middlesex, Hertford, Buckingham and for the New Forest* (London, 1909), 133, 13, 41.

[2] F. W. Morgan, 'The Domesday geography of Berkshire', *Scot. Geog. Mag.*, LI (1935), 358.

[3] J. Stevenson (ed.), *Chronicon Monasterii de Abingdon*, II (Rolls Series, London, 1858), 10, 113–14, 219–20, 247. See E. M. Jope, 'Saxon Oxford and its region' in D. B. Harden (ed.), *Dark-Age Britain* (London, 1956), 247.

FORESTS AND OTHER HUNTING DISTRICTS

Hunting played a great part in the life of Norman England, and this is reflected in a variety of Domesday entries. The names of people with the epithet *venator* appear both among the tenants-in-chief and among the under-tenants. The fief of Waleran the huntsman, for example, lay in Dorset, Hampshire and Wiltshire, and comprised nearly one hundred hides;[1] and he was only one of a number of royal huntsmen. The royal forests, the deer parks both of the king and his subjects, and the references to deer 'hays' in many woods – all provide an indication of the importance of the chase to King William and his barons. Then, too, the mention of hawks, and their great value, show that falconry was greatly esteemed.

The royal forests

The Anglo-Saxon kings had taken pleasure in hunting, and Domesday Book occasionally makes reference to these earlier activities. We hear, for example, that King Edward had freed a tenant from dues at Kintbury in south-west Berkshire (61b) in consideration of the wardenship of the forest (*pro forestam custodiendam*); and there were foresters holding land in 1066 at Woking (30) in Surrey and at Withypool (*479b*, 98b) in Exmoor. The Norman kings, in turn, had a passionate love of the chase, and the forest law and forest courts of Normandy were introduced into England. As the Anglo-Saxon Chronicler wrote under the year 1087, King William made 'large forests for deer'. In the next century, Richard fitz Neal, the Treasurer of England, could say that these were to be found in certain well wooded counties, and that they were subject to their own law which protected the wild beasts within them.[2]

As they were game preserves protected by special law, forests are rarely specified or described in Domesday Book. When we do hear of them it is in an incidental way, usually through a reference to the fact that a manor or a holding, or its wood, had been placed *in foresta* or *in foresta regis*. At the lost *Haswic* (247b) in Staffordshire, for example, there was land for 8 teams which was waste because it had been placed in the forest (*Modo est wasta propter forestam regis*). A number of entries

---

[1] R. R. Darlington in *V.C.H. Wiltshire*, II (1955), 103.
[2] C. Petit-Dutaillis, *Studies and notes supplementary to Stubbs' Constitutional History*, 2 vols (Manchester, 1915), II, 149 *et seq.*

do not specifically use the word forest but say that a holding was in the king's enclosure (*in defensione regis*) or in the king's hands (*in manu regis*), or, maybe, in the king's wood (*in silva regis*), and there are other variants. There are a number of such entries in the Herefordshire folios.[1] Other entries speak of the woodland itself being taken out of a manor as at Feckenham (180b) in Worcestershire: *silva hujus maneriae foris et missa ad silvam regis*. At Ellington (204b), in Huntingdonshire, one out of ten hides was likewise waste (*una wasta per silvam regis*). In the land beyond the Mersey, two entries for the hundreds of West Derby (269b) and Salford (270), most unusually, measure the forest in terms of linear dimensions.[2] These entries may imply not forest but wood, for the corresponding entries for the other hundreds speak of *silva* not *foresta*. The only other entry in which *foresta* is so measured is that for the Flintshire hundred of Atiscros (268b).

References to foresters sometimes provide clues to what had happened. The only hint we have of the Forest of Essex is that Robert Gernon had taken a swineherd from the manor of Writtle (5b) and made him forester of the king's wood (*forestarius de silva regis*); and at Walton on Thames (36) in Surrey, not far from Windsor Forest, a forester paid 10s (*Ibi unus forestarius de x solidis*). On the royal manors of Hanley Castle and Bushley (180b), in Worcestershire, two foresters had been placed outside the manors for the keeping of the woods (*propter silvas custodiendas*). Situated between these places were Ripple and Upton upon Severn (173) held by the bishop of Worcester. Their wood was at Malvern (*In Malferna*) to the west; from this the bishop formerly had the honey, the hunting and all profits, but it had been placed in the forest, leaving him only with its pannage and its wood for fuel and for the repair of houses. Only rarely are the details spelt out in this way.

In the palatine earldom of Chester, five places were said to be in Earl Hugh's forest (*in foresta comitis*); they were all in *Roelau* hundred, in what was later Delamere Forest. To the west, in Atiscros hundred (now in Flintshire), the earl had put all the woods into his forest (268b), whereby the manors were much depreciated (*unde maneria sunt multum pejorata*). Further west still, he and his tenant Robert of Rhuddlan shared between them all the forests which did not belong to any vill in the manor of Rhuddlan (269 *bis*).

The references to these various forests, either explicit or implied, are

[1] *D.G.M.E.*, 86–7.   [2] *D.G.N.E.*, 357–8.

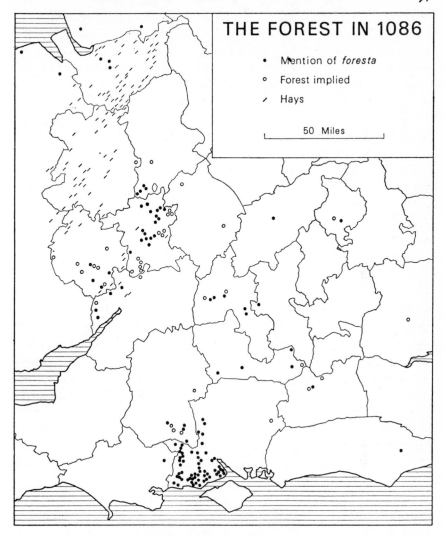

THE FOREST IN 1086

- Mention of *foresta*
○ Forest implied
⁄ Hays

50 Miles

Fig. 65. Royal forests in 1086.

For places with both forests and hays, only the former are plotted.

set out on Fig. 65 and in Appendix 9 (pp. 354–5). But possibly the list does less than justice to the hints that Domesday Book may be giving us. The entry for Botley (47) in Hampshire says that the wood was wanting (*silva deest*); this may mean not that there was no wood but that it had been put outside the manor and was in what later became the Forest of Bere by Porchester. Something similar may have happened at Durley (50b) on the margin of the New Forest; its wood had once rendered 6 swine but it did so no longer (*Silva de vi porcis fuit sed non est*). Or again, at Chilworth (47b) not far away, the value of an estate had fallen from £10 to £8 and then to £4 because its holder had no power to use its wood (*quia non habet potestatem in silva sua*). The entry for Oakhanger (49b) in the north-east of Hampshire records no wood but says that the holder could not have 'pasture or pannage in the king's wood except by authority of the sheriff'. Might the 'king's wood' have been in Woolmer Forest or Alice Holt Forest, neither of which Domesday Book mentions?

Only a few forests are specifically mentioned by name. The Forest of Dean appears as *Dene* (167b), which had been held by 3 thegns in 1066, and we are told that King Edward had freed its lands from geld *pro foresta custodienda*. Wood at Windsor (56b) had been placed *in defensa*, but the name *foresta de Windesores* appears only in the entry for Cookham (56b). In Wiltshire, we hear of *foresta de Gravelinges* (74), and in Dorset of *foresta de Winburne* (78b) which may have been part of Holt Forest mentioned in later records; the earliest reference to Holt comes from the twelfth century in the form of *Winburneholt*.[1] The Oxfordshire entries provide the names of five 'demesne forests of the king' – Shotover, Stowood, Woodstock, Cornbury and Wychwood (154b); they lay in two groups, the first two to the east of Oxford and the others to the north-west.

The New Forest

The New Forest is the only forest for which Domesday Book gives some detail. Its description forms a special section of the Hampshire folios, under the heading *In Nova Foresta et circa eam* (51–51b). This unusual section has attracted a good deal of attention. The chroniclers of the twelfth century declared that William reduced a flourishing district to a waste by the wholesale destruction of villages and churches. But against this view there is the evidence provided by the poor soils of the district and by Domesday Book itself. The evidence of soil is clear enough. The greater part of the area is covered by infertile sands and gravels which cannot ever have supported a flourishing agriculture. In the middle of the Forest there are great stretches that seem always to have been

[1] A. Fägersten, *The place-names of Dorset* (Uppsala, 1933), 82.

uninhabited. The evidence of Domesday Book likewise shows that the making of the forest involved much less destruction than the traditional accounts would have us believe. By distinguishing between those settlements placed wholly in the forest and those only partly so, F. H. Baring produced a reasonable interpretation of what may have taken place.[1]

It would seem that about 30 to 40 villages (involving 46 holdings) were placed entirely under forest law, except sometimes for a few acres of meadow.[2] Only about a half of these place-names appear on Fig. 66 because the rest cannot be identified. Nothing is said about the population and teams of all these afforested villages, but we are almost always told of their assessments, their 1066 values and their ploughlands; these latter (for at least 27 villages) amounted to 110. Taking Hampshire as a whole there were just over 3 recorded people per ploughland, so that the figure of 110 may have represented, very roughly of course, about 350 male adults, which implies a total of population of some 1,500 or so. The total would be somewhat higher if we made allowance for those entries with no mention of ploughlands. What had happened to these people? If their settlements were entirely deserted, who provided the Inquest officials with the details of assessment, ploughlands and values? And what of the phrase 'except *n* acres of meadow' which occurs in nearly a half of the entries? Who used the meadow? Is it possible that transference 'into the forest' meant disappearance only from the record and not from the land itself? Whatever view we take, the fact that over a dozen place-names remain unidentified suggests appreciable damage to the local economy, but not to the extent envisaged by the early chroniclers.

There were another 40 or so villages (involving 56 holdings) with only a portion of each 'in the forest'. Some inhabitants of these villages remained outside the forest; and village life continued though apparently in a reduced form. For 31 of these partially afforested holdings, values are given for three dates – *tunc*, *post* and *modo*. On ten of these, there was a decline in value between *tunc* and *post*. For another twelve, the *tunc* and *post* values were the same, and decline came only between *post* and *modo*. This immediately suggests the possibility that the extension of the forest may not have been all of one date. Another six holdings showed a decline during both periods, and there were three exceptional entries.

---

[1] F. H. Baring, 'The making of the New Forest', *Eng. Hist. Rev.*, XVI (1901), 427–38. Reprinted in *Domesday Tables*, 194–205.
[2] *D.G.S–E.E.*, 324–38.

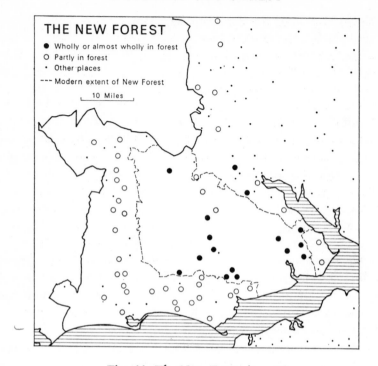

Fig. 66. The New Forest in 1086.

Presumably the wood (and sometimes the pasture) taken into the forest was still physically in existence in 1086. But what of the inhabitants of these afforested portions? Six entries, only, break the silence and tell us about the people and the teams taken into the forest. The totals amount to 69 people and 19 teams; they are spoken of in the past tense (*manserunt, erant, manebant*) but their values are sometimes given in the present tense (*valet, appreciantur*). Does this mean that these people and their teams were physically present 'in the forest'? And if so, what about those of the other afforested portions for which we are not given such detail; their values were sometimes high enough to arouse our suspicion that being 'in the forest' did not always or necessarily imply eviction and destruction, but this is no proof and it might well be an unjustified suspicion. Just across the border, at Downton in Wiltshire, the Geld Rolls tell of '2 hides from which the inhabitants have fled because of the king's forest' (*ii hidas de quibus homines ibi manentes fugati sunt propter forestam regis*). Could *fugati* have meant not dispossessed but merely lost to the manor? In any case, the corresponding Domesday entry (65b) says nothing of these inhabitants. Whatever be the answers to these questions, we can only conclude by saying that, although its limits have greatly shrunk, the New Forest still covers some 92,000 acres, and remains a unique memorial of Norman England.

Other hunting districts

We hear not only of forests but of 'parks' which, presumably, were enclosed in some way by fences for the preservation of the game within. The word *parcus* is sometimes used alone, but in about a third of the entries it appears as *parcus bestiarum silvaticarum* or *parcus ferarum silvaticarum*. The Domesday total is certainly incomplete, and does not include, for example, the park that William de Braiose had made at Bramber in Sussex.[1] What seems to have been 'half a park' was entered for Bentley (287) in Suffolk, but the text here may be corrupt. A number were on royal holdings and *parcus regis* is specifically mentioned in entries for Oakley (Bucks., 149), Stoke next Guildford (Sy., 30) and Watchingwell (Hants., 52b). To what extent these were under forest law is difficult to say, but it may be relevant to note that the royal park at Oakley was near Brill (143b) for which a forest is recorded. An entry for the royal manor of Hollow Court (180b) in Worcestershire certainly seems to imply afforestation: *Ibi est parcus ferarum sed missus est extra manerium cum tota silva*; this therefore appears in the lists of both forests and parks. Most parks, however, were held by the great magnates of the realm. The greater number were in the south-eastern part of the realm, and there was no mention of any in the midland and northern circuits (Fig. 67).

We also hear of hunting at places for which neither forests nor parks are mentioned or implied. On Countess Judith's estate of Fotheringhay (228) in Northamptonshire, the wood yielded 10s when it bore mast and the king did not hunt in it (*cum oneratur et rex in ea non venator*). We cannot say what relation this bore to the Forest of Rockingham, first recorded by name in 1157.[2] In Worcestershire, it was the bishop who had all the proceeds from hunting and other things in the woods of Bredon (173) and Fladbury (172b).

General references to hunting are frequent in the Herefordshire folios (Fig. 69). The city of Hereford (179) itself supplied beaters when the

[1] J. H. Round and L. F. Salzman in *V.C.H. Sussex*, I (1905), 366.
[2] J. E. B. Gover *et al.*, *The place-names of Northamptonshire* (Cambridge, 1933), I.

Fig. 67. Places with parks in 1086 (by Domesday counties).

The names of the places with parks are given opposite.

king went hunting (*ad stabilitionem in silva*), a service similar to that
mentioned among the customs of Shrewsbury (252) and Berkshire (56b).
Some six miles to the south-west of Hereford was the royal manor of
Kingstone (179b); its entry tells of 'a wood called Treville', and says that
the villeins who dwelt there in 1066 had rendered no service beyond that
of carrying venison to the city; at a later date Treville appears as the
name of a forest. Near the Welsh border, at Ailey (187), Gilbert fitz
Turold had a large wood for hunting (*Silva magna ad venandum*); and not
far away on the very marches of Wales (*in Marcha de Walis*) Osbern
fitz Richard hunted on the devastated land of eleven vills which were overgrown with wood (186b). Along the border to the north, in Shropshire
near Montgomery (254), the wasted lands of thirteen vills (two unidentified) had been used for hunting (*ad venandum*) in 1066; they still lay waste
in 1086 and were presumably used for the same purpose. Another indication of hunting in the western parts of the realm comes from the entries

Places with parks in 1086

(Key to Fig. 67)

Bedfordshire
  1 Stagsden (212b)
Buckinghamshire
  2 Long Crendon (147)
  3 Oakley (149)
Cambridgeshire
  4 Burrough Green (195b)
  5 Kirtling (202)
Devonshire
  6 Winkleigh (*109*, 101b)
Essex
  7 Rayleigh (43b)
Gloucestershire
  8 Sodbury (163b)
Hampshire
  9 Bishop's Waltham (40)
  10 Sobberton (48b, 49)
  11 Watchingwell (52b)
Herefordshire
  12 Weobley (184b)
Hertfordshire
  13 Bennington (141)
  14 St Albans (135b)
  15 Ware (138b)
Kent
  16 Chart Sutton (18)
  17 Wickhambreux (7b, 9,
    12 *bis*)

Middlesex
  18 Enfield (129b)
  19 Ruislip (129b)
Norfolk
  20 Costessey (145)
Shropshire
  21 *Marsetelie* (252)
Somerset
  22 Donyatt (*270*, 92)
Suffolk
  23 Bentley (287)
  24 Dennington (328)
  25 Eye (319b)
  26 Ixworth (438b)
Surrey
  27 Stoke next Guildford (30)
Sussex
  28 Rotherfield (16)
  29 Tortington (25)
  30 Up Waltham (25b *bis*)
  31 Walberton (25)
  32 Wilting (18b)
Worcestershire
  33 Hollow Court (180b)
  34 Salwarpe (174, 176)
  35 Wadborough (175)

for three royal manors in Gloucestershire – Barton, Cheltenham and Cirencester (162b); each had to find 3,000 loaves for the hounds (*ter mille panes canibus*) but the render had been commuted into a payment of 16*s*. In the north of England an entry for the twelve devastated vills of Longdendale (273) in north-west Derbyshire, without indicating the amount of their wood, merely says it was suitable not for pannage but for hunting (*silva est ibi non pastilis, apta venationi*); Longdendale was later one of the three divisions of Peak Forest.

That there was also hunting in many other woods we may assume from the references to 'hays' or hedged enclosures constructed to control the driving and capture of animals. The usual formula runs *Ibi n haiae*, and it usually follows the statement about wood. The connexion is made explicit in some entries. At Rushock (185b) in Herefordshire there was a hay in a large wood (*Ibi est una haia in una magna silva*); and at Titley (186b) nearby there was another in a small wood (*ibi i haia in silvula*). The number of hays on a holding was usually one or two, and never more than seven. Although hays were usually associated with wood, there are entries which record them without wood. This is so for 16 out of the 42 places with hays in the Shropshire folios, which provokes a suspicion that the record of wood may not be complete. The three hays connected with Lee (Salop., 254b) are said to be fixed (*haiae firmae*). Some entries expand their references to explain the purpose for which a hay was made – for catching wild beasts or roe-deer or whatever could be taken. Here are three examples:

Kington (Worcs., 176b): *i haia in qua capiebantur ferae.*
Lingen (Salop., 260): *iii haiae capreolis capiendis.*
Bernoldune (Heref., 187): *Ibi est una haia in qua quod potest capere captat.*

In the land beyond the Mersey (269b–270), the thegns of West Derby hundred had, among other things, to make enclosures and hays in the wood (*faciebant in silva haias et stabilituras*); and the freemen of Newton and Blackburn hundreds were subject to similar services. The men of Leyland and Salford hundreds, on the other hand, had to make only one hay (*Tantummodo i haiam in silva faciebant*). In Salford hundred, there were many hays (*plures haiae*).

The record of places with hays presents some strange features (Fig. 68). By far the greater number appear in the folios for Cheshire and Shropshire with 52 and 42 places respectively. There are another 10 for Herefordshire but only 3 each for Gloucestershire and Worcestershire; and there are the references to the making of hays in South Lancashire. Apart from these, there is the solitary reference for the unidentified *Donnelie* (240) in Warwickshire; it is unusual in that the hay is measured: *Ibi haia habens dimidia leuua longa et tantundum lata.* Could it be that here *haia* was a slip of the pen for *silva*? In view of the widespread hunting activity in Domesday England, it is difficult to believe that there were not many more which were never recorded. What about, for example, the entries

PLACES WITH HAYS IN 1086

Number in each Domesday county

—— Circuit boundary

50 Miles

Fig. 68. Places with hays in 1086 (by Domesday counties).

for Ailey (Heref., 187) and other places which mention hunting in wood-lands but not hays? Are the frequent references for Cheshire and Shrop-shire the result of some idiosyncrasy on the part of those who compiled the returns for these counties (Fig. 69), or do they reflect the great import-ance of hunting outside the royal forests in the thinly populated counties near the Welsh border?

Falconry, like hunting, was a favourite sport in Anglo-Saxon times, and so it was after the coming of the Normans. In several entries no less than £10 appears as the alternative render for a hawk – for the counties of Leicester (230), Northampton (219), Oxford (154b), Warwick (238), Wiltshire (64b) and Worcester (172); that for Worcestershire was said to be a Norway (*norresc*) hawk. Renders of hawks appear for a number of other places. Some entries mention nests of hawks usually following upon statements about wood, which is not surprising in view of the arboreal habits of the hawk. The connection is occasionally made explicit as in the

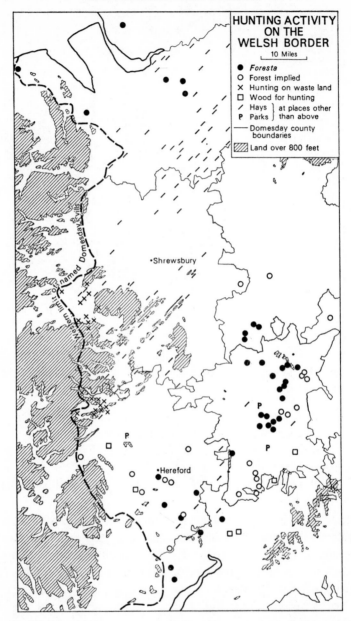

Fig. 69. Hunting activity on the Welsh border (by Domesday counties).

PLACES WITH HAWKS' NESTS IN 1086

Number in each Domesday county

—— Circuit boundary

50 Miles

Fig. 70. Places with hawks' nests in 1086 (by Domesday counties).

For the list, see Appendix 10 (p. 356 below).

three following entries, that for Limpsfield being unusual in that it uses *nidi* instead of *airea*:

Chalfont (Bucks., 152): *in eadem silva una Area Accipitris.*
Forthampton (Gloucs., 180b): *in defenso silvae regis est ibi airea Accepitris.*
Limpsfield (Sy., 34): *iii nidi accipitris in silva.*

The references occur most frequently for places along the Welsh border and they are especially numerous for Cheshire – Fig. 70 and Appendix 10 (p. 356). Again, we have to ask whether this represents a physical fact or an idiosyncrasy on the part of those who made the returns for these counties.

CHAPTER VII

ANNUAL VALUES

One of the questions about a manor in the preamble to the Ely Inquest was: 'How much was the whole worth, and how much is it worth now?' The list of questions, moreover, is followed by a general statement to the effect that the information should be provided for three dates – 1066, 'afterwards' and 1086 (see pp. 4–5). Broadly speaking, the answers from the counties within each circuit show similar features, and indicate annual values either at two or at three dates (Fig. 71). The double-valuation counties sometimes include a number of entries with three valuations – e.g. about 30% of the entries for Shropshire, 18% for Herefordshire, 17% for Warwickshire, 13% for Oxfordshire and 12% for Worcestershire.[1] To these generalisations there are exceptions. Some entries are incomplete, and give only one valuation, e.g. several on folio 182b for Herefordshire seem to refer only to 1086; other single values, on the other hand, clearly refer only to 1066.[2] Occasionally when Domesday Book gives only one value, the Exeter text shows that it refers to two dates.[3] No valuation is given for a number of holdings, e.g. for Radwell (141) in Hertfordshire and for Chilton (59, 61b) in Berkshire, but many of these formed part of manorial complexes and their values were included in grand totals. In some entries there are blank spaces in which figures for values were never inserted.[4] Only occasionally was a value specifically said to be *per annum*, e.g. for Great Bowden (230b) and Rothley (230) in Leicestershire.

THE VARIETY OF THE ENTRIES

Methods of accounting

Values were normally stated in terms of pounds, shillings and pence. Neither of the first two existed as coins; they were accounting units at the rate of twenty shillings to the pound and twelve pence to the shilling.

---

[1] For the eastern counties, see R. Welldon Finn, *The Norman Conquest and its effects on the economy: 1066–86* (London, 1971), 242–75.

[2] *D.G.N.E.*, 42–3, 124–5, 199. [3] *D.G.S–W.E.*, 96, 167, 252.

[4] *D.G.N.E.*, 41, 198.

Another method of accounting, especially in Scandinavian districts, was in terms of the Danish *ora* of 16*d*, as seen in the 2*s* 8*d* entered for Kinoulton (293) and the 5*s* 4*d* entered for Aslockton (291, 293), both in Nottinghamshire. Other units were the mark of silver (13*s* 4*d*) which appears, for example, in the entry for Somersall Herbert (Derby., 274b), and the mark of gold (£6) in that for Singleton (Sx., 23). We also hear of ounces of gold (*unciae auri*), e.g. at Birstall (232, 232b) in Leicestershire. Ottery St Mary and Rawridge (*195b*, 104), in Devonshire, held by the abbey of Rouen, were valued in terms of the Rouen penny which, at a later date, was worth one half an English penny.[1]

Some entries specify values by tale or number (*ad numerum*) when coins were reckoned at their nominal value, e.g. for Slaughter (163) in Gloucestershire. But in view of the circulation of worn coins and debased coins, various methods of compensation were adopted. One method was to reckon by weight (*ad pensum* or *ad pondus*) to allow for light-weight coins, and it would seem that something of the order of about 6% had to be added to their nominal value.[2] Debased coins were assayed and weighed to produce blanched or white money. The usual phrases are *ad ignem et ad pensum*, *ad arsuram et pensum*, *librae albae*, *librae blancae*, *librae candidae*, with variants. An entry for Bosham (Sx., 16) implies that £65 was worth only £50 when assayed and weighed, which means a surprising depreciation of over 20%. A third method of compensation, frequent on royal manors, was to reckon not 16*d* but 20*d* to the *ora*, that is to say, 'for every 16*d* due, 20*d* was collected';[3] thus £10 at 20*d* to the *ora* would need £12 10*s* in nominal value to produce it. The equation of such *orae* with blanched money is implicit in such entries as this for Chedworth and Arlington (164) in Gloucestershire: *xl librae alborum nummorum de xx in ora*.

Values were often round sums such as £3, or 20*s*, which suggest estimates or approximations rather than exact totals. Other sums, however, seem to indicate careful appraisal and the addition of individual renders, e.g. the 53*s* at Chiltley (38) and the £12 3*s* 2*d* at Clere (41), both in Hampshire. On the other hand, an impression of detail may simply be the result of counting in terms of the ora of 16*d* or 20*d*. As well as the

---

[1] O. J. Reichel in *V.C.H. Devonshire*, I (1905), 435n.

[2] J. S. Forbes and D. B. Dallaway, 'Composition of English silver coins (870–1130)', *British Numismatic Jour.*, XXX (1962), 82–7.

[3] J. S. Harvey, 'Royal revenue and Domesday terminology', *Econ. Hist. Rev.*, 2nd ser., XXII (1967), 221–8.

annual value of an estate, we hear frequently of separate money renders from such resources as mills, meadow or pasture. To what extent these were included in the total annual value is not clear, but we can only suppose they were included from such phrases as *in totis valentiis* for Aylesbury (143), Taplow (144) and Wendover (143b) in Buckinghamshire, or as *in totis redditionibus per annum* for Hambleden (152b) in the same county. The phrase *totum valet* appears in the first five entries on folio 155b for Oxfordshire. The fifth of these, that for Yarnton, expands the statement: *Totum T.R.E. valebat x libras. Modo cum piscaria et cum pratis valet xiiii libras,* but while meadow appears in the body of the entry, the fishery does not; furthermore, the body of the entry mentions pasture and we are left to conjecture whether that was included in the valuation. Other entries also leave us in doubt as to what was included. Here are details for two Berkshire manors producing cheese in the Vale of White Horse:

	Buckland (58b)			Shellingford (59b)		
	£	s	d	£	s	d
Mill		12	6		2	6
Fisheries	1	0	6		—	
Meadow		?			12	6
Dues of cheese	1	12	4	4	16	8
Sum of above	3	5	4	5	11	8
Domesday *valet*	8	0	0	12	0	0

We can only speculate whether the miscellaneous renders were included in the total value of each manor, thus leaving the differences to be accounted for by the four teams at work at Buckland and the seven at Shellingford. Only rarely is an item specifically excluded from the main valuation of a holding: Rayleigh (43b) in Essex was said to be worth £10 in 1086 apart from the wine (*praeter vinum*) from its vineyard.

In the same way, it is sometimes impossible to be sure of what is included in the main valuation of an estate with component holdings. The annual values of components are frequently given separately, and some of these are said to be included within the valuation (*in pretio*) for a complex as a whole, e.g. for Mendlesham (285b–286) in Suffolk. But when no such statement is made, can we be sure whether or not the value of a component is so included? Doubts of this kind arise from the entries for Norton (284b–286) in Suffolk, Hitchin (132b–133) in Hertfordshire, Houghton (40b) in Hampshire, Taunton (*174,* 187b) in Somerset and for a host of other places. Such entries must each be considered on its own merits. Clearly, two people equally familiar with the Domesday text might well arrive at different totals.

There were sometimes differences of opinion about values. Newton Tony (70), in Wiltshire, was valued at £18 in 1086, but the Englishmen said it was only worth £12 (*Ab anglicis appreciatur xii libras*). Or again, the Englishmen put the value of Barking (18), in Essex, at £80 but the Frenchmen put it as high as £100. One curiosity is the entry for Aldwincle (222) in Northamptonshire. Its value had risen from 20s to 30s but this could reach 100s if it were well worked (*Si bene exerceretur*). These few examples, and there are quite a number of others,[1] show that there must have been many an argument about what Domesday Book usually tersely records as the annual value or render of a holding.

The renting out of manors

Many manors were 'rented out' or 'farmed out', e.g. in Cambridgeshire, Litlington (190) with a *valet* of £22 and Woodditton (189b) with one of £12 were said to be *ad firmam*. Frequently there is mention not of *valet* but of *reddit* which more explicitly indicates a rent rather than a valuation. In all eight counties of the eastern and south-eastern circuits, many new landowners obtained rents greatly in excess of the values of some manors, and sometimes we are told specifically that the manor was 'at farm'. Here are some examples from Kent: Pluckley, valued (*valet*) at £15 in 1086, paid £20 in rent (*et tamen reddit xx libras*); Bilsington, valued (*valet*) at £50, paid £70 to the farm (*et tamen reddit de firma lxx libras*); Wadholt (i.e. *Platenovt*), valued (*valet*) at only 20s, paid 40s becuase it was at farm (*tamen appreciatur xl solidis eo quod sit ad firmam*). The complete figures for these three places are representative of many others:

	Valet			Reddit
	1066	'post'	1086	1086
Pluckley (3b)	£12	£8	£15	£20
Bilsington (10b)	£10	£30	£50	£70
Wadholt (12b)	20s	20s	20s	40s

Such excess amounts are entered for 172 places in the five south-eastern counties, that is about 12% of the total number. The corresponding figures for the three eastern counties are 46 places or 2½%.

[1] E.g. *D.G.M.E.*, 18–19.

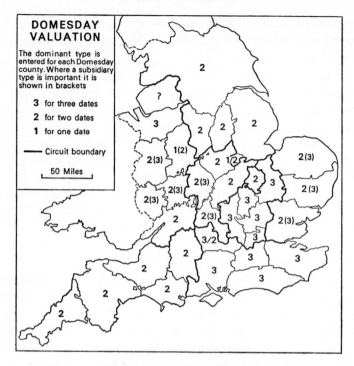

Fig. 71. Domesday valuation: Main types of entries
(by Domesday counties).

It is not surprising that there were complaints. In Sussex, the payment of £80 instead of £60 at Pagham (16b) was considered too heavy (*sed nimis grave est*); and the sum from Preston (17), near Brighton, had been kept at £18 because the farm of £25 could not be borne (*sed non poterat reddere*). Pettaugh (440), in Suffolk, had been at farm for £3 15*s* but this was reduced to 45*s* because the men were thereby ruined (*sed homines inde fuerunt confusi*). The entry for Thaxted (38b), in Essex, is unusually detailed. Its value had risen from £30 in 1066 to £50 in 1086, and it had been leased by Richard fitz Gilbert to 'a certain Englishman' for £60, but he appears to have lost £10 by the transaction (*Ricardus dedit cuidam anglico ad Censum pro lx libris; sed unoquoque anno deficiunt illi ad minus x librae*). The Anglo-Saxon Chronicle, under the year 1087, has a famous passage about the high rents extracted by the king, but it is clear that such extortion was also practised by other landowners, both lay and ecclesiastical.

Outside the eastern and south-eastern circuits, excessive rents are very rarely mentioned; here are a few scattered examples:

Bausley (Salop., 255 b): *Valuit et valet ii solidos et tamen est ad firmam pro vi solidis et viii denariis.*

Damerham (Wilts., 66b): *Totum manerium T.R.E. valebat xxxv libras. Modo reddit lxi libras, sed ab hominibus non appreciantur plusque xlv libras propter confusionem terrae et propter firmam quae nimis est alta.*

Marsh Gibbon (Bucks., 148b): *Valet et valuit semper lxx solidos. Istement tenuit T.R.E. sed modo tenet ad firmam de Willelmo [filius Ansculfi] graviter et miserabiliter.*

Melbourne (Derby., 272b): *T.R.E. valuit x libras; modo vi libras, tamen x reddit.*

Stotfold (Beds., 213): *In totis valentiis valet xxv libras. Quando recepit xii libras. T.R.E. xx libras. Die qua Radulphus tallebosc obiit pro xxx libras erat ad firmam.*

Is it likely that extortion outside the south and south-eastern circuits was confined to a few sporadic places? Or does its frequent mention in the folios for these two circuits merely reflect the method employed by their respective commissioners?

We might assume that in the eastern and south-eastern circuits rents were only stated when they exceeded values. But in that case we must also assume that extortion outside these two circuits was confined to a very few sporadic places. This is most unlikely. Moreover, when the Domesday text for these other counties makes no reference to *ad firmam* and speaks only of *reddit*, can we be sure that a manor was not farmed? Reginald Lennard, in a detailed discussion of Domesday values, came to the conclusion that the renting of manors was more prevalent than is apparent from the specific references to it, and that 'the *reddit* of Domesday indicates the payment of a definite rent or farm and not the actual or estimated profits of direct exploitation by the lord'.[1] Furthermore, there is evidence that some *valets*, at any rate, were really *reddits*. At Exning (189b) in Domesday Cambridgeshire one holding was worth (*valet*) £53, and it is only from the I.C.C. (p. 4) that we know that it was held *ad firmam de rege.* Likewise, Thurrock (63) in Essex was valued (*valet*) at £30 in 1086, but its 7 houses in London were said to be included *in hac firma.* Or again, Wantage (57), in Berkshire, was said to be worth (*valet*) £61, and it is only incidentally, in a separate entry for Betterton (57) nearby, that we hear of *firma de Wanetinz.* In the same way Norton (286)

---

[1] R. Lennard, *Rural England, 1086–1135* (Oxford, 1959), 123.

in Suffolk was valued (*valet*) at £16 blanch, and we hear of *firma de Nortuna* only in an entry for Ashbocking (285).

A comparison of the Exchequer and Exeter texts yields some additional evidence. The *reddit* of the Exchequer text appears as a *firma* in the Exeter text, e.g. for Bluehayes (*398*, 113) in Devonshire. Moreover, when the Exchequer text uses *valet*, the Exeter version sometimes uses *reddit*, e.g. in entries for Ashmore (Do., *29b*, 75b) and Leonard (Devon, *395b*, 112). Furthermore the Exeter version itself sometimes interlines *reddit* above *valet* and vice versa, e.g. *reddit* above *valet* in entries for Horwood (Devon, *336*, 114) and Westowe (Som., *428b*, 93b), and *valet* above *reddit* in those for Nether Stowey (Som., *373*, 97) and Eleigh (Som., *426b*, 93b); the Exchequer text in all four entries uses *valet*. There is no means of knowing whether these Exeter emendations were based upon real differences or whether the two terms were used indifferently, but two entries invite comparison with their Exchequer versions:

Foddington (Som.)
Exch. D.B. (99): *Olim et modo valet xx solidos.*
Exon D.B. (*466b*): *reddit per annum xx solidos et quando Escelinus accepit ad firmam de rege valebat tantundem.*
Lympstone (Devon)
Exch. D.B. (113): *Olim x librae. Modo valet* (*reddit* interlined) *viii libras.*
Exon D.B. (*460*): *reddit viii libras ad firmam Willelmo et quando Ricardus hanc mansionem* (? *recepit*) *valebat x libras.*

The *valet* of the Exchequer entry for Foddington does not reveal the fact that it was held *ad firmam*. The Exchequer entry for Lympstone, on the other hand, emends *valet* by interlining *reddit* above.

Comparison of the Domesday folios for Kent with the alternative text of the Domesday Monachorum also raises a number of points. The Domesday *reddit* sometimes appears as a *reddit de firma* in the Monachorum text, e.g. for Malling and Wrotham.[1] Furthermore, the distinction between *valet* and *reddit* is not always clear. The Domesday text gives a valuation of £16 17s 6d for Appledore (5); the corresponding entry in the Monachorum says that it was worth (*valet*) £12, but that it rendered (*sed tamen reddit*) £16 16s 7d [*sic*].[2] Something similar appears in the entry for Boughton under Blean (3b). Its Domesday *valet* was £30 16s 3½d but the Monachorum entry puts its *valet* at £20 and goes on to

[1] D. C. Douglas (ed.), *The Domesday Monachorum of Christ Church, Canterbury* (Roy. Hist. Soc., London, 1944), 87.   [2] D. C. Douglas, 91.

say that it rendered (*reddit ad firmam*) £25 and also a rent (*gablum*) of £5 15*s* 3*d*, thus making a total of £30 15*s* 3*d*.[1] Or again, the Domesday entry for Adisham (3) puts its *reddit* at £46 16*s* 4*d* but the Monachorum speaks of a *valet de firma* of £30 and a *gablum* of £16 16*s* 4*d*.[2] Both texts say the *valet* of Wingham (3b) was £100, but a schedule included with the Monachorum refers to £100 *de firma*, a *gablum* of £29 10*s*, and customs (*constumes*) to the value of £3 17*s*.[3] Such entries make us inclined to think that Domesday valuations may not be as straightforward as at first sight they appear to be.

When we see that the distinction between *reddits* (and *valets*) and higher *reddits* is practically confined to two circuits, we may well wonder whether their absence from the other circuits reflects differences of method or of fact, and whether some Exchequer *reddits* were in excess of the true *valets*. Consider, for example, the *reddits* for three royal manors in Buckinghamshire described on folios 143–143b:

Aylesbury: T.R.E. £25 *ad numerum*
    T.R.W. £56 *arsae et pensatae* and from toll
    £10 *ad numerum*.
Risborough: T.R.E. £10 *ad numerum*
    T.R.W. £46 18*s* 8*d de argento albo*
Wendover: T.R.E. £25 *ad numerum*
    T.R.W. £38 *arsae et pensatae*

Such large increases are remarkable. Could these manors have been at farm in 1086 for sums beyond their reasonable annual values?

Some *reddits* and *valets* seem to have been artificial in character. A group of fifteen royal manors in Somerset had formerly belonged to the house of Godwine, and the renders of ten of them, and possibly of all fifteen, were multiples of 23*s de albo argento*; Crewkerne, for example, rendered (*reddit*) 40 such units, North Curry rendered 20, and Capton rendered two (*103–107*, 86b–87). This strange unit has never been explained; certainly its incidence bore no reasoned relationship to agricultural resources.[4] An artificial element has also been postulated for the *reddits* of groups of royal manors in Devonshire and Cornwall,[5] and also for the 1066 *reddits* of royal manors in Northamptonshire.[6] Other evidence

---

[1] D. C. Douglas, 84–5.   [2] D. C. Douglas, 89–90.
[3] D. C. Douglas, 83, 98. See R. Lennard (1959), 119.
[4] *D.G.S–W.E.*, 168–9. See also J. H. Round in *V.C.H. Somerset*, 1 (1906), 397–8.
[5] J. H. Round, *The commune of London and other studies* (Westminster, 1899), 70–1.
[6] J. H. Round in *V.C.H. Northamptonshire*, 1 (1902), 273.

of artificiality is seen in the values of nine large manors forming part of the fief of Drogo de Brevere in Holderness (323b–324). Each had been worth (*valuit*) £56 in 1066, and some were valued at £10 and others at £6 in 1086; again there is no explanation of this conventional element.[1] A number of other large Yorkshire manors had been worth (*valuit*) £56, a sum more consistent with the idea of 'a *firma* pre-determined by the lord than with the assumption that it represents an approximate calculation of potential revenue on the part of the local jurors'.[2]

The implication of Domesday 'values' is complicated by the fact that a holding often made other payments in addition to its rent. One such payment was the *tailla* or tallage, not to be confused with the later medieval due of that name.[3] It is mentioned occasionally in connexion with estates in a number of counties, e.g. for Gunthorpe (Notts., 285b) and for Conisbrough (Yorks., 321), but it is a special feature of the Lincolnshire text. On folio after folio there are entries similar to that for Dowsby (340) with a *valet* in 1086 of £4 and also with *Tailla xx solidi*. The great manor of Folkingham (355b) was worth (*valet*) £40 but its *tailla* amounted to no less than £50. Such additional sums appear in 267 Lincolnshire entries. In these entries, with both a *valet* and *tailla*, the sum of the latter amounts to as much as 45% of the former. The variation amongst the Lincolnshire divisions is as follows:

Lindsey:	North Riding	38%
	West Riding	32%
	South Riding	78%
Kesteven		35%
Holland		48%

Another payment was the *gersuma*, more occasional in character.[4] It is mentioned only very infrequently in the main Domesday Book (e.g. on folio 180b for Martley in Worcestershire), but appears again and again in the folios of Little Domesday Book. Thus in Essex, Peter the sheriff received from Havering (3) £80 *de censu* and £10 *de gersuma*. Reginald

---

[1] *D.G.N.E.*, 197–8. See also F. W. Maitland, *Domesday Book and beyond* (Cambridge, 1897), 473.

[2] F. M. Stenton, *Types of manorial structure in the northern Danelaw* (Oxford, 1910), 34.

[3] F. M. Stenton in C. W. Foster and T. Longley, *The Lincolnshire Domesday and the Lindsey Survey* (Lincs. Record Soc., 1924), xxiii.

[4] R. Lennard (1959), 180–2.

Lennard suggested that sometimes a 'value' may have been 'artificially low because a *gersuma* had been paid' when a rent-paying tenant entered into occupation.[1] As we explore more deeply the relationship of value to rent and of either to total renders, the real annual worth of a manor becomes increasingly obscure.

Renders in kind

Some valuations provide glimpses of an archaic system of food rents which had almost disappeared by 1086. This was the arrangement by which the king received a *firma unius noctis* (sometimes called *firma unius diei*), that is one day's provision or 'feorm' for the royal household during its journeying throughout the realm. The levy usually came from large and wealthy manors on the royal demesne. Some manors were responsible for only fractions of a night, usually leaving us without a clue to the remaining fractions; groups of manors, on the other hand, were sometimes combined to provide the necessary resources. Surviving examples in 1066 or 1086 were to be found especially in the Wessex counties of Dorset, Hampshire, Somerset and Wiltshire, and these manors were said never to have been hidated or to have paid geld. Frequently by 1086 a feorm had been commuted for a money payment which was of the order of £100 to £110, but sums as low as £76 16s 8d were recorded. The specific references to these and the other feorms are set out in Appendix 11 (pp. 357–8).

Other entries for manors in these Wessex counties may also indicate a feorm of a night or day, although they do not specifically say so. Such are the entries for the royal manors of Broughton (38b) and Neatham (38) in Hampshire: the annual value of each in 1066 was £76 16s 8d which is exactly double the value of the half-day farms at Barton Stacey and Eling (38b) in the same county. Or again, Bedminster (Som., *90b*, 86b), with no recorded render in 1066, may have been combined with the three quarters of a night at Milborne Port (*91b*, 86b); their combined renders in 1086 amounted to £100 10s 9½d.[2]

Occasional *firmae noctis* were to be found in a number of other counties, but with values less than the £100 or so on the Wessex manors. There was, moreover, much variation in circumstance. The feorms from three Gloucestershire manors had not been commuted in 1086; those from

[1] R. Lennard in a review, *Eng. Hist. Rev.*, LXXIX (1964), 396.
[2] J. H. Round, *Feudal England* (London, 1895), 111–12.

three Sussex manors, on the other hand, had been entirely commuted. Then again, three manors in Bedfordshire paid in 1086 partly with sums of money and partly with half-day feorms in 'grain, honey and other things pertaining to the feorm (*aliis rebus ad firmam pertinentibus*)'; conceivably, these were full feorms that had been partly commuted. In the same way, the royal manors of Soham and Fordham in Cambridgeshire had each paid, in 1066, a sum of money and a three-days feorm in 'grain, honey, malt and other small dues (*aliis minutis consuetudinibus*)'; but by 1086 the feorm had been commuted for £13 8s 4d. References to the same sum from five other royal manors in the Cambridgeshire area show that commutation had also taken place on them. Elsewhere, we hear of feorms from the counties of Northampton and Oxford, and from manors in Herefordshire, Shropshire and the three counties of Little Domesday Book. In the latter, entries for Norfolk and Suffolk refer to payments both in sums of money and in days or nights of honey and other dues (*dies de melle cum consuetudinibus*) in 1066, but these lingering vestiges of feorms in kind had all been commuted by 1086. There is a hint of the system in Cornwall where the canons of St Piran in 1066 had a feorm of four weeks (*206b*, 121).

Many and varied renders in kind often appear in entries that make no specific references to feorms of a day or night. Thus the Gloucestershire manors of Cheltenham, Barton and Cirencester (162b) rendered in kind as well as in money. Honey renders are sporadically mentioned for places widely scattered from Derbyshire to Suffolk, to Sussex and to Devonshire (see pp. 277–9). There were also renders in lead in 1066 from the Derbyshire manors of Bakewell, Ashford and Hope (272b–273). An unnamed holding (*436b*, 97), identified as Charlton Horethorne in Somerset, paid £18 when Robert fitz Gerald acquired it, but in 1086 it rendered 100 cheeses and 10 bacon pigs (*c casei et x bacones*); an entry in the 'Summaries' of the *Liber Exoniensis* (530b) shows that the missing value was £17.[1] The majority of renders in kind are set out not as part of the total value of a manor but separately in connection with such resources as mills or fisheries; these include grain, eels and even iron. We can only suppose that, like the corresponding money renders, they were subsumed within the total annual value of a manor. Finally, there were curious renders in money or kind such as the ancient grain renders that had been commuted on some Oxfordshire royal manors (154b),[2] or the

[1] *D.G.S–W.E.*, 168.   [2] *D.G.S–E.E.*, 233.

renders of sheep, lambs or iron made 'to some royal or some comital manor by the holders of other manors' in Somerset and Devonshire.[1]

Hundredal manors

The profits of some manors, particularly royal manors, were derived not only from economic exploitation but from the rights of jurisdiction attached to them. The soke of a hundred or hundreds was said to belong to a manor and was 'feormed' with that manor. Generally speaking, two thirds of the proceeds of justice in the shire courts and hundred courts went to the king and one third to the earl. 'And just as the king's rights as the lord of a hundredal court become bound up with, and are let to farm with, some royal manor, so the earl's third penny will be annexed to some comital manor.'[2]

In the Oxfordshire folios (154b) we hear of seven great royal manors, and of various payments due to them, and of the fact that to each 'pertained' two or three hundreds. Then follows a statement of the render of each: *Inter totum reddit per annum n libras*, with variants. These renders ranged from £18 to £85, and 'represented a revenue drawn from many sources. The profits of justice done in the courts of the annexed hundreds must have formed an important part of it, although the Survey gives no indication of their amount.'[3] In Shropshire, the nine hundredal manors, which had once belonged to King Edward, were in the hands of Earl Roger in 1086. The details are fuller than for the Oxfordshire manors; and here are the relevant parts of four of the Shropshire entries in the order in which they come on folios 253–253b:

Wrockwardine: *Huic manerio pertinebat T.R.E. de Hundredo Recordine ii denarii; Comes habebat tercium denarium. T.R.E. reddebat vi libras et xiii solidos et viii denarios. Modo reddit xii libras et x solidos de firma.*

Condover: *Huic manerio pertinebat ii denarii de hundredo Conendoure. Reddebat x libras; modo reddit cum hundredo x libras.*

Hodnet: *T.R.E. reddebat hoc manerium iii libras et vi solidos et viii denarios. Modo reddit viii libras cum Hundredo quod ad manerium pertinet.*

Corfham: *Huic manerio pertinet totum Comestane hundredum et Patinton hundredum. T.R.E. cum ii denarios de hundredo reddebat x libras de firma. Modo cum hundredis reddit comite vi libras.*

[1] F. W. Maitland, 169–70. See also *D.G.S–W.E.*, 210–12.

[2] F. W. Maitland, 95, 411. See also R. S. Hoyt, *The royal demesne in English constitutional history: 1066–1272* (Cornell, 1950), 11–13.

[3] F. M. Stenton in *V.C.H. Oxfordshire*, 1 (1939), 374–5.

Among many other examples we may name that of Slaughter (163) in Gloucestershire: *Reddit nunc de manerio ipso et de hundredo xxvii libras ad numerum.*

Manors with 'pertinent' hundreds or manors said to receive 'third pennies' are widely scattered throughout the country, as may be seen from the evidence assembled by H. M. Cam.[1] One entry of particular interest is that for the Somerset manor of Taunton (*174*, 87b). The manor as a whole rendered £153 1s 1d, including all its dependencies and their customary dues (*cum omnibus appendiciis et consuetudinibus suis*), and among these customs were *denarii de hundredo*.[2] Wider in scope than these hundredal profits were those, occasionally, from the shire itself. To Puddletown (*Piretone, 25b*, 75) belonged 'the third penny of the whole shire of Dorset'; its total render amounted to £73. Coton (238), in Warwickshire, had received 'the third penny of the pleas of the shire' in 1066 when it rendered £17. A few years later it was at feorm for £30, and likewise in 1086 with all that pertained to it (*Modo tantundem cum omnibus quae ibi pertinet*).[3]

The evidence for 'hundred pennies' is least abundant in the north – none for the counties of Lincoln, Nottingham and York; but here again profits of justice from sokeland formed an important element in the 'value' of a manor. Moreover, the values of many large sokes are round sums such as £60, £50 or £30. 'Figures of this type, it is clear, do not result from the addition of a number of casual payments, nor shall we readily believe that they represent chance estimates of manorial value on the part of the local jurors.'[4]

THE DISTRIBUTION OF ANNUAL VALUES

How does the statement about annual value or render compare with the other information given in a Domesday entry? Generally speaking, the greater the number of teams and men on a holding, the higher its value; but there are wide variations and it is impossible to discern any consistent relationship. Manors with identical annual values show great differences in their recorded resources. The following figures are for seven Warwickshire

[1] H. M. Cam, 'Manerium cum hundredo: the hundred and the hundredal manor', *Eng. Hist. Rev.*, XLVII (1932), 353–76. See also F. W. Maitland, 91–2.
[2] E. B. Demarest, 'The hundred-pennies', *Eng. Hist. Rev.*, XXXIII (1918), 67–9.
[3] For this entry see J. H. Round in *V.C.H. Warwickshire*, I (1904), 290–1.
[4] F. M. Stenton (1910), 32.

estates, each worth (*valet*) £2 in 1086; they have been chosen because they are likely to be without the complications of large and composite manors:

	Teams	Men	Other resources
Binton (243b)	2	4	mill
Bericote (241b)	3	9	meadow, mill
Ashow (241b)	4	22	meadow, wood, mill
Wolfhamcote (240b)	5	21	meadow
Rugby (241)	6	18	meadow, mill
Grendon (242)	8	40	meadow, wood, mill
Nuneaton (241b)	11	22	meadow, wood

On such simple manors as these, the lack of correlation with an annual value of £2 may be the result not so much of the complications already discussed as of the presence of unrecorded resources such as pigs, dairy cattle and, more especially, sheep.

The Little Domesday Book, however, goes a long way towards providing such information in that it gives details about demesne live-stock for 1066 and 1086. The number of variables on a holding compli-cates any comparison between the two dates, but here are some details for places each with rather similar resources in both years. At Harpley (161b), in Norfolk, an increase in the number of demesne sheep from 180 to 308 was accompanied by a rise in value from 60s to 70s; and at Wratting (396b), in Suffolk, an increase from 60 to 700 sheep was also accompanied by a rise in value but only from 50s to 60s. Many other entries, however, show no such correlations. Thus the circumstances of Quendon (51), in Essex, were also very similar at both dates except for a great increase in livestock (from 80 to 200 in the case of sheep), yet its value fell from £8 to £6; and at Bowers Gifford (71b), in the same county, the sheep and other resources were comparable at both dates but the value of the holding had doubled. J. H. Round confessed himself baffled by the 'incomprehensible advances' in the values of many Essex manors.[1]

The Exeter Domesday Book also records demesne livestock, and when we look at some sample entries from both it and Little Domesday Book, no constant relationship between resources and values appears, although we must remember that it is only about demesne livestock that we are told. The table on p. 222 sets out the figures for ten holdings each worth

[1] J. H. Round in *V.C.H. Essex*, I (1903), 364–5.

Sample holdings worth £2 a year in 1086 from Exeter D.B. and Little D.B.

The abbreviations stand for meadow, pasture and wood

	Place	Folio	Men	Teams	Demesne sheep	Other livestock	Other resources
Somerset	Clatworthy	357	23	7	100	59	M.P.W. Mill
	Redlynch	276	14	2	20	21	M.W.
Devon	Cheriton	337	8	2	30	35	P.W.
	Feniton	214b	14	¼	15	5	M.P.W.
Norfolk	Banham	201b	11	1¼	30	61	M.W.
	Lexham	165	24	6	200	36	W. Mill
Suffolk	Ilketshall	301b	18	2¼	40	21	M.W. Mill
	Old Newton	374	3	1	40	8	M.
Essex	Bowers Gifford	71b	1	1	100	20	P.
	Bromley	40b	3	0	11	—	M.W.

£2 a year in 1086. Their variety can only lead us to suppose that many considerations now lost to us entered into manorial valuations. We can however plot the valuations if only with the idea of marshalling the information of Domesday Book rather than with the hope of penetrating through that information to the geographical reality of eleventh-century England.

We can do this in full awareness of the fact that, as we have seen, the valuations present many problems that may never be properly resolved. Leaving these obscure questions aside, there are three practical difficulties involved in mapping. One arises from the varied way in which values are expressed. This can be overcome to some extent by reckoning in terms of number (*ad numerum*) and bringing the figures of the other methods approximately to this base; the excessive *reddits* in the eastern and south-eastern circuits can be ignored in favour of their accompanying *valets*. The uncommuted feorms can be allowed for, but not the various renders in kind. Imprecise though our arithmetic must be, it may provide a very generalised picture of Domesday information as opposed to eleventh-century reality.

A second difficulty results from the existence of composite entries covering a number of places. This is an ever-present problem in the handling of Domesday statistics, but it is especially acute for values. The values of the great Lincolnshire sokes are not usually given separately but are concealed in totals for the chief manors. Thus the value of Greetham (349), in the southern part of the Wolds, was £60 in 1086, but this figure covered not only Greetham itself but territory in 33 widely separated villages; the converse of this is that many a Lincolnshire holding has no value specifically entered for itself. There are also frequent groups of berewicks included in only one valuation. A like state of affairs is found in other northern counties – Derbyshire, Nottinghamshire and Yorkshire.[1] A similar problem is encountered in East Anglia. The valuation of Necton (235–236b) in Norfolk, for example, covered holdings at 21 other places scattered over seven hundreds; that of Kettleburgh (293b–294), in Suffolk, covered holdings in 19 other places. Moreover, in both counties a single holding is frequently said to be included in the valuation (*in pretio*) of another holding elsewhere.[2]

---

[1] F. M. Stenton (1910), 31. See also *D.G.N.E.*, 254, 301.
[2] *D.G.E.E.*, 118–19, 172–5. See also R. Welldon Finn, *Domesday studies: the eastern counties* (London, 1967), 161.

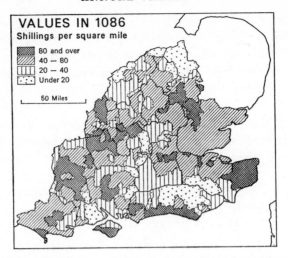

Fig. 72. The distribution of annual values over part of England in 1086.

A third difficulty arises from the unsatisfactory information for the boroughs. We have therefore attempted to exclude borough rents and profits, and to restrict our calculations to the annual values of rural properties alone. But the nature of the information does not always make this possible. Some boroughs formed part of rural manors and the valuations of both manor and borough were combined in one total which we have included, e.g. for Bedwyn (Wilts., 64b), Buckingham (143) and Newport Pagnell (Bucks., 148b). Yet another complication arises from the fact that the so-called 'contributory properties' in boroughs were valued in with the rural manors to which they belonged, e.g. those at Warwick (238) – see p. 309.

There is little we can do about these three groups of complications except exclude from our calculations those counties where the problems are most acute. The result of the calculations can be seen on the accompanying maps. The basic map (Fig. 72) is that showing the distribution of shillings per square mile. Many of its features recall those of the distributions of population and teams (Figs. 35 and 41), e.g. high densities in eastern Kent, along the Sussex coastal plain and in parts of southern Cambridgeshire. The two subsidiary maps have been plotted in quintiles in order to emphasise the highest and lowest values. On Fig. 73 (shillings per man) the areas with very high values are more scattered, but the chalklands of Dorset and Wiltshire stand out as prosperous areas. Of the three maps, Fig. 74 may be the most instructive in that a high value per team may indicate the non-arable element in the valuations. Part of this non-arable element could be the result of those obscure and intractable problems already discussed; but part of it could also reflect, as Professor Sawyer has emphasised, the presence of rural activities associated with pig-rearing, dairy farming and especially sheep-farming.[1] The map shows two outstanding features. One is the high density over the greater part of Kent. Could this be, in part, a reflection of non-arable activity in the Weald and the coastal marshes? Or, is it to be associated with the position of Kent in relation to the continent? Or might it result from some idiosyncrasy in the returns for the county? The 'Monachorum' shows that the *valets* (as opposed to the *reddits*) at three places in the county were lower than Domesday Book records. The excessive *reddits* for 55 places in the county have been disregarded in the construction of Figs. 72–4. Could other *reddits* have also been in excess without our knowing it?

The other outstanding feature is the high density in the chalklands of Dorset, Wiltshire and Hampshire. The Exeter Domesday Book leaves us in no doubt about the importance of sheep in the chalk county of Dorset (Fig. 59) and there is no reason to doubt that the downlands of Hampshire and Wiltshire also provided good sheep pasture. But other factors may have helped to increase values here. The chalklands of Dorset and Wiltshire included over a dozen places from which a *firma unius noctis* was due, and in our reckoning these have been put down at high sums (see p. 217). Below the chalk escarpment in northern Berkshire was an adjoining area of high values in the Vale of White Horse with its abundant meadows, its dairying and its cheese-making. Another area with a high density lay below the chalk in Buckinghamshire. Was this the result of economic activity or of the fact that here was the royal manor of Aylesbury responsible in 1086 for a render, *in totis valentiis*, of £56 whereas in 1066 it had paid only £25? As we think about such questions we cannot be surprised that commentator after commentator has been puzzled over the implications of the Domesday *valet* and *reddit*.

[1] P. H. Sawyer in a review, *Econ. Hist. Rev.*, 2nd series, XVI (1963–4), 155–7.

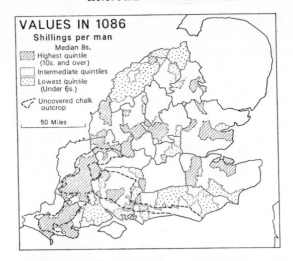

Fig. 73. The distribution of annual values per man (by quintiles, and adjusted for slaves) over part of England in 1086.

ANNUAL VALUES BY DOMESDAY COUNTIES

As we have seen, some of the uncertainties over annual values spring from the nature of the Domesday entries themselves. Others arise from the fact that so often the value of an estate covers holdings widely scattered over the face of a county, and there is no means of apportioning the amounts among the different places. It might be argued, however, that we could side-step the latter difficulties by considering not the totals for each of the 715 units upon which the density maps are based, but the totals for each of the Domesday counties. The result would not give a detailed picture but, at any rate, it would give some picture. It is with this possibility in mind that Appendix 12 (p. 359) has been prepared.

Total values for each of 21 counties were assembled by C. H. Pearson as long ago as 1867.[1] These were adopted by Maitland who also used R. W. Eyton's totals for Somerset and Staffordshire, making a total of 23 counties.[2] Other writers have also produced fresh totals for a number

---

[1] C. H. Pearson, *History of England during the early and middle ages*, I (1867), 661–70.
[2] F. W. Maitland, *Domesday Book and beyond* (Cambridge, 1897), 401, 464n; R. W. Eyton, *Domesday studies: an analysis and digest of the Somerset Survey*, 2 vols. (London, 1880); R. W. Eyton, *Domesday studies: an analysis and digest of the Staffordshire Survey* (London, 1881), 109.

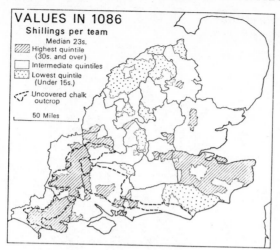

Fig. 74. The distribution of annual values per team (by quintiles) over part of England in 1086.

of these counties e.g. Derbyshire and Gloucestershire,[1] and also for Yorkshire not included in the 23.[2] The table on p. 359 covers 33 Domesday counties – that is taking Yorkshire as one and excluding the unit of *Roteland* and the Cheshire appendix on south Lancashire because their information is too fragmentary. Generally speaking, the present figures are of the same order of magnitude as the earlier estimates of Pearson, Eyton and others. In recording the early attempts to estimate values, we must not forget the outstanding analysis by W. J. Corbett of 'the rental of England in 1086', 'exclusive of the revenue arising from the towns'. His conclusion was that the total revenue from rural properties was about £73,000 a year. This compares with the £72,000 of the present count.[3]

We must be under no illusion about the precarious nature of these county totals. Into them enter all the uncertainties inherent in the entries themselves – the difficulties involved in the relation of *valets* to *reddits*, the artificial nature of some amounts, the complication of additional

[1] F. M. Stenton in *V.C.H. Derbyshire*, I (1905), 319; C. S. Taylor, *An analysis of the Domesday Survey of Gloucestershire* (Bristol and Gloucestershire Archaeol. Soc., 1889), 334.

[2] W. Farrer in *V.C.H. Yorkshire*, II (1912), 189.

[3] W. J. Corbett, 'The development of the duchy of Normandy and the Norman conquest of England', being chapter 5 of J. R. Tanner *et al.*, *The Cambridge Medieval History*, V (Cambridge, 1926), 507.

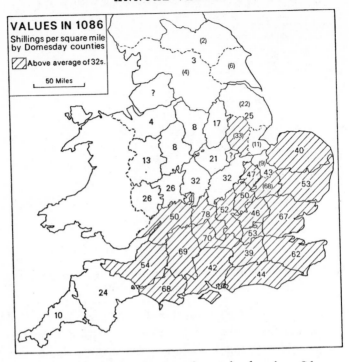

Fig. 75. The distribution of annual values in 1086
(by Domesday counties).

renders such as the *tailla*, the impossibility of evaluating renders in kind, especially those of some *firmae noctis*, and, not least, the fact that some values include profits from justice as well as the fruits of economic activity.

But granted that the county totals may provide, to use Maitland's words, some 'distant approach towards the truth',[1] their interest lies in their relation to the areas of the Domesday counties and to the county totals for teams and for men, i.e. recorded population 'adjusted for slaves'. In an attempt to make the figures per square mile, per man and per team as satisfactory as possible, two totals were calculated for some counties based upon maximum and minimum interpretations of such entries as those for Norton and other places discussed above (see p. 210). This was done in order to see to what extent differing interpretations of the figures might affect the averages per square mile, per

[1] F. W. Maitland, 407.

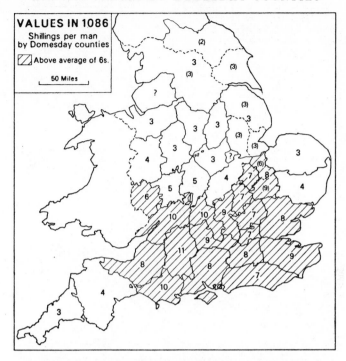

Fig. 76. The distribution of annual values per man in 1086
(by Domesday counties, and adjusted for slaves).

man and per team. Almost invariably the differences were negligible
when taken to the nearest shilling, and did not affect the general picture
taken county by county.

The resulting averages have been transferred to Figs. 75–7. Averages
for the broad Domesday divisions of a few counties have also been
shown – Yorkshire has been divided into its three ridings, Lincolnshire
with its three 'parts', and in Cambridgeshire 'the two hundreds of Ely'
(i.e. the Fenland) have been separated from the rest of the county. The
counties along the Welsh border present certain problems in view of the
unsatisfactory nature of much of the evidence for the Welsh districts,
especially for North Wales and for the lands beyond the Wye. It so
happens that the figures per square mile, per man and per team are the
same (to the nearest shilling) whether one includes or excludes places now
in Wales for Cheshire, Shropshire and Herefordshire. The figures for
Gloucestershire are 50s per square mile (including Wales) as compared

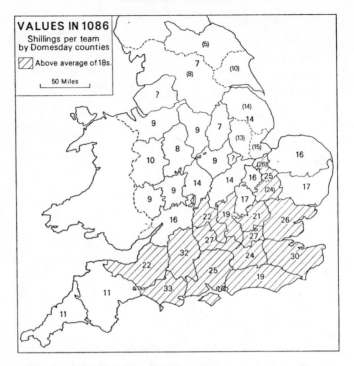

Fig. 77. The distribution of annual values per team in 1086
(by Domesday counties).

with 51*s* (excluding Wales); the corresponding figures per man are 10*s* as compared with 8*s*; and the figures per team are the same – 16*s*.

The basic map (Fig. 75) shows the distribution of shillings per square mile. In a very general way this agrees with the detailed maps showing the distribution of population (Fig. 34) and ploughteams (Fig. 41), but there are some surprises. Norfolk comes below Suffolk and much below the heavily wooded Essex. Might this be explained by the fact that so much of western Norfolk consisted of marsh and heath before the hand of the improver touched them in the eighteenth century? This explanation could hold also for Lindsey with its large tracts of light soil. On Fig. 76, showing values per man, the relative position of Norfolk falls even lower as compared with Suffolk and Essex but the fenland portions of Cambridgeshire and Lincolnshire are relatively wealthy as compared with the upland around.

Of the three maps, Fig. 77 (shillings per team) may be the most instructive in that a high value per team presumably reflects the non-arable element in its valuations. The high place of Dorset and Wiltshire and of Kent is in agreement with the more detailed distributions of Fig. 74. The relatively high place of the 'two hundreds of Ely' also prompts reflections upon the non-arable activities within the Fenland, as does the high place of Essex with its coastal pastures. But to press any detailed interpretations of this map, as of the other two, would be to strain the credibility of the evidence. Both the table and the maps are given here for the interest of those future workers who might attempt to unravel the obscurities and perplexities of the Domesday record.

CHAPTER VIII

DEVASTATED LAND

As we have seen, the annual values given in Domesday entry after entry raise many problems (see pp. 208–31). However enigmatic they may be, the fact that they are normally recorded for more than one date presents the possibility of comparing the earlier with the later, and so of obtaining an idea of changes between 1066 and 1086. We may thus see the effects of the Norman Conquest upon the fortunes not only of individual places but of whole districts.

But it is a possibility that is fraught with difficulties. One of these is uncertainty about the arithmetical accuracy of some entries; thus when we read that the combined values of Bramshill and Swallowfield (Hants., 48) at three dates were 40s, 20s 5d, 25d, can we be sure that 25d was not a mistake for 25s, especially as the mill itself rendered 25d? What is more important is uncertainty about the implications of many entries. When we see such figures as £9, £8, £24 for Newbury (*Ulvritone*, 62b) in Berkshire, can we be sure that the greatly increased value for 1086 was not the result of an alteration in the composition of the manor? Such alterations may well account for the changes, or apparent changes, in the valuations of many manors.[1] Furthermore, as we shall see, the formulae themselves contain many ambiguities.

CHANGING VALUES

The variety of entries

The entries for many counties give the annual values of manors for three dates – *tunc, post* and *modo* – that is for 1066, for some subsequent date, and for 1086 (Fig. 71). There are variations. Sometimes, *tunc* is replaced by the specific *T.R.E.*; and sometimes the intermediate date is specified not as *post* but as *olim* (formerly) or as *quando recepit* (i.e. when the existing owner received the estate), or occasionally in some other way, e.g. at Ilminster (Som., *188*, 91) when Abbot Leofweard died. Thus it is that the intermediate dates do not all refer to exactly the same

[1] R. Welldon Finn, *The Norman Conquest and its effects on the economy: 1066–86* (London, 1971), 8–10.

year, but most of them would seem to lie between 1066 and 1070. The phrase *val' semper* sometimes occurs and, presumably, may be taken to imply an unchanged value at all three dates. But does another formula, *valuit et valet* also imply this or merely *tunc* and *modo* or even *post* and *modo?*

The entries for other counties give values for only two dates, for 1086 and for some earlier date, but it is not always clear whether the latter (*valuit* or *valebat*) implies *tunc* or *post* or even both. In contrast with the Exchequer version, that of the Exeter text (for the south-western circuit) almost invariably gives the earlier date as *quando recepit*. To what extent *valuit* implies an intermediate date in other counties with double valuations is not entirely clear. A common formula in the four counties of the midland circuit is *Valuit – Modo*, and it has been held that for Leicestershire (where, except for Leicester itself, *T.R.E.* never occurs) the first valuation refers not to 1066 but to an intermediate date.[1] This could conceivably also be true of many Northamptonshire double valuations, but for this county *T.R.E.* is explicitly mentioned in the entries for a number of royal estates (219–220). The occasional entries with three valuations for Oxfordshire and Warwickshire can only leave us to conjecture what is meant by *Valuit et Valet* and *Valuit – Modo* which are found in the greater number of entries for those counties. The formulae of the western circuit are very diverse. Here again, there is an intermingling of triple with double valuations, but the occasional occurrence of *T.R.E. – Modo* seems to indicate a 1066 date for the *Valuit* of their entries in general; it is possible that it may also refer to an intermediate date. Finally, the northern circuit with its repetitive *T.R.E. – Modo* leaves no room for doubt.

On those manors with triple valuations, the amounts sometimes increased or sometimes remained the same at all three dates. But a very frequent pattern was a decrease immediately after the Conquest, followed by recovery or partial recovery; thus the figures for Buckland (144), in Buckinghamshire, were £10, £3, £8. Some manors had more than recovered, e.g. Wooburn described on the same folio with amounts of £12, £5, £15; others had continued to fall as at Ashendon (147), another Buckinghamshire manor, with amounts of £5, £4, £3. Among other variants was Yalding (14), in Kent, with values of £30, £30, £20, and the *post-modo* fall was because the land had been despoiled of its stock

---

[1] F. M. Stenton in *V.C.H. Leicestershire*, I (1907), 282–4. See p. 242 below.

(*eo quod terra vastata est a pecunia*), but we are not told how or why. Manors with double valuations displayed a similar variety; the figures for 1086 were sometimes higher, sometimes lower and sometimes the same as for 1066.

The valuations of some manors fell so low that they yielded no income, and were said to be *wasta* or *wastata*. This was true, for example, of Bexhill (18) in Sussex, a county characterised by triple valuations: *Totum manerium T.R.E. valebat xx libras, et post wasta fuit. Modo xviii libras et x solidos*. Then again in the counties with double valuations there are many entries such as the following for five vills in Morley wapentake (Yorks., 318); *Wasta est. T.R.E. valuit xl solidos*. It so happens that there is a duplicate entry on the same folio which runs: *Archil tenebat T.R.E. et valebat xl solidos; modo est nil*. Clearly, the waste was not that of mountain, heath or marsh, but land that had gone out of cultivation mainly, it seems, as a result of deliberate devastation but also perhaps because of some local vicissitude that is lost to us.

That some vills were only partly waste we may conclude from two kinds of evidence. In the first place, there were those vills comprising two or more holdings of which at least one was waste. Thus of two at Chesthill in Shropshire, one was tilled (258b) and the other was waste (252). Or again, at Bushbury in Staffordshire, two out of three were tilled (247b, 250), while the third (250) was said to be completely waste (*vasta est omnino*). In the second place, some single holdings were themselves partly waste. Addlethorpe (Lincs., 360), for instance, was assessed at 1 carucate and 1 bovate, but 4 bovates of this were waste; as a berewick, no separate values were entered for the holding. The value of Bickerton (Ches., 264b) had dropped from 18*s* in 1066 to 11*s* in 1086; two villeins ploughed with one team on its 4 ploughlands, and we are told that it was for the most part waste (*Wasta fuit et est ex maxima parte*). There were also 4 ploughlands at Bratton (Salop., 257b) which had been worth 24*s* in 1066, but its 5 bordars were said to have nothing (*nil habent*), and it was almost entirely waste (*pene wasta est*). These and some such similar phrases are encountered in many other entries – e.g. *cetera wasta* at Bridlington (Yorks., 299b), *Haec terra ex multa parte est wasta* at Cooksey (Worcs., 177b), and *reliqua est wasta* at Manfield (Yorks., 309).

Even when a holding was 'waste' it was not necessarily devoid of some value, and we are sometimes told that this was in spite of, or 'notwithstanding', its condition. Here is a selection of characteristic entries:

Charlton (N'hants., 223b): *Vasta est. Tamen valet et valuit v s.*

Fleckney (Leics., 234b): *Vasta est et tamen valet xii d.*

Great Braham (Yorks., 328b): *Wasta est sed xvi d reddit.*

Halton (Yorks., 315): *Wasta est. T.R.E. valuit xx s. Modo ii s reddit.*

Loynton (Staffs., 249b): *Vasta est. Valet vi s.*

Newthorpe (Notts., 287b): *Wasta est. T.R.E. valuit v s; modo ii s.*

Thulston (Derby., 275b): *Wasta est sed tamen valet iii s.*

Walford near Ross (Heref., 182): *Villani reddunt x s pro wasta terra.*

What could account for these renders from devastated land? Is a clue provided in the entry for a tiny subsidiary holding with one bordar at Mullacott in Devonshire? The Exchequer text (117) makes no mention of waste, but the Exeter version (469) adds *terra iacet vastata ad pasturam.* This seems to imply that the devastated land was used for grazing. Or is another possibility indicated by two entries for Butley in Cheshire? The value of one holding (267b) had fallen from 30s in 1066 to 2s in 1086, and we are told *Wasta est praeter vii acras seminatas*; something similar is said for the other holding (264b). Who could have sown these acres, because no men are entered for either holding? Is any light thrown upon the question by such entries as that for Elsthorpe and Bulby (Lincs., 368)? Here were two bovates empty yet tilled (*vacuae sunt sed tamen coluntur*); we can only assume by men from elsewhere, and it so happens that there was another holding at Elsthorpe (358) with men and teams. The entry for the unidentified *Curdeslege* (187b), in Herefordshire, is unusual; its two ploughlands had been waste except for 3 acres lately tilled there (*Wasta fuit et est praeter iii acras terrae nuper ibi aratas*), but we are not told by whom or with what oxen. There were certainly a number of other vills with land specifically said to have been tilled by teams from elsewhere (see pp. 122–3). With these may perhaps be included Strefford (255) in Shropshire. It had yielded 30s in 1066; after this it was waste but by 1086 it was yielding 20s although it had no population – *Non sunt homines ibi et tamen Rainaldus habet xx s.*

There were yet other holdings with waste but with resources such as wood or meadow or pasture; some had small values entered for them, but whether such amounts resulted from these other resources or from some use of the devastated arable, we cannot say. Here are some examples; and only for Cogshall is the source of the value made explicit:

Chellaston (Derby., 275): *Terra dimidiae carucae. Wasta est. Ibi iii acrae prati. T.R.E. valuit xii s; modo iii s.*

Cogshall (Ches., 267): *Terra est i carucae. De pastura exeunt iii s. Wasta est terra.*

Hartington (Derby, 274): *Terra ii carucis. Wasta est. Ibi xvi acrae prati. Silva minuta iii quarentenis longa et lata. T.R.E. valuit xl s.*

Trowell (Notts., 292b): *Terra iiii bobus. Wasta est. Alden habet. Ibi ii acrae prati. T.R.E. x s valuit; modo v s et iiii d.*

Akin to such entries is that for Cradwell (Yorks., 322) which was uninhabited in 1086 (*Willelmus habet nunc sed non inhabitatur*). It had been worth 20s and was still worth 5s 4d in 1086. Could this latter sum have come from its *silva pastilis*, one league by one? These obscurities and variations are perhaps not surprising when we remember the compressed nature of the Domesday text, and also all the possible local circumstances of which we have no record. All the waste holdings with small annual values or some resources, or both, have been regarded not as 'partly waste' but as entirely waste in the sense that all their arable seems to have been devastated and that they had no recorded population.

The causes of devastation

Devastated land had formed a conspicuous element in the geography of England during the period of Anglo-Danish warfare, and it did not cease to be so after 1042 when a member of the royal house of Wessex, Edward the Confessor, once more ruled over England. During his reign, the complicated politics of the great earldoms resulted in much conflict. Earl Godwine and his sons, banished overseas, returned in 1052 to raid along the south coast. Raids from Ireland, from Wales and from Norway also resulted in the devastation of various parts of the realm. The sources are obscure, and we can only repeat what the Anglo-Saxon chronicler wrote under the year 1058: 'it is tedious to relate how it all happened'. An echo of some of the complications comes in the Hampshire folios which tell us that Edward the Confessor had reduced the geld liability of Fareham (40b) from 30 hides to 20 'on account of the Vikings, because it is by the sea' (*causa Wichingarum quia super mare*).

From the north of the realm, Earl Morcar of Northumbria marched south in 1065 to Northamptonshire and he was joined by Earl Edwin of Mercia with a Mercian and Welsh host. They did much damage around Northampton, wrote the Anglo-Saxon chronicler:

They slew men and burned houses and grain, and took all the cattle which they might come at, that was many thousand; and many hundred men they

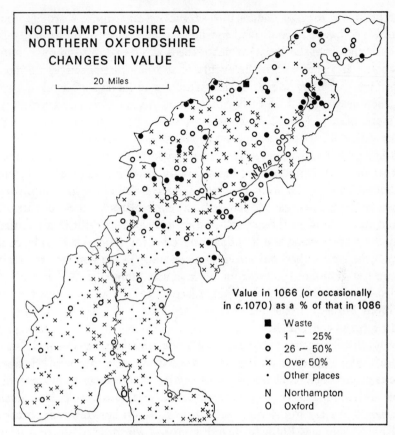

NORTHAMPTONSHIRE AND
NORTHERN OXFORDSHIRE
CHANGES IN VALUE

20 Miles

Value in 1066 (or occasionally
in c.1070) as a % of that in 1086

■   Waste
●   1 — 25%
○   26 — 50%
×   Over 50%
·   Other places

N   Northampton
O   Oxford

Fig. 78. Northamptonshire and northern Oxfordshire:
Changes in value, 1066–86.

took and led north with them; so that the shire and the other shires around
were for many years the worse.

The Domesday valuations bear witness to this devastation, and, in
particular, to his advance up the valley of the Nene. The earlier valuations
for the county were very low as compared with those of 1086, and it
would seem that the great increases over 20 years or so were due not so
much to a basic improvement in prosperity as to recovery after the events
of 1065.[1] The values of many holdings had at least doubled by 1086,
and the increase was sometimes as much as four-fold and more. Fig. 78

[1] J. H. Round in *V.C.H. Northamptonshire*, I (1902), 261–3.

tells its own story of the results of the descent upon Northampton. The tale of havoc is confirmed by the so-called Northamptonshire Geld Roll (dating from the 1070s) which records about one third of the county as waste.[1] In order to put the events of 1065 into perspective, we must remember that there was to be devastation again. The Pipe Roll of 1156 returned nearly one third of Northamptonshire as waste, and even a half or more of some counties, as a result of civil war in Stephen's reign (1137–54), but by 1162 recovery was almost complete.[2]

Some of the valuations in north Oxfordshire show a similar contrast to that in Northamptonshire, being low in 1066 and high in 1086; but the differences are not so marked nor so extensive. These have also been attributed to the ravages of the northern rebels of 1065, some of whom it is said came south to the city of Oxford to negotiate.[3] But it seems that only the leaders came south and, in any case, the Domesday evidence is not conclusive.[4] Other indications of devastation in the years immediately before the Conquest come from the counties along the Welsh border, raided by the Welsh and their kings (see p. 321). The evidence for the northern borders of the realm is not so clear, but there are echoes of raiding Scots and Danes.[5]

With the Conquest, the evidence of devastation becomes clearer. There is, for example, the marginal note in the Exeter text (*323*) which tells of nine manors which had been laid waste by Irish raiders some time between 1066 and 1086: *hae ix predictae mansiones sunt vastatae per Irlandinos homines*. They lay in the extreme south of Devon between the estuaries of Kingsbridge and Bigbury Bay (Fig. 79). Two manors had recovered to their former values, but the other seven had far from recovered, and three of these were worth only a quarter of their values when Judhell of

---

[1] J. H. Round (1) *Feudal England* (London, 1895), 147–56; (2) *V.C.H. Northamptonshire*, I, 258–60. See also D. G. Douglas and G. W. Greenaway (eds.), *English historical documents, 1042–1189* (London, 1953), 483–6.

[2] H. W. C. Davis, 'The anarchy of Stephen's reign', *Eng. Hist. Rev.*, XVIII (1903), 630–41; H. C. Darby (ed.), *An historical geography of England before A.D. 1800* (Cambridge, 1936), 172–3.

[3] F. H. Baring, 'Oxfordshire traces of the northern insurgents of 1065', *Eng. Hist. Rev.*, XIII (1898), 295–7; G. H. Fowler, 'The devastation of Bedfordshire and the neighbouring counties in 1065 and 1066', *Archaeologia*, LXXII (1922), 41–50.

[4] R. Welldon Finn (1971), 117–18. See also F. M. Stenton, *Anglo-Saxon England* (Oxford, 1943), 571.

[5] L. F. Salzmann in *V.C.H. Yorkshire*, III (1913), 395; K. C. Bayley in *V.C.H. Durham*, II (1907), 134–5.

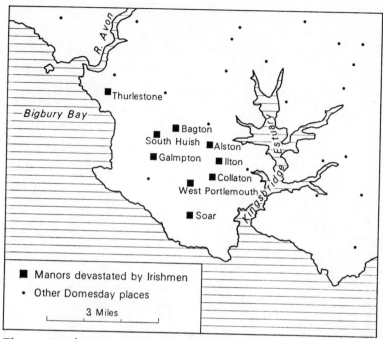

Fig. 79. South Devonshire: Manors devastated by Irishmen after 1066 (*321b–323*, 109).

	Valuit	*Valet*
Bagton	15s	15s
South Huish	25s	25s
Galmpton in South Huish	40s	30s*
Thurlestone	£4	£3
Alston	20s	10s
Soar	40s	20s
Collaton in Malborough	20s	5s
West Portlemouth	40s	10s
Ilton	20s	5s

*The Exchequer text reads 50s

Totnes had received them, as the table above shows. Raiding may also account for the fact that to the west, in the Lizard Peninsula, the Exeter version says that Trembraze (*226*) was waste and Skewes (*225b*) altogether waste (*penitus vastata*); furthermore, of the 23 manors in the peninsula 12 had no teams and 6 had no inhabitants in 1086 (Fig. 80).

On the other side of the realm, for Wrangle (*367b*), in Lincolnshire, there is an unusual reference to wasting due to the action of the sea:

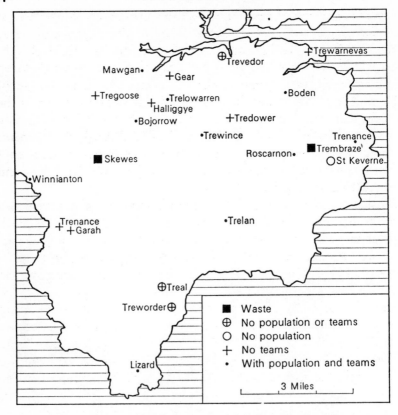

Fig. 80. Devastation in the Lizard Peninsula after 1066.

Wastum est propter fluxum maris. The waste in some of the other coastal villages of Lincolnshire may also have been due to the sea, that is unless it was the result of Danish raids. Inland in Lincolnshire, we can only assume that the waste found in occasional villages reflected the hazards of farming or was due to some other local cause. At the sokeland of Little Grimsby (340b) belonging to Covenham, there had been recovery on land for 3 oxen; it had formerly been waste but was cultivated by 1086 (*Wasta fuit, modo colitur*). Such specific entries are rare. Generally speaking, we are left to assume recovery from a rise in value. Another unusually specific entry is that for Yalding (14) in Kent; this attributes a fall in value from £30 to £20 to the destruction of livestock (*eo quod terra vastata est a pecunia*), but from what cause we are not told.

Another cause of waste, or of land withdrawn from cultivation, was enclosure in the king's forest. This was true of land for 2 ploughteams at Chasepool (249b) in the Staffordshire forest of Kinver; it was also true of the lost *Haswic* (247b), not far away; here was land for 8 plough-teams which was waste because it had been placed in the king's forest (*Modo est wasta propter forestam regis*). The entry for Ellington (204b) in Huntingdonshire implies the same when it says that one out of the ten hides there was *wasta per silvam regis*. Sometimes, land that already lay waste was included in the forest as at *Aldredelie, Done* and *Kenardeslie* (263b) in what was later to be called Delamere Forest in Cheshire.[1] Similar references are encountered for *Brocote* (181) and for Didley and *Stane* (181b) in Herefordshire.

Outside the royal forests, devastated vills and their woods were also used for hunting. Longdendale (273) with its twelve vills in north Derbyshire was said to be completely waste (*Wasta est tota*) and its wood was described as suitable for hunting, not pannage (*Silva est ibi non pastilis, apta venationi*). Along the Welsh border, thirteen wasted vills near Montgomery (254) provided opportunities for hunting (*ad venandum*). Something similar was true of the eleven wasted vills along the north-west border of Herefordshire (186b) where Osbern fitz Richard hunted on devastated land overgrown with wood (*In his wastis terris excreverunt silvae in quibus isdem Osbernus venationem exercet*). Not far to the south, the wasted land at Harewood in Clifford (187) had also become overgrown with wood (*Haec terra in silvam est totam redacta*); we are told nothing of hunting here, but it may well have taken place. Another indication of hunting on devastated land is the presence of 'hays' on waste holdings, sometimes with wood, sometimes without, as at Horton (257b) and Minton (258) in Shropshire, and at *Mateurdin* (187b) and Titley (186b) in Herefordshire (Fig. 69).

Of all the causes of devastation and waste, easily the most important was the passage of armies. Yet we are explicitly told so only on one occasion in Domesday Book. The entry for Harbury (239), in Warwick-shire, records land for one team which was waste because of the army of the king (*Vasta est per exercitum regis*). Yet the indirect evidence meets our eyes on page after page, not only in the waste holdings recorded for 1086 and earlier dates, but also in frequent falls in value on many manors – between *tunc* and *post* or between *post* and *modo*. Invasion, conquest and rebellion could not fail to bring ruin to many localities, sometimes

[1] *D.G.N.E.*, 357–8.

for only a few years, sometimes for decades. As we have seen, the facts are not always easy to interpret because of the uncertainty of some of the figures and the ambiguities of some of the formulae. Moreover, the evidence of the chronicles for the movement of armies is fragmentary and not without its difficulties. It is possible to interpret the distribution of falls in value in different ways, and sometimes a fall may be the net result of campaign and recovery at different times.[1] Consider the example of Leicestershire. Its low early values (unlike those of Northamptonshire) probably refer not to 1065 but to 'some time of disorder that followed the Conquest'.[2] This time has been suggested as that of the Conqueror's march from Warwick to Nottingham in 1068.[3] But can we be sure that the low values were not in part the result of the Northumbrian descent upon Northamptonshire in 1065, especially in view of the reference in the Anglo-Saxon Chronicle to the shires around being waste for many years?

Furthermore, intermingled with the consequences of moving armies were the hazards of bad weather and poor harvests and also a variety of local vicissitudes about which we can never know. Amidst many doubts about details, the fact of destruction is clear enough, and there are three main groups of evidence characteristic of different parts of the realm. The south-eastern counties saw the first campaigns of the Conquest in 1066. The north midlands and Yorkshire saw the ferocious suppression of rebellion in 1069–70. And, in the third place, the counties along the Welsh border saw the continuation of that long-standing conflict between the Welsh and the lowlanders to the east. Circumstances in these three areas must now be considered.

DEVASTATION IN THE SOUTH-EAST

A striking feature of the valuations of manors in the south-eastern counties is that they frequently show a substantial reduction between *tunc* and *post*. Thus the figures for Ashburnham (18) in Sussex are £6, 20s, £9, and those for Bexhill (18) nearby are £20, *wasta*, £18 10s. When two or more entries relate to one place, they sometimes differ, one entry showing a decrease, and the other an increase. In constructing Figs. 81 and 82,

---

[1] R. Welldon Finn (1971), 94, 100, 117, 228, 237.
[2] F. W. Maitland, *Domesday Book and beyond* (Cambridge, 1897), 469.
[3] F. M. Stenton (1907), 282–4.

the values at each date for one place have been added together, with the result that similar totals for all three dates occasionally conceal changes. F. H. Baring attributed the very frequent post-Conquest reductions to the passage of Duke William's forces. 'It is obvious that a large army living, as his did, on the country it passes through must move on a wide front and leave a broad strip of ravaged country behind.' Consequently he believed that the great reductions marked 'the Conqueror's footprints', or rather those of his soldiers.[1]

The Norman forces landed in the bay of Pevensey, without opposition, at nine o'clock on the morning of Thursday, 28 September. After some days they transferred their base to Hastings, and what the Berkshire folios, in an incidental reference (60b), call *bellum de Hastinges* took place on 14 October at a place where Battle Abbey was afterwards founded to commemorate the victory. Five days later, William set out by way of Romney to Dover where he stayed for eight days before proceeding via Canterbury towards London. Places in the neighbourhood of Hastings had suffered considerable reductions in value, and some had been completely wasted. The values of places in eastern Kent, especially to the north of Dover, had likewise been greatly reduced, and there was also a series of depreciated manors in northern Kent and especially in north-eastern Surrey. William did not cross the Thames into London but, after some of his forces had burnt Southwark, he began a great encircling movement westward into northern Hampshire and Berkshire, and he reached the Thames at Wallingford towards the end of November. Some of the depreciated manors in Hampshire and west Sussex may have been the result of reinforcements moving inland from Fareham and Chichester.

From Wallingford, William turned north-eastwards to complete the encirclement of London and to prevent any possible help from the Midlands. His route immediately after Wallingford cannot be traced because the Oxfordshire folios do not give intermediate values; but there is abundant evidence of depreciated manors in Buckinghamshire and Hertfordshire. Baring thought that it was near Little Berkhamsted, among the depreciated manors of eastern Hertfordshire, that William received the submission of the Anglo-Saxon leaders who had come out

---

[1] F. H. Baring, 'The Conqueror's footprints in Domesday', *Eng. Hist. Rev.*, XIII (1898), 17–25. Reprinted with 'some additions and alterations' in *Domesday Tables* (London, 1909), 207–16.

Fig. 81. South-eastern counties: *Tunc et post* values in the west.

For the key, see Fig. 82. The category of 'other places' includes those for which information is lacking as well as those with constant or increased values.

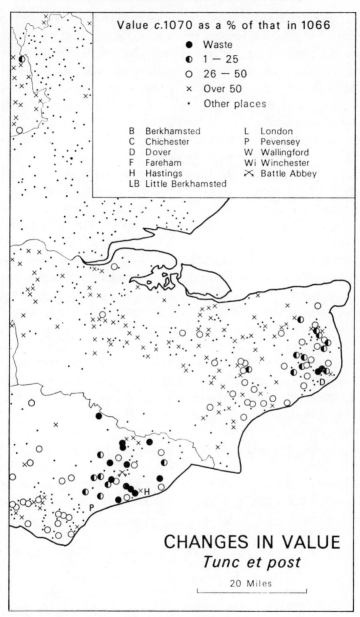

Value *c.*1070 as a % of that in 1066

● Waste
◐ 1 — 25
○ 26 — 50
× Over 50
· Other places

B Berkhamsted L London
C Chichester P Pevensey
D Dover W Wallingford
F Fareham Wi Winchester
H Hastings ✕ Battle Abbey
LB Little Berkhamsted

CHANGES IN VALUE
Tunc et post

20 Miles

Fig. 82. South-eastern counties: *Tunc et post* values in the east.

from London to surrender the city. In support of this view there is the statement of William of Poitiers (who wrote before 1071) that the submission was made at a point where the army had just come in sight of London.[1] From a hill of about 350 ft above sea-level, to the south-east of Little Berkhamsted, one could have seen the smoke of London some 15 miles away. A number of other writers have agreed with Baring that the place of surrender was Little Berkhamsted.[2] William then moved into London to be consecrated king on Christmas Day in Edward the Confessor's new church of Westminster Abbey.

We can only speculate how far north the campaign of 1066 extended, and whether the Normans went into northern Buckinghamshire and even into Bedfordshire and Cambridgeshire before coming south into eastern Hertfordshire. Depreciated manors were certainly to be found here, and some scholars have argued for this wide extension of the campaign.[3] But it is possible that the depreciations in the values of some of these manors were due to other movements of troops unknown to us, e.g. those associated with Hereward's revolt in the Isle of Ely in 1070–1.

The Anglo-Saxon Chronicle, under the year 1066, briefly summarises these events by saying that William 'harried all that part which he overran, until he came to *Beorh-hamstede*'. Writers before and after Baring have thought that this was not Little Berkhamsted but Great Berkhamsted (called simply Berkhamsted today) in the extreme west of Hertfordshire, and that William's forces came there more or less direct from Wallingford.[4] Great Berkhamsted is some 27 miles from London Bridge, and it does not so conveniently fit either the statement of William of Poitiers or the postulated wasting of northern Buckinghamshire, Bedfordshire, Cambridgeshire and eastern Hertfordshire. But it could be said that *Beorh-hamstede* obviously refers to the greater rather than the smaller place, and that William of Poitiers' words should not be taken in too literal a sense.

---

[1] William of Poitiers, *Gesta Willelmi Ducis*, ed. J. A. Giles (London, 1845), 141.

[2] E.g. C. H. Lemmon in D. Whitelock *et al.*, *The Norman Conquest* (London, 1966), 122; D. Butler, *1066: The story of a year* (London, 1966), 278.

[3] E.g. C. H. Lemmon, 121; D. Butler, 276–7.

[4] E.g. E. A. Freeman, *History of the Norman Conquest of England*, III (Oxford, 1869), 544–8; G. J. Turner, 'William the Conqueror's march to London in 1066', *Eng. Hist. Rev.*, XXVII (1912), 209–25; W. J. Corbett in *The Cambridge medieval history*, V (1926), 501–2.

Baring's reconstruction of the route followed by the Norman forces involved, as he said, 'an element of conjecture'. The evidence certainly does not lend itself to interpretation in any rigid way. There was not one army but several forces, and there must also have been foraging bands. Then again, it is unlikely that the forces always laid waste wherever they went. Moreover, it seems as if the English themselves may have been responsible for a certain amount of destruction.[1] We know, too, from an entry under 1067 in the Anglo-Saxon Chronicle, that some devastation by the Normans took place after William had become king. Furthermore, the dates at which the tenants of 1086 had received their lands must have varied. And, as Baring himself wrote in his account of Berkshire, a subjective element may often have entered into the judgement of juries assessing values.[2] Not least, we must remember that many vicissitudes unknown to us may have caused the depreciation of this or that manor. A number of manors seem to have survived the troubles of 1066 only to decline in value later; such were Warfield (57), in Berkshire, with valuations of £12, £12, £6, and Yalding (14), in Kent, where the figures were £30, £30, £20. But when all these uncertainties are borne in mind, and while we might hesitate to mark on a map the exact itineraries of William's forces, the widespread damage that is revealed in the post-Conquest valuations must, in general, be attributed to the campaign and the turbulence by which William won his kingdom.

By 1086, however, recovery was well on the way. It is true that some manors still remained in their depleted condition; the valuations of Solton (11) in Kent, for example, were £15, 30s, 30s. But, generally speaking, the devastated manors had recovered either in part or wholly; thus the valuations of Farnham (31), in Surrey, were £55, £30, £47; and those of Gatton (31b), also in Surrey, were £6, £3, £6. Other manors had increased beyond their 1066 valuation; such was Basing (45), in Hampshire, with figures of £12, £8, £16. However severely some localities in the south suffered in 1066, agricultural production in general was not impaired for long. The countryside was soon yielding as much as ever, and in places far more than ever, under its new masters.

[1] G. J. Turner, 211.　　　　[2] F. H. Baring (1909), 48.

THE HARRYING OF THE NORTH

Six months after his landing, by the end of March 1067, the organisation of his new kingdom had proceeded far enough to allow William to visit Normandy where he stayed until St Nicholas's Day, i.e. December 6th. During his absence, a rising in Kent had been suppressed, though many other parts of England were on the verge of rebellion and there was always the threat of a Danish landing. Upon his return, William marched to Devon and put down an outbreak at Exeter; the Anglo-Saxon Chronicle tells us how 'he let his men plunder all the country through which they passed'. He then proceeded to Winchester for Easter, and went on to Westminster where the queen, who had now come over from Normandy, was consecrated on Whit Sunday 1068. In spite of a year and a half or so of Norman rule, the kingdom was far from being under complete control, and its remoter parts – in the Midlands and the North – had not yet felt the power of the new king's arm. The next two years were to be spent in incorporating these outer regions into the realm, and it is to this phase of William's reign that the devastation of the north belongs.

In order to deal with strong anti-Norman feeling in Yorkshire, William marched north in the latter half of 1068. After building – founding would be a better word – castles at Warwick and then at Nottingham, he reached York and raised the castle-mound on which Clifford's Tower now stands. His presence, for the moment, quelled resistance without a battle, and he was able to turn southward again, establishing castles at Lincoln, Huntingdon and Cambridge.

Early in the following year, renewed rebellion in the north brought William once more to York. After relieving the garrison, he began the building of a second castle on the opposite bank of the Ouse, on the site where the Baile Hill now stands. He then returned south once more to Winchester for the Easter of 1069.

Later in the year, the standard of revolt was again raised in the north, and the rebels were aided by the arrival of a Danish fleet in the Humber. York was attacked and occupied, and William once more went north. As he drew near, the Danes abandoned the city, fell back upon the Humber, and established themselves in the Isle of Axholme, to which he then directed his march. In the meantime, simmering discontent in Mercia had broken out into open revolt which was aided by the Welsh.

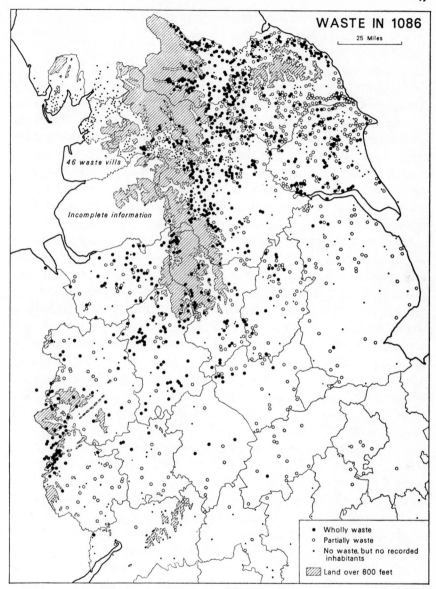

Fig. 83. The distribution of waste in 1086.

Leaving a force to watch the Danes in the neighbourhood of the Humber, William set out for Stafford, where he seems to have won an easy victory over the Mercian insurgents (see p. 328).

He then began his return to the neighbourhood of the Humber. At Nottingham he learned that the Danes were preparing to reoccupy York, so he struck directly north, but was held up for three weeks at the crossing of the Aire near the modern town of Pontefract, where the bridge was broken, the river in flood and the northern bank held against him. At last he drew near to York itself and seems to have devastated the land to the north and west, before entering the city where he spent the Christmas of 1069. Early in the New Year he continued operations right up to the Tees, and received the submission of the northern rebels.

Mercian resistance had survived the defeat at Stafford, and rebel forces were still active in the Midlands. Leaving York in safe hands, William then marched across the Pennines to the Cheshire plain. The campaign was difficult, and the earliest accounts of it tell of wet weather and of a shortage of provisions. After a threat of mutiny, the army reached Cheshire where the last flickering fires of rebellion were put out. Founding a castle at Chester, William moved to Stafford to found another, and so proceeded southward to Salisbury. By the Easter of 1070, the campaign was over. The last resistance of the Anglo-Saxons was yet to come in the winter of 1070–1 with a rallying on the Isle of Ely under Hereward; but from the spring of 1070, the Midlands and the North could be counted effective parts of the realm.

The devastation wrought by the campaigns of 1069–70 was no ordinary reprisal. William deliberately left the countryside in a condition in which it could give him no trouble again. The entry under 1069 in the Anglo-Saxon Chronicle is brief, and merely says that the king 'laid waste all the shire', but other chronicles of Norman times tell of the ferocity with which the harrying had been carried out. Yorkshire suffered most, but we are told, in one early account, that the harrying extended over Cheshire, Derbyshire, Shropshire and Staffordshire; nor did Nottingham-shire escape.[1] The chronicler of an abbey as far away as that of Evesham in Worcestershire described how fugitives from William's devastation – old men and young men, women and children – crowded into the town, and how many died of their hunger and misery and were buried by the

[1] F. M. Stenton (1943), 596–7.

prior.[1] To the harrying by the king's armies must be added the damage done by the Scots and the Danes in the north – in the Cleveland district and elsewhere – and by the Welsh in the west.

The general statements of the chroniclers are borne out in a vivid manner by the evidence of Domesday Book. Seventeen years or so had not sufficed to obliterate the result of William's work, and entry after entry, on folio after folio, reads *Wasta est*. Some vills were wholly waste, without teams or population but occasionally of some small value and with amounts of wood or meadow. Other vills were only partly waste. Over one half of the vills of the North Riding, and over one third of those of both the East and the West Ridings, were wholly or partly waste, and about one fifth of those of Cheshire, Derbyshire and Nottinghamshire.

It may well be, however, that the total of waste entries does not give a complete picture of the empty countryside of 1086. A large number of vills are not specifically described as waste, yet they have no population (and almost invariably no teams) entered for them. It is conceivable, however, that occasionally the absence of any reference to population was accidental, or was the result of the summarised nature of many entries. It may be difficult to believe, for example, that almost the whole of what is now north Lancashire was uninhabited but that is what the account of the area around Preston (301b) implies when it says that 16 vills were inhabited by a few people (*a paucis incoluntur*) and that the remaining 46 were waste. Fig. 83 shows both waste or partly waste vills and uninhabited vills not said to be 'waste'; but even this may not give a complete picture of the devastation because as well as wasted and uninhabited holdings there were many others with greatly reduced values.[2] One at Kearby (322) in the West Riding had dropped from 20*s* in 1066 to 16*d* in 1086, and one at Snelston (275) in Derbyshire from £8 to £2. The occasional increases in value may have been due to such facts as the transference of men and stock from poorer settlements or to recovery or even to clerical error.

It has been suggested that the distribution of these waste vills does not directly reflect the movement of William's armies.[3] According to this

---

[1] W. D. Macray, *Chronicon Abbatiae de Evesham* (Rolls Series, London, 1863), 90–1. See R. R. Darlington, 'Aethelwig, Abbot of Evesham', *Eng. Hist. Rev.*, XLVIII (1933), 177.
[2] R. Welldon Finn (1971), 177–209 *passim*.
[3] T. A. M. Bishop, 'The Norman settlement of Yorkshire' in R. W. Hunt *et al.* (eds.), *Studies in mediaeval history presented to Frederick Maurice Powicke* (Oxford, 1948), 1–14.

view, the harrying took place mainly in the lowland districts, and then, between 1070 and 1086, the peasantry of the upland vills migrated to the empty vills on the more fertile plain, such migration being organised by individual landholders. Many of the waste places of 1086 were, according to this view, the result not of devastation but of abandonment. It has also been suggested that some Yorkshire tenants-in-chief may have transferred populations from their holdings in other counties to their empty vills in Yorkshire.[1]

That some migration did take place between non-wasted and wasted vills is very possible, but it is difficult to prove conclusively.[2] If only the folios for Yorkshire (and also those for Derbyshire and Nottingham-shire) gave the values of holdings at the time when their Norman holders received them, we should then know what was the distribution of waste *c.* 1070 as opposed to that in 1086, and so could argue much more clearly about these matters. But we have this information for only one northern county; the Cheshire folios alone give valuations for *tunc*, *post* and *modo*. From this information, we see that the devastation of Cheshire in 1070 was considerable, and that waste vills were then abundant throughout the county, in both lowland and upland alike (Fig. 85). Whatever be the precise vicissitudes that lay behind the entries of the other northern counties, the fact of large-scale desolation is clear enough. Fig. 83 leaves us in no doubt about the importance of devastation as an element in the economic geography of northern England in the eleventh century.

RAIDING ON THE WELSH BORDER

The counties along the Welsh border traditionally formed a land of conflict. The vicissitudes of the frontier can be seen from the fortunes of the three manors of Chirbury, Maesbury and Whittington in the west of Shropshire (253b). They had rendered half a night's feorm 'in the time of Ethelred, the father of King Edward', i.e. about the year 1000; but in 1066 they were lying waste, only to be restocked by 1086. There is specific mention of one raid in the Herefordshire entry (181) which tells how King Grifin and Blein had devastated the district of Archenfield in the time of King Edward. This presumably refers to the events of 1055

---

[1] T. Beddoe and T. H. Rowe, 'The ethnology of West Yorkshire', *Yorks. Archaeol. Jour.*, XIX (Leeds, 1907), 58–9. See also T. A. M. Bishop, 9.

[2] *D.G.N.E.*, 450–4.

when Gruffydd ap Llewellyn, king of Gwynedd and Powys had plundered Hereford and the countryside around; Blein, or Bleddyn, was Gruffydd's immediate successor. We also hear in a Gloucestershire entry (162) of four vills beyond the Wye wasted by King Caraduech, and this probably refers to the raid in 1065 upon Portskewett on the shores of the Severn estuary by King Caradoc ap Gruffydd of Gwynllwg. Non-Domesday sources give records of other raids.[1]

After the Conquest, amid the complicated politics of the time, Welsh princes were sometimes in league with the English against the Conqueror. In 1069 Bleddyn and Rhiwallon joined the Mercians under Edric 'the Wild', and were able to burn Shrewsbury before William arrived from the north to defeat the rebels at Stafford. In view of this conflict with all its complications, it is not surprising that the folios for the border counties contain many references to devastated land. Moreover, many entries give information not only for 1086 but also for some earlier year or years.

There is no doubt about the date implied by the phrase *wasta est*; it can only refer to 1086. In the same way, the phrase *T.R.E. wasta fuit* refers to 1066. The phrases *wastam invenit* or *post fuit wasta* are also explicit in that they imply an intermediate date when a Norman holder acquired an estate, in, say, 1070 or so. References to such intermediate dates are frequent for Cheshire and Shropshire, but they occur only three or four times in the Herefordshire folios – for the see of Hereford (181b), Caerleon (185b), Pembridge (186) and possibly Thornbury (186). So much is clear, but what of the phrase *wasta fuit* without *T.R.E.*? Does it refer to 1066 or 1070 or both?

The examples set out on p. 258 illustrate the problem. The entry for Weston Rhyn gives details for three dates, and the phrase *wasta fuit* clearly refers to 1066; so does that for Tetton. The entry for Spoonley also gives details for three dates, but its reference to *wasta fuit* seems to imply 1070 because another valuation is assigned to *T.R.E.* But at which of the two dates was there waste at Audley? And does *wasta fuit* in the entries for Eyton and Sawbury refer to two dates (1066 and 1070), or to one; and if only to one, which one? In constructing Figs. 84–5, these *wasta fuit* entries have been shown in a separate category. That the phrase may have referred to both dates seems to be suggested by the entry for

---

[1] J. E. Lloyd, 'Wales and the coming of the Normans (1039–1093)', *Trans. of the Honourable Society of Cymmrodorion*, 1898–99 (1900), 134–7. See also R. Welldon Finn (1971), 140–1, 172n.

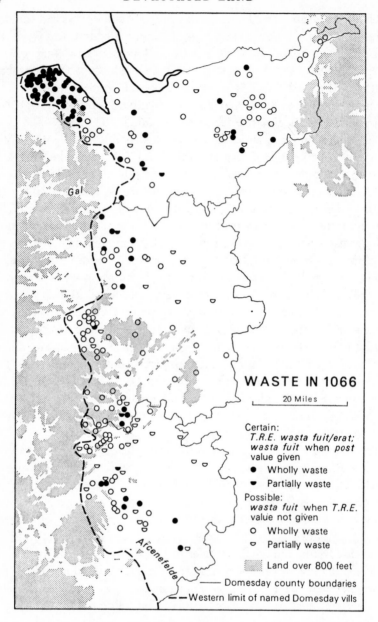

Fig. 84. The Welsh border: Distribution of waste in 1066.

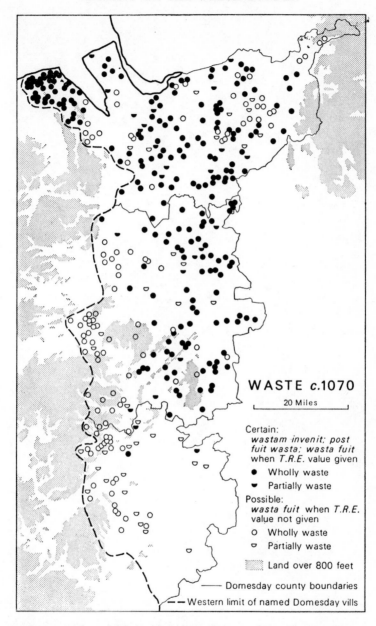

WASTE c.1070

20 Miles

Certain:
*wastam invenit; post
fuit wasta; wasta fuit*
when *T.R.E.* value given
● Wholly waste
◥ Partially waste

Possible:
wasta fuit when *T.R.E.*
value not given
○ Wholly waste
▽ Partially waste

▒ Land over 800 feet
— Domesday county boundaries
— — Western limit of named Domesday vills

Fig. 85. The Welsh border: Distribution of waste *circa* 1070.

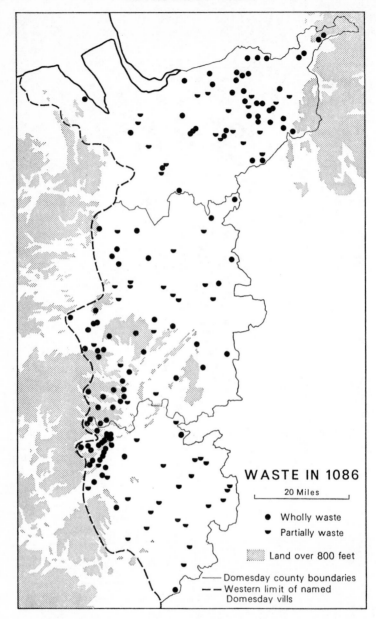

WASTE IN 1086

20 Miles

● Wholly waste
▼ Partially waste

Land over 800 feet

——— Domesday county boundaries
— — Western limit of named
Domesday vills

Fig. 86. The Welsh border: Distribution of waste in 1086.

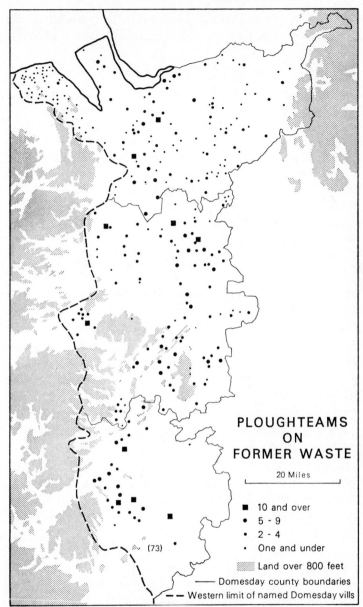

Fig. 87. The Welsh border: Ploughteams in 1086 on former waste.
The number (73) refers to the combined total of the teams of the 'king's men' of
Archenfield, and their location is uncertain.

Goostrey with its 'always was and is waste'; for all such entries, the phrase *valuit semper* has been plotted as certainly waste at both dates.

Selected waste entries for places on the Welsh border

Weston Rhyn (Salop., 254b): *Wasta fuit et wastam invenit. Valet modo x s.*
Tetton (Ches., 267): *T.R.E. et post wasta fuit. Modo valet x s.*
Spoonley (Salop., 259): *Wasta fuit et est. T.R.E. valebat xx s.*
Audley (Salop., 256): *Valuit vi s. Modo ii s. Wasta fuit.*
Eyton in Baschurch (Salop., 256): *Wasta fuit. Modo valet v s.*
Sawbury (Heref., 185): *Wasta fuit et est.*
Goostrey (Ches., 266b): *Wasta fuit semper et est.*
Marton (Ches., 266b): *Wasta fuit semper.*
Rostherne (Ches., 266): *Wasta fuit . . . T.R.E. valebat iiii s.*
Barnston (Ches., 266): *Valet x s. Wastam invenit.*
Huntington (Ches., 263): *T.R.E. fuit wasta. Modo valet xvi s.*
Oulton (Ches., 263b): *Wasta est.*

Other variants in phrasing also raise difficulties. The entry for Marton is similar to that for Goostrey, but makes no reference to 1086; that for Rostherne also makes no reference to 1086; both these holdings have been regarded as waste in 1086 because neither is credited with teams or population for that year. The entry for Barnston, on the other hand, says nothing about conditions in 1066, while that for Huntington says nothing about 1070. Can we assume that such holdings were waste at these dates? In constructing the maps we have not made this assumption, but have taken the text as it literally reads, i.e. regarded Barnston as waste only in 1070 and Huntington only in 1066. There are yet other phrases which invite speculation. The information for Oulton, for example, is confined to the phrase *wasta est*, and we are told nothing of its condition in 1070 or 1066; again we have plotted the information literally and not shown it as waste at those earlier dates, although it may well have been.

Fig. 84 shows the places that were waste and possibly waste in 1066. As might be expected, the greater number lay towards the west, although there were quite a few in the eastern part of the Cheshire plain. The effect of the disorders of 1069–70 can be seen on Fig. 85; the Evesham Chronicle specifically mentions Cheshire and Shropshire among the devastated counties of the time (see p. 250). The concluding entry at the foot of folio 254b of the Shropshire text tells of two manors waste 'as many others were' (*ut multa alia*). By 1086, as Fig. 86 shows, there had been considerable recovery, but many places were still in a devastated condition and some of these, along the Welsh border in Herefordshire and Shropshire, provided opportunities for hunting (see p. 202).

The extent of the recovery can be seen on Fig. 87 which shows the teams at work in 1086 on holdings that had been wasted at some earlier time. The number of teams restored (together with their associated people) constituted a considerable fraction of the total teams and population of the district as the following table shows:

	Teams in 1086		Population in 1086	
	On former waste	% of total teams	On former waste	% of total population
Cheshire	208	46	676	44
Shropshire	325	18	884	18
Herefordshire	252	10	475	11
Now in Wales	91	59	299	75
Total	876	18	2,334	20

These figures raise many questions about the restocking that had taken place. Could the empty vills of 1066 and 1070 have acquired all these oxen and people over a single generation or so? Were the devastated vills completely empty when they were described as *wasta*? In some ways, on the other hand, Fig. 86 may not be conveying the full extent of the desolation of 1086. Some vills not described as waste had no population (and usually no teams) entered for them. It is possible that their territories may have been utilised by men from elsewhere, or that the omission of any reference to population may have been accidental. Fig. 83 shows the combination of waste or partly waste vills and uninhabited vills not specifically said to be waste.

CHAPTER IX

INDUSTRY

Although industry was not important in eleventh-century England, we might expect to hear more of it than we do. Even so, the fragments of information that are available provide hints of that fuller picture we can never have. In the first place, there were the extractive industries providing raw material for salt-making, iron-working and lead-working. There were also the 'agricultural industries' of grain-milling and the making of wine and honey. Then there was fishing both in rivers and at sea. Finally some other non-agricultural activities are revealed by a few miscellaneous references.

SALT-MAKING

Salt was an indispensable item in the economy of the Middle Ages, especially for the preservation of meat and fish to be eaten during the winter. Rock salt was not discovered in Britain until 1670 during explorations for coal at a depth of about 100 feet near Northwich in Cheshire. Before then, salt was obtained by evaporation either from inland brine springs or from sea water.

Inland brine springs

The inland centres of production were in Worcestershire and Cheshire, and the brine springs were derived from the Keuper Marl beds of the Triassic system. The Worcestershire industry was centred on the borough of Droitwich for which brine-pits (*putei*) and salt-pans (*salinae*) are recorded; we also hear of mysterious *hocci*, the meaning of which is not clear.[1] At least 236½ salt-pans are said to have been in Droitwich itself; the Worcestershire folios mention another 68½ pans entered among the details for various villages, and these, or some of them at any rate, may also have been in or near the borough. The annual render of a pan or pans is usually stated, sometimes in money or sometimes in *mittae* of salt, an obscure measure which may have been equal to 8 bushels.[2] There is no information about the processes of manufacture, but six

[1] *D.G.M.E.*, 252–8.
[2] E. B. Pillans in *V.C.H. Worcestershire*, II (1906), 257.

leaden vats (*vi plumbi*) are entered for Bromsgrove (172) and two for Tardebigge (172b). The entry for Northwick and Tibberton (173b) mentions a *fabrica plumbi* which could be a lead works for making the vats. At Droitwich itself (174b) there were four furnaces (*furni*) belonging to Westminster Abbey. Such references are casual and isolated; no leaden vats, for example, are entered for Droitwich itself, and there is only one reference in the Worcestershire folios to the salt-workers (*salinarii*) employed in the industry – at Bromsgrove (172). There are, however, four references to the fuel that sustained the Droitwich industry – in the entries for Bromsgrove (172), Northwick and Tibberton (173b), Fladbury (172b) and Martin Hussingtree (174b); the last-named, for example, tells of an annual render of 100 cartloads made by the villeins – *reddunt per annum c caretedes lignorum ad salinas de Wich*. Two Herefordshire entries for Much Marcle (179b) and Leominster (180) also connect wood and salt, though not so explicitly (see pp. 189–90).

As well as the total of 305 pans recorded in the Worcestershire folios, 33 villages in other counties possessed salt-pans or the right to a number of *mittae* or of loads (*summae*) of salt; a total of several dozen pans may be implied (Fig. 88). Some of these entries specifically mention Droitwich, others do not; the most distant of these places was the Buckinghamshire village of Princes Risborough (143b) which had a salt-worker in Droitwich (*unus salinarius de Wicg*) about seventy miles away. All this suggests some interesting reflections on the movement of commodities in Domesday England. The salt was presumably transported by wagon or by packhorse; and names such as Saltway, Salter's Corner and Salford are preserved on the One-Inch Ordnance Survey maps of today. Possible saltways from Droitwich have been traced by linking up such placenames.[1] The entry for Chedworth (164), in Gloucestershire, refers to a toll brought to the hall (*theloneum salis quod veniebat ad aulum*).

The Cheshire salt industry is described in one and a quarter columns on folio 268. It was centred at the 'Wiches' of Northwich, Middlewich and Nantwich; all three had suffered greatly from the disturbances of 1070 and they were waste when Earl Hugh received them, except for a single salt-pan at Nantwich. They had far from recovered by 1086, and their combined renders amounted to less than a third of what they had been in 1066. In contrast to the description of Droitwich, we hear nothing of

[1] A. Mawer et al., *The place-names of Worcestershire* (Cambridge, 1927), 4–9; A. H. Smith, *The place-names of Gloucestershire*, pt. 1 (Cambridge, 1964), 19–20.

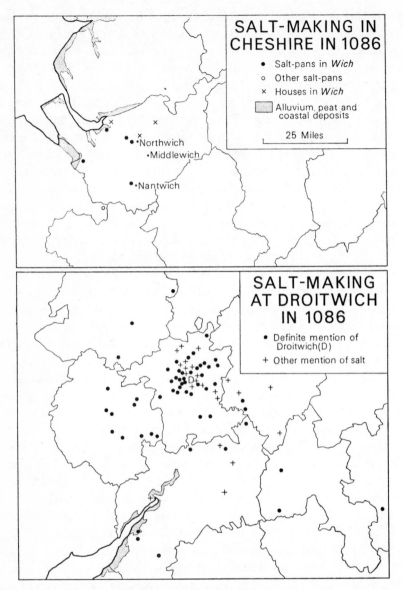

Fig. 88. Salt-making in Cheshire and Worcestershire in 1086.

their population or resources apart from their salt-pans. There are, however, a few incidental allusions to the processes of manufacture, and we are told of a brine-pit at Nantwich for making salt (*puteus ad sal' faciendum*) and of boilings (*bulliones*).[1]

Five rural manors held salt-pans in one or other of the Wiches, and in the same way three other manors held houses, two of which were waste (Fig. 88); no reference is made to salt in these three latter entries, but the manors or their owners may have had some connection with the industry. Furthermore, the main entry (268) says that a number of men of the county held salt-pans in Nantwich, but there is a gap where the number should have been inserted: *In eodem Wich habebant* [ ] *salinas plurimi homines patriae.* These arrangements resembled those at Droitwich, in which rural manors also held *salinae.*

A large part of the main entry is occupied with details of the tolls levied on those who transported the salt away, whether on foot or on horseback or by oxcart. The tolls increased with the distance from which a purchaser came, whether from the same hundred or from another hundred or from another county. There is also a reference to the toll paid by traders who carted salt about the county to sell. These glimpses imply an organised trade that extended far beyond the Wiches themselves. As in the case of Droitwich, place-names suggest a system of ways along which the salt was distributed through neighbouring counties.[2]

Coastal salt-pans

Domesday entries for many places along the east and south coasts mention *salinae*, and usually state their number and their render, mostly in money but occasionally in bushels of salt as at Chislet (12) in Kent, and Washington (28) in Sussex; the Little Domesday Book is exceptional in that it merely states the number of pans and never the render. The number at any one place varied greatly, from one or two to as many as 30 or 40, and occasionally even more; at Rye (17) in Sussex there were 100 pans yielding £8 15*s* a year. There is no consistency about the render; two pans at Bedhampton (43), in Hampshire, yielded 37*s* 8*d*, while eleven at Seaton (*Flueta*, *184*, 104), in Devonshire, yielded only 11*d*. Occasionally, we hear of a waste salt-pan, e.g. at Bicker (Lincs., 340). Fractions

---

[1] *D.G.N.E.*, 362–4.

[2] W. B. Crump, 'Saltways from the Cheshire Wiches', *Trans. Lancs. and Cheshire Antiq. Soc.*, LIV (1939), 84–142.

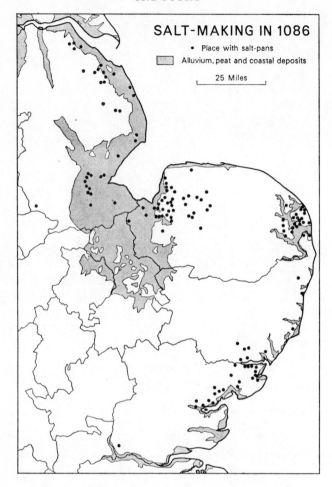

Fig. 89. Salt-making in eastern England in 1086.

are sometimes given, but it is only rarely possible to combine them in such a way that suggests that adjoining villages shared a salt-pan; there was, for example, a twelfth of a pan at Shernborne (268) in Norfolk, but there is no clue to the other eleven twelfths. We are told nothing of the processes or the circumstances of the manufacture from sea-water, but occasionally there is a reference to the salt-workers (*salinarii*) themselves. Along the Dorset coast, for example, there were 27 at Lyme Regis (77b and 85), 16 at Charmouth (80), and 13 at Ower (*44b*, 78); those at Ower formed the only population recorded for the village. Another 61 salt-workers are recorded for places along the Devonshire coast.[1]

A striking feature of the distribution of salt-working along the coast is the great cluster of pans in western Norfolk (Fig. 89). Some of the pans could not possibly have been at the inland villages for which they are entered; they must have been on the coast at some distance away. Salt-pans are also recorded for many villages in the Lincolnshire Fenland, and it is clear that salt-making must have been an important activity around the shores of the Wash. Later evidence shows its continued existence throughout the Middle Ages.[2] Further along the east coast there was another conspicuous cluster of salt-making villages in Norfolk Broadland and quite a number along the estuaries of Suffolk and Essex.

To the south, there was a number of salt-making villages associated with the alluvial areas of northern Kent, and, in Sussex, with Romney Marsh, the Pevensey Levels and various estuaries (Fig. 91). Here again, the pans entered for some inland manors must have been physically situated elsewhere. Further west, there were salt-making villages in the neighbourhood of Poole Harbour and along the estuaries of the Devon-shire rivers (Fig. 90). On the north coast of the south-west peninsula, they are limited to a few places in the estuaries of the Taw and the Torridge in Devonshire, and to a solitary Cornish manor.

How complete is the record of coastal salt-pans? That we cannot tell, but we may well suppose that Domesday Book does not give a full picture. In Devonshire, for example, the entry for Salcombe Regis (*118b*, 102) makes no reference to salt-pans, although the name means 'salt valley' and is mentioned in a pre-Domesday charter;[3] the other Salcombe, to the west of Dartmouth, is not mentioned in the Domesday text. Likewise in Essex no salt-pan is entered for the Domesday village of *Salcota* (65) in Virley on a creek of the Blackwater estuary. What is more, the salt-pans along the Essex coast appear only for the three northern hundreds; none are entered for the three southern hundreds where conditions for salt-making were equally suitable. Could this absence reflect some idiosyncrasy in the hundred returns?

[1] *D.G.S–W.E.*, 271.
[2] E. H. Rudkin and D. M. Owen, 'The medieval salt industry in the Lindsey marshland', *Rep. and Papers, Lincs. Archit. and Archaeol. Soc.*, N.S. VIII (1959–60), 76–84; H. E. Hallam, 'Salt-making in the Lincolnshire Fenland during the Middle Ages', ibid. 85–112.
[3] J. E. B. Gover, *The place-names of Devon*, pt II (Cambridge, 1932), 595.

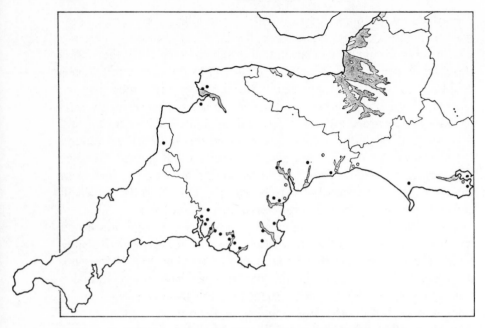

Fig. 90. Salt-making in south-west England in 1086.

For the key, see Fig. 91.

IRON-WORKING

Iron-ware must have been in widespread use in the eleventh century, but we hear little, in Domesday Book, of the extraction and forging of the iron itself. An unusually explicit reference is that to the iron mines (*mineriae ferri*) in the district around Rhuddlan (269), surveyed in the Cheshire folios. Iron-working in the Forest of Dean is presumably reflected in the renders of iron and of rods of iron, for making nails for the king's ships, that are mentioned in the account of Gloucester (162), and also in the renders of iron at Alvington (185b) on the shores of the Severn estuary. For the Wealden iron area, the only reference is to a *ferraria* somewhere in East Grinstead hundred (22b) in Sussex. In the north of the realm, the six iron-workers (*ferrarii*) at Hessle (316), to the south-east of Wakefield, may have been engaged in working the iron-stone deposits to be found in the Coal Measures of the West Riding. But it is not so easy to conjecture from whence came the raw

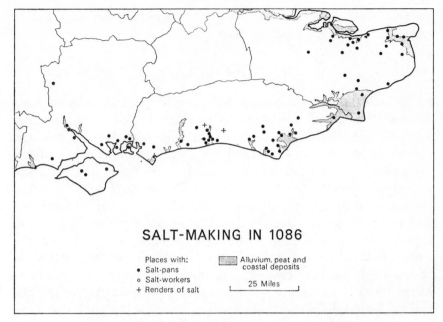

Fig. 91. Salt-making in south-east England in 1086.

material for the four iron-workers at North Molton in Devonshire (*94b*, 100). The iron works belonging to the manors of Corby and Gretton (219b) in the Northamptonshire area were 'wanting' in 1086, possibly because they had been taken into the forest later known as Rockingham.

Ferrariae and *fabricae ferri* are also mentioned for a number of other places, but we cannot tell whether they were smelting furnaces or merely forges. Such were those at Stratfield (45b) in north Hampshire, at Stow (344) and Bytham (360b) in Lincolnshire, at Chertsey (32b) in Surrey, at Wilnecote (240) in Warwickshire, and at Fifield Bavant (70b) in Wiltshire. We also hear of six smiths (*fabri*) each with a forge (*forgia*) at Hereford (179) and each making 120 horseshoes (*ferra*) out of the king's iron in 1066. These cannot have been the only forges at work, nor can the 64 recorded smiths (25 in Herefordshire alone) have been the only ones in Domesday England. Renders of ploughshares (*ferra carucis*) or of *blomae* or *plumbae* or *massae* of iron are sporadically mentioned among the details for a number of holdings – Appendix 13 (p. 360). They come from pasture, wood and mills, and convey the impression that iron was in general use throughout the country.[1]

LEAD-WORKING

In Roman times lead was worked in the Mendips, Flintshire, Shropshire, Derbyshire and north Yorkshire. Of these, Derbyshire is the only area for which *plumbariae* are mentioned in Domesday Book. Three are entered for Wirksworth (272b) and one each for Ashford and its twelve berewicks (272b), for Bakewell and its eight berewicks (272b), for Crich and Shuckstonefield (277) and for Matlock Bridge (272). The term *plumbaria* has been translated sometimes as lead mine and sometimes as lead works.[2] That lead was certainly smelted and cast may be gathered from the account of the combined render in 1066 from the three royal manors of Bakewell, Ashford and Hope (273), each with its complement of berewicks; the three gave not only money and honey but also 5 cart-loads of lead of 50 slabs (*v plaustratae plumbi de l tabulis*), but by 1086 this had been replaced entirely by a money render. It is possible that there is one indirect reference to lead-working. The combined render, in 1086, of five other royal manors (Darley, Matlock Bridge, Wirksworth, Ashbourne, Parwich, 272b) was £40 of pure silver (*puri argenti*), and it has been suggested that this unique entry 'may point to some metallurgical connexion between the working of silver and lead'.[3] The places with *plumbariae* lie on or near the outcrop of Carboniferous Limestone which contains veins of metalliferous ores from which the lead must have been derived (Fig. 92). We are told nothing of the methods by which the finished lead was produced; nor is there any hint of the customs of the industry which was to become such a feature of the Derbyshire uplands in later times.

There is also mention of a *fabrica plumbi* in the entry for Northwick and Tibberton (173b) in Worcestershire, and it is possible that this referred to lead works for making the vats used in the manufacture of salt at Droitwich nearby. That there was trade in lead throughout the realm we may infer from a casual but interesting reference in the *Inquisitio*

---

[1] *D.G.M.E.*, 49, 106; *D.G.S–E.E.*, 31, 167; *D.G.S–W.E.*, 126, 211.
[2] G. J. Fuller, 'Early lead smelting in the Peak District: another look at the evidence', *East Midland Geographer*, V (1970), 1–8.
[3] F. M. Stenton in *V.C.H. Derbyshire*, I (1905), 316.

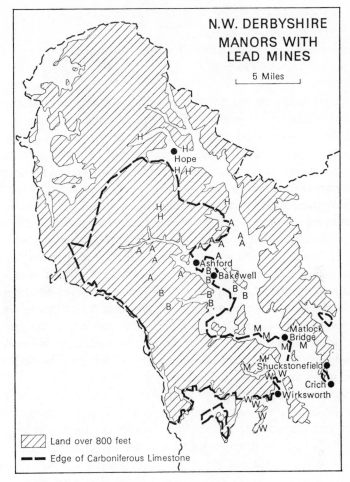

Fig. 92. Lead mines in north-east Derbyshire in 1086.

The respective berewicks of the manors are indicated by initials. Note that the information for Hope relates only to 1066.

Eliensis. This compares the weight of a 'fodder' of Peak lead (*carreta plumbi del pec*) with that of a London 'fodder', and it would seem that the abbey of Ely may have had its supply of lead for roofing and other purposes from Derbyshire.[1]

---

[1] N. E. S. A. Hamilton, *Inquisitio Comitatus Cantabrigiensis . . . subjicitur Inquisitio Eliensis* (London, 1876), 191.

GRAIN-MILLING

The earliest reference to a water-mill in England comes from a document referring to Chart in Kent, and dating from 762. References to water-mills become relatively numerous after about 800 or so.[1] The first mention of a windmill, on the other hand, does not appear until 1191 in a document relating to the abbey of Bury St Edmunds.[2] We may therefore assume that the mills of Domesday Book were water-mills. They numbered several thousand; their spread was one of 'the greatest economic achievements' of the four centuries before 1086, and yet one that is 'completely unrecorded'.[3] In spite of this achievement, it is probably true to say that much grain was still ground by hand.

Sometimes, as for the counties of the Little Domesday Book, we are merely told the number of mills on a holding, but elsewhere we usually hear of their renders which ranged from a few pence per mill to a few pounds. Some mills rendered nothing (*nil reddit*), e.g. at Aston Eyre (255) in Shropshire. Occasionally a mill is said to be unrented (*sine censu*), and in the Exeter version such a mill is said to grind its own grain (*molit annonam suam*).[4] Other variants which imply the same thing include *ad aulam molens, serviens ad hallam, serviens curiae* and *in dominio serviens*.[5] On the other hand there is a rare reference to the mills of the villeins (*molini villanorum*) at Leeds (7b) in Kent.

We sometimes hear of renders in kind as well as, or instead of, money renders. Such renders were usually in eels presumably from the mill pond or mill stream; and for Barking (382b) and for Creeting (304b), both in Suffolk, there is mention of a mill dam or sluice (*exclusa*). Other mill renders in kind include honey at Cleeve Prior (Worcs., 174), salt at Wasperton (Warw., 239), malt at Bledlow (Bucks., 146), rye at Ryton (Salop., 257b), and grain, either *frumentum* as at Kyre Magna (Worcs., 176b) or *annona* as at Bunford (Salop., 260). The 4 mills on 3 holdings at Lexworthy in Somerset (*282, 432, 432b*; 91b, 94 *bis*) paid a mysterious render of 6 blooms of iron (*plumbae ferri*). At Shelford (191) in Cambridgeshire 2 mills paid 45*s* and 2 pigs which the I.C.C. (p. 48)

[1] H. P. R. Finberg in H. P. R. Finberg (ed.), *The agrarian history of England and Wales*, I (1972), 498–9.
[2] H. E. Butler (ed.), *The chronicle of Jocelin of Brakelond* (London, 1949), 59.
[3] J. H. Clapham, *A concise economic history of Britain from the earliest times to 1750* (Cambridge, 1949), 68.
[4] *D.G.S–W.E.*, 190–1.   [5] *D.G.S–E.E.*, 458; *D.G.S–W.E.*, 276.

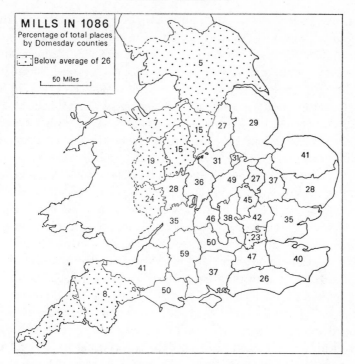

Fig. 93. The distribution of places with mills in 1086
(by Domesday counties).

explains by saying that 2 pigs were fattened from the mills (*ii porci impinguantur de molinis*). At Much Marcle (Heref., 179b) a mill rendered nothing beyond the sustenance of its keeper (*nisi tantum victum ejus qui eum custodit*). There is also an unusual entry for Rudford (Gloucs., 170b) where the mill rendered as much grain as it could (*reddit annonam quantum potest lucrari*).

Occasional mills were said to be waste (*wastum*), e.g. at North Muskham (Notts., 284). There was a broken mill that yielded nothing (*fractum molinum quod nichil reddit*) at Shillington (210b) in Bedfordshire; there was also a broken mill at Duxford (196) in Cambridgeshire, but we are told that this could be repaired (*modo confractum sed potest restaurari*). The Little Domesday Book tells of a number of mills that had disappeared since 1066;[1] and elsewhere we hear of sites (*sedes*) of mills.[2] An unusual

[1] *D.G.E.E.*, 136, 188, 248, [2] *D.G.E.E.*, 72; *D.G.N.E.*, 269–70, 319.

entry is that which refers to the mill at Evenlode (Worcs., 173) in the past tense (*fuit*). Conversely we are very occasionally told of new mills, e.g. at Chetton (Salop., 254) and Croxby (Lincs., 376). Sometimes, there is reference to a winter mill (*molinum hiemale*) e.g. at Frodsham (263b) and at Golborne (265) in Cheshire; the entry for Welbatch (255b), in Shropshire, is more specific in saying *molinum hiemale non aestivum*. Such restrictions reflected the seasonal nature of their streams. Millers (*molinarii*) themselves are mentioned in the entries for Berrington (Worcs., 176b), Chiddingly (Sx. 22b), Doddenham (Worcs., 176b), Feckenham (Heref., 180b), Stokesay (Salop., 260b), and Tilston (Ches., 264). A joint entry for Morton and two other places (276b) in Derbyshire refers to a mill-keeper (*custos molini*), and, as we have seen, another is implied in the entry for Much Marcle (Heref., 179b). We can only suppose that millers elsewhere were included in one or other of the main categories of population.

It is impossible to be precise about the exact number of mills in Domesday England because of the frequency of fractions – that is of mills held jointly by two or more people. Thus each of the three holdings at Coleshill (59b, 61, 63), in Berkshire, had a third of a mill (*tercia pars molini*), and each third yielded 10s; but the renders were sometimes unequal, and two halves of a mill at Tellisford (*148*, 88b) in Somerset paid 7s 6d and 9s respectively. Other fractions included quarters, fifths, sixths and eighths.[1] A freeman in the unidentified Suffolk vill of *Langhedana* (404b) had a fourth share in a mill every third year (*in tercio anno quarta pars molini*). On some occasions it would seem as if the fractions were the result of the subdivision of an estate among heirs.[2] Occasionally, adjoining villages shared a mill; Rivenhall (27) and Braxted (49), in Essex, each had half a mill, and J. H. Round was able to show that they were parts of one mill on the River Blackwater between the two villages.[3] Only too often, however, the fractions do not so easily combine, and, in Hampshire for example, we are given no clue to the missing portions of the 1½ mills at Leckford (42) on the Test, or of the 1½ at Itchen Stoke (44) on the Itchen. Bearing all these difficulties in mind, and taking the Domesday figures at their face value, the total number of mills recorded in Domesday Book amounts to just over 6,000 (see Appendix 14, p. 361).

Difficult as it may be to estimate the total number of mills in the realm,

---

[1] *D.G.E.E.*, 136; *D.G.S–E.E.*, 345, 360, 395.
[2] R. Lennard, *Rural England, 1086–1135* (Oxford, 1959), 286–7.
[3] J. H. Round in *V.C.H. Essex*, I (1903), 379.

it is perhaps even more difficult to be sure of the total of places with mills. This is because some mills were entered for anonymous holdings, and, even more important, a substantial number was recorded in entries covering two or more places, frequently the berewicks or other members of a manor. One mill appears in an entry for Henbury and 4 other places (164b) in Gloucestershire; and we can therefore assume that the mill was at one place. For the same county, however, 3 mills are entered for Foxcote and 6 other places (165). Were they all at one place, or were they distributed among two or three places? Similar queries arise over other Gloucestershire entries. What, for example, of the 8 mills entered for the 21 berewicks of Berkeley (163)? If one assumes that each group of vills was at one place, the total number of places with mills in Gloucestershire was 123. If, on the other hand, one assumes that each mill was at a separate place, the total becomes 140. The correct number lies somewhere between these two figures. This is so because it is clear that many villages with mills had more than one apiece, and often two or three or even more. Thus Meldreth (191, 193b, 194b, 198b, 199b) and Shepreth (193, 194b, 197, 198), two adjoining Cambridgeshire villages on the River Cam or Rhee, seem to have had 8 and 5 mills respectively. The table in Appendix 14, therefore, sets out three totals for each county – minimum, maximum and average. The average total for Domesday Book as a whole is 3,550, that is to say just over one quarter of the Domesday settlements had a mill or mills recorded for them. Their distribution county by county is shown on Fig. 93. The figures include boroughs. Of the 112 boroughs recorded in Domesday Book, mills were entered for 58, and we also hear of two other boroughs with mills in 1066 – Tewkesbury (163) and York (298). The numbers on Fig. 93 may be not far from the reality, but there is yet a further complication. Even when there is no reference to dependencies in a Domesday entry, we may strongly suspect their existence on manors with large totals for men, teams and other resources. Thus a large number of mills entered for one manor creates a suspicion that more than one settlement may be involved; this is so for the 13 mills at Chippenham (64b, 73) in Wiltshire and the 9 mills at Neatham (38) in Hampshire.

There are other ways of considering the distribution of Domesday mills. On the one hand there is their location in villages along streams, and the county maps in other volumes of this series demonstrate this, often in a striking fashion. On the other hand, there is the relation of the mills to the population they served and to the arable which produced their

Fig. 94. Mills in 1086 per 1,000 men
(by Domesday counties, and adjusted for slaves).

raw material. In Huntingdonshire, Kimbolton (205b) with 30 teams had only one mill yielding 5s, yet Hartford (203b), in the same county, with only 12 teams had 2 mills yielding £4. Could the reason be that the former was on the small stream of the Kym while the latter was on the Ouse below Huntingdon? In any case, was the grain of Kimbolton ground mainly by hand or sent elsewhere to be ground by mill? Battersea (32), in Surrey, provides a contrast. It had 17 teams and yet its 7 mills yielded as much as £42 9s 8d out of a total render from the manor of £75 9s 8d. These mills must surely have drawn their grain from beyond their manor, and they must have sent their produce elsewhere. Could it have been to London?

These marked contrasts between individual manors prepare us for more general contrasts over the country as a whole. Figs. 94–5 are very imperfect but, even allowing for a wide margin of error, the facts they convey are most striking. Over the whole of Domesday England there were 25 mills to every 1,000 households. Cornwall, however, had only

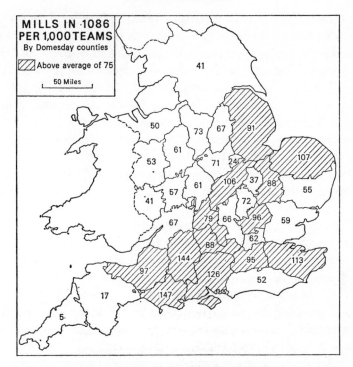

Fig. 95. Mills in 1086 per 1,000 teams (by Domesday counties).

one per 1,000. The corresponding figure for Devonshire was 7 as opposed to 34 for Somerset, 43 for Dorset and 50 for Wiltshire. The number of mills per 1,000 teams conveys the same impression. Can we believe that the record for the south-western circuit was unusually defective for Cornwall and Devonshire? Or would it be wiser to fall back on the hypothesis that grinding was done largely by hand and that the water-mill was but little used in these remote areas?[1] The same questions could be asked about the northern and western parts of the realm.

VINE-GROWING

Vineyards are recorded for about 45 places in Domesday England – Appendix 15 (pp. 362–3). It is impossible to be precise because of two multiple entries and because of the doubts associated with another three entries. At

[1] M. T. Hodgen, 'Domesday water mills', *Antiquity*, XIII (1939), 261–79.

Lomer (Hants., 43), in 1066, a certain Alward had rendered ten sesters of wine a year, but we are not told whether this wine was produced locally and whether the render continued to be paid by his successor in 1086. Then, again, we cannot be sure that the vineyard entered on fo. 127 was really at Holborn.[1] An even more uncertain allusion appears in the entry for Wandsworth (36) in Surrey. Here, among the sub-tenants, a certain Walter held one hide, and the word *vinitor* is interlined above his name; this has been variously translated as 'vine-yard keeper' or 'vintner', but even if the former is implied we cannot be sure that the vineyard was at Wandsworth itself. There is only one reference to yield; the vineyard at Rayleigh (43b) in Essex was said to produce 20 *modii* of wine 'if it did well'; that at Wilcot (69) in Wiltshire was said to be a good one.

J. H. Round argued that the culture of the vine was reintroduced after Roman times by the Normans, and he based this view on the facts that the Domesday vineyards were normally on holdings in the direct hands of Norman tenants-in-chief; that they were usually measured by the foreign unit of the arpent, which seems to have been approximately the same as an acre; and that we are sometimes told that they had been planted only recently.[2] This view cannot be maintained because we hear of vineyards in England in the eighth, ninth and tenth centuries;[3] moreover, the entry for Lomer seems to imply the existence of a vineyard in Edward the Confessor's day.

On the other hand, however, it is true that vineyards were almost all on estates held directly by tenants-in-chief, usually Norman nobles but sometimes abbeys. It is also true that they were measured in arpents except in five places where they were measured in acres and in three places where no measurements were given. It is also true that the vineyards at Ware (138b) in Hertfordshire, and at Kempton (129) and Westminster (128) in Middlesex, had but lately (*noviter* or *nuperrime*) been planted. Portions of others at Belchamp (77), Debden (73b) and Stebbing (74), in Essex, were not in bearing, and those at a number of places in Essex and Suffolk are recorded only for 1086 (*modo*). It would seem as if the Normans had not so much reintroduced the vine into England as extended, possibly greatly extended, its cultivation.

---

[1] J. H. Round, 'Essex vineyards in Domesday', *Trans. Essex Archaeol. Soc.*, N.S. VII (1900), 249–51; *V.C.H. Essex*, I (1903), 382–3.
[2] *D.G.S–E.E.*, 134.
[3] G. Ordish, *Wine growing in England* (London, 1953), 20–1.

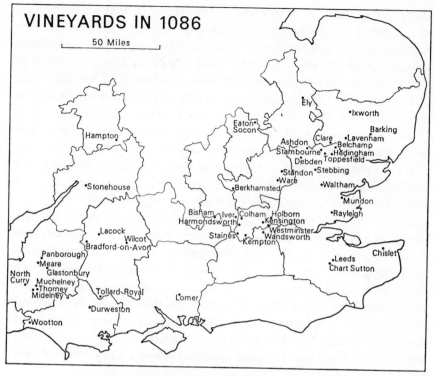

Fig. 96. Domesday vineyards in England.

For the list, see Appendix 15 (pp. 362–3 below).

Fig. 96 shows that the recorded vineyards were restricted to the south of the country and that they were most numerous in the counties around London. The most northerly place with a vineyard was Ely.

BEE-KEEPING

The care of bees was an important feature of rural life in Anglo-Saxon and Norman times. In the absence of sugar, honey was of considerable value, and it was an ingredient both in mead and in various medicinal preparations. Wax was employed in making candles not only for the wealthy but also for use in churches. Beehives were regularly entered in the Little Domesday Book, along with the livestock, under the name *vasa apum* or, very rarely, *ruscae apum*. Taking the three counties together, as many as 1,370 hives were recorded at 267 places (i.e. at about 12% of the total number of places); over a dozen are sometimes entered for one holding, e.g. the 27 at Methwold (Norf., 136). Their numbers fluctuated; thus at Saffron Walden (Ess., 62b) there were only 4 in 1066 but 30 in 1086; and conversely the number at Clavering (Ess., 46b) had fallen from 12 to 5. Hives are not enumerated in the Exeter text nor in the Exchequer Domesday Book itself, apart from an occasional rare mention, e.g. the 12 *vasculi* at Suckley (180b) in Worcestershire; but a variety of entries in both texts indicate the importance of honey.

Honey renders formed a characteristic feature of the newly conquered districts described in the folios for Gloucestershire and Herefordshire. In the former, beyond the Wye, there were groups of Welsh villages or 'trefs' rendering not manorial services but food-rents among which were sesters of honey (162). In the latter, in the districts of Archenfield and Ewias, honey renders, often from Welshmen, were frequent.[1] In addition to the separate mention of renders at individual places, we are told that there were 96 king's men in Archenfield who rendered 41 sesters of honey (181); and we also hear of penalties for those who tried to conceal their honey (179). There were, moreover, honey renders at other places in the two counties and also in other counties. Altogether, indications of bee-keeping, either in 1086 or 1066, appear at places widely scattered over twenty counties.[2]

Some honey renders were mentioned in connection with woods, e.g. at Bredon (173) in Worcestershire, at Greens Norton (219b) in Northamptonshire, and at Eling (38b) in the New Forest; the honey may well have come from nests of wild bees. Honey renders occasionally appear as part of a day's feorm, as on the royal manor of Luton (209) in Bedfordshire; but more often such renders had been commuted for money payments, e.g. on the royal manors of Cambridgeshire (189–189b) (see p. 218). Part of the dues from some boroughs took the form of payments commuted from honey renders since 1066: Colchester (107), Gloucester (162), Ipswich (290), Leicester (230), Norwich (117), Oxford (154b), Thetford (119), and Warwick (238). The bee-keepers themselves were only rarely mentioned. There were 5 *mellitari* at Southbrook (*347*, 111b) in Devonshire, and another 9 at Westbury (65) in Wiltshire; and there was a *custos*

---

[1] *D.G.M.E.*, 54, 75, 106.
[2] Beds., Cambs., Derby., Devon, Do., Ess., Gloucs., Hants., Heref., Leics., Norf., N'hants., Notts., Oxon., Salop., Suff., Sx., Warw., Wilts., Worcs.

apium at Stokesay (260b) in Shropshire and another at Suckley (180b) in Worcestershire. It is possible that the *serviens* who rendered 7 sesters at Bradford on Avon (67b), in Wiltshire, was yet another. The incompleteness of the Domesday record may be seen from the fact that the entries for Westbury and Stokesay mention neither hives nor honey renders; and we must suppose that for the most part bee-keepers were silently included among the other peasantry.

INLAND AND COASTAL FISHING

Fish, salted or otherwise, must have played an important part in the life of an eleventh-century community. The preamble to the *Inquisitio Eliensis* includes the question 'How many fisheries?'; and fisheries are recorded in a variety of ways in many Domesday entries. Sometimes, as for the counties of the Little Domesday Book, we are merely told the number of fisheries; but, more usually, their render is also stated, in money or eels or both. The render of eels is sometimes given either as a straightforward figure or in terms of *stiches*, the medieval stick of eels comprising twenty-five. Only rarely, as at Cleeve (179b), in Herefordshire, did a fishery yield nothing (*nil reddit*). Another at Kingston (30b), in Surrey, was said to be very good although it yielded no rent (*valde bona sed sine censu*). A few fisheries were specifically said to be *in dominio* (Tidenham, Gloucs., 164) or *ad hallam* (Swanscombe, Kent, 6); a few others were likewise specially said to be rented by the villeins or *in censu villanorum* (*Udeford* and Ruyton, Salop., 257b). Moieties or halves of fisheries are frequent, but it is not always possible to assemble the fractions of neighbouring holdings together in any comprehensible fashion. Where, for example, in Nottinghamshire along the Trent was the missing portion of the $3\frac{1}{2}$ fisheries at Rampton (287) or the remainder of the third part of the fishery at Radcliffe (288)?

A fishery is usually called *piscaria*, but *piscina* also appears; the latter is often translated as fishpond, but the I.E. frequently uses *piscina* where the Domesday text speaks of *piscaria*.[1] It would seem that they are but variant forms; when the Essex folios extend *pisc'* it is always to *piscina*. Another variant at Kilverstone (153b) in Norfolk, and Hollesley (39) in Suffolk, was *piscatio*; and other variations occur in the Exeter Domesday Book.[2] A number of entries make no mention of fisheries as such but refer to

[1] R. Lennard, 248. [2] *D.G.S–W.E.*, 271.

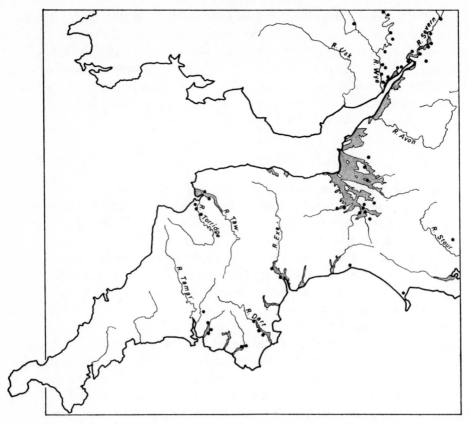

Fig. 97. Fisheries in south-west England in 1086.

renders of eels in connection with mills, and these eels, presumably, were from mill ponds or mill streams; the eleven places with fisheries in Warwickshire are all characterized by this formula.[1]

It seems as if the mention of a fishery in Domesday Book may imply some kind of fixed contrivance such as a weir or fish-trap. A number of entries for Cambridgeshire, Hertfordshire and Middlesex speak not of fisheries but of weirs (*gurt, guort, gurges* with its plural *gurgites*).[2] Occasional entries mention a fish-stew (*vivarium piscium*) as for the holding of Osbern the fisherman at Sharnbrook (216b) in Bedfordshire, and for

[1] *D.G.M.E.*, 300–1.
[2] *D.G.E.E.*, 306; *D.G.S–E.E.*, 82, 128.

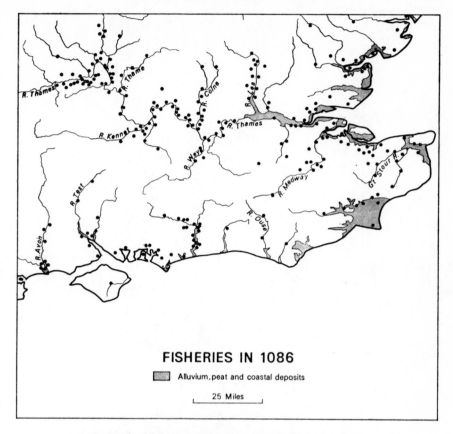

FISHERIES IN 1086

▨ Alluvium, peat and coastal deposits

└─── 25 Miles ───┘

Fig. 98. Fisheries in south-east England in 1086.

other places.[1] Some kind of fixed apparatus is also suggested by the reference to a new fishery at Monkton (4b) in Kent, or to the making of two in the Wye (*crevit in Waiam*) at Tidenham (164) in Gloucestershire, or to the construction of one by force (*vi construxit eam*) at Mortlake (31) in Surrey, or to the waste fishery (*piscaria wasta*) at Barnby Dun (319b) in the West Riding, or to the fishery at Chadwell (23b), in Essex, which had disappeared but which could be restored (*modo nulla est sed potest fieri*), or to the site of a fishery (*sedes piscariae*) at, for example, Morton upon Swale (309b) in the North Riding.

Only rarely do we encounter references to the actual operations

[1] *D.G.E.E.*, 198; *D.G.S–E.E.*, 39, 83, 223.

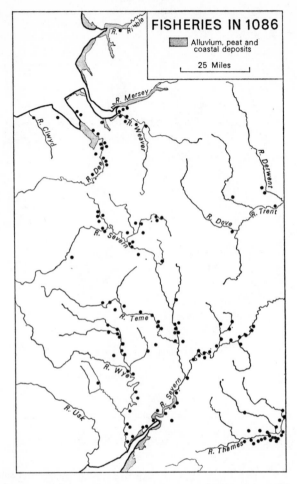

Fig. 99. Fisheries in part of western England in 1086.

involved in fishing. There is, it is true, the description of Whittlesey Mere
with its fishermen and their boats (*naves*) owned by the abbeys of Peterborough, Ramsey and Thorney (Hunts., 205); and the account of the
fishermen with their boats (*naves*) and nets (*sagenae*) in Soham Mere.[1]
There was also a fishing boat (*navis ad piscandum*) belonging to Laken-
heath (392) on the Suffolk edge of the Fenland; and an entry for Swaffham
(190b) in Cambridgeshire mentions a toll of 6*s* from fishing nets (*de*

---

[1] *D.G.E.E.*, 306.

theloneo retis vi s.) which, says the I.C.C. (p. 13), came from the landing of boats (*de appulatione navium*). On the Thames at Hampton (130) in Middlesex there were dues from seines and dragnets (*De sagenis et tractis in aqua temisiae*); and boats and nets (*navicula/navis et rete*) are also entered for three villages along the Dee above Chester–Cheveley (263), Eccleston (267) and Huntington (263).

The species normally mentioned is that of eels, but the render from Petersham (32b) in Surrey comprised not only 1,000 eels but 1,000 lampreys (*lampridulae*). Salmon are recorded for a few places in the west—for Gloucester (165b) along the Severn, for Eaton (263b) on the Dee near Chester, and in south Devonshire for Cornworthy (*323b*, 109) and Dartington (*368b*, 111) along the Dart, and for Loddiswell (*321b*, 109) along the Avon.

The Domesday evidence is clearly incomplete. No fisheries are recorded for Leicestershire, yet it is difficult to believe that there were not some along the Soar and the Wreak. Wiltshire, Cornwall and Rutland are other counties for which fisheries are not recorded. Or again, can we believe that in Staffordshire there were only two vills with fisheries, or in Dorset only 3 vills, or in Northamptonshire only seven vills?[1] Furthermore, there must have been much fishing at places without the equipment which the Domesday *piscaria* seems to have implied.

The Domesday fisheries were located along the main rivers such as the Thames, the Trent, the Nene, the Bedfordshire Ouse, the Wye, the Severn and its tributaries, the Avon and the Teme (Figs. 97–100). On the northern shore of the Severn estuary, Tidenham (Gloucs., 164, 166b, 167b) was outstanding with nearly 70 fisheries, mostly in the Severn (*in Saverna*) but also in the Wye (*in Waia*). There was another group of fishing villages in and around the Somerset Levels, and an immensely more important group in the Fenland, and especially around its margin and along the rivers that flow from the nearby counties.

The annual renders, whether of eels or money, were often considerable, and it is clear that fishing activities gave a distinctive character to the economies of a number of localities. At Eaton (263b) on the Dee above Chester, six fishermen (out of a total recorded population of ten people) rendered 1,000 salmon annually. Two fisheries belonging to the abbey of Muchelney (*189*, 91) in Somerset, rendered 6,000 eels. The 20 fisheries at Tudworth (321), in Hatfield Chase in the West Riding, rendered 20,000

[1] *D.G.M.E.*, 209; *D.G.S–W.E.*, 110; *D.G.M.E.*, 208.

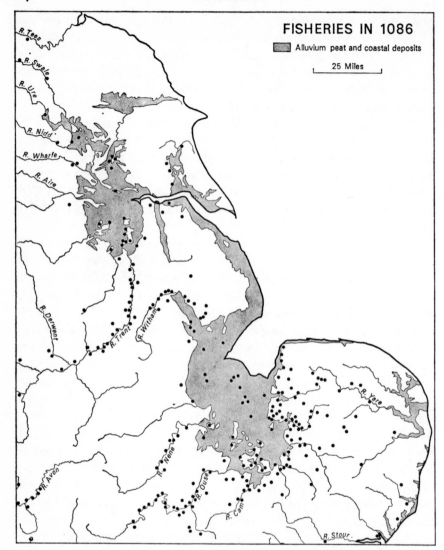

Fig. 100. Fisheries in part of eastern England in 1086.

eels. In the East Riding, along the valley of the Hull, 17 fisheries at Beverley (304), Cottingham and Pillwood (328) and Leconfield (306, 322b) rendered a total of 21,400. Similar large renders came from some of the Fenland villages. In Cambridgeshire, 17,000 eels came from Littleport, 24,000 from Stuntney, 27,150 from Doddington, and 33,260 from Wisbech.[1] It is not surprising that Ely, 'the eel district', obtained its name from its most characteristic product.

The majority of these fisheries were along rivers, but some were certainly not. The bishop of Salisbury's holding at Lyme Regis (75b), on the Dorset coast, was occupied by an unspecified number of fishermen; further to the east, at Bridge (83, 83b, 84b), there were 4 fishermen and one villein; they were without teams but they rendered 20s between them. Groups of coastal fishermen such as these may well have been engaged in sea-fishing, but the evidence is rarely explicit. The 24 fishermen at Yarmouth (283) are likely to have been seamen. Not far away, Thorpe St Andrew (137b) had rendered 2,000 herrings (allecti) in 1066; and to the south of Yarmouth, the three Suffolk hundreds of Blything, Lothingland and Wangford contained 18 places (five unidentified) with herring renders in 1086 (Fig. 101); 25,000 came from Southwold (371b), 60,000 from Beccles (370), and as many as 68,000 from Dunwich (312). There were also references to fishing activity along the shore itself. At Southwold (371b), the abbey of Bury St Edmunds had a moiety of a sea-weir and the fourth part of the other moiety (medietas unius heiemaris et quarta pars alterius medietatis), but there is no clue to the remaining three eighths. There also belonged to the manor of Blythburgh nearby the fourth penny from the rent of the 'hay' of the unidentified 'Riseburc' (quartus denarius de censu de heia de riseburc). These references imply some arrangement of fences with nets along the shore, and such 'hays' may well have been a feature of other coastal fisheries.[2]

To the south, we hear of herring renders at London (34, 35) and Southwark (35) on the Thames, at Luddenham (10b) and Sandwich (3) in Kent, and at Brighton (26b), Iford (26), Rodmell (26) and Southease (17b) in Sussex. At Southease and at Stone (5b) in Kent, we hear of porpoises (marsuins) as well as of the more prosaic herring; the Domesday Monachorum also mentions porpoises at Gillingham.[3] Fragmentary though the sum total of this evidence is, it enables us to glimpse something of the activity along the rivers and off the shores of eleventh-century England.

[1] D.G.E.E., 306.
[2] J. H. Round, 'The coast fisheries in Domesday' in V.C.H. Essex, I (1903), 424–5.
[3] D. C. Douglas (ed.), The Domesday Monachorum of Christ Church, Canterbury (Roy. Hist. Soc., London, 1944), 96, 98.

Fig. 101. Herring renders in east and south-east England in 1086.

MISCELLANEOUS ACTIVITIES

Among the miscellaneous industrial activities, quarrying is represented by entries for seven places. The quarry at Taynton (157) in Oxfordshire was well known for its Great Oolite freestone which is to be found in surviving pre-Domesday masonry in villages up to 30 miles and more from the outcrop;[1] the render from the quarry was incongruously grouped with those from meadow and pasture. The quarries at Bignor (25) in Sussex and at Whatton (290b) in Nottinghamshire produced mill-stones from the Upper Greensand and Keuper beds respectively. The remaining quarries in Surrey and Sussex must have been in Lower Greensand beds. These seven quarries obviously formed only a small fraction of the total worked throughout the realm in 1086.

Domesday quarries

Nottinghamshire
    Whatton (290b)   *Ibi una molaria ubi molae fodiuntur de iii markis argenti.*
Oxfordshire
    Taynton (157)   *Inter quadrariam et prata et pascua reddit xxiiii s et vii d.*
Surrey
    Limpsfield (34)   *Duae fossae Lapidum de ii s.*
Sussex
    Bignor (25)   *una molaria de iiii s.*
    Grittenham (23b)   *Quadraria de x s et x d.*
    Iping (29b)   *quadraria de ix s et iiii d.*
    Stedham (23)   *Quadraria de vi s et viii d.*

Domesday potters

Gloucestershire
    Haresfield (168b)   *v figuli reddunt xliiii d* (*poters* interlined above *figuli*).
Oxfordshire
    Bladon (156)   *de ollaria x s* (*potaria* interlined above *ollaria*).
Wiltshire
    Westbury (65)   *Ibi potarii reddunt xx s per annum.*

So, too, the potteries and potters entered for Bladon (Oxon., 156), Haresfield (Gloucs., 168b) and Westbury (Wilts., 65) must stand for a large number in the country as a whole.

[1] E. M. Jope, 'The Saxon building-stone industry in southern and midland England', *Medieval Archaeology*, VIII (1964), 92.

Stray hints of other occupations come in the description of Bury St Edmunds (372) in Suffolk with its bakers, tailors, shoemakers, robe-makers and others; among these were *cervisarii*, the only other Domesday use of the word being the reference to the forty at Helston (*100b*, 120) in Cornwall; it has been translated either as ale-brewers or as those who paid their dues in ale. A baker (*pistor*) and a bakery (*furnus*) are entered for Cheverton (52b) in the Isle of Wight. In Hereford (179) in 1066 a due of 10*d* had been paid by everyone whose wife brewed ale (*braziabat*) 'within or without the city'. At Chester (262b) anyone who brewed inferior beer (*mala cervisia*) was either put in the cucking-stool or had to pay 4*s* to the reeves. Then there are the occupational designations attached to the names of land-holders such as Erchenger the baker (202b) and 'two of the king's carpenters' (202) in Cambridgeshire. The recorded population in entry after entry includes very few non-agricultural workers apart from the small number of fishermen, millers, potters, salt-workers and smiths. Why, for example, should we be suddenly told of a carpenter at Fown-hope (187) in Herefordshire? There must have been many others else-where, concealed apparently among other categories of population. The record of all these craftsmen is meagre, even for an unindustrialised society like that of eleventh-century England.

CHAPTER X

BOROUGHS AND TOWNS

Whatever the difficulties of interpretation, the Domesday information for rural England is systematically presented and is remarkable for the detail it provides. When we turn from the countryside to the towns all is different. No instructions about towns appear in the preamble to the Ely Inquest, and the information presented to us is as unsystematic as it is incomplete. It is usually impossible to form any clear idea of the size of a town or of the economic and other activities that sustained it.

The Anglo-Saxon word 'burh' or borough signified a fortified centre, and the fact that it later came to mean town does not justify the conclusion that all burh-building resulted in the creation of urban settlements. There has been much debate about whether defence or trade provided the impetus to urban development, but surely both were important. The security of fortified centres encouraged trading activity, while, in turn, trading centres needed to be fortified for protection. Some sites were favourable for trade, and here burhs, or maybe villages, developed into flourishing towns – at bridgeheads on rivers, at the confluences of tributaries, at the crossing-places of route-ways, or near convenient gaps in hill country. Long before the Norman Conquest, a force had begun to operate which was to give to the English town its essential character – that of a trading centre. As well as the fort or castle, the market came to be important, and also the mint to provide a trustworthy coinage for the purposes of trade.

THE VARIETY OF INFORMATION

The number of places that seem to have been regarded as boroughs in 1086 was 112 (Fig. 102). They were described by different terms – *civitas*, *burgus*, *villa* – but we must not attach too much importance to these differences. The entries for Stafford use all three (246, 247b) and Lydford in Devonshire is styled *burgus* in the Exchequer folios (100) but both *burgus* and *civitas* in the Exeter version (*87b*). Moreover, many a small village is styled *villa*. It is true that *civitas* usually designates one of the larger towns, but not always. Norwich (116), greater than most towns, is merely a *burgus*, and Ipswich (290, 290b) a *burgus* or a *villa*. Some places with burgesses are not specifically designated as boroughs but are merely entered under their manors. Unusual terms are *burbium* for Berkhamsted (Herts., 136b), *suburbium* for Hertford (132) and Torksey (337), and *portus* for Chester (262b) and Dover (1).

The total of 112 is a somewhat arbitrary one, and it may come as a surprise that different lists of Domesday boroughs are not identical. Thus for Somerset, Round and Eyton agreed in naming eight boroughs – Axbridge, Bath, Bruton, Frome, Ilchester, Langport, Milborne Port and Taunton.[1] Ballard, on the other hand, omitted Frome from his list.[2] It is true that Frome is not called a borough, nor are burgesses recorded for it, but the payment of the 'third penny' suggests burghal status, and Tait included it. Tait also included Milverton which likewise paid the 'third penny' and which, moreover, was styled a borough in the entry for Oake in the Exeter version (*433*); but, as he said, both Frome and Milverton 'had practically ceased to be boroughs by the date of Domesday, though Milverton retained some burghal features'.[3] Claims to burghal status in 1086 have also been put forward for two other places in Somerset – Watchet and Yeovil – but these have not been included in the total of 112.[4]

Similar doubts arise over other places. Thus Ballard did not regard Windsor (56b), in Berkshire, as a borough because its Domesday entry does not call it one;[5] but it had 95 *hagae*, and Round described it as 'a typical example of a town dependent upon a great castle'.[6] The burghal status of other places in Berkshire and elsewhere has also been debated.[7] Looking backwards towards the tenth century, it is clear that burghal status was far from constant, especially in the south-west, that 'land of petty boroughs'.[8] The potentialities of the Anglo-Danish boroughs varied. Not all survived as such by 1086, and not all Domesday boroughs retained their status into the twelfth century. Conversely, in each century new boroughs emerged.[9] It is not surprising that the cross-section that is

---

[1] J. H. Round in *V.C.H. Somerset*, I (1906), 420–1; R. W. Eyton, *Domesday Studies: an analysis and digest of the Somerset Survey*, II (London, 1880), 3.
[2] A. Ballard, *The Domesday boroughs* (Oxford, 1904), 9.
[3] J. Tait, *The medieval English borough* (Manchester, 1936), 55.
[4] *D.G.S.–W.E.*, 196–9.   [5] A. Ballard (1904), 10.
[6] J. H. Round in *V.C.H. Berkshire*, I (1906), 13.
[7] *D.G.S–E.E.*, 273–4; F. W. Maitland, *Domesday Book and beyond* (Cambridge, 1897), 181.   [8] J. Tait, 55.
[9] C. Stephenson, *Borough and town* (Cambridge, Mass., 1933), 74–5; J. Tait, 18.

Domesday Book presents us with doubts about the status of a number of places.

While the entries for rural settlements follow a fairly regular pattern, those for boroughs vary in their positions in the county texts, in the amounts of information they provide, and in the way in which it is presented. For the greater part of England north of the Thames, the descriptions of the 'county boroughs' appear at the beginning, even before the lists of tenants-in-chief, e.g. Leicester before Leicestershire and Warwick before Warwickshire. To this generalisation there are four exceptions. The Lincolnshire text begins with an account not only of Lincoln but of Stamford and Torksey (336–337). The Gloucestershire text similarly begins not only with Gloucester but also with a brief statement about Winchcomb, once the capital of its own shire (162–162b).[1] The Derbyshire text is preceded by a blank folio (271), and the description of its borough comes at the end on the same folio as that of Nottingham (280) which comes before the list of tenants-in-chief of Nottinghamshire. Fourthly, the text for Middlesex is preceded by a blank folio (126), presumably intended for an account of London which was never inserted.

The folios for the counties south of the Thames, on the other hand, show no attempt at consistency. The Wiltshire text opens with an account of Malmesbury (64b); that for Devonshire with an account of Exeter (100); that for Dorset with very brief accounts of Dorchester, Bridport, Wareham and Shaftesbury (75); that for Kent (1 and 2) with long accounts of Dover and Canterbury and a very brief reference to Rochester, but here, too, come entries for some rural holdings of the church of St Martin of Dover. The surveys of Berkshire and Surrey are different in that the accounts of Wallingford (56) and Guildford (30) do not precede but follow the lists of tenants-in-chief. The text for Sussex is preceded by a blank folio (15) possibly meant for Hastings which is mentioned only incidentally among the rural entries. The Hampshire text is likewise preceded by a blank folio (37) which may have been meant for Winchester, also mentioned only incidentally in the body of the text; Southampton (52) comes after the survey of mainland Hampshire and before the second instalment of the account of the Isle of Wight. The surveys of Somerset and Cornwall are preceded by blank folios (85b, 119) and their boroughs are described in the body of the text. Finally, the treatment of the boroughs of Little Domesday Book also shows no consistency. The long account of

---

[1] H. P. R. Finberg, *Gloucestershire studies* (Leicester, 1957), 49–51.

Colchester (104–107b) comes at the end of the Essex text, and Norwich and Ipswich are described after the royal estates of Norfolk (116–118) and of Suffolk (290) respectively.

The reasons for these variations may lie in the differing histories of the various parts of England, or in the administrative status of different boroughs in relation to their counties, or, maybe, in the circumstances of the compilation of Domesday text, or in other circumstances unknown to us.[1] The compilers of the circuit Domesday Books may well have been perplexed about how to describe their towns and boroughs.

The 'county boroughs', described either at the beginning or elsewhere in the county texts, form only a fraction of the total of 112. Many other boroughs are described in connection with rural manors. Thus the entry for the large manor of Steyning (Sx., 17) includes a statement about what was *in burgo*, i.e. 123 *mansurae*; that for the large manor of Taunton (Som., *173b*, 87b) refers to 64 burgesses; that for Okehampton (Devon, *288*, 105b) mentions only 4 burgesses; that for Berkhamsted (Herts., 136b) tells of 52 burgesses in the *burbium* of the vill; and that for Bedwyn (Wilts., 64b) says that 25 burgesses belonged to the manor (*Huic manerio pertinent xxv burgenses*).

Boroughs did not necessarily bear the same names as the manors on which they grew up. The borough of Langport (Som., *89b*, 86) was in the manor of Somerton (*Ibi Burgus quod vocatur Lanporth*); and, in the same county, that of Axbridge (*170*, 86) was in the manor of Cheddar. The borough of Hythe (Kent, 4b) was in the manor of Saltwood, and borough and manor were valued together (*Inter burgum et manerium*); Quatford (Salop., 254) was part of Eardington; and in the manor of *Rameslie* (Sx., 17) there was 'a new borough' which was to grow into Rye. Windsor Castle was built on half a hide of the manor of Clewer (Berks., 62b). Other boroughs are also mentioned in connection with castles. At Tutbury (Staffs., 248b) there was a borough around the castle (*circa castellum*); and at three places in Herefordshire we may discern something similar: 2 *mansurae* at Ewias Harold (185) *in castello*; 16 burgesses at Clifford (183) *in hac castellaria*; and the borough at the recently built castle of Wigmore on the waste land which was called *Merestun* (183b). There was also 'a new borough', with 18 burgesses, at the recently built castle of Rhuddlan (269). The entry for Rhuddlan is of especial interest for its burgesses were granted the same laws and customs as those of Hereford and

[1] F. W. Maitland (1897), 178; *Domesday rebound* (H.M.S.O., London, 1954), 28.

Breteuil.[1] Some boroughs are barely mentioned; thus Seasalter (Kent, 5) is described merely as 'a small borough' which belonged to the archbishop's kitchen;[2] all we hear of Cricklade, in Wiltshire, is that it had burgesses;[3] and Romney in Kent, and Tamworth in Staffordshire, are named only in connection with their 'contributory burgesses' belonging to other manors.[4] For yet other boroughs (e.g. Marlborough and Salisbury) we are told even less, and can infer their borough status only from the payment of the 'third penny'.[5]

Some boroughs certainly had a strong agricultural flavour. Arable, meadow or pasture are entered for many of them, and also such categories of population as villeins and bordars. Thus Cambridge (189) was a fairly substantial town in the context of the time, yet its burgesses in 1066 'used to lend their ploughs to the sheriff three times a year', and in 1086 he was demanding that this be increased to nine times. At Huntingdon (203) the burgesses cultivated (*colunt*) land; at Shrewsbury (253), two burgesses worked on the land (*in hac terra laborantes*); at Tamworth (Staffs., 246b) eight burgesses worked like the other villeins (*ibi operantur sicut alii villani*); and at Steyning (Sx., 17) the burgesses seem to have worked in a similar fashion in 1066. At Totnes (Devon, *334*, 108b) there were burgesses who worked on land outside the borough (*extra burgum terram laborantes*). At York there was also land tilled by the burgesses (298).

In envisaging the towns of the eleventh century, we must not forget the walls or ramparts of many of them. We hear of *mansurae* within the wall (*intra murum*) at Stafford (246), of houses below (*infra*) the walls at Colchester (106), and of the repair of walls at Chester (262b) and at Oxford (154). That the built-up area had expanded, in some towns at any rate, we may suppose from references to houses outside the wall (*extra murum*) at Colchester (107), Hereford (179), Leicester (230b), Oxford (158) and outside the city (*extra civitatem*) at Canterbury (2), and Lincoln (336); there is also a reference to 4 *suburbani* at Winchester (39). There is mention of a gate (*porta*) at Hereford, and the entry for the Essex manor of Waltham Holy Cross (15b) refers to one at London. With these may be grouped the references to the ditches of the town (*fossatum civitatis/ burgi/urbis*) at Canterbury (2), Nottingham (280) and York (298). At

[1] M. Bateson, 'The laws of Breteuil', *Eng. Hist. Rev.*, xv (1900), 73–8, 302–7.
[2] *D.G.S–E.E.*, 554; J. Tait, 67.   [3] *D.G.S–W.E.*, 55–6.
[4] *D.G.S–E.E.*, 553; *D.G.M.E.*, 208–9. See p. 309 below.
[5] *D.G.S–W.E.*, 55, 57.

Norwich (117) there was a man named *Hereberd fossator*; but the certain ditcher (*quidam fossarius*) at Berkhamsted (Herts., 136b) was employed, we may suppose, in connection with the defence of the castle.

Entries for some of the larger towns record administrative divisions. Cambridge (189) was said to comprise ten wards (*custodiae*); Stamford (336b) had six wards, five in Lincolnshire and the sixth 'across the bridge' in Northamptonshire; Huntingdon (203) had four quarters (*ferlingi*); York had seven divisions (*scyrae*). We obtain hints of internal government from the references to *judices* at Chester (262b) and York (298), and to lawmen (*lagemanni*) at Cambridge (189), Lincoln (336) and Stamford (336b). Other information about boroughs is extremely diverse and ranges from laconic references up to long and involved statements about services, customs, fines and other legal matters. Lengthy statements are mostly to be found in the descriptions of 'county boroughs', e.g. Chester (262b), Hereford (181b), Lincoln (336) and Oxford (154); but, on the other hand, the account of Bedford (209) is very brief. The information about the number of inhabitants and the amount of their property is likewise varied, unsystematic and clearly incomplete. For some boroughs, such as Colchester (104–107b), there are long and detailed lists of groups of individuals and their properties. For others, such as Derby (280), we are merely given bare totals.

The various terms for properties are *mansurae, mansiones, hagae* and *domus*. These have been described as 'practically synonymous'[1] but this may not be so. At Nottingham (280) there were *iii mansiones in quibus sedent xi domus*; and at Chichester (Sx., 23) where *mansurae* and *hagae* seem to be equated, we are told that on 97½ of them there were 60 more houses (*domus*) than there had been. The relation of properties to inhabitants raises further problems, for in the entry for Guildford (Sy., 30) we hear of 75 *hagae* on which 175 men (*homines*) lived. At Shaftesbury (Do., 75) 151 burgesses seem to have lived in 111 houses;[2] but the burgesses are not mentioned in the Exeter text (11). On the other hand, the 5 *hagae* entered under Brightwalton (59b) appear as 5 *mansurae* in the account of Wallingford (Berks., 56); a burgess entered under Risborough (Bucks., 143b) appears as a *mansio* in the account of Oxford (154);[3] and at Warwick (238) 19 burgesses had 19 *mansurae*.

Even if we could safely add up, for each borough, all the various pro-

[1] A. Ballard (1904), 13.   [2] *D.G.S–W.E.*, 121.
[3] *D.G.S–E.E.*, 276, 230.

perties (or all the properties and inhabitants together), the resulting totals could be used only with caution. For some boroughs we are given what are obviously incomplete figures, e.g. for Winchcomb (Gloucs., 162b) and Hereford (179) or no figures at all as for Bedford (209). Furthermore, the entries for some boroughs give two or more sets of figures, and it is not always clear whether one set is included in another, e.g. for Buckingham (143), Malmesbury (Wilts., 64b) and York (298), or whether properties said to exist in 1066 were additional to those entered for 1086, e.g. at Norwich (116–118). Then again, when a borough is entered for a manor, it is impossible to say how the non-burgess population should be divided between manor and borough, e.g. at Bedwyn (64b) and Calne (64b) in Wiltshire. The evidence is assembled in Appendix 16 (pp. 364–8). Unsatisfactory though this evidence is, it does show that many Domesday settlements were being sustained by something more than local agriculture. It also provides information about the fortunes of some boroughs – how houses had been destroyed for one reason or another, and how, on the other hand, new forces were at work to hasten the transference of boroughs into towns and trading centres. Furthermore, it may enable us to form some idea of what were the largest and most important towns in the realm. But we must recognise that our estimates of size based upon such imperfect statistics will probably always be too low.

CHANGES: 1066–86

Destruction in the boroughs

The immediate effect of the Norman Conquest on some boroughs was the destruction of houses to make room for the building of castles. One of the seven wards of York (298) had been wasted for this purpose. At Lincoln (336b), 166 *mansiones* had been destroyed; at Norwich (116b), 98 *mansurae*; at Shrewsbury (252), 51 *mansurae*; and there had been similar destruction on a smaller scale at Cambridge (189), Canterbury (2), Gloucester (162), Huntingdon (203), Stamford (Lincs., 336b), Wallingford (Berks., 56) and Warwick (238). The castles at Rhuddlan (269) in North Wales and at Clifford (183) and Wigmore (183b) in Herefordshire were also built on wasted land (*wasta terra*). These were not the only Domesday boroughs with castles; there were others which bring the total up to 27.[1]

[1] D. F. Renn, *Norman castles in Britain* (London, 2nd edn, 1973), 109, 185, 272.

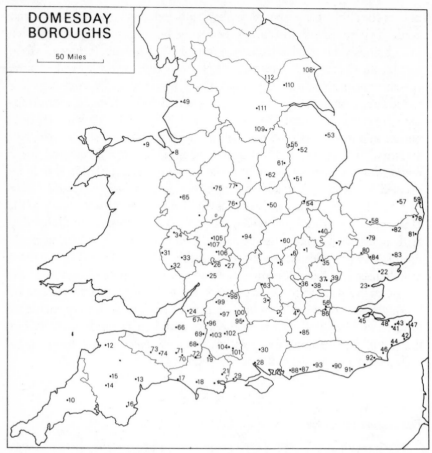

Fig. 102. Domesday boroughs.

The names of the boroughs are given opposite.

We hear also of other wasted houses and properties, but only occasionally are the reasons given. At Canterbury (3b) 27 *mansurae* had been destroyed to make room for the new residence of the archbishop. At Lincoln (336b) apart from the 166 *mansiones* wasted on account of the castle, there were another 74 wasted 'because of misfortune, poverty and the ravage of fires' (*propter infortunium et paupertatem et ignium exustionem*). At Norwich (116–118) there were not only 98 *mansurae* wasted for the castle but another 199 empty for other reasons; twenty-two burgesses had gone to live in Beccles, and another 10 had left for other places. Both those

DOMESDAY BOROUGHS

(Key to Fig. 102)

Bedfordshire
  1 Bedford
Berkshire
  2 Reading
  3 Wallingford
  4 Windsor
Buckinghamshire
  5 Buckingham
  6 Newport Pagnell
Cambridgeshire
  7 Cambridge
Cheshire
  8 Chester
  9 Rhuddlan
Cornwall
  10 Bodmin
Derbyshire
  11 Derby
Devonshire
  12 Barnstaple
  13 Exeter
  14 Lydford
  15 Okehampton
  16 Totnes
Dorset
  17 Bridport
  18 Dorchester
  19 Shaftesbury
  20 Wareham
  21 Wimborne Minster
Essex
  22 Colchester
  23 Maldon
Gloucestershire
  24 Bristol
  25 Gloucester
  26 Tewkesbury
  27 Winchcomb
Hampshire
  28 Southampton
  29 Twynham
  30 Winchester
Herefordshire
  31 Clifford
  32 Ewias Harold
  33 Hereford
  34 Wigmore
Hertfordshire
  35 Ashwell

36 Berkhamsted
37 Hertford
38 St Albans
39 Stanstead Abbots
Huntingdonshire
  40 Huntingdon
Kent
  41 Canterbury
  42 Dover
  43 Fordwich
  44 Hythe
  45 Rochester
  46 Romney
  47 Sandwich
  48 Seasalter
Lancashire
  49 Penwortham
Leicestershire
  50 Leicester
Lincolnshire
  51 Grantham
  52 Lincoln
  53 Louth
  54 Stamford
  55 Torksey
Middlesex
  56 London
Norfolk
  57 Norwich
  58 Thetford
  59 Yarmouth
Northamptonshire
  60 Northampton
Nottinghamshire
  61 Newark
  62 Nottingham
Oxfordshire
  63 Oxford
Shropshire
  64 Quatford
  65 Shrewsbury
Somerset
  66 Axbridge
  67 Bath
  68 Bruton
  69 Frome
  70 Ilchester
  71 Langport
  72 Milborne Port

  73 Milverton
  74 Taunton
Staffordshire
  75 Stafford
  76 Tamworth
  77 Tutbury
Suffolk
  78 Beccles
  79 Bury St Edmunds
  80 Clare
  81 Dunwich
  82 Eye
  83 Ipswich
  84 Sudbury
Surrey
  85 Guildford
  86 Southwark
Sussex
  87 Arundel
  88 Chichester
  89 Hastings
  90 Lewes
  91 Pevensey
  92 Rye
  93 Steyning
Warwickshire
  94 Warwick
Wiltshire
  95 Bedwyn
  96 Bradford on Avon
  97 Calne
  98 Cricklade
  99 Malmesbury
  100 Marlborough
  101 Salisbury
  102 Tilshead
  103 Warminster
  104 Wilton
Worcestershire
  105 Droitwich
  106 Pershore
  107 Worcester
Yorkshire
  108 Bridlington
  109 Dadsley
  110 Pocklington
  111 Tanshelf
  112 York

that fled and those that remained had been ruined (*vastati*) partly on account of forfeitures after Earl Ralf's rebellion, partly through fire, partly owing to the king's geld and partly because of the oppression of Waleran the sheriff. At Exeter, 2 houses (*domus*) had been destroyed by fire (*120b*, 101b) and another 48 had been laid waste (*88*, 100) presumably to make room for the castle which William built after the rebellion of 1068, although Domesday Book says nothing of its existence. Oxford (154) had also suffered grievously. As many as 478 houses (*domus*) had been destroyed (*vastae et destructae*) and there were also other waste properties in the city; some of this wasting may have been the result of the building of the castle in 1071, which, again, Domesday Book does not mention. There had also been substantial damage in the four Dorset boroughs of Bridport, Dorchester, Shaftesbury and Wareham (75); a total of as many as 350 out of some 800 or so houses (*domus*) had lain waste since the time of Hugh fitz Grip, the sheriff, but we are not told why. Nor is any reason given for the heavy damage at Ipswich (290) where at least 328 *mansiones* out of a total of about 540 had been wasted. Indications of waste also appear for other boroughs. Altogether, waste due to one cause or another was entered for as many as 33 of the 112 Domesday boroughs.

Commerce in the boroughs

Alongside these set-backs there were long-term tendencies of a different kind at work. Some people have believed that the pre-Domesday borough had little or no really urban character, and that the origin of commercial towns (as distinct from fortified boroughs) was essentially a development of the years after 1066.[1] Others have challenged this view which, they have said, under-estimates the amount of trade and urban growth before 1066; they point to the development of the Anglo-Saxon coinage and to various hints of internal and foreign trade, and they have concluded that there was no new urban concentration in the years immediately after the Conquest.[2] While this may be true in a general sense, the fact remains that there are many indications of commercial activity within the Domesday boroughs, some of it certainly new. The urban trend of the later Anglo-Scandinavian period continued to develop and perhaps even to accelerate.

One indication is the establishment of new boroughs alongside the old at Norwich (118), Northampton (219) and Nottingham (280); that at

[1] C. Stephenson, 70–1.   [2] J. Tait, 130–8.

Norwich included 124 French burgesses. A new borough (*novus burgus*) had also been established at Rye in the manor of *Rameslie* (17) in Sussex. Groups of Frenchmen or French burgesses had also settled at Cambridge (189), Dunwich (311b), Hereford (179), London (127b), St. Albans, Shrewsbury (252), Southampton (52), Stanstead Abbots (Herts., 138b), Wallingford (Berks., 56) and York (298). Rather different in character was the growth of Bury St. Edmunds (Suff., 372) around its monastery, with the built-up area extending over what had been arable in 1066.

There are also references to trading activities at a number of places. In the borough around the castle at Tutbury (Staffs., 248b) there were 42 men who devoted themselves wholly to trade (*In Burgo circa castellum sunt xlii homines de mercato suo tantum viventes et reddunt cum foro iv libras et x solidos*). At Eye (Suff., 319b), 25 burgesses lived around the market place which had not existed in 1066 (*modo i mercatum . . . et in mercato manent xxv burgesses*). Then, again, there were 25 houses rendering 100s a year around the market place (*in foro*) of Worcester (173b). We also hear of merchants' houses (*domus mercatorum*) at Nottingham (280), and of stalls in the provision market (*banci in macello*) at York (298). Of the markets mentioned in Domesday Book, only 17 are entered for boroughs, an example of the incompleteness of the record.

Hints of external trade are not many. It is true that the description of Chester (262b) refers to the coming and going of ships, and to trade in marten pelts which, we know from other sources, came from Ireland.[1] But there is no reference to the trade of Bristol or Gloucester or Exeter, although it seems, again from other sources, that Bristol was exporting slaves to Ireland in the eleventh century,[2] and that there were foreign merchants in Exeter in 1068.[3] In the south-east, London must have been the scene of varied activities, but nothing is said about traffic along its river, apart from that to Southwark (23) on the south bank. Foreigners (*extranei mercatores*) were frequenting Canterbury (2) in 1066, but no reference is made to their presence in 1086. A variety of miscellaneous hints, however, point to considerable activity in the south-east, as may be seen if we follow the ports around the coast. The annual value of Rochester (2) had increased four times. At Sandwich (3) the number of *mansurae*

[1] J. H. Round, *Feudal England* (London, 1895), 465–7.
[2] W. Cunningham, *The growth of English industry and commerce during the early and middle ages* (Cambridge, 5th edn, 1910), 86.
[3] J. Tait, 118.

had increased by a quarter, and it was also liable to the same service at sea as Dover. In 1066 the burgesses of Dover (1) had supplied King Edward with 20 ships, each with 21 men for 15 days every year; and the Excerpta adds *ad custodiendum mare*.[1] Whenever the king's messengers came, they paid 3*d* for the passage of a horse in winter and 2*d* in summer, the burgesses supplying a helmsman and one assistant (*stiremmanus et unus alius adjutor*); presumably this was the charge for crossing the Channel. Soon after the arrival of King William, the town had been burnt, but it had obviously recovered and prospered. We hear of its *gilhalla burgensium* and of its port and shipping and of an increase from £8 to £22 from toll in 1086. The annual value of Hythe (4b) had also greatly increased, and at Rye (17) there was a new borough. At Pevensey (206) the number of burgesses had doubled and the proceeds from tolls had increased four times. The annual value of Lewes (26) had increased by a third, and we are told of its trade in horses, oxen and slaves. That of Steyning (17) had increased by a quarter. That of Arundel (23), if we read aright, had greatly increased, and we hear of its port and shipping dues and of tolls from foreigners (*de hominibus extraneis*). That of Chichester (23) had doubled, and it had far more houses than in 1066. Further west, Southampton (52) had acquired a French colony 'after King William came to England', but there is no detail about its activities. We can only conclude that increased traffic with Normandy had brought prosperity with it. To these fragments of information we must add the references to hithes or harbours (*hedae id est portus*) at four places in Kent along the Thames estuary – Dartford (2b), Gravesend (7b), Milton near Gravesend (7b) and Swanscombe (6).

To what extent this quickening of activity was felt elsewhere along the coast, we cannot say. There is a reference to a seaport (*i portus maris*) at Frostenden (414b) some three miles to the north-west of Southwold in Suffolk, but nothing that throws light on its activities.[2] There is also a strange reference to 'one port' at Holt (111b) in Norfolk; the text here may be corrupt, but it should be noted that Holt had berewicks at Cley and Blakeney. We are told nothing of the maritime activity of Dunwich (311b) beyond a reference to its herrings, and nothing of Yarmouth beyond a reference to its fishermen (283). Lynn was not a borough in 1086

---

[1] A. Ballard (ed.), *An eleventh-century inquisition of St Augustine's Canterbury* (British Academy, London, 1920), 24.

[2] C. Morley and E. R. Cooper, 'The sea port of Frostenden', *Proc. Suffolk Inst. Archaeol. and Nat. Hist.*, XVIII (Ipswich, 1924), 167–79.

and there was no mention at all of Boston; but, further north, there is a reference to disputes about new tolls on ships at three small places along the Lincolnshire coast – at Saltfleet, Mere Haven and Swine (375b); this entry refers to dues in respect of 24 ships from Hastings which does a little to compensate for the absence in the Sussex folios of any information about the maritime life of this port. There were also tolls that, apparently, had not existed in 1066 at Barton upon Humber (375b), Grimsby (376) and South Ferriby (375b). We also hear of ferries at these places and at Winteringham (343, 354, 354b *ter*, 363); all four seem to have been crossing-places on the Humber (Fig. 103). But of coastal traffic around the shores of England in general, Domesday Book is silent.

There are, however, a few indications of navigation along the inland waters of the realm. One indication comes in the description of Wallingford (56) on the Thames. In 1066 its burgesses did service for the king with horses or by water (*cum equis vel per aquam*) upstream to Benson and Sutton Courtenay, downstream to Reading, and overland to Blewbury. There is more detail about navigation along some northern rivers. The Witham and the Trent are connected by Foss Dyke, an artificial channel, some seven miles long, constructed by the Romans. It leaves Witham near Lincoln and joins the Trent at Torksey, so providing a connection by water between the Wash, Lincoln and York (Fig. 103). In 1066, the burgesses of Torksey (337) had the duty of conducting the king's messengers to York with their ships and other aids (*cum navibus et aliis instrumentis navigationes*). By 1086, the 213 burgesses had declined to 102. Domesday Book offers no explanation but it may be that the decline was due to some obstruction in Foss Dyke; at any rate we hear of its being cleared in 1121.[1] Other evidence of movement along the Trent occurs in the account of Nottingham (280): 'the water of the Trent, and the Foss (*fossa*) and road towards York are so regulated (*custodiuntur*) that if anyone impedes the passage of boats or if anyone ploughs or makes a ditch within two perches of the king's road, he has to pay a fine of £8'. Downstream from Nottingham there was a toll and a boat (*theloneum et navis*) rendering 30s 8d at Gunthorpe (285b). Farther downstream still there was a ferry (*passagium*) also yielding money at Fiskerton (288) and at Southwell (283); the latter is on the Greet, a minor tributary of the Trent, but as the entry also covers twelve unnamed berewicks, the ferry may well have been on the

[1] F. M. Stenton in C. W. Foster and T. Longley, *The Lincolnshire Domesday and the Lindsey Survey* (Lincoln Record Society, 1924), xxv.

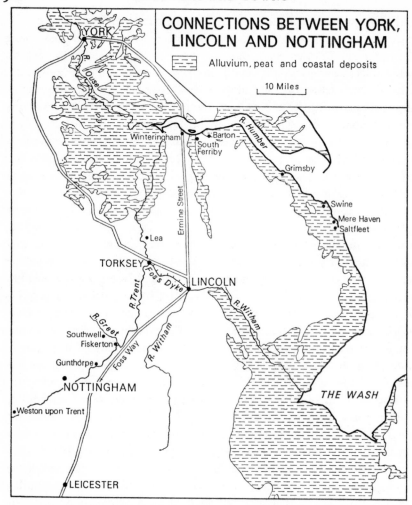

Fig. 103. Connections between York, Lincoln and Nottingham in 1086.

Trent itself. Then again, below Torksey there was a ferry at Lea (347).
Upstream from Nottingham, at Weston upon Trent (Derby, 273), there
was another ferry, described as *passagium aquae*.

BOROUGHS IN ORDER OF SIZE

By far the largest borough must have been London. It is therefore particularly unfortunate that Domesday Book contains no account of it. The

126th folio, where this should have come, is blank, and there are only a few incidental references to London elsewhere in the Book.[1] It had been a Roman city, and after the confusion of the Anglo-Saxon invasions was over, its advantages of site and location reasserted themselves. By the eighth century it had become, in the words of Bede, 'the market place of many peoples coming by land and sea', and, for the eleventh century, there is evidence of its wide trading connections with the continent.[2] It is true that the idea of a capital city had not yet become current in western Europe, and that the centre of government moved about with the court of the king. But London already had a distinct place among the boroughs of England, a place emphasised by its role as a centre of resistance against Danish invasion in the early years of the eleventh century.[3] A guess might place the number of its inhabitants at over 10,000, but any attempt to estimate how much over becomes even more hazardous. Fire was always a danger here as in other cities. The Anglo-Saxon Chronicle, under the year 1077, records an extensive fire in London, greater than any 'since the town was built'; and ten years later there was another fire which destroyed 'the greatest and fairest parts of the whole city'. We must picture it as lying almost entirely within its Roman walls. Not far away was the *villa* of Westminster where stood the church of St Peter founded by Edward the Confessor. Fig. 104 gives some idea of what has been covered by the changes of later times.

There are likewise only incidental Domesday references to Winchester, the city to which the results of the Inquest were brought and in which the Domesday Book was at first kept. There are, however, two early surveys of the city, dating from c. 1110 and 1148, which tell us a little about it. We hear, among other things, of a merchants' guildhall, of a market and shops and stalls, of a hospital, of mints, of forges, of a prison, and of shanties (*bordelli*) erected outside the walls. Its maximum population at this time has been estimated at between 5,500 and 8,000, but this seems large.[4] Of the other boroughs, we can only conjecture from the unsatisfactory Domesday evidence that the following had at least 4,000, and maybe over 5,000, inhabitants each in 1086: York, Lincoln, Norwich and possibly Thetford. To this group Oxford had belonged in 1066, but twenty years later it appears to have been in a very reduced position.

---

[1] *D.G.S–E.E.*, 131–4.   [2] J. Tait, 118.

[3] F. M. Stenton, *Anglo-Saxon England* (Oxford, 1943), 531–3; J. Tait, 118.

[4] M. Biddle (ed.), *Winchester in the early middle ages* (Oxford, 1976.)

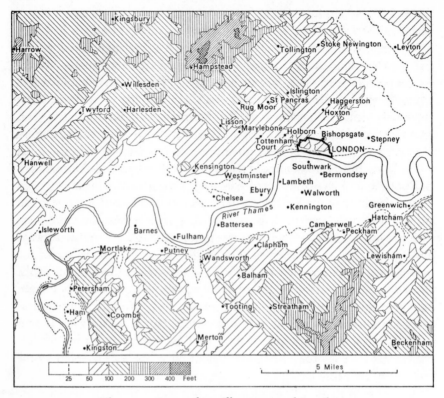

Fig. 104. Domesday villages around London.

The boundary of London follows the Roman Wall and the north bank of the Thames.

York (298) had been a great Danish centre, and, set on a tidal waterway, it had benefited from trade across the North Sea; there is record of merchants frequenting the city around the year 1000.[1] In 1066 it had perhaps 8,000 or more inhabitants, but the houses in one of its seven wards were destroyed to make room for two castles, and there were also 940 other wasted or empty houses. By 1086, its population may well have been not more than 5,000. Yet it was the seat of an archbishopric, and we hear of eight churches, of a provision market (*macellum*) and of what seems to have been a French colony occupying 145 *mansiones*. There is, on the other hand, no Domesday reference to the mint which we know was there. Although we cannot be clear about the scope of its administrative, eccle-

[1] J. Tait, 118.

siastical, military and commercial activities, the city, in spite of its set-back, was easily the most important regional centre in northern England.

Lincoln (336–336b) had been one of the Five Boroughs of the Dane-law. In 1066 its population was probably about 6,000, but, like York, it suffered in the years following the Conquest. Some of its *mansiones* had been destroyed to make room for the castle; other dwellings were waste 'because of misfortune, poverty and the ravages of fires'. Altogether, about one fifth of its houses had been wasted, and by 1086 the population of the city may have been reduced to about four to five thousand. On the other hand, its mint yielded as much as £75 annually, it had at least five churches, and to it had been transferred the seat of a large bishopric from Dorchester in Oxfordshire. The city, moreover, was beginning to expand beyond its limits. Thirty-six houses and two churches had recently been built outside the city limits (*extra civitatem*), presumably to the south of the Witham.

Norwich (116–118) seems to have been a city of some six to seven thousand people in 1066, but the description is very involved. In one place we are told that the burgesses used to hold (*tenebant*) 15 churches, and in another place that they were then holding (*tenent*) 43 chapels. There is also reference to the houses which King William had given 'for the principal seat of the bishopric', but the see itself was not translated here from Thetford until 1094. A hint of the amenities of the time is given by the reference to 'one bear and six dogs for bear (baiting)'. From such unsatisfactory fragments as these, two facts stand out.

In the first place, the town had fallen upon evil days. We hear of a total of 297 empty messages (*mansurae vacuae*) and of 50 houses (*domus*) which paid no dues. Some of these empty dwellings were *in occupatione castelli*. Twenty-two burgesses had gone to live in Beccles, and another ten had also left (*dimiserunt*) the borough. 'Those fleeing and the others remaining have been entirely ruined (*vastati*) partly by reason of the forfeitures of [the lands] of Earl Ralf; partly by reason of fire, partly by reason of the king's geld and partly by Waleran the sheriff.' In the second place, the Normans had added a new borough (*novus burgus*) to the old, and by 1086 this included 124 French burgesses, 36 other burgesses, 6 Englishmen and a waste *mansura*. In spite of its misfortunes, Norwich, with its bishop, its castle and its French colony, must have been a substantial centre in 1086 with probably nearer 5,000 than 4,000 inhabitants, and possibly more than 5,000.

Thetford (118b–119) stands at the junction of the Thet and the Little Ouse, and where the Icknield Way crosses them. It does not seem to have emerged into prominence until the late ninth century; the Danish army wintered there in 869–70, and the place played an important part in Danish strategy. It had become moreover a centre for the making of pottery, and archaeological evidence shows its trading connections with the Low Countries and the Rhineland.[1] In 1066 it may have been a town of about 5,000 inhabitants, but by 1086 we hear of 228 *mansurae vacuae*, which may imply a reduction to 4,000 or even under. The seat of the bishop of East Anglia had moved here from North Elmham about 1072, but it was to move to Norwich in 1094. Even so, in 1086 there were at least 13 churches in the town, and it kept its mint which was yielding as much as £40 a year to the king. Yet in spite of its place among the largest half a dozen Domesday towns, it lacked enduring qualities. Its potentialities as an economic centre were slender, and by the middle of the next century it had ceased to be one of the major towns of the realm.

In 1066, Oxford (154) was another city with maybe over 5,000 inhabitants, and it must then have been the largest and most prosperous town in midland England. But by 1086 it had become greatly reduced. Over one half its *mansurae* and *domus* had been wasted and destroyed (*vastae et destructae*). Whether all of them had completely disappeared is another matter, but whatever view we take, Oxford in 1086 seems to have been only one half its former size. The cause is not known. Some dwellings may have disappeared to make room for the castle which was built in 1071, and which Domesday Book does not mention; but this could not have accounted for so great a reduction and there is no record of any catastrophe – siege, fire or epidemic – that might explain the decline. One suggestion is that 'the King and his court no longer resorted there' as in pre-Norman days.[2] Even in its decline, Oxford was still a substantial city, with not less than 5 churches and a mint that yielded £20 a year to the king. We also hear of its suburbs beyond the wall (*extra murum*).

It is difficult to place the remaining Domesday boroughs (that is by far the majority) in any certain order of size. The example of Gloucester (162) illustrates the difficulty. The Domesday record for the city accounts for

[1] G. M. Knocker and R. G. Hughes, 'Anglo-Saxon Thetford', *Archaeol. News Letter*, 2 (1950), 117–22; Part II, ibid., 3 (1950), 41–6; G. C. Dunning, 'The Saxon town of Thetford', *Archaeol. Jour.*, CVI (1951), 72–3; R. R. Clarke, *East Anglia* (London, 1960), 169–72.

[2] H. E. Salter, *Medieval Oxford* (Oxford, 1936), 22.

73 burgesses, 23 *mansiones*, 2 *domus* and another 30 *domus* which had been wasted. The presence of a mint rendering £20 each year serves to warn us that this record might not give a complete picture. The extent of this incompleteness is shown by the fact that the Evesham Abbey Survey, closely related to the Domesday account, enters no less than 528 burgesses, one house and 82 waste houses, from which we can assume that Gloucester may have had not less than 2,500 to 3,000 inhabitants. Winchcomb (162b) provides another example. The brief Domesday entry tells us nothing about its inhabitants, and we hear of 29 burgesses only incidentally in other entries; the Evesham Survey, on the other hand, tells us of as many as 141 burgesses.[1] In view of such difficulties, a ranking list of Domesday boroughs is clearly impossible. But we may perhaps obtain some idea of the order of magnitude involved if we select a number of middle-rank towns, each with detailed entries and with what seem to be over a thousand inhabitants each. After this we can name a number of the smaller boroughs with populations of less than a thousand. But in making this distinction, we must acknowledge the frailty of our evidence.

One distinctive group of middle-rank boroughs is that of the midland 'county towns' which have given their names to the districts or shires around them, and which display what Maitland called 'an exceedingly neat and artificial scheme of political geography'.[2] Those of the Danelaw had come to prominence as centres of the various Danish armies – Derby, Leicester, Nottingham and others. Those of the West Midlands resulted from reorganisation by the Wessex kings and include Shrewsbury and Warwick. A number of these midland towns may have had 2,000 inhabitants or more, e.g. Leicester and Nottingham; and, as we have seen, Oxford, in its reduced condition, had more than this. Chester also had suffered but its population in 1086 cannot have been less than 1,500, and this was true also of Cambridge, Huntingdon and Northampton. If we included Bedford and Buckingham with this group, it would be only on the grounds of analogy, for there is not enough information to allow us even to guess what their size was. As well as these 'county towns', there were other midland centres with maybe as many as 3,000 or so inhabitants each – Stamford where the Great North Road crossed the Welland, and Wallingford in a strategic position in the Thames valley, with connections to north and south in Oxfordshire and Berkshire.

[1] H. B. Clarke, 'Domesday slavery (adjusted for slaves)', *Midland History*, vol. 1, no. 4 (1972), 38. [2] F. W. Maitland (1897), 187.

Towns of a comparable size were to be found elsewhere in England. In East Anglia, apart from Norwich and Thetford, there were a number of important centres. Dunwich, in spite of the threat of the sea, may have had 2,000 people; and Ipswich and Maldon between 1,000 and 2,000 each. In the south-east, Canterbury, an important centre for obvious reasons, had at least 2,500. Along the coast, Sandwich and Lewes had over 2,000 each, and Chichester and Hythe over 1,000. Dover, Southampton and such places as Hastings would surely come within the 1,000–3,000 range, but their details are too fragmentary to permit an estimate. To the west was Exeter with over 2,000 inhabitants, and Bath and Shaftesbury with at least 1,000 apiece.

At the lower end of the scale were small boroughs with populations to be reckoned in hundreds not thousands, boroughs such as Ashwell and Berkhamsted in Hertfordshire, Fordwich in Kent, and Calne and Malmesbury in Wiltshire. A number of the smallest boroughs were on the verge of losing their burghal status in the next century. Such were Bruton and Frome in Somerset, Tilshead in Wiltshire, and Lydford in Devonshire. Other small boroughs seem to have come into being on manors not long before 1086, and we are specifically told of 'the new borough' on the manor of *Rameslie* (17), i.e. Rye. Sometimes the association of growing boroughs with castles or markets is more explicit – with castles at Ewias Harold (185) and Wigmore (183b), and with markets at Eye (319b) and Tewkesbury (163b), and with both at Tutbury (248b) in Staffordshire.

If we hope for a clear idea of what sustained the Domesday boroughs, we shall be disappointed. Some had markets or mints or were ports for overseas trade, but their economic activities never come clearly into focus. Others had castles; others were centres of administration for hundred or county; yet others had cathedrals or monasteries which needed to be maintained. A number seem to have been centres of a sea-fishing industry – Yarmouth (283) in Norfolk, Beccles (370) and Dunwich (312) in Suffolk, Sandwich (3) in Kent. The west midland borough of Droitwich was unusual in being an industrial centre producing salt; on the basis of its Domesday record, it had under a thousand inhabitants, but there may well have been more.[1] There are a few references to such miscellaneous activities as the making of horseshoes at Hereford (179) and brewing at Hereford (179) and Chester (262b), while mills are recorded for 58 of the 112 boroughs. But only for one centre – Bury St Edmunds (372) in

[1] *D.G.M.E.*, 263–5. See p. 368 below.

Suffolk – does something of the bustle of a town show through the Domesday text, and this was a place not specifically termed a borough although we have counted it as one. The town had grown around the monastery of St Edmund 'king and martyr of glorious memory'. It had been a substantial community in 1066, but the next twenty years were to see another 342 houses cover land which had been under the plough. We hear not of its burgesses but of its clergy and of its 'bakers, ale-brewers, tailors, washerwomen, shoemakers, robe-makers, cooks, porters, agents (*dispensatores*)'. It may have been a centre of some 3,000 people. It probably had a market and a mint, although Domesday Book does not mention them.[1] But in spite of the incompleteness of the information, the veil is lifted, for a moment at any rate, to give a glimpse of the growth of a commercial centre in the eleventh century.

URBAN–RURAL CONNECTIONS

One feature of many boroughs was that some of their burgesses and properties were recorded as belonging to magnates who held lands in the districts around. To such burgesses and properties Ballard gave the name 'contributory'.[2] In Warwick (238), for example, the king had 113 properties, and his barons another 112 which were valued with their holdings outside the borough (*Hae mansurae pertinent ad terras quas ibi ipsi barones extra burgum et ibi appreciatae sunt*). Sometimes, as for Barnstaple (*87b*, 100) and Exeter (*88*, 100), in Devonshire, these properties are indicated not in the description of a borough itself but in the accounts of various fiefs, mostly either at the beginning or at the end of the usual rural entries, as if, wrote Ballard, 'the commissioners had noted them down when entering the rural properties, added them up, and then entered them in one total'.[3] But for most boroughs the information is usually specific in that such urban properties are recorded in connection with named rural manors. The record, however, is quite unsystematic in that this detail appears sometimes in the account of the borough itself, or sometimes in the relevant entries for rural manors, or sometimes in both. Here are some examples of this variety:

(1) The account of Northampton (219) says that Suain the son of Azur had 21 houses belonging to Stoke Bruerne (*xxi domus de ii solidis*

---

[1] M. D. Lobel, *The borough of Bury St Edmunds* (Oxford, 1935), 11–15.
[2] A. Ballard (1904), 14.   [3] A. Ballard (1904), 27; *D.G.S–W.E.*, 280–3.

pertinentes ad Stoches), but there is no mention of this fact in the entry for the vill itself (228).[1]

(2) The account of Lewes (26) makes no reference to contributory properties but they appear in 37 entries for 31 villages in Sussex; thus among the statistics for Keymer (27) we read: *In Leuues vi hagae de xxvi denariis.*[2]

(3) The account of Colchester (104–107b) refers to properties belonging to holdings at 8 vills. The body of the Essex text also contains entries for 6 vills which specify the houses connected with them in Colchester. The two lists, incidentally, have the names of two vills in common.[3]

That these arrangements were no Norman innovation is shown by the fact that pre-1066 owners are sometimes named, e.g. at Canterbury and Wallingford.[4]

Much of the information relating to boroughs thus appears not in the accounts of the boroughs themselves but hidden away, so to speak, in entries for various rural manors. There are even boroughs for which such rural entries form the only Domesday evidence, e.g. Wimborne Minster in Dorset, and Milverton in Somerset.[5] Thus although Domesday Book contains no accounts of London and Winchester, we hear of some of their properties in entries for rural manors. Those for London lay in Middlesex, Essex and Surrey; those for Winchester were scattered throughout Hampshire.[6] One further point must be mentioned. It is clear that the Domesday evidence for contributory properties is not complete. This was certainly so at Oxford,[7] and it seems likely to be true of Colchester.[8] There is somewhat similar evidence for Lydford in Devonshire.[9]

This relationship between borough and rural manor has attracted a great deal of discussion. Maitland believed that it was a vestige of earlier arrangements by which the great ones of a shire held properties and men within a borough to maintain its ramparts and secure its place in the national defence.[10] This so-called 'garrison theory' harked back to the fortified burhs of the tenth century. It was wholeheartedly adopted by

---

[1] *D.G.M.E.*, 415. [2] *D.G.S–E.E.*, 466–9. [3] *D.G.E.E.*, 252–3.
[4] *D.G.S–E.E.*, 549, 277; F. M. Stenton (1943), 523–4.
[5] *D.G.S–W.E.*, 122, 204. [6] *D.G.S–E.E.*, 131–2, 353–4.
[7] *D.G.S–E.E.*, 230–1.
[8] J. H. Round in *V.C.H. Essex*, I (1903), 412, 418.
[9] H. P. R. Finberg, *Tavistock Abbey* (Cambridge, 1951), 74.
[10] F. W. Maitland (1897), 178–88.

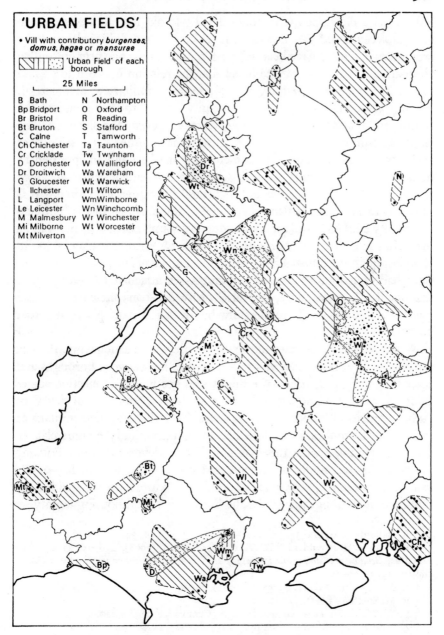

'URBAN FIELDS'

- Vill with contributory *burgenses, domus, hagae* or *mansurae*

'Urban Field' of each borough

25 Miles

B Bath	N Northampton
Bp Bridport	O Oxford
Br Bristol	R Reading
Bt Bruton	S Stafford
C Calne	T Tamworth
Ch Chichester	Ta Taunton
Cr Cricklade	Tw Twynham
D Dorchester	W Wallingford
Dr Droitwich	Wa Wareham
G Gloucester	Wk Warwick
I Ilchester	Wl Wilton
L Langport	Wm Wimborne
Le Leicester	Wn Winchcomb
M Malmesbury	Wr Winchester
Mi Milborne	Wt Worcester
Mt Milverton	

Fig. 105. 'Urban fields' in 1086: Leicestershire to Somerset.

Ballard who developed it in some detail.[1] It did not, however, secure general acceptance. Tait described it as 'more than dubious',[2] and the arguments against it have been set forth on more than one occasion.[3] The alternative theory rests on the belief that the relation between town and manor in the eleventh century was not so much military as commercial. A rural landowner acquired property in a nearby town because of the trading rights and benefits it brought, or, maybe, even for residence.[4] 'The elaborate economy of a large Old English manor implied the possibility of access to something more than a mere rural market; and an appurtenant house in a neighbouring borough formed a convenient centre at which goods needed on the estate could be brought together and stored.'[5] It is only fair to say that Maitland met some of the criticism of his 'garrison theory' by confessing that it could not serve for all boroughs, and that he had said too little of the borough as a market.[6] Finally, it may be useful to reflect upon the unusual and extreme arrangements in Droitwich. It not only had contributory houses and burgesses attached to nearby rural manors in Worcestershire, but also many salt-pans attached to rural manors not only in Worcestershire but in far distant places in other counties.[7]

Whatever view one takes of this old battlefield of scholarship, the fact remains that both theories envisage a connection between boroughs and their surrounding districts. We might well see in this connection something of what the language of a later age was to call 'urban fields' or 'urban spheres of influence', and spheres that, whatever their military or jurisdictional implications, were becoming increasingly commercial. In trying to envisage what the economic life of eleventh-century England was like, that fact might be remembered as one looks at Figs. 105–6. We can see, for example, how much of southern Oxfordshire came within the influence of Wallingford, across the border in a neighbouring county.

---

[1] A. Ballard (1904), 11–36.   [2] J. Tait, 342.
[3] E.g. (1) J. H. Round in *V.C.H. Herefordshire*, 1 (1908), 296–7; (2) C. Petit-Dutaillis, *Studies and notes supplementary to Stubbs' Constitutional History*, 1 (Manchester, 1923), 79–83.
[4] J. H. Round in *V.C.H. Surrey*, 1 (1902), 285–6.
[5] F. M. Stenton (1943), 523–4.
[6] F. W. Maitland, *Township and borough* (Cambridge, 1898), 210.
[7] *D.G.M.E.*, 252–8, 263–5. See pp. 260–1 above.

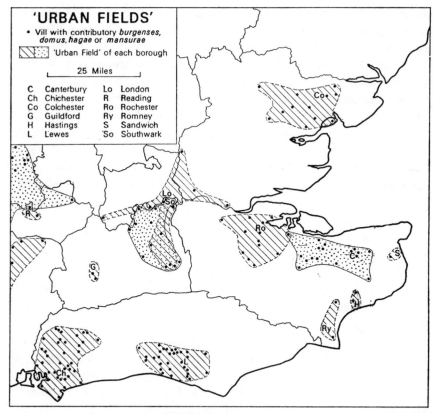

'URBAN FIELDS'

• Vill with contributory *burgenses, domus, hagae* or *mansurae*

⬚ 'Urban Field' of each borough

25 Miles

C	Canterbury	Lo	London
Ch	Chichester	R	Reading
Co	Colchester	Ro	Rochester
G	Guildford	Ry	Romney
H	Hastings	S	Sandwich
L	Lewes	So	Southwark

Fig. 106. 'Urban fields' in 1086: South-east England.

CASTLES

The earliest Norman castles were usually of the motte-and-bailey type. The motte, or mound, was made of earth or rubble around which was a ditch and upon which was a wooden tower. This looked down over a bailey, or courtyard, surrounded by a palisade, a bank and its own ditch; within the bailey were huts for workshops, stables and accommodation. It was by means of castles of this type that the king and his barons accomplished the Norman Conquest of England; stone structures came later.[1] Castles are named, or implied, in Domesday Book in connexion with 48

[1] E. S. Armitage, *The early Norman castles of the British Isles* (London, 1912); A. Hamilton Thompson, *Military architecture in England during the Middle Ages* (London, 1912); D. F. Renn, *Norman castles in Britain* (London, 2nd edn, 1973).

places, of which 27 were boroughs. At eleven of these boroughs properties had been cleared to make room for the castles; on the cleared land at
York two castles had been erected on opposite banks of the Ouse (*vastata
in castellis*). In addition to the eleven, there were also three other boroughs
with castles built upon devastated land (see p. 295). Some castles were
founded not only on rural manors but on quite unimportant ones, e.g. at
Dunster in Somerset (*359*, 95b) and Rayleigh in Essex (43b), and at
Rockingham in Northamptonshire (220) which lay waste when William
ordered a castle to be built there. One castle – that at Berkeley in Gloucestershire (mentioned under *Nesse*, 163) – was specifically described as a small
one (*unum castellulum*). Castles are mentioned in successive entries for
Tutbury and *Burtone* in the Staffordshire folios (248b), but it w ould seem
that they both refer to the same castle – i.e. that at Tutbury.[1]

At two of the 48 places, castles had been built before the Conquest 'by
Norman lords under the Confessor'.[2] One was at Ewias Harold in
Herefordshire; its pre-Conquest lord is not mentioned, but Domesday
Book says that it had been refortified (*refirmaverat*) by William fitz
Osbern (186) which implies at some date between 1066 and 1071 when he
died. The other was Richards Castle, in the same county, which took its
name from Richard (son of Scrob) who settled in Herefordshire in 1052
and who was succeeded by his son Osbern fitz Richard. Three castles are
designated by the names of their owners not by those of their localities,
but these can be identified as Clitheroe in Lancashire and Tanshelf and
Richmond, in Yorkshire,[3] although doubt has been expressed about the
first-named identification.[4] There is also no specific reference to a castle
at Pevensey where William landed and where we know he built one, but
entries for Eastbourne (206) and West Firle (21) refer to warders of the
castle (*custodes castelli*), which seem to imply that of Pevensey. Then
again, the Devonshire folios (*118*, 101b) refer to the manors of Benton
and Haxton which had been exchanged for 'the castle of Cornwall', but
it is practically certain that this refers to the castle at *Dunhevet*, i.e. Launceston, which is named in the Cornish folios (*264b*, 121b).[5] The Stafford-

---

[1] C. F. Slade in *V.C.H. Staffordshire*, IV (1958), 58n.

[2] J. H. Round in *V.C.H. Herefordshire*, I (1908), 273; F. M. Stenton (1943), 554n.

[3] E. S. Armitage, 129–30, 187–8, 193–4; D. F. Renn, 146, 281, 294–5.

[4] J. McNulty, 'Clitheroe castle and its chapel: their origins', *Trans. Hist. Soc.
Lancs. and Cheshire*, XCIII (Liverpool, 1942), 45–53.

[5] H. P. R. Finberg, 'The castle of Cornwall', *Devon and Cornwall Notes and
Queries*, XXIII (Exeter, 1949), 123.

shire folios tell us that the king had ordered a castle to be built on 'the land of Stafford' belonging to the manor of Chebsey (248b), but that it had since been destroyed (*modo est destructum*). Finally, with this enumeration of castles must be mentioned the two very unusual references to *domus defensabilis* in the entries for Ailey (187) and Eardisley (184b) in the Herefordshire folios.

It is clear that the mention of castles in Domesday Book was far from systematic or complete. Thus we hear of the castle at Lewes in Sussex only incidentally in the folios for Norfolk, and of that at Eye in Suffolk only in a reference to a dispute about markets. Among the castles which we know to have existed only from non-Domesday sources were those at Barnstaple, Chester, Exeter and Oxford. At each of these places we hear of wasted houses which may have been the result of castle-building, although Domesday Book does not specify the cause of the destruction. There were yet others that went unmentioned, e.g. that at Nottingham which, the Anglo-Saxon Chronicle tells us, William raised in 1070. Nor is the castle at Hereford mentioned, although this, like Ewias Harold and Richards Castle, was almost certainly of pre-Conquest date.[1] It is difficult to be precise about the total number of castles that had been raised in Domesday England by 1086, but it would seem to be between 70 and 80 (Fig. 107).

Taken together, these castles commanded the chief towns and main routes of southern England, with terminals at Norwich, York, Chester and Exeter, although the last two do not appear in the Domesday folios. In the west, along the Welsh border, there were a number that commanded the approaches to and from Wales – in Shropshire, Herefordshire and Gloucestershire. In the south, along the coasts of Kent and Sussex, there was another group that secured communications with Normandy.

The term *castellaria*, implying the area of jurisdiction of a castle or the area intended for its maintenance, is occasionally encountered in the Domesday folios. It occurs in the entries for Caerleon, Clifford, Dudley, Ewias Harold, Montgomery and Richards Castle. It is also found in one of the entries for Hastings (18), and the phrases *pro castallatione* or *de castaellatione*, mentioned unexpectedly in the Norfolk folios (162b, 163), imply the same thing for Lewes; a similar organisation existed for each of the other Sussex rapes, but there are no specific references to their *castellariae*.[2]

[1] E. S. Armitage, *passim*; D. F. Renn, *passim*.
[2] L. F. Salzman in *V.C.H. Sussex*, I (1905), 351–3; R. Welldon Finn, *The Domesday Inquest* (London, 1961), 13.

CASTLES
IN 1086

● Domesday castles
x Other castles

50 Miles

Fig. 107. Castles in 1086.
The names of the Domesday castles are given opposite.

The phrase *infra metam castelli* implies like arrangements for Tanshelf, as does *in castellatum* for Clitheroe. Both *castellaria* and *castellatum* appear for Richmond, and the Summary for the North Riding tells us it included 199 manors of which 108 were waste. In the same way we hear that the castle of Rhuddlan was the head of a district (*caput est huius terrae*). Domesday Book mentions no castle for Tonbridge in Kent but makes frequent reference to its *leuua* or lowy, but that this was also a *castellaria* we may suppose from the reference to *infra castellum* in the

Domesday Monachorum.[1] It is clear that there were yet other *castellariae* unmentioned in Domesday Book.[2]

DOMESDAY CASTLES

(Key to Fig. 107)

An asterisk indicates a borough

Berkshire
 1 Wallingford (56)*
 2 Windsor (62b)*
Cambridgeshire
 3 Cambridge (189)*
Cheshire
 4 Rhuddlan (269)*
Cornwall
 5 Launceston (*Dunhevet, 264b,* 121b)
 6 Trematon (*256,* 122)
Derbyshire
 7 Peveril (*Pechefers* 276)
Devonshire
 8 Okehampton (*288,* 105b)*
Dorset
 9 Corfe Castle (*castellum Warham,* 78b)
Essex
 10 Rayleigh (43b)
Gloucestershire
 11 Berkeley (*Nesse,* 163)
 12 Caerleon (185b)
 13 Chepstow (*Estrighoiel,* 162)
 14 Gloucester (162)*
Hampshire
 15 Carisbrooke (Alvington, 52b)
Herefordshire
 16 Clifford (183, 184)*
 17 Ewias Harold (181b, 184, 185, 186)*
 18 Monmouth (180b)
 19 Richards Castle (*Auretone,* 185, 186b)
 20 Wigmore (180, 183b)*
Huntingdonshire
 21 Huntingdon (203)*
Kent
 22 Canterbury (2)*
 23 Rochester (2b)*
Lancashire
 24 Clitheroe (Roger of Poitou, 332 *bis*)

 25 Penwortham (270)*
Lincolnshire
 26 Lincoln (336b)*
 27 Stamford (336b)*
Norfolk
 28 Norwich (116b)*
Northamptonshire
 29 Rockingham (220)
Shropshire
 30 Montgomery (254)
 31 Oswestry (*Luvre,* 253b)
 32 Shrewsbury (252)*
 33 Stanton Holdgate (258)
Somerset
 34 Dunster (*Torre, 359,* 95b)
 35 Montacute (*280,* 93)
Staffordshire
 36 Stafford (248b)*
 37 Tutbury, *Burtone* (248b *bis*)*
Suffolk
 38 Eye (379)*
Sussex
 39 Arundel (23)*
 40 Bramber (28)
 41 Hastings (18)*
 42 Lewes (L.D.B., 163, 163b, 164b, 165)*
 43 Pevensey (20b, 21)*
Warwickshire
 44 Warwick (238)*
Worcestershire
 45 Dudley (177)
Yorkshire
 46 Tanshelf (Ilbert de Laci, 373b)*
 47 Richmond (Count Alan, 381)
 48 York (two castles, 298)*

[1] D. C. Douglas, *The Domesday Monachorum of Christ Church, Canterbury* (Roy. Hist. Soc., London, 1944), 88; *D.G.S–E.E.*, 486–8, 556.
[2] F. M. Stenton, *The first century of English feudalism* (Oxford, 1932), 193–4; F. M. Stenton (1943), 619–20.

MARKETS

Markets are recorded or implied in Domesday Book in connection with 60 places of which 19 were boroughs—Appendix 17 (pp. 369–70). Clearly, the record is very incomplete. There are entire counties for which no markets are entered; such, for example, are those of Cambridge, Dorset, Shropshire and Sussex, yet they must have had markets not only in their boroughs but elsewhere. An obvious illustration of this incompleteness is the Sunday market at Otterton in Devon, entered in the Exeter (*194b*) but not in the Exchequer text. The usual designation is *mercatum*, but *forum* is also used, and *portus* is entered for Lewisham in Kent, and a provision market (*macellum*) for York. Not included in the total of 60 places is Aspall, in Suffolk, for which a fair (*feria*) is entered (418), and Methleigh in Cornwall for which the Exchequer text enters a *forum* (120b); the latter appears in the Exeter version as *annuale forum* (*199*), and in the *Terrae Occupatae* (507b) as *quaedam feria*.

All we hear in some entries is the bald statement that there was a market; but usually its annual render is also given, and this ranged from 4*s* to £11. These renders were not always to a single lord. A quarter of the market at Beccles, for example, was owned by the king and the remainder by the abbey of Bury St Edmunds. Fractional parts are also entered for Dunham and Litcham in Norfolk, for Haverhill in Suffolk, and for Tealby in Lincolnshire, but for none of these is there any clue to the remaining fractions. Occasionally, there is a little further information. We hear of dwellers around the market places at Berkeley (Gloucs.), Eye (Suff.) and Worcester, and of merchants before the gates of Abingdon Abbey (Berks.), and also of men living by trade alone in the borough around the castle at Tutbury (Staffs.). There is no mention of a market at Cheshunt, but the presence of ten merchants, rendering 10*s* in customary dues, may well indicate the presence of one. The record of 48 merchants' houses at Nottingham (280) is also indicative, but this has not been included in our count.

Markets at Bolingbroke (Lincs.), Cirencester (Gloucs.), Cookham (Berks.) were 'new'; others at Hereford and Kelsale (Suff.) likewise seem to have been new creations, and one at Tewkesbury (Gloucs.) was also recent, being founded by the late Queen. The establishment of a new market could lead to difficulties. At Hoxne, in Suffolk, there had been a Saturday market belonging to the bishop of Thetford; but at Eye, some three miles away, William Malet built a castle and set up (*sedebat*) another Saturday market, around which, incidentally, 25 burgesses dwelled. This so spoiled the bishop's market that it was of little value and so he tried to avoid the competition by moving it to Friday. There was similar trouble in Cornwall. There, the bishop of Exeter's Saturday market at St Germans had been rendered worthless because the count of Mortain had established another at his castle of Trematon some four miles to the east. The count had also injured the canons of St Stephens by placing the market of St Stephens within the jurisdiction of his castle at Launceston. These are the only echoes of what must have been many conflicts of interest, and they emphasise the incomplete nature of the Domesday evidence. Often, for example, when we hear of a toll, it may well imply a toll from a market, e.g. at Arundel (23) and Pevensey (20b) in Sussex, and at Berkhamsted (136b) and St Albans (135b) in Hertfordshire, for all of which no markets are entered.

MINTS

The characteristic features of the English coinage on the eve of the Conquest went back to the laws of Athelstan in the middle of the tenth century. His words ran: 'there shall be one coinage throughout the realm, and there shall be no minting except in a *port*', i.e. a borough.[1] On the one hand, a degree of uniformity was secured by the rule that every moneyer should receive his dies from London. On the other hand, there was decentralisation in the minting of the coins themselves. A coin came to bear the names of both moneyer and minting place, and the evidence suggests that there were some 60 or so minting places in the late Anglo-Saxon period.

The Norman Conquest did not interrupt these arrangements. It is true that a few mints disappeared and a few others were resuscitated, but the basic organisation remained, and there seem to have been about the same number of minting places as before.[2] Domesday Book, however, records or implies the existence of mints at only 28 of these places – Appendix 18 (p. 371). Sometimes, it mentiones a *moneta*, and sometimes the moneyers (*monetarii*) themselves, and sometimes both. A few of these entries refer

---

[1] F. M. Stenton (1943), 527–30; G. C. Brooke, *Catalogue of English coins in the British Museum: the Norman kings*, I (London, 1916), clx–clxxxviii; R. H. M. Dolley (ed.), *Anglo-Saxon coins* (London, 1960).

[2] R. H. M. Dolley, *The Norman Conquest and the English coinage* (London, 1966).

explicitly only to 1066, and we are left to conjecture what the position was in 1086. The payment for the privilege of coinage was sometimes substantial, and ranged from £75 at Lincoln downwards to £1 each at Lewes and Pevensey. Furthermore, a fee was charged for new dies when the design was changed, e.g. with each new king; the amount varied, but it was frequently 20s. The fragmentary evidence may do less than justice to many boroughs in 1086, but at any rate it points to their function as minting places and to their role as centres of economic life.

CHAPTER XI

THE WELSH MARCH

Like the English, the Welsh in the Dark Ages were divided into a number of small kingdoms. At times during the ninth and tenth centuries, two or more of the kingdoms had been brought together under a single rule, but the details are obscure. In the eleventh century Gruffydd ap Llewellyn of Gwynedd succeeded in uniting the various divisions.[1] Thus strengthened, he faced the common enemy to the east, and the Anglo-Saxon Chronicle, under the year 1052, tells how 'Griffin the Welsh king' plundered western Herefordshire almost as far as Leominster. To Gruffydd must also be attributed many of the wasted villages that, in 1066, stretched from Rhuddlan southwards towards Gwent (Fig. 84). The Herefordshire folios (181) speak of the ravaging of Archenfield by 'Grifin and Blein' (see pp. 252–3), and we also hear of his control of Gwent (162). After further warfare along the Herefordshire border, an attempt at conciliation was made by a group of English notables, and the Anglo-Saxon Chronicle records, under the year 1056, how Gruffydd swore to be a faithful under-king to Edward the Confessor. We do not know whether an entry in the Cheshire folios (263) refers to this time. It says that King Edward gave Gruffydd all the land beyond the river Dee (*tota terra iacebat trans aquam quae De vocatur*), and there is specific reference in another entry to his manor of Bistre (269). It is conceivable that this was merely the recognition of the existing state of affairs. In any case it was a remarkable cession of a substantial stretch of country characterised by English names such as Axton, Calcot, Fulbrook and the like. They appear later as Domesday villages for, as the entry on folio 263 goes on to say, Gruffydd (presumably after his defeat and death in 1063) forfeited his lands which were restored to the bishop of Chester and to others who had formerly held them.

In the meantime, Gruffydd had played a part in the politics of the English earldoms and had helped to reinstate Earl Alfgar of Mercia whose daughter he had married. The end came in 1063 when, as a result of dissensions among the Welsh and pressure from the English, he was killed. Wales once more fell into its political divisions. The main units were Gwynedd, Powys, Deheubarth, Morgannwg and Gwent, but there

[1] J. E. Lloyd, *A history of Wales*, II (London, 3rd edn, 1939), 357–71.

were also a number of smaller units each with its own prince; such, for example, were Buellt and Gwynllwg (Fig. 108).

With their conquest of England, the Normans inherited the problem of the frontier with Wales, and the Norman Conquest could never be complete until Wales had also been subdued. What is more, the divided condition of the Welsh offered ample opportunities to the restless energies of the Norman barons. The most important of the barons were the three earls whom William established along the frontier. From these border earldoms of Hereford, Shrewsbury and Chester, the conquest of Wales proceeded in a piecemeal fashion. There were no fixed boundaries but a frontier that shifted with the fortunes of raiding. In the south, even in the time of Edward the Confessor, Norman lords had come to defend the frontier in Herefordshire; and, in 1067, after the Conquest, William fitz Osbern was made earl of Hereford. He left England never to return in 1070, and his premature death in 1071, followed by the treason of his son in 1075, brought the earldom back into the hands of the king. The result is that the work of Earl William does not stand out so clearly in the Domesday folios as that of his fellow earls along the border. In the north, Hugh of Avranches became earl of Chester in 1070 and, together with his kinsman Robert of Rhuddlan, he had pressed the frontier against the Welsh far along the coast by 1086. Between these two earldoms of north and south, that of Shrewsbury, in the central part of the March, was created for Roger of Montgomery in 1071. By 1086 he had penetrated into the district of the upper Severn valleys.

It has been said that in the eleventh century the English shires along the Welsh border showed certain social characteristics peculiar to themselves.[1] Among these was the frequency of radmen, *bovarii* and *hospites*. 'These classes appear within the Welsh frontier, and virtually nowhere else in Domesday England.' This, we have already seen from Figs. 28, 30 and 32. The functions of radmen, it has been claimed, were 'semi-military, and they acted much in the character of a frontier militia'; they were relics from Anglo-Saxon times and by 1086 they were disappearing as a class. *Bovari* represented another adjustment to the frontier in that they may have been 'men who combined the arms of a free man with the duties of a slave'. Unfortunately, such statements must remain conjectures rather than proved facts. It is the same with *hospites* who seem to have

---

[1] L. H. Nelson, *The Normans in South Wales, 1070–1171* (University of Texas, Austin, 1966), 44–60.

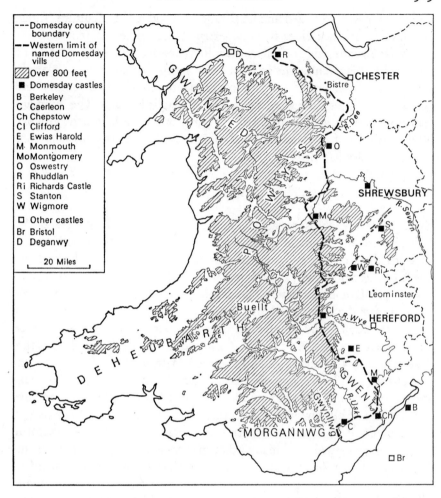

Fig. 108. Wales and the Welsh March in 1086.

been colonists whom lords invited to settle on their lands. They may well
have represented an attempt to populate a thinly-settled frontier; but it is
possible that colonists in other counties and other circuits passed under
other designations.

Whatever view we take of these matters, the folios for the border
counties convey the impression of a wild country where the chase was
important (Fig. 69). It is true that forests themselves are rarely mentioned but there are many references to 'hays' and, in Cheshire especially,

to hawks' nests, recorded amidst details of wood and agriculture. Again we have to ask ourselves to what extent these references represent the state of the countryside or reflect the idiosyncrasies of those who made the returns for this circuit. The frontier districts were certainly more sparsely occupied than most of the rest of England. Overlooking empty and populated villages alike were the castles of the border earls. The Normans had not only moved the frontier forward, but were in touch with the Welsh princes of the lands beyond. The first phase of the Norman conquest of Wales had begun.

THE EARLDOM OF HEREFORD

Strong defensive measures against the Welsh had been taken in Herefordshire before the Norman conquest. Two castles had been built under Edward the Confessor – at Ewias Harold and Richards Castle; and the castle of Hereford itself, though not mentioned in Domesday Book, was also of pre-Domesday date.[1] The desolate condition of the frontier may be seen from the widespread distribution of waste in pre-Domesday times (Fig. 84). Much of the countryside does not seem to have recovered since the onslaught of the Welsh king, Gruffydd ap Llewellyn, in the 1050s.[2] The fate of this district was now placed in the hands of William fitz Osbern who had been one of Duke William's companions in the Conquest (Fig. 109). When the Conqueror returned to Normandy in 1067, he left the care of his new kingdom in the hands of William fitz Osbern and Bishop Odo of Bayeux; fitz Osbern was moreover made earl of Hereford. Although concerned with many other matters up to his death in 1071, he left a mark upon the Welsh March. It was during this period that Edric 'the Wild', the holder of several manors in northern Herefordshire, allied with the Welsh and, so the Anglo-Saxon Chronicle tells us, 'fought with the men of the castle of Hereford' in 1067, and maintained resistance until he finally submitted in 1070.

The chronicles speak of Earl William as actively waging war against the kings of the Welsh,[3] and something of his activity is reflected in Domesday Book. He refortified the castle of Ewias Harold (186), and the phrase *refirmaverat* suggests that it had suffered since its first foundation. He also

[1] F. M. Stenton, *Anglo-Saxon England* (Oxford, 1954), 554n.
[2] J. H. Round in *V.C.H. Herefordshire*, 1 (1908), 264–5.
[3] J. E. Lloyd (1939), 375.

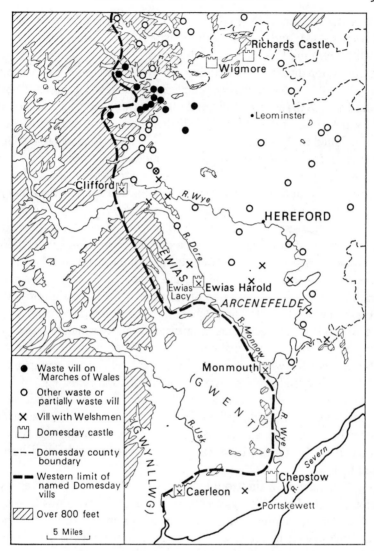

Fig. 109. The earldom of Hereford in 1086.

Names in brackets are not mentioned in Domesday Book.

built castles at Wigmore (183b) and at Clifford (183), both on land that
had been wasted; and to the south he likewise established castles at Monmouth (180b) and *Estrighoiel* or Chepstow (162). To the west, he seems
to have occupied part of the kingdom of Gwent between the Wye and the
Usk.[1] By 1086 the Normans had established a castle as far west as Caerleon
on the Usk (185b) where William de Scohies was resettling wasted land,
but by this time Earl William had died abroad in 1071, and his son had
been banished for treason in 1075. The earldom was forfeited to the Crown
and it is as *Terra regis* that it appears in Domesday Book.

Gwent is never mentioned by name in Domesday Book, but it is
described in an untidy and anomalous section that follows the account of
Gloucester on folio 162. This refers sporadically to population and to
teams and other resources, and names only seven places.[2] Yet the evidence
leaves us in no doubt that here was a district (*inter Huscham et Waiam*)
with an economy and a social order quite different from that of England.
It had never been assessed in hides, and when the Normans divided out
much of it, they did so in terms of carucates. We have a glimpse of the
process when we hear that fitz Osbern gave to Ralph de Limesei 50 carucates of land as it occurs (i.e. is measured) in Normandy – *sicut fit in
Normannia*. Other entries make no reference even to carucates but to the
Welsh system by which groups of vills or 'trefs', each group under a
prepositus, rendered not manorial services but food rents, e.g. of honey,
pigs and cows. There were 13 such vills under Waswic, 14 under Elmui,
13 under Blei and 14 under Idhel. There were yet other vills that made no
renders but had been allowed by Earl William to retain the privileges
granted them by Grifin, i.e. Gruffydd ap Llewellyn, who had been defeated in 1063.

Some indication of the troubled history of the district is given by the
reference to the four vills wasted by King Caraduech who was Caradoc ap
Gruffydd of the neighbouring kingdom of Gwynllwg and who raided as
far as Portskewett in 1065. We also hear of another *wasta terra* and of a
number of other vills. It would seem that 'the river Wye separated by a
sharp line the Saxon land, on which the manorial land system prevailed,
from the Welsh land, on which the Welsh tribal system prevailed'.[3] To

---

[1] W. Rees, 'Medieval Gwent', *Jour. British Archaeol. Assoc.*, N.S. XXXV (1930),
189–206; C. S. Taylor, 'The Norman settlement of Gloucestershire', *Trans. Bristol
and Gloucs. Archaeol. Soc.* XL (1917), 82–5.   [2] *D.G.*, 542.
[3] F. Seebohm, *The English village community* (London, 1883), 208.

what extent the Normans had penetrated beyond the Usk we cannot say. Caerleon (185b) itself was certainly on the west bank of the river, with Welshmen living under Welsh law (*Walenses lege Walensi viventes*). We also hear of 6 carucates *ultra Uscham* and of 7 vills *in Wales*.

To the north of Gwent lay Archenfield or, to use its Welsh name, Erging. Although situated to the west of the Wye, it had become part of Herefordshire in pre-Conquest times, but without losing its Welsh character. 'The customs of the Welsh T.R.E. in Archenfield' are set out in an anomalous section following the account of Hereford itself (179). They include various references to Welshmen, including one to the three priests who acted as the king's envoys into Wales (*ferunt legationes regis in Walis*). The description of the district comes on folio 181 under *Terra regis*, and it shows us a land lying waste in 1066 as a result of devastation by 'King Grifin and Blein', that is Gruffydd ap Llewellyn and his successor Bleddyn. But it had recovered, or recovered in part, by 1086 (Fig. 87). It retained its Welsh character under the Normans, and its economy seems to have resembled that of Gwent. It is true that we do not hear of clusters of Welsh vills, but the district was not assessed in hides, and its holdings were characterised by renders in honey and sheep, even on those holdings with Norman under-tenants. Some holdings specifically enumerate Welshmen among their population.

To the north-west was another district called by an old Welsh territorial name – Ewias. It lay to the west of the valley of the river Dore, and Domesday Book says so little about it that it must still have been largely in Welsh hands or in a wasted condition or both. At its southern end was Ewias Harold with its castle refortified by Earl William (186) and with four waste carucates in its *castellaria*. To the west, beyond the castellany, was Ewias Lacy (now Longtown). From both these places came renders of honey, and from the latter a render of swine 'when the men are there' (184). To the north of Ewias was Clifford where Earl William built a castle on wasted land (183), and there were four waste carucates in its castellany (184). Although part of the English realm (*de regno Angliae*), it did not belong to any hundred nor did it render customary dues (183). Not far away the wasted land at Harewood (187) had become all covered with wood (*Haec terra in silvam est tota redacta*). Further north still there were fourteen places with a total of 54 waste ploughlands (183b, 186b) which were said to lie on the Marches of Wales (*in Marcha de Wales*); at eleven of these places 36 ploughlands had also become overgrown with woods, where Osbern fitz Richard hunted (186b). Not far from these scenes of desolation were the castles at Richards Castle and Wigmore, the former of pre-Conquest date, and the latter built by Earl William, again on wasted land (183b).

It would seem that at times the Normans attempted a policy of conciliation, and there is the strange spectacle of grants of land in Herefordshire by Earl William to King Mariador – at Kenchester (187), Bunshill, Lye, Mansell Gamage, Mansell Lacy and two unidentified places (187b). This Welsh king appears to have been none other than Maredudd ab Owain who ruled Deheubarth between 1067–72; the lands, moreover, were confirmed to his son Gruffydd after his father's death.[1]

Looking at this southern area as a whole, we can see that the frontier against the Welsh had advanced but little since the death of Earl William in 1071. It still ran from the neighbourhood of Wigmore castle by way of Ewias and Archenfield to Caerleon. It is true that in 1081 King William had ridden west as far as St David's. According to the monks of St David's, this was a pilgrimage to venerate their saint; but the Anglo-Saxon Chronicle says that the king 'led an army' and set free 'many hundred men'. After this show of force, William left Morgannwg and Deheubarth in the hands of a Welsh prince called Rhys ap Tewdwr who may have been the *Riset de Wales* who rendered £40 (179).[2] There was also another district (*terra Calcebuef*) from which the king received 10s (179), and this has been connected with the cantref of Buellt, or Builth, with its own line of princes.[3]

THE EARLDOM OF SHREWSBURY

The rebellion of Edric 'the Wild' in 1067 flared up once more in 1069 when, again in alliance with Welsh princes, Bleddyn and Rhiwallon, he was able to besiege Shrewsbury. The movement spread eastward to Stafford, and was not suppressed until King William arrived from the North (see p. 253). Soon after this, the traditional conflict between upland and lowland took a new turn when, in 1071, William created the earldom of Shrewsbury for Roger who came from Montgomeri in central

---

[1] J. E. Lloyd (1939), 376–7, 398; J. H. Round (1908), 280.
[2] J. E. Lloyd (1939), 394; J. G. Edwards, 'The Normans and the Welsh March', *Proc. British Academy*, XLII (1956), 161.
[3] J. E. Lloyd, 'Wales and the coming of the Normans (1039–1093)', *Trans. of the Hon. Soc. of Cymmrodorion*, Session 1898–99 (1900), 163.

Normandy. Earl Roger soon made his presence felt (Fig. 110). He destroyed 51 properties in Shrewsbury to make room for a castle (252), and also built another, in the upper Severn valley, at Montgomery, called after his home. It lay amidst thirteen wasted settlements (two unidentified) over which three English thegns had hunted in the time of Edward the Confessor (254). Other entries for places along the Shropshire border referring to waste, to woods and to hays also indicate the character of the March against the Welsh (Figs. 69 and 84–6).

Earl Roger extended his activities right into the Welsh upland. We read, on folio 253b, that he received £6 from a certain district in Wales (*de uno fine de Walis*) belonging to the *castellaria* of Montgomery. This nameless district was probably the hundred of *Arvester* which is mentioned in the Cheshire folios (269) and which has been identified as the cantref of Arwystli which was in dispute between Earl Roger and Robert of Rhuddlan.[1] Control over Arwystli implies control over the intervening districts of Ceri and Cydewain. On folio 253b we also read that 'Tuder, a certain Welshman, holds of the Earl a district of Welsh land (*fines terrae Walensis*)'. It seems likely that this was the Welsh commote of Nanheudwy in the Vale of Llangollen.[2] There was a third extension, for Roger also held the land of Gal in Wales (*in Walis terra de Gal*); this was the Welsh commote of Ial or Yale (254).[3] It had lain waste in 1066 and also when Earl Roger granted it to Earl Hugh of Chester, but by 1086 it had been resettled and restocked with men and teams.

Earl Roger also granted out other border estates to those vassals who aided him in his warfare against the Welsh. Among them was Warin the Bold who, on his death, was succeeded as sheriff by Rainald.[4] The description of the customs of Shrewsbury (252) tells us that when the sheriff marched into Wales, anyone who was given notice and did not accompany him, forfeited 40s. Rainald had estates throughout the whole county but they were especially numerous in the border hundred of *Mersete* (254b–255). Many of these lay waste both in 1066 and when he received them, but by 1086 they were being cultivated by a population that included Welshmen, presumably brought from elsewhere. It was in this area that Rainald built a castle called, as yet, merely 'the work' (*Luvre*, 253b) but later known as Oswestry. To the west of *Mersete* he

[1] J. Tait in *V.C.H. Shropshire* I (1908), 287–8; J. G. Edwards, 160.
[2] J. E. Lloyd (1939), 389.   [3] J. E. Lloyd (1900), 160.
[4] J. E. Lloyd (1939), 388–9.

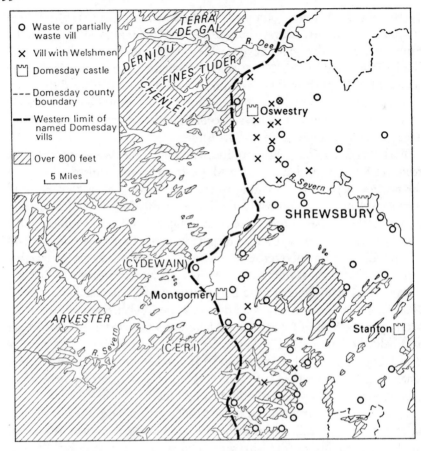

Fig. 110. The earldom of Shrewsbury in 1086.

Names in brackets are not mentioned in Domesday Book.

held the two Welsh commotes of Cynllaith and Edeyrnion (*Chenlei* and *Derniou*); from the former he received 60*s* by way of rent, and from the Welshmen in the latter he received 8 cows (255). To sum up, the year 1086 found Earl Roger poised for an invasion of Deheubarth seven years later.[1]

[1] J. E. Lloyd (1939), 390, 400–1.

THE EARLDOM OF CHESTER

King William first gave the city and county of Chester, with the title of earl, to his stepson, Gherbod of Flanders, but Gherbod resigned within a year, and was succeeded, in 1071, by Hugh of Avranches who came to dominate the affairs of the northern part of the March for the next thirty years until his death in 1101.[1] The county that he thus acquired extended far to the west of modern Cheshire, and included the whole of what later became Flintshire and also much of Denbighshire; but the area that was assessed in hides extended only up to Wat's Dyke (Fig. 111). Much of western Cheshire had suffered from the raids of Gruffydd ap Llewellyn, king of Gwynedd. He had been defeated and killed in 1063 but the result of his work was still to be seen in the devastated manors of 1066 which were still lying waste in 1071 when Earl Hugh acquired them.

By 1086 there had been great changes, and most of the wasted manors had been restocked by their Norman lords. Figs. 85–7 show the transformation that had taken place, and the table below summarises the numbers of people and teams involved in that part of Domesday Cheshire now in Wales:

	Recorded population	Teams
Exestan (in part)	45	8
Dudestan (in part)	48	20
Hidated Atiscros	72	$16\frac{1}{12}$
Unhidated Atiscros	159	36
	324	$80\frac{1}{12}$

There is no clue to the origin of these people and their teams.

A prominent leader in the advance to the west was Earl Hugh's cousin named Robert who held a great part of the district of Englefield, or Tegeingl, as sub-tenant. The settlements of the district were berewicks of the extensive manor of Rhuddlan, and Earl Hugh and Robert shared between them the profits from the church, the mint, the tolls, fisheries, mills, iron mines and forests. What is more, they established and shared a castle and a new borough (269). Rhuddlan, it is true, was but a small borough with 18 burgesses and tolls yielding only 3s a year, but it has a

[1] J. E. Lloyd (1939), 381.

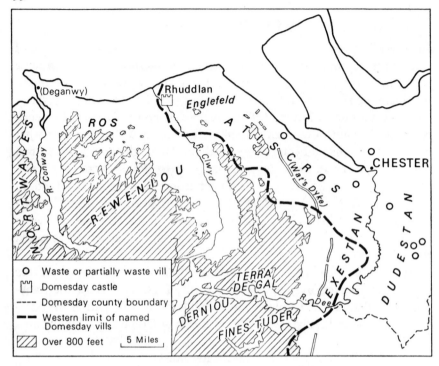

Fig. 111. The earldom of Chester in 1086.

Names in brackets are not mentioned in Domesday Book.
The Dee estuary is approximately that of 1086, but can only be hypothetical.

place in urban history because, as Domesday Book records, it was granted
laws and customs as they were in Hereford and Breteuil; the mark of
Breteuil upon the constitutions of the English borough was thus felt at an
early date.

From this base there was advance westward beyond the Clwyd up to
the Conway, and Robert of Rhuddlan held directly from the king in fee
(*de feudo*) *Ros* and *Reweniou*, that is the two Welsh cantrefs of Rhos and
Rufoniog (269). Here, there was land for 20 teams and this brought in
£12 a year; all the rest consisted of woods and moors which could not be
tilled (*Omnis alia terra est in silvis et moris, nec potest arari*). Further west
still, beyond the Conway, was 'Nortwales' which Robert held of the
king at farm (*ad firmam*) for £40 a year, the same amount, incidentally,
that *Riset de Wales* was paying for Deheubarth (179). 'Nortwales' was

the kingdom of Gwynedd whose prince, Gruffydd ap Cynan, had been held prisoner by Robert since 1081. In 1088 the Welsh made a daring attack, and Robert was killed near his castle of Deganwy which he had recently built and which is not mentioned in Domesday Book.[1]

[1] J. E. Lloyd (1939), 391.

APPENDICES

APPENDIX 1

GENERAL STATISTICAL SUMMARY BY DOMESDAY COUNTIES

Assessment, ploughlands, ploughteams and rural population of boroughs are included in these totals, but it must be emphasised that the information for the boroughs is often fragmentary.

The figures for the assessment are hides unless otherwise stated – c for carucates, s for sulungs. Ploughland totals are impossible for some counties owing to the form of their entries.

	Settlements	Assessment	Ploughlands	Ploughteams	Rural population	Boroughs
Bedfordshire	141	1,186	1,588	1,405	3,591	1
Berkshire	189	2,495	2,114	1,885	6,139	3
Buckinghamshire	206	2,210	2,296	2,056	5,103	2
Cambridgeshire	142	1,297	1,688	1,501	4,868	1
Cheshire (now in England)	266	492; 5c	940	458	1,528	1
Cheshire (now in Wales)	100	53	128	80	324	1
Cornwall	332	424	2,557	1,221	5,368	1
Derbyshire	346	699c	768	939	2,836	1
Devonshire	980	1,142	7,934	5,735	17,246	5
Dorset	314	2,357	2,287	1,858	7,382	5
Essex	444	2,799	?	3,909	14,004	2
Gloucestershire (now in England)	372	2,468	?	3,895	8,191	4
Gloucestershire (now in Wales)	7	30c	18	90	58	—
Hampshire	454	2,785	2,932	2,747	9,780	3
Herefordshire (now in England)	302	1,168; 24c	?	2,417	4,326	4
Herefordshire (now in Wales)	9	31; 10c	19	48	15	—
Hertfordshire	171	1,119	1,739	1,372	4,556	5
Huntingdonshire	85	808	1,177	1,009	2,500	1
Kent	347	1,152s	?	3,153	11,753	8
(Lancashire, South)	55	153c; 54	22	94	260	1
Leicestershire	292	2,233c; 26	?	1,876	6,423	1
Lincolnshire	754	4,206c	5,027	4,810	21,462	5
Middlesex	62	880	677	546	2,177	1
Norfolk	730	2,423c	?	5,006	26,309	3
Northamptonshire	354	1,280	2,869	2,461	7,663	1
Nottinghamshire	297	563c	1,231	1,978	5,608	2
Oxfordshire	250	2,568	2,857	2,584	6,713	1
Roteland	16	40c	144	249	859	—
Shropshire (now in England)	435	1,364	3,075	1,750	4,709	2
Shropshire (now in Wales)	24	66	55	26	48	—
Somerset	622	2,933	4,815	3,924	12,991	9
Staffordshire	342	507; 29c	1,468	1,063	3,028	3
Suffolk	639	2,411c	?	4,480	19,070	6
Surrey	144	2,002	1,263	1,276	4,105	2
Sussex	336	3,204	3,134	3,200	9,600	7
Warwickshire	247	1,297	2,272	2,033	6,277	1
Wiltshire	344	4,032	3,475	3,003	9,944	10
Worcestershire	275	1,432	?	2,120	4,604	3
Yorkshire	1,993	10,609c	5,710	2,927	7,566	5
Totals	13,418			81,184	268,984	112

APPENDIX 2

SUMMARY OF CATEGORIES OF RURAL POPULATION

Villeins	109,230	*Mercatores*	20
Bordars	81,849	*Hospites*	17
Slaves	28,235	Bee-keepers	16
Sokemen	23,324	*Bedelli*	14
Freemen	13,553	*Consuetudinarii*	11
Cottars	5,205	*Angli*	11
Coscets	1,742	Shepherds	10
Priests	1,027	Flemings	9
Coliberts	840	Thegns	9
Buri	65	*Rustici*	8
Oxmen	759	*Franci homines*	8
Free oxmen	12	*Franci*	4
Men (*homines*)	595	Drengs	6
King's men	96	Millers	6
Men with gardens	23	*Alodiarii*	5
Swineherds	556	Potters	5
Radmen	546	*Clerici*	5
Francigenae	259	Foresters	4
Censores	160	*Francones homines*	3
Gablatores	7	*Vavassores*	3
Salt-workers	121	Cowmen	2
Knights	106	Mill-keepers	2
English knights	6	Carpenter	1
French knights	3	Deacon	1
Welshmen	111	Huntsman	1
Fishermen	92	*Serviens*	1
Prepositi	68	*Mercennarius*	1
Fabri	64	Others (*alii*)	6
Ferrarii	10	Uncertain	54
Cervisarii	40		
Servientes	21		
Francigenae servientes	16	Total	268,984

APPENDIX 3

CATEGORIES OF RURAL POPULATION BY DOMESDAY COUNTIES

This summary includes the apparently rural element in the boroughs
A query refers to an unspecified number.

	Villeins	Bordars	Slaves	Sokemen	Freemen	Cottars
Bedfordshire	1,854	1,147	480	107	—	—
Berkshire	2,685	1,859	793	—	—	734
Buckinghamshire	2,899	1,321	845	20	—	10
Cambridgeshire	1,937	1,408	541	177	—	770
Cheshire (now in England)	557	463	141	—	—	—
Cheshire (now in Wales)	124	118	44	—	—	—
Cornwall	1,704	2,426	1,149	—	—	—
Derbyshire	1,858	738	20	128	—	—
Devonshire	8,472	4,866	3,318	—	—	36
Dorset	2,632	2,990	1,244	—	—	198
Essex	4,056	7,007	1,809	600	432	—
Gloucestershire (now in England)	3,819	1,859	2,140	—	21	—
Gloucestershire (now in Wales)	16	32	7	—	—	—
Hampshire	3,900	4,000	1,765	—	—	—
Herefordshire (now in England)	1,704	1,231	722	—	15	19
Herefordshire (now in Wales)	—	2	10	—	—	—
Hertfordshire	1,799	1,130	591	43	8	855
Huntingdonshire	1,935	482	—	20	—	—
Kent	6,829	3,372	1,160	44	2	309
(Lancashire, South)	119	81	20	—	—	—
Leicestershire	2,630	1,371	402	1,903	6	—
Lincolnshire	7,029	3,379	—	10,882	—	—
Middlesex	1,163	364	112	—	—	464
Norfolk	4,607	9,886	973	5,410	5,227	—
Northamptonshire	3,874	1,982	737	971	3	—
Nottinghamshire	2,634	1,180	24	1,704	—	—
Oxfordshire	3,671	1,948	1,002	—	26	—
Roteland	730	114	—	8	—	—
Shropshire (now in England)	1,818	1,141	918	—	20	15
Shropshire (now in Wales)	15	14	10	—	—	—
Somerset	5,273	4,826	2,120	—	—	392
Staffordshire	1,786	939	240	—	16	—
Suffolk	3,094	6,438	892	859	7,753	—
Surrey	2,389	936	503	—	—	276
Sussex	5,883	2,519	416	—	—	766
Warwickshire	3,514	1,823	781	—	19	—
Wiltshire	3,497	2,783	1,588	—	—	285
Worcestershire	1,694	1,868	718	—	3	60
Yorkshire	5,030	1,806	—	448	2	16
Totals	109,230	81,849	28,235	23,324	13,553	5,205

Coscets	Priests	Coliberts	*Buri*	Oxmen	Free oxmen	Men	King's men	Men with gardens
—	—	—	—	—	—	1	—	—
—	6	24	18	—	—	—	—	—
—	—	—	4	—	—	—	—	—
—	2	—	—	—	—	—	—	—
—	24	—	—	161	—	3	—	—
—	6	—	—	2	—	3	—	—
—	—	49	—	—	—	—	—	—
—	47	—	—	—	—	1	—	—
70	1	32	4	—	—	3	—	—
196	4	33	—	—	—	10	—	—
—	28	—	—	—	—	32	—	—
—	52	85	—	—	—	58	—	—
—	—	—	—	—	—	—	—	—
—	2	98	—	—	—	8	—	—
—	44	16	19	113	11	134	96	—
—	—	—	—	—	—	—	—	—
—	51	—	—	—	—	—	—	—
—	48	—	—	—	—	9	—	—
—	12	—	—	—	—	16	—	—
—	2	—	—	12	—	8	—	—
—	43	—	—	—	—	10	—	—
—	122	—	—	—	—	27	—	—
—	18	—	—	—	—	34	—	—
—	11	—	—	—	—	160	—	—
—	68	—	—	—	—	6	—	—
—	63	—	—	—	—	—	—	—
—	1	—	17	—	—	1	—	23
—	7	—	—	—	—	—	—	—
9	53	13	—	389	1	16	—	—
—	—	—	—	2	—	—	—	—
56	3	208	—	—	—	4	—	—
—	33	—	—	—	—	—	—	—
—	4	—	—	—	—	24	—	—
—	—	—	—	—	—	—	—	—
—	5	—	—	—	—	—	—	—
—	68	6	—	1	—	13	—	—
1,411	3	270	—	—	—	?	—	—
—	60	6	3	79	—	1	—	—
—	136	—	—	—	—	13	—	—
1,742	1,027	840	65	759	12	595	96	23

12

	Swine-herds	Radmen	Franci-genae	Censores	Gabla-tores	Salt-workers	Knights
Bedfordshire	—	—	—	—	—	—	2
Berkshire	—	1	—	—	—	—	3
Buckinghamshire	—	—	1	—	—	—	—
Cambridgeshire	—	—	2	—	—	—	—
Cheshire (now in England)	—	119	31	—	—	—	—
Cheshire (now in Wales)	—	15	10	—	—	—	1
Cornwall	—	—	—	—	—	—	—
Derbyshire	—	—	—	42	—	—	—
Devonshire	370	—	—	—	—	61	—
Dorset	—	—	—	11	—	56	—
Essex	1	—	—	36	—	—	—
Gloucestershire (now in England)	4	126	12	—	—	—	6
Gloucestershire (now in Wales)	—	—	—	—	—	—	1
Hampshire	—	5	—	—	—	—	—
Herefordshire (now in England)	1	53	23	—	—	—	—
Herefordshire (now in Wales)	—	—	—	—	—	—	—
Hertfordshire	—	—	48	—	—	—	12
Huntingdonshire	—	—	—	—	—	—	—
Kent	—	—	3	—	—	—	3
(Lancashire, South)	—	9	—	—	—	—	—
Leicestershire	—	—	33	—	—	—	14
Lincolnshire	—	—	7	14	—	—	1
Middlesex	—	—	9	—	—	—	11
Norfolk	—	—	—	—	—	—	—
Northamptonshire	—	—	3	—	—	—	14
Nottinghamshire	—	—	—	2	—	—	—
Oxfordshire	—	—	8	—	—	—	6
Roteland	—	—	—	—	—	—	—
Shropshire (now in England)	—	174	34	—	—	—	9
Shropshire (now in Wales)	—	4	—	—	—	—	—
Somerset	84	—	—	—	7	—	—
Staffordshire	—	—	—	—	—	—	4
Suffolk	—	—	—	—	—	—	—
Surrey	—	—	—	—	—	—	—
Sussex	—	—	—	—	—	—	—
Warwickshire	—	—	12	—	—	—	16
Wiltshire	87	—	—	—	—	—	2
Worcestershire	9	40	23	—	—	4	1
Yorkshire	—	—	—	55	—	—	—
Totals	556	546	259	160	7	121	106

English knights	French knights	Welshmen	Fishermen	Prepositi	Fabri	Ferrarii	Cervisarii	Servientes
—	—	—	—	—	—	—	—	—
1	—	—	—	—	—	—	—	—
—	—	—	—	—	1	—	—	—
—	3	—	28	—	—	—	—	—
—	—	—	14	6	4	—	—	1
—	—	—	—	—	—	—	—	1
—	—	—	—	—	—	—	40	—
—	—	—	2	—	1	—	—	—
—	—	—	4	—	2	4	—	—
—	—	—	1	—	1	—	—	—
—	—	—	—	2	2	—	—	—
—	—	2	—	—	—	—	—	—
—	—	—	—	—	—	—	—	—
—	—	39	—	31	24	—	—	9
—	—	3	—	—	—	—	—	—
—	—	—	—	4	—	—	—	—
—	—	—	5	—	1	—	—	—
—	—	—	—	2	—	—	—	—
—	—	—	—	—	—	—	—	—
—	—	—	—	—	—	—	—	—
—	—	—	24	—	—	—	—	—
—	—	—	—	1	2	—	—	2
—	—	—	—	—	—	—	—	—
—	—	—	4	—	—	—	—	—
—	—	—	—	—	—	—	—	—
—	—	64	—	9	8	—	—	6
—	—	3	—	—	—	—	—	—
—	—	—	10	—	8	—	—	—
—	—	—	—	1	—	—	—	2
—	—	—	—	—	—	—	—	—
—	—	—	—	—	—	—	—	—
5	—	—	—	—	2	—	—	—
—	—	—	—	—	—	—	—	—
—	—	—	—	12	8	—	—	—
—	—	—	—	—	—	6	—	—
6	3	111	92	68	64	10	40	21

	Francigenae servientes	Merca-tores	Hospites	Bee-keepers	Bedelli	Consuetu-dinarii	Angli
Bedfordshire	—	—	—	—	—	—	—
Berkshire	—	10	—	—	—	—	—
Buckinghamshire	—	—	—	—	—	—	—
Cambridgeshire	—	—	—	—	—	—	—
Cheshire (now in England)	—	—	3	—	—	—	—
Cheshire (now in Wales)	—	—	—	—	—	—	—
Cornwall	—	—	—	—	—	—	—
Derbyshire	—	—	—	—	—	—	—
Devonshire	—	—	—	5	—	—	—
Dorset	2	—	—	—	—	—	—
Essex	—	—	—	—	—	—	—
Gloucestershire (now in England)	—	—	—	—	—	—	—
Gloucestershire (now in Wales)	—	—	—	—	—	—	—
Hampshire	—	—	—	—	—	—	—
Herefordshire (now in England)	—	—	7	—	9	—	—
Herefordshire (now in Wales)	—	—	—	—	—	—	—
Hertfordshire	—	10	—	—	—	—	2
Huntingdonshire	—	—	—	—	—	—	—
Kent	—	—	—	—	—	—	—
(Lancashire, South)	—	—	—	—	—	—	—
Leicestershire	9	—	—	—	—	—	—
Lincolnshire	—	—	—	—	—	—	—
Middlesex	—	—	—	—	—	—	1
Norfolk	—	—	—	—	—	11	—
Northamptonshire	—	—	—	—	—	—	—
Nottinghamshire	—	—	—	—	—	—	—
Oxfordshire	—	—	—	—	—	—	—
Roteland	—	—	—	—	—	—	—
Shropshire (now in England)	3	—	7	1	—	—	—
Shropshire (now in Wales)	—	—	—	—	—	—	—
Somerset	—	—	—	—	—	—	—
Staffordshire	—	—	—	—	—	—	6
Suffolk	—	—	—	—	—	—	—
Surrey	—	—	—	—	—	—	—
Sussex	—	—	—	—	—	—	—
Warwickshire	—	—	—	—	—	—	—
Wiltshire	—	—	—	9	—	—	2
Worcestershire	2	—	—	1	5	—	—
Yorkshire	—	—	—	—	—	—	—
Totals	16	20	17	16	14	11	11

Shepherds	Flemings	Thegns	Rustici	Franci homines	Franci	Drengs	Millers	Alodiarii
—	—	—	—	—	—	—	—	—
—	—	—	—	—	—	—	—	5
—	—	—	—	—	—	—	—	—
—	—	—	—	—	—	—	—	—
—	—	—	—	—	—	—	1	—
—	—	—	—	—	—	—	—	—
—	—	—	—	—	—	—	—	—
—	—	—	—	—	—	—	—	—
—	—	—	1	—	—	—	—	—
—	—	—	—	—	—	—	—	—
—	—	—	—	—	—	—	—	—
—	—	—	—	1	—	—	—	—
—	—	—	—	—	—	—	—	—
—	—	—	—	—	—	—	—	—
—	—	—	2	—	—	—	—	—
—	—	—	1	—	—	—	—	—
—	—	3	—	—	—	6	—	—
—	—	—	—	—	—	—	—	—
—	—	—	—	1	—	—	—	—
—	—	—	—	—	1	—	—	—
—	—	—	—	—	—	—	—	—
—	—	—	—	1	—	—	—	—
—	—	—	—	—	—	—	—	—
—	—	—	—	—	—	—	1	—
—	—	—	—	—	—	—	—	—
—	—	1	—	—	—	—	—	—
—	—	—	—	5	1	—	—	—
—	—	—	—	—	—	—	—	—
10	—	—	—	—	—	—	1	—
—	9	5	—	—	—	—	—	—
—	—	—	4	—	2	—	—	—
—	—	—	—	—	—	—	3	—
—	—	—	—	—	—	—	—	—
10	9	9	8	8	4	6	6	5

	Potters	Clerici	Foresters	Francones homines	Vavas- sores	Cowmen	Mill- keepers
Bedfordshire	—	—	—	—	—	—	—
Berkshire	—	—	—	—	—	—	—
Buckinghamshire	—	—	—	—	2	—	—
Cambridgeshire	—	—	—	—	—	—	—
Cheshire (now in England)	—	—	—	—	—	—	—
Cheshire (now in Wales)	—	—	—	—	—	—	—
Cornwall	—	—	—	—	—	—	—
Derbyshire	—	—	—	—	—	—	1
Devonshire	—	—	—	—	—	—	—
Dorset	—	—	—	—	—	—	—
Essex	—	—	1	—	—	—	—
Gloucestershire (now in England)	5	—	—	—	—	—	—
Gloucestershire (now in Wales)	—	—	—	—	—	—	—
Hampshire	—	—	—	—	1	—	—
Herefordshire (now in England)	—	3	—	—	—	1	1
Herefordshire (now in Wales)	—	—	—	—	—	—	—
Hertfordshire	—	1	—	—	—	—	—
Huntingdonshire	—	—	—	—	—	—	—
Kent	—	—	—	—	—	—	—
(Lancashire, South)	—	—	—	—	—	—	—
Leicestershire	—	1	—	—	—	—	—
Lincolnshire	—	—	—	—	—	—	—
Middlesex	—	—	—	—	—	—	—
Norfolk	—	—	—	—	—	—	—
Northamptonshire	—	—	—	—	—	—	—
Nottinghamshire	—	—	—	—	—	—	—
Oxfordshire	—	—	—	—	—	—	—
Roteland	—	—	—	—	—	—	—
Shropshire (now in England)	—	—	—	—	—	—	—
Shropshire (now in Wales)	—	—	—	—	—	—	—
Somerset	—	—	—	—	—	—	—
Staffordshire	—	—	—	—	—	—	—
Suffolk	—	—	—	—	—	—	—
Surrey	—	—	1	—	—	—	—
Sussex	—	—	—	—	—	—	—
Warwickshire	—	—	—	3	—	—	—
Wiltshire	?	—	—	—	—	—	—
Worcestershire	—	—	2	—	—	1	—
Yorkshire	—	—	—	—	—	—	—
Totals	5	5	4	3	3	2	2

Carpenter	Deacon	Huntsman	Serviens	Mercennarius	Alii	Uncertain	Total
—	—	—	—	—	—	—	3,591
—	—	—	—	—	—	—	6,139
—	—	—	—	—	—	—	5,103
—	—	—	—	—	—	—	4,868
—	—	—	—	—	—	—	1,528
—	—	—	—	—	—	—	324
—	—	—	—	—	—	—	5,368
—	—	—	—	—	—	—	2,836
—	—	—	—	—	—	—	17,246
—	—	—	—	—	—	—	7,382
—	—	—	—	1	—	—	14,004
—	—	—	—	—	—	—	8,191
—	—	—	—	—	—	—	58
—	—	—	—	—	—	—	9,780
1	—	—	—	—	—	—	4,326
—	—	—	—	—	—	—	15
—	—	—	—	—	—	—	4,556
—	—	—	—	—	—	—	2,500
—	—	—	—	—	—	—	11,753
—	—	—	—	—	—	—	260
—	1	—	—	—	—	—	6,423
—	—	—	—	—	—	—	21,462
—	—	—	—	—	—	—	2,177
—	—	—	—	—	—	—	26,309
—	—	—	—	—	—	—	7,663
—	—	—	—	—	—	—	5,608
—	—	—	—	—	6	—	6,713
—	—	—	—	—	—	—	859
—	—	—	—	—	—	—	4,709
—	—	—	—	—	—	—	48
—	—	—	—	—	—	—	12,991
—	—	—	—	—	—	—	3,028
—	—	—	—	—	—	—	19,070
—	—	—	—	—	—	—	4,105
—	—	—	—	—	—	—	9,600
—	—	—	—	—	—	—	6,277
—	—	—	1	—	—	—	9,944
—	—	1	—	—	—	—	4,604
—	—	—	—	—	—	54	7,566
1	1	1	1	1	6	54	268,984

APPENDIX 4

CHURCHES AND PRIESTS
BY DOMESDAY COUNTIES

(1) Number of churches. (2) Number of priests. (3) Number of places with churches. (4) Number of places with priests but no churches. (5) Total of columns (3) and (4). (6) Total places. For the priests in Cornwall, see p. 56.

	(1)	(2)	(3)	(4)	(5)	(6)
Bedfordshire	4	—	4	—	4	141
Berkshire	64	6	57	1	58	189
Buckinghamshire	4	—	4	—	4	206
Cambridgeshire	3	2	3	2	5	142
Cheshire (now in England)	13	24	10	14	24	266
Cheshire (now in Wales)	9	6	9	2	11	100
Cornwall	—	?	—	—	—	332
Derbyshire	47	47	43	5	48	346
Devonshire	12	1	9	1	10	980
Dorset	14	4	12	4	16	314
Essex	17	28	17	20	37	444
Gloucestershire (now in England)	11	52	11	42	53	372
Gloucestershire (now in Wales)	—	—	—	—	—	7
Hampshire	129	2	104	—	104	454
Herefordshire (now in England)	14	44	12	27	39	302
Herefordshire (now in Wales)	1	—	1	—	1	9
Hertfordshire	4	51	3	50	53	171
Huntingdonshire	54	48	53	—	53	85
Kent	186	12	147	2	149	347
(Lancashire, South)	7	2	7	2	9	55
Leicestershire	1	43	1	42	43	292
Lincolnshire	242	122	228	2	230	754
Middlesex	3	18	3	18	21	62
Norfolk	249	11	219	5	224	730
Northamptonshire	3	68	3	64	67	354
Nottinghamshire	86	63	72	4	76	297
Oxfordshire	6	1	2	1	3	250
Roteland	8	7	4	—	4	16
Shropshire (now in England)	29	53	24	25	49	435
Shropshire (now in Wales)	—	—	—	—	—	24
Somerset	18	3	17	—	17	622
Staffordshire	2	33	2	29	31	342
Suffolk	427	4	352	2	354	639
Surrey	68	—	62	—	62	144
Sussex	109	5	94	1	95	336
Warwickshire	1	68	1	62	63	247
Wiltshire	29	3	29	2	31	344
Worcestershire	10	60	10	52	62	275
Yorkshire	177	136	167	10	177	1,993
Totals	2,061	1,027	1,796	491	2,287	13,418

APPENDIX 5

THE SHROPSHIRE PLOUGHLAND FORMULAE

Fief by fief and folio by folio

a *possent esse*   c *T.R.E. carucae*
b *Terra carucis*   d *carucae fuerunt*
　　o No mention of ploughlands

Bishop of Chester	(252)	o o o a b o o a b
Bishop of Hereford	(252)	a c
Church of St Remy	(252)	d
	(252b)	o a o o o a a a o o o a a o o o a a a a o o o b b b
	(253)	o a a b b o o o a a a o o a o o o o
Earl Roger	(253)	o a a a o b a a a b
	(253b)	a b a b o o a b o a o o a a o o o a o a o a a
	(254)	a a a o a a a b o o a a a a o a a a o o a a a
	(254b)	o a a a a o a o a a a o a a a o a a a a a b b b b b
	(255)	b b b b b o b a a a b o o o o a b a o a o a b o o o a a a a a a
	(255b)	a o b o b a o o o o o b a o a a a o a o a a (ba)[1] o o a o a
	(256)	a o b a o a o a a a a o a o o o a o o o b a a a a a a a
	(256b)	o a a o a a a a o o a a o o o a a b a a a a a a o b
	(257)	a o a a b b a o o b o o b b b b a b b b b b b b b b b b b b b b
	(257b)	b b a b b b b b b b b b b b b b b b o b b b b b b b b a b b b b
	(258)	b b b b b b b b b b b d b b b b b o o b b b b b b b b b b b b b
	(258b)	b b b b b b b b b b b b b b b b b b b b b b b b b b b b b o b
	(259)	b b b b b b b b b b b b b b b b o b b o o b b b b b b b b b o b
	(259b)	o b b b b b b o b o b b b b b b b b b b b b b b b b b b b b b o
		o b
Osbern fitz Richard	(260)	b b b b b b b b
Ralf de Mortemer	(260)	b b o o b b b b b b b b b b b b b b b
	(260b)	b b b b b b b b o b b b o o
Roger de Laci	(260b)	b o b b b b
Hugh Lasne	(260b)	b b
Nigel the Physician	(260b)	b b

[1] Both formulae occur in the same entry.

APPENDIX 6

THE LEICESTERSHIRE
PLOUGHLAND FORMULAE

Fief by fief and folio by folio

a   *possent esse*   c   *T.R.E. carucae*
b   *Terra carucis*   d   *carucae fuerunt*
o   No mention of ploughlands
bˣ   Defective entry

The king	(230)	o o o o o
	(230b)	(o o o o o o o o o o o o o o o o o o o o)¹ o (o o o o o o
		o o o o)² o o o o o o o o o b
Archbishop of York	(230b)	o o o o o o o
Bishop of Lincoln	(230)	o
	(231)	b o a a b b b b o o b o o b b
Bishop of Coutances	(231)	b
Abbey of Peterborough	(231)	b b o
Abbey of Coventry	(231)	o b o o o o
Abbey of Crowland	(231)	b b
The king's alms	(231)	o b o o o
Count of Mellend	(231b)	c o b o o
Earl Aubrey	(231b)	b o o o o o o o b b b b b b b b b o
Countess Godeva	(231b)	b b c
Countess Alveva	(231b)	c c
Hugh de Grentemaisnil	(232)	b b b o b o b b b b b b b b b b b b b b b b b b b b b b
	(232b)	b b b b b b b b b b b b b b b b b b b b b b b b b b b
		b b b b b b
	(233)	b b b b b b b b b b
Henry de Ferrers	(233)	c c c o c c o o c c c c c c o c c
	(233b)	o c c o o c o o c o o o c c c c c o
Robert de Todeni	(233b)	c c o c c c c c b b o o o b b
	(234)	b b b
Robert de Veci	(234)	c c c c b c c o c o
Robert de Buci	(234)	b b b c c o o b b b c c c o b o o c c c
	(234b)	c c c c o b c o c c c b c c
Roger de Busli	(234b)	c c c c c
Robert Dispensator	(234b)	b bˣ b bˣ bˣ bˣ o o bˣ o bˣ bˣ c c
	(235)	c o o o o o
Robert the Usher	(235)	b b b o
Ralf de Mortemer	(235)	b b
Ralf fitz Hubert	(235)	b
Guy de Reinbudcurt	(235)	b b b b b b
Guy de Credun	(235)	c o b
William Peverel	(235)	b b b b b
William Buenvaslet	(235)	o
William Loveth	(235b)	b c c
Geoffrey Alselin	(235b)	c c c c o c
Geoffrey de Wirce	(235b)	c c o (c c c c c c c)³ d d d o d o d d d d d d o o d d d o
Godfrey de Cambrai	(235b)	d

Gunfrid de Cioches	(235b)	o
Humfrey the Chamberlain	(236)	d d
Gilbert de Gand	(236)	d
Girbert	(236)	d d
Durand Malet	(236)	d d o
Drogo de Beurere	(236)	d d
Maino the Breton	(236)	d d d
Oger the Breton	(236)	d
Nigel de Albingi	(236)	o b
Countess Judith	(236)	d d d d o d d d d d d o d o d d d d
	(236b)	o d d d d d d d d d o d d d d d d o o o d d
Adeliz wife of Hugh de Grentemaisnil	(236b)	b b b
The king's Serjeants	(236b)	d o d o d o b b o o
Earl Hugh	(237)	(c c c c c c c c c c c c c c c c c c c)⁴ o o o o o
Men of Count of Mellend	(237)	o o d d d d d d d d d d

¹ Members of Rothley.
³ Members of Melton Mowbray.

² Members of Great Bowden.
⁴ Covered by one total.

APPENDIX 7

THE YORKSHIRE PLOUGHLAND FORMULAE

Fief by fief and folio by folio

a *Ubi possunt esse* b *Terra carucis*
o No mention of ploughlands

The king	(299)	a a a a a a a a a a a a
	(299b)	a a a a a a a b b a a a a a a a a
	(300)	b b b b b b b b b b o b b b b b b b b b b b b b b b b b b b b b b b b o b b b b b b b b b b b o b b b b b o b b b b b b b b b b b
	(300b)	b b b b b b b b b b b b b b b b b b b b o b b o b o b b b b b b b o b b b b b b b b b b b b b b b b b b b b b b b b b b b b b b b b
	(301)	b b b b b b o b b o b b b b b b o b o b b b b b b b b b b b b o o b b b b b b b o b b o o b b b o b b b b b b b b b b b b b b b b b b b b b b b b b b b b b b b b b b b b b b o o
	(301b)	b b b b b b b b b b b o b b b b b b b b b b b b b b b o o o o o o o
	(302)	o o o o o
Archbishop of York	(302)	b b b o
	(302b)	a a a a a a a a a a o a a a
	(303)	a a a a o a o a a a a a a o a a a a a a a
	(303b)	b b o o o a a a a a a a a a a a a o
	(304)	o a a o a a a a a o a a o a a a a b b b b b b o b o b b b b b o o o o b o b o o b
Bishop of Durham	(304b)	a a a a a a a o o a a a a a a a b b b
Earl Hugh	(305)	a a a a a a a o a
Count of Mortain	(305)	o a a a a a a a a a a a a a
	(305b)	a a a a a a a a a a a a a a a a a a a a a a o a o a a b b
	(306)	a a o a a a o o o a a a a a o o a a a o a o a o a o a a
	(306b)	a a a o a a a a a o o a a a a o a o o o a o a a a a o a a a
	(307)	o a a a o a a a o o o o a a o o o o o o o o o a a o a o o a
	(307b)	a o a a a a a a a o a a a a a a a a
	(308)	a a a a a a a a a a a b b b b o o a
	(308b)	a a a a o a a
Count Alan	(309)	a a a a a a a a a a a a a a
	(309b)	a a o a a a a a a a a a a a a a a a a
	(310)	a a a a a a a a a a a a a a a a a a o a
	(310b)	a a a a a a a a a a a a a a a a a
	(311)	a a a a a a a a a a a a a a a a a a a a a a a a a a a
	(311b)	a a a a a a a a a a a a a a a a a a a o a
	(312)	a a a a a a a a a a a a a a a a a a a a a a
	(312b)	a a a a a a a a a o a a a a a a a a
	(313)	a a a a a a a a a a a

	(313b)	Blank
Robert de Todeni	(314)	a a
Berenger de Todeni	(314)	b b b b b o b b b b b b b b b b b b b b b b b
	(314b)	o b o o b b b b b b b
Ilbert de Laci	(315)	a a a a a a a b b b a a a a a a a a a a a
	(315b)	b b b b a a a a a a a a a b a a a a a a b a a
	(316)	a a a a a a a a a a a a a a a a a a
	(316b)	a a a a a a a a a a a a a a a a a
	(317)	a a a a a a a a a a o a a a a a a a a a
	(317b)	a a a a a a a a a a a a a a a a a a a a a a
	(318)	a a a a a a a a a a a a a a a a a a a a a b
	(318b)	Blank
Roger de Busli	(319)	a a a a a a a a a a a a a a a a a
	(319b)	a o a a a a a a a a a a a a a a a a a a a
	(320)	a a a a a a
Robert Malet	(320)	a a a a a o o o o a o a a a a a o b o o o a a a ̧a b o a a
	(321)	b b b
William de Warene	(321)	b b
William de Perci	(321b)	a a a a a a a a a a a a a a a a a a
	(322)	a a a a a a a a a a a o a a a a a a a a a a a a a o o o o o o o
	(322b)	a a a a a a a a a a a a a a a a a a a a a
	(323)	o a a a a a a a a a a a a
Drogo de Beurere	(323b)	a a a a a a a a a a a a a a a
	(324)	a a a a a a a a a a a a a a a a a a
	(324b)	a a o a a a a a a a a a a a a a a a a o a
	(325)	a a a b b b b
Ralf de Mortemer	(325)	b b b b b b b b o b b b b b
	(325b)	b b b b b
Ralf Pagenel	(325b)	b b b b b a b b b b
	(326)	b b b
Goisfrid de la Wirce	(326)	b
Goisfrid Alselin	(326)	b b b
Walter de Aincurt	(326)	b b b
Gislebert de Gand	(326)	b b b b b
Gislebert Tison	(326b)	b b b b b b b b b b b b b b b b b b b o b b o b b b b
	(327)	b b b o o o
Richard fitz Erfast	(327)	b b b b b o
Hugh fitz Baldric	(327)	b b b b b b b b b
	(327b)	b b b b b b b b b b b o b b b b b b b b b
	(328)	b b b b b b b b b b b b b b b b b b b b b b
Erneis de Burun	(328b)	b b b o b b b b b o b b b b b b b b o b b b b b
Osbern de Arches	(329)	b b b o b b o b b b b b b b b b b b b b
	(329b)	b b b b b b b b o b o
Odo the Crossbowman	(329b)	b b b b o b b b b b b
Aubrey de Coucy	(329b)	b b
Gospatric	(330)	b b o b b b b b b b b b b b b b b b b b b b b b b b b b o b b b b b b b b b o
King's thegns	(330b)	b b b b b b o b b b b o b b b b b b b b b b b b b b b b b b
	(331)	b b b b b b b o b o b b b b b b b b b b b b b b b b b b b b b b b
	(331b)	b b b b b b b b b b b b b b b o o o o o o o o o o o o
Roger the Poitevin	(332)	o o o o o o o o o o o o o o o o o o o o o o o o o o o o o o o o o o o o o o o
Robert de Bruis	(332b)	o o o o o o o o o o o o
	(333)	o o o

APPENDIX 8

REFERENCES TO MARSH

Cambridgeshire

Bottisham (196)	*De maresc iii soci et cccc anguillae*
Cherry Hinton (193b)	*De maresc xxv denarii*
Chesterton (189b)	*De maresch mille anguillarum*
Cottenham (192b)	*De maresch quingentae anguillae et de presentatione xii denarii*
(201b)	*De maresc cl anguillae*
Croxton (202)	*De Maresch quingentae anguillae per annum*
Landbeach (195)	*Maresch ccccl anguillae*
(201b)	*De maresch mille anguillarum et xii denarii de presentatione*
Long Stanton (197b)	*De maresch iii millia et cc anguillarum et ii solidi et viii denarii*
Milton (201b)	*De maresch sexcentae et l anguillae et xii denarii*
Over (192b)	*De maresch vi solidi et iiii denarii*
Swaffham (190b)	*De maresc vi denarii*
Swavesey (197b)	*De maresch ccxxv anguillae*
Wilburton (192)	*De juncis xvi denarii*
Willingham (191b)	*De maris vi solidi*

Essex

Canfield (35)	*xlviii acrae prati inter pratum et maresc*
Greenstead (104)	*Tunc xxiiii acrae prati et maresc et modo*
Parndon (78b)	*xlv acrae inter pratum et maresc*
Peldon (94b)	*De his v hidis tulit hamo dapifer lxxx acras de arabili terra et cc acras de maresc quod totum adjacebantur huic manerio t.r.e. et post adventum regis Willelmi*
Tilty (56b)	*xxx acrae prati, xx acrae de maresc*

Huntingdonshire

Colne (204)	*Silva pastilis i leuua longa et dimidia lata et maresc tantundem*
Holywell (204)	*Maresc i leuua longa et i lata*
Warboys (204b)	*Maresc i leuua longa et dimidia leuua lata*

Kent

Six unnamed holdings (13)	*in Maresc de Romenel*

Lincolnshire

Axholme, Isle of (369b)	*Ad hanc insula adjacent maresc x leuuis longa et iii lata*
Baston (346b)	*Maresc xvi quarentenis longa et viii lata*
Candlesby (348b)	*c acrae maresc*
Coteland (369b)	*Maresc x quarentenis longa et vi quarentenis lata*
Elvedon (344b)	*c acrae maresc*
(357b)	*xl acrae maresch*
(369b)	*xl acrae maresch*
Ewerby Thorpe, Howell, Heckington, Quarrington (337b)	*xx acrae maresch*
Grainsby (347)	*Toruelande v solidi et iiii denarii*
Hasthorp (355)	*xxx acrae maresch*
Langtoft (346b)	*Maresc ii leuuis longa et ii lata*
Morton (350)	*Morae*
North Thoresby and Autby (342b)	*toruelande reddens x solidos*

Lincolnshire (*cont.*)
  South Ferriby (354b)   *cclx acrae maresc*
  South Kyme (337b)   *septies c acrea maresc*
  Willoughby on the Marsh (355)   *xl acrae maresc*
Norfolk
  Heckingham (205)   *Maresc lx ovibus*
  Marham (212b)   *in Maresc nescit mensuram*
  Raveningham (273b)   *i maresc*
Somerset
  Adsborough (*356*, 95b)   *x acrae morae*
  Fiddington (*441b*, 94b)   *xliii acrae morae*
  Huntworth (*371b*, 97)   *x acrae morae*
  Milborne Port (*91*, 86b)   *una leuga Morae*
  North Newton (*477b*, 98b)   *xx acrae morae*
  Seavington (*265b*, 91b)   *xxv acrae morae et prati*
  Tuxwell (*441b*, 94b)   *xli acrae morae*
  Wedmore (*159b*, 89)   *ibi morae quae nichil reddunt* (in Exon. D.B. only)
  Wells (*157b*, 89)   *iii leugae morae*
  Weston in Gordano (*142b*, 88)   *vi quarentenae morae*
  Yatton (*159b*, 89b)   *Morae una leuua in longitudine et latitudine*

APPENDIX 9

REFERENCES TO FORESTS

	Foresta mentioned	Forest implied
Berkshire	Bucklebury (61b)	Windsor (56b)
	Cookham (56b)	
	Kintbury (61b)	
	Winkfield (59)	
Buckinghamshire	Brill (143b)	
Cheshire (now in England)	*Aldredelie* (263b)	
	Done (263b)	
	Kenardeslie (263b)	
	Kingsley (267b)	
	Weaverham (263b)	
Cheshire (now in Wales)	Atiscros hd (268b)	
	Bistre (269)	
	Rhuddlan (269 *bis*)	
Dorset	Wimborne Minster (78b)	
Essex		Writtle (5b)
Gloucestershire	*Dene* (167b)	Forthampton (180b)
	Hewelsfield (167)	Staunton (181)
	Taynton	
	Wyegate (166b)	
Hampshire	See pp. 198–201 above and	
	D.G.S–E.E., 327–30	
Herefordshire	Bullingham (184, 186)	*Brocote* (181)
	Cleeve (179b)	Burton (181b)
	Harewood, in Archenfield	Didley (181b)
	(181)	Dinedor (183)
	Turlestane (179b)	Madley (181b)
	William fitz Norman (181)	Moor (182b)
		Much Cowarne (186)
		Ross (182)
		Stane (181b)
		Stradel hd (182b)
Huntingdonshire	Brampton (208)	Ellington (204b)
(Lancashire, South)	Salford hd (270)	
	West Derby hd (269b)	
Northamptonshire	Brixworth (219b)	
Oxfordshire	Cornbury (154b)	Shipton under Wychwood
	Shotover (154b)	(154b)
	Stowood (154b)	Wootton (154b)
	Woodstock (154b)	
	Wychwood (154b)	
Shropshire		Albrighton (259)

	Foresta mentioned	Forest implied
Staffordshire	Chasepool (249b)	Coven (249b)
	Cippemore (249b)	
	Enville (249)	
	Haswic (247b)	
Surrey	Pyrford (32)	Walton on Thames (36)
		Woking (30, 31)
Sussex	Dallington (18b)	
Warwickshire		Erdington (243)
		Southam (238b)
Wiltshire	Downton (65)	Britford (65)
	Grovely (74)	Collingbourne Ducis (65)
	Laverstock (68)	South Newton (68)
	Milford (71, 74)	Washern (68)
Worcestershire	Aston (174)	Alvechurch (173)
	Baddington (174)	Barley (173)
	Bellington (177)	Bushley (180b)
	Bredicot (173b)	Eldersfield (180b)
	Chadwick (172)	Feckenham (180b)
	Churchill (173b)	Hanley Castle (180b)
	Cofton Hackett (174, 177b)	Hollow Court (180b)
	Crowle (174)	*Ovretone* (174)
	Hanbury (174)	Queenhill (180b)
	Hindlip (173b)	Shell (176b)
	Huddington (173b)	*Tonge* (174)
	Kidderminster (172)	West Hill (174)
	Malvern (173)	
	Offerton (173b)	
	Perry Wood (173b)	
	Stoke Prior (174)	
	Willingwick (172)	
	Woodcote (177b)	

APPENDIX 10

REFERENCES TO HAWKS AND RENDERS OF HAWKS

A. Hawks' nests

Buckinghamshire
  Chalfont (144, 151b)
Cheshire (now in England)
  Acton (265b), Adlington (264), Audlem (265), Austerson (265b), Barthomley (265b), Blakenhall (267), Bredbury (265), Buerton (265b), Dutton (267b), Hale (266b), Hassal (265b), Kingsley (267b), Minshull (265b *bis*), Mottram (268), Odd Rode (268), Peover (267), Wilkesley (265), Wincham (267), Wrenbury (265b)
Cheshire (now in Wales)
  Atiscros hd (268b), Bistre (269), Dyserth *et al.* (269), Gresford (268)
Gloucestershire
  Avening (163b), Forthampton (180b)
Herefordshire
  Leominster (180)
(Lancashire, South)
  Blackburn hd in T.R.E (270), Leyland hd (270 *bis*), Newton hd (269b), Penwortham (270), Roby *et al.* (269b), Salford hd (270), West Derby hd (269 *bis*)
Shropshire
  Little Wenlock (252b), Rushbury (256b), Wem (257)
Surrey
  Limpsfield (34)
Worcestershire
  Bromsgrove (172), Hanley Castle (180b)

B. Renders of hawks

Bach (Heref., 187), Berkshire (56b), Calverhall (Salop., 259), Gloucestershire now in Wales (162), Hampton (Ches., 264), Kingstone (Heref., 179b), Kinnerley (Salop., 259), Kirkby Fleetham (Yorks., 310b), Leicestershire (230), Northamptonshire (219), Oxfordshire (154b), *Pechingeorde* (Sy., 36b), Warwickshire (238), Wiltshire (64b), Worcestershire (172), Yarmouth (Norf., 118b)

APPENDIX II

REFERENCES TO FIRMA UNIUS NOCTIS/DIEI

(No distinction is made between *ad numerum*, *ad pondus*, *de albo argento* etc.)

South-west circuit

Devonshire
    Walkhampton *et al.* (*86b*, only in Exon D.B.)   T.R.E. one night; T.R.W. £5
Dorset
    Burton Bradstock *et al.* (*27*, *75*)   T.R.W. one night
    Wimborne Minster *et al.* (*27*, *75*)   T.R.W. one night
    Dorchester *et al.* (*27b*, *75*)   T.R.W. one night
    Pimperne *et al.* (*27b*, *75*)   T.R.W. ½ night
    Winfrith Newburgh *et al.* (*27b*, *75*)   T.R.W. ½ night
    Dorchester borough (*11b*, *75*)
    Bridport borough (*12*, *75*)   } T.R.E. incidental reference in each entry to one
    Wareham borough (*12b*, *75*)   night, probably elsewhere.[a]
Somerset
    Somerton *et al.* (*90*, 86)   T.R.E. one night; T.R.W. £100 10s 9½d
    North Petherton *et al.* (*89*, 86)   T.R.E. one night; T.R.W. £106 0s 10d
    Williton *et al.* (*89*, 86b)   T.R.E. one night; T.R.W. £105 16s 6½d
    Frome *et al.* (*91*, 86b)   T.R.E. one night; T.R.W. £106 0s 10d
    Milborne Port *et al.* (*91b*, 86b)   'T.R.E. ¾ night; T.R.W. £79 10s 7d[b]
Wiltshire
    Calne (64b)   T.R.W. one night
    Bedwyn (64b)   T.R.W. one night
    Amesbury (64b)   T.R.W. one night
    Warminster (64b)   T.R.W. one night
    Chippenham (64b)   T.R.W. one night, *valet* £110
    Tilshead (65)   T.R.W. one night, *valet* £100

Western circuit

Gloucestershire
    Awre (163)   T.R.E. and T.R.W. ½ night
    Bitton *et al.* (162b)   T.R.E. and T.R.W. one night
    Westbury on Severn (163)   T.R.E. and T.R.W. one night *per iiii annos*
Herefordshire
    Linton (179b)   T.R.E. ¼ night; *Modo est valde imminutum*
Shropshire
    Whittington *et al.* (253b)   ½ night *Tempore Adelredi patris Edwardi regis*;
                  T.R.E. *wasta*; T.R.W. £15 15s

South-east circuit

Hampshire
    Barton Stacey *et al.* (38b)   T.R.E. ½ day, *valuit* £38 8s 4d; T.R.W. £33
    Eling (38b)   T.R.E. ½ day, *valuit* £38 8s 4d; T.R.W. £20
    Basingstoke *et al.* (39)   T.R.W. one day[c]

South-east circuit (cont.)

Sussex
  Beddingham (20b)   T.R.E. one night; T.R.W. £36
  Beeding (28)   T.R.E. one day, *valuit* £95 5s 6d; T.R.W. £40
  Eastbourne (20b)   T.R.E. one night; T.R.W. £43 7s

Midland circuit

Northamptonshire (219)   T.R.W. 3 nights, *valet* £30; and other dues.
Oxfordshire (154b)   T.R.W. 3 nights, *hoc est* £150; and other dues

Bedford–Middlesex circuit

Bedfordshire
  Leighton Buzzard (209)   T.R.W. £22 and ½ day of grain, honey etc.
  Luton (209)   T.R.W. £30 and ½ day of grain, honey etc.
  Houghton Regis (209b)   T.R.W. £10 and ½ day of grain, honey etc.
Cambridgeshire
  Soham (189)   T.R.E. £25 and 3 days of grain, honey, malt,
                        etc.; T.R.W. £25 and £13 8s 4d for grain,
                        malt, honey etc.
  Fordham (189b)   T.R.E. £10 and 3 days of honey, grain, malt;
                        T.R.W. £10 and £13 8s 4d for honey, grain,
                        malt
  Isleham (189b)   ⎫
  Cheveley (189b)   ⎪ T.R.E. 3 days not specified but indicated by
  Wilbraham (189b)   ⎬ T.R.W. render of £13 8s 4d for honey, grain,
  Haslingfield (189b)   ⎪ malt etc.
  Chesterton (189b)   ⎭

Eastern circuit

Essex
  Writtle (5b)   T.R.E. 10 nights and £10; T.R.W. £100 and
                        £5 *de gersuma*
  Brightlingsea *et al.* (6)   T.R.E. 2 nights; T.R.W. £22
  Lawford (6)   T.R.E. 2 nights; T.R.W. £11
  Newport *et al.* (7)   T.R.E. 2 nights; T.R.W. £25 16s
  Baddow (21b)   T.R.E. 8 nights; T.R.W. £17
Norfolk
  Saham Toney *et al.* (110)   T.R.E. £12, and ½ day of honey, and *consue-*
                        tudines mellis; T.R.W. £20
  Holt *et al.* (111b)   T.R.E. £20, and one night of honey and 100s
                        de consuetudine; T.R.W. £50
  Broome (211b)   T.R.E. (?) 2 days; T.R.W. 20s
  Necton *et al.* (235b)   T.R.E. 6 nights; T.R.W. £60
Suffolk
  Diss (282)   T.R.E. £15, and the soke of 1½ hundreds, and ½
                        day of honey *cum consuetudinibus*; T.R.W. £30
  Blythburgh (282)   T.R.E. £30, and one day of honey *cum tota*
                        consuetudine; T.R.W. £23

ᵃ J. H. Round, *Feudal England* (London, 1895), 114.
ᵇ Conceivably, the remaining ¼ could have been at Bedminster (90b, 86b) with £21 0s 2½d,
making a total of £101 10s 9½d. See *D.G.S–W.E.*, 170.
ᶜ Later evidence shows that the value of the T.R.E. *firma* was £104 12s – J. H. Round in *V.C.H.*
Hampshire, I (1900), 401–2.

APPENDIX 12

ANNUAL VALUES FOR RURAL HOLDINGS IN 1086 BY DOMESDAY COUNTIES

	Area in square miles	Value in £s	Shillings per		
			square mile	man	team
Bedfordshire	461	1,164	50	7	17
Berkshire	720	2,524	70	9	27
Buckinghamshire	741	1,947	52	9	19
Cambridgeshire	861	1,847	43	8	25
Cheshire (now in England)	1,008 }	203 }	4	3	9
Cheshire (now in Wales)	295	44			
Cornwall	1,348	670	10	3	11
Derbyshire	1,043	430	8	3	9
Devonshire	2,585	3,145	24	4	11
Dorset	981	3,110	68	10	33
Essex	1,514	5,047	67	8	26
Gloucestershire (now in England)	1,218 }	3,094 }	50	10	16
Gloucestershire (now in Wales)	59	110			
Hampshire	1,620	3,415	42	8	25
Herefordshire (now in England)	816 }	1,078 }	26	6	9
Herefordshire (now in Wales)	27	37			
Hertfordshire	640	1,458	46	7	21
Huntingdonshire	356	827	47	7	16
Kent	1,544	4,770	62	9	30
(Lancashire, South)	Incomplete value for 1086				
Leicestershire	821	842	21	3	9
Lincolnshire	2,646	3,253	25	3	14
Middlesex	278	740	53	7	27
Norfolk	2,037	4,094	40	3	16
Northamptonshire	1,076	1,744	32	4	14
Nottinghamshire	839	731	17	3	7
Oxfordshire	734	2,878	78	10	22
Roteland	Incomplete value for 1086				
Shropshire (now in England)	1,298 }	846 }	13	4	10
Shropshire (now in Wales)	55	6			
Somerset	1,615	4,361	54	8	22
Staffordshire	1,194	449	8	3	8
Suffolk	1,453	3,828	53	4	17
Surrey	778	1,533	39	8	24
Sussex	1,431	3,116	44	7	19
Warwickshire	875	1,409	32	5	14
Wiltshire	1,379	4,770	69	11	32
Worcestershire	745	969	26	5	9
Yorkshire	7,024	1,084	3	3	7
	44,118	71,573	32	6	18

APPENDIX 13

REFERENCES TO IRON AND RENDERS
OF IRON

A. Iron works or workers

Cheshire (now in Wales)	Rhuddlan (269b): *mineriae ferii*
Devonshire	North Molton (*94b*, 100b): *iiii ferrarii*
Hampshire	Stratfield (45b): *ferraria de ii s et ii d.*
Herefordshire	Hereford (179): *vi forgiae* (in 1066)
Lincolnshire	Stow (344): *iii ferrariae*
	Castle Bytham (360b): *fabrica ferri xl s.*
	Little Bytham (360b): *fabrica ferri de xl s et viii d.*
Northamptonshire	Corby (219b): *Multa desunt huic manerio quae T.R.E. ibi adjacebant in silva et ferrariis et aliis causis*
	Gretton (219b): *Plurima desunt huic manerio quae T.R.E. appendebat ibi tam in silva et ferrariis quam in aliis reditibus*
Surrey	Chertsey (32b): *una ferraria quae operatur ad hallam*
Sussex	East Grinstead hd (22b): *una ferraria*
Warwickshire	Wilnecote (240): *ferraria v s.*
Wiltshire	Fifield Bavant (70b): *i ferraria reddit xii d per annum*
Yorkshire	Hessle (316b): *Ibi sunt vi ferrarii*

B. Renders of iron

Bedfordshire	Cranfield (210b), Wilshamstead Coton End (214)
Buckinghamshire	Aston Clinton (150b), Bledlow (146), Burnham (151), Chesham (150b), Hampden (148b)
Gloucestershire	Alvington (185b), Gloucester (162), Pucklechurch (165)
Herefordshire	*Turlestane* in 1066 (179b)
Somerset	Alford (*277b*, 92b), Bickenhall (*270b*, 92), Cricket St Thomas (*88b*, 86), Lexworthy (*282*, *432*, *432b*, 91b, 94 *bis*), Seaborough in 1066 (*154*, 87b), Whitestaunton (*265b*, 91b)
Wiltshire	Fifield Bavant (70b)

APPENDIX 14

STATISTICAL SUMMARY OF MILLS BY DOMESDAY COUNTIES

	Total places	Places with mills				Total mills	Mills per	
		Min. no.	Max. no.	Average no.	% of total		1,000 teams	1,000 men
Bedfordshire	141	64	64	64	45	101	72	31
Berkshire	189	94	94	94	50	166	88	30
Buckinghamshire	206	78	78	78	38	135	66	30
Cambridgeshire	142	53	53	53	37	132	88	30
Cheshire (now in England)	266	18	18	18	} 7	19	} 50	} 16
Cheshire (now in Wales)	100	7	7	7				
Cornwall	332	5	5	5	2	6	5	1
Derbyshire	346	52	53	53	15	69	73	24
Devonshire	980	78	78	78	8	96	17	7
Dorset	314	151	165	158	50	274	147	43
Essex	444	153	153	153	35	230	59	18
Gloucestershire (now in England)	372	123	140	132	} 35	252	} 67	} 39
Gloucestershire (now in Wales)	7	2	2	2		6		
Hampshire	454	165	167	166	37	346	126	41
Herefordshire (now in England)	302	71	79	75	} 24	98	} 41	} 27
Herefordshire (now in Wales)	9	1	1	1		3		
Hertfordshire	171	72	72	72	42	132	96	32
Huntingdonshire	85	23	23	23	27	37	37	15
Kent	347	139	139	139	40	356	113	33
(Lancashire, South)	55	—	—	—	—	—	—	—
Leicestershire	292	89	90	90	31	133	71	22
Lincolnshire	754	204	225	215	29	439	91	20
Middlesex	62	14	14	14	23	34	62	16
Norfolk	730	294	298	296	41	538	107	21
Northamptonshire	354	172	176	174	49	261	106	37
Nottinghamshire	297	80	81	81	27	132	67	24
Oxfordshire	250	114	114	114	46	203	79	34
Roteland	16	5	5	5	31	6	24	7
Shropshire (now in England)	435	87	87	87	} 19	94	} 53	} 23
Shropshire (now in Wales)	24	—	—	—		—		
Somerset	622	254	255	255	41	381	97	34
Staffordshire	342	52	52	52	15	65	61	23
Suffolk	639	175	176	176	28	246	55	13
Surrey	144	67	67	67	47	121	95	33
Sussex	336	87	87	87	26	167	52	18
Warwickshire	247	89	89	89	36	123	61	22
Wiltshire	344	201	202	202	59	433	144	50
Worcestershire	275	72	84	78	28	120	57	30
Yorkshire	1,993	92	102	97	5	120	41	16
	13,418			3,550	26	6,082	75	25

APPENDIX 15

REFERENCES TO VINEYARDS

Bedfordshire
    Eaton Socon (212)   *ii acrae vineae*
Berkshire
    Bisham (60b)   *xii arpendi vineae*
Buckinghamshire
    Iver (149)   *ii arpendi vineae*
Cambridgeshire
    Ely (192)   *iii arpendi vineae*
Dorset
    Durweston (83)   *Ibi ii acrae vineae*
    Wootton (83)   *ii arpenz vineae*
Essex
    Ashdon (71)   *i acra vinea*
    Belchamp (77)   *Modo xi arpenni vineae, i portat*
    Debden (73b)   *modo ii arpenni vineae portantes et alii ii non portantes*
    Hedingham (76b)   *modo vi arpenni vineae*
    Mundon (49b)   *ii arpenni vineae*
    Rayleigh (43b)   *vi arpenni vineae et reddit xx modios vini si bene procedit*
    Stambourne and
       Toppesfield (55b)   *i arpendus vineae*
    Stebbing (74)   *ii arpenni vineae et dimidia, et dimidia tantum portat*
    Waltham (58)   *modo x arpenni vineae*
Gloucestershire
    Stonehouse (166b)   *Ibi ii arpenz vineae*
Hampshire
    ? Lomer (43)   *reddebat abbati per annum x sextaria vini*
Hertfordshire
    Berkhamsted (136b)   *Ibi ii arpendi vineae*
    Standon (142b)   *Ibi ii arpendi vineae*
    Ware (138b)   *iiii Arpendi vineae nuperrime plantatae*
Kent
    Chart Sutton (8)   *Ibi iii arpendi vineae*
    Chislet (12)   *Ibi sunt iii arpenni vineae*
    Leeds (7b)   *Ibi ii Arpendi vineae*
Middlesex
    Colham (129)   *i arpendus vineae*
    Harmondsworth (128b) *i arpendus vineae*
    ? Holborn (127)   *Willelmus camerarius reddit vicecomiti regis per annum vi solidos pro terra ubi sedet vinea sua*
    Kempton (129)   *viii arpenni vineae noviter plantatae*
    Kensington (130b)   *iii Arpenni vineae*
    Staines (128b)   *ii arpenni vineae*
    Westminster (128)   *Ibi iiii arpenni vineae noviter plantatae*
Somerset
    Glastonbury (*172*, 90)   *iii arpenz vineae*
    Meare (*172*, 90)   *ii arpenz vineae*
    Panborough (*172*, 90) *iii arpenz vineae*

Somerset (*cont.*)
  Muchelney, Midelney and
    Thorney (*189*, 91)   *unus arpentus vineae*
  North Curry (*105*, 86b) *vii acrae vineae*
Suffolk
  Barking (382b)   *ii arpenni vineae*
  Clare (389b)   *Modo v arpenni vineae*
  Ixworth (438b)   *iii arpenni vineae*
  Lavenham (418)   *i arpentum vineae*
Surrey
  ? Wandsworth (36)   Walter (*vinitor* interlined above) 1 hide
Wiltshire
  Bradford on Avon (67b) *Ibi unus arpendus vineae*
  Lacock (69b)   *dimidia acrae vineae*
  Tollard Royal (73)   *Ibi ii arpenni vineae*
  Wilcot (69)   *vinea bona*
Worcestershire
  Hampton near Evesham
    (175b)   *vinea novella ibi*

APPENDIX 16

STATISTICAL SUMMARY OF BOROUGHS

The numbering of the boroughs is the same as that for Fig. 102

Bedfordshire
1 Bedford (*villa*) — *burgenses de bedeford* entered in the list of tenants-in-chief of the county

Berkshire
2 Reading (*burgus*) — 29 *mansurae*; 30 *hagae*. Also a manor here
3 Wallingford (*burgus*) — 93 *mansurae*; 22 *mansurae francigenarum*; a *monetarius*; 404 *hagae;* 26 domus + unspecified number of *domus*; 1 *haga wasta*; 8 *hagae destructae* on account of the castle

4 Windsor (*villa*) — 95 *hagae*. Also a manor here

Buckinghamshire
5 Buckingham (*burgus*) — 25 *burgenses* (and probably another 27 *burgenses*). Also a manor here

6 Newport Pagnell — Unspecified number of *burgenses*. Also a manor here

Cambridgeshire
7 Cambridge (*burgus*) — 324 *mansurae* (probably including 29 *burgenses*); unspecified number of *lagemanni*; 49 *mansurae vastae*; 27 *domus destructae* on account of the castle; *plures domus destruuntur* on account of 3 mills

Cheshire
8 Chester (*civitas, burgus*) — 282 *domus*; 205 *domus vastae*. The following may be in addition: 33 *burgenses*; 4 *burgenses ultra aquam* (presumably in Handbridge); 1 *domus*; 2 *mansurae wastae*

9 Rhuddlan (*novus burgus*) — 18 *burgenses*

Cornwall
10 Bodmin — 68 *domus* (probably the 68 *burgenses* mentioned in the Exon D.B. Summary). Also a manor here

Derbyshire
11 Derby (*burgus*) — 100 *burgenses*; 40 *burgenses minores*; 16 *mansurae*; 103 *mansiones wastae*

Devonshire
12 Barnstaple (*burgus*) — 58 *burgenses intra burgum*; 9 *burgenses extra burgum*; 2 *domus* (*mansurae* in Exon D.B.); 38 *domus vastae*
13 Exeter (*civitas*) — 399 *domus* (probably including 11 *burgenses*); 51 *domus vastae*
14 Lydford (*civitas, burgus*) — 28 *burgenses intra burgum*; 41 *burgenses extra burgum*; 40 *domus vastae*
15 Okehampton — 4 *burgenses*. Also a manor here
16 Totnes (*burgus*) — 96 *burgenses intra burgum*; 15 *burgenses extra burgum terram laborantes*

Dorset
17 Bridport — 101 *domus*; 20 *domus destitutae*
18 Dorchester — 1 *burgensis*; 89 *domus*; 100 *domus penitus destructae*. Also a manor here
19 Shaftesbury (*burgus*) — 151 *burgenses*; 177 *domus* (the *burgenses* may have been on 111 of these); 20 *mansiones vacuae*; 80 *domus destructae, penitus destructae* or *omnino destructae*

Dorset (*cont.*)

20 Wareham (*villa*)   4 *burgenses*; 142 *domus*; 1 *bordarius*; 150 *domus destructae, penitus destructae* or *vastae*

21 Wimborne Minster   8 *burgenses*; 14 *domus*; 3 *bordarii*. Also a manor here

Essex

22 Colchester (*civitas, burgus*)   6 *burgenses*; 433 *domus*; unspecified number of *prebendarii*

23 Maldon (*burgus*)   Unspecified number of *burgenses*; 180 *domus quos tenent burgenses*; 3 *domus*; 18 *mansurae vastatae*. Also a manor here

Gloucestershire

24 Bristol   Unspecified number of *burgenses*; 12 *domus*. Also a manor here

25 Gloucester (*civitas*)   73 *burgenses* (another 8 *burgenses* appear in the past tense); 23 *mansiones* + unspecified number of *mansiones*; 2 *domus*; 14 *domus wastatae*; 16 *domus modo desunt* on account of the castle

26 Tewkesbury   13 *burgenses*. Also a manor here

27 Winchcomb (*burgus*)   29 *burgenses*

Hampshire

28 Southampton (*burgus*)   55 *domus*; 79 *homines*; 65 *francigenae*; 31 *angligani*.

29 Twynham (*burgus*)   39 *mansurae*. Also a manor here

30 Winchester (*civitas*)   20 *burgenses*; 35 *mansurae*; 9 *mansiones burgensium*; 39 *hagae*; 7 *domus*; 4 *suburbani*

Herefordshire

31 Clifford (*burgus*)   16 *burgenses*

32 Ewias Harold   2 *mansurae in castello*. Also a manor here

33 Hereford (*civitas*)   10 *burgenses*; unspecified numbers of *anglici burgenses* and *francigenae vero burgenses*. (The following are recorded for 1066: 27 *burgenses*; 98 *mansurae*; 103 *homines intus et extra murum*; 7 *monetarii*; 6 *fabri*)

34 Wigmore (*burgus*)   *burgus quod ibi est*

Hertfordshire

35 Ashwell (*burgus*)   14 *burgenses*. Also a manor here

36 Berkhamsted (*in burbio hujus villae*)   52 *burgenses*; *quidam fossarius*. Also a manor here

37 Hertford (*burgus, suburbium*)   18 *burgenses*; 36 *domus*

38 St Albans (*villa*)   46 *burgenses*. Also a manor here

39 Stanstead Abbots   7 *burgenses*. Also a manor here

Huntingdonshire

40 Huntingdon (*burgus*)   256 *burgenses* (including 80 *hagae*); 100 *bordarii*; 3 *piscatores*; 112 *mansiones wastae*; 21 *mansiones quae modo absunt* on account of the castle. The following may be in addition: 104 *burgenses*; 2 *mansiones*; 18 *domus*; 1 *tofta*

Kent

41 Canterbury (*civitas*)   438 *burgenses*; 95 *mansurae*; 2 *mansurae terrae*; 15 *hagae*; 4 *domus*; 45 *mansurae extra C*; 11 *burgenses* [i.e. *domus*] *vastati in fossato*; *mansurae destructae* for the new residence of the archbishop

42 Dover (*villa*)   Unspecified number of *burgenses*; 29 *mansurae*; 420 *homines*

43 Fordwich (*parvus burgus*)   6 *burgenses*; 80 *mansurae terrae*

44 Hythe (*burgus*)   231 *burgenses*. Part of manor of Saltwood

45 Rochester (*civitas*)   5 *burgenses*; 80 *mansurae terrae*; 3 *mansiones terrae*; 10 *hagae*; 13 *domus* + unspecified number of *domus*; 4 *domus juxta R*

46 Romney (*burgus*)   156 *burgenses*

47 Sandwich (*burgus*)   383 *mansurae hospitatae*; 32 other *mansurae* (? + 30 *mansurae* in Excerpta)

48 Seasalter (*parvus burgus*)   *parvus burgus nomine Seseltre quod proprie pertinet coquinae archiepiscopi*. Also a manor here

(Lancashire, South)

49 Penwortham — 6 *burgenses*

Leicestershire

50 Leicester (*civitas, burgus*) — 65 *burgenses*; 318 *domus*; unspecified number of *monetarii*; 4 *domus vastae*

Lincolnshire

51 Grantham (*villa*) — 111 *burgenses*; 77 *toftes sochemanorum teignorum* (unique phrase in D.B.); 8 *toftes*. Also a manor here

52 Lincoln (*civitas*) — 3 *burgenses*; 900 *mansiones*; unspecified number of *lagemanni*; *extra civitatem* 36 *domus*; 240 *wastae mansiones* (including 166 on account of the castle)

53 Louth — 80 *burgenses*. Also a manor here

54 Stamford (*burgus*) — 9 *burgenses*; 405½ *mansiones* (including 77 *mansiones sochemanorum* and 50½ belonging to 9 *lagemanni*); unrecorded *mansiones* in the sixth ward; 5 *wastae mansiones* on account of the castle; 1 *wasta mansio* belonging to the lawmen

55 Torksey (*suburbium, villa*) — 102 *burgenses*; 111 *wastae mansiones*

Middlesex

56 London — 78 *burgenses*; unspecified numbers of *francigenae* and *burgenses*; 59 *mansurae*; 30 *domus* (another 17 *domus* appear in the past tense)

Norfolk

57 Norwich (*burgus, novus burgus*) — 665 *burgenses anglici*; 480 *bordarii pauperes*; a possible *monetarius*; 50 *domus*; 297 *mansurae vacua*, including 98 *in occupatione castellii* (In 1066 there had been 1,320 *burgenses*)
In novo burgo: 36 *burgenses*; 124 *burgenses franci*; 6 *anglici*; 1 *mansura vasta*

58 Thetford (*burgus*) — 725 *burgenses*; 2 *mansurae*; 23 *domus*; 33 *homines*; 2 *prebendarii*; 228 *mansurae vacuae*

59 Yarmouth — 70 *burgenses*

Northamptonshire

60 Northampton (*burgus, novus burgus*) — 47 *burgenses habentes totidem mansiones*; 209 *domus*; 14 *mansiones wastae*; 21½ *domus vastae*
40 *burgenses in novo burgo*

Nottinghamshire

61 Newark — 56 *burgenses*. Also a manor here

62 Nottingham (*burgus, novus burgus*) — 3 *mansiones* (*in quibus sedunt xi domus*); 3 *mansiones burgi*; 141 *domus*; 48 *domus mercatorum*; 25 *domus equitum*; 120 *homines*
13 *domus in novo burgo*

Oxfordshire

63 Oxford (*civitas*) — 1 *burgensis*; 41 *mansiones*; 138 *mansiones murales*; 1 *haga*; 11 *domus*; 42 *domus hospitatae tam intra murum quam extra* (may include 13 *hagae*); 243 *domus tam intra murum quam extra* (may include 1 *burgensis*); 32 *mansiones vastae*; 81 *mansiones murales vastae*; 478 *domus vastae et destructae*; 2 *domus vastae*

Shropshire

64 Quatford (*burgus*) — *Nova domus et burgus Quatford dictus nil reddit*. Part of manor of Eardington

65 Shrewsbury (*civitas*) — 151 *domus* (including 39 *burgenses* and 43 *francigenae burgenses*); 50 *mansurae vastae*; 51 *mansurae vastae* on account of

Shropshire (*cont.*)

the castle. The following may be in addition: 33 *burgenses*+ unspecified number of *burgenses*; 7 *mansurae*; 12 *domus canonicorum*; 10 *mansurae vastae*

Somerset

66 Axbridge	32 *burgenses*. Part of manor of Cheddar
67 Bath (*burgus*)	178 *burgenses*; 7 *domus*. The following may be in addition: 1 *borgisum* (Exon. D.B.); 12 (Exon. D.B.) or 13 (Exch. D.B.) *burgenses*; 6 *domus*; 1*mansura vacua*; 6 *domus vastae*
68 Bruton	17 *burgenses*. Also a manor here
69 Frome	No information, but paid third penny. Also a manor here
70 Ilchester	108 *burgenses*
71 Langport (*burgus*)	39 *burgenses*. Part of manor of Somerton
72 Milborne Port	67 *burgenses*; 2 *mansurae*. Also a manor here
73 Milverton (*burgus*)	1 *domus*. Also a manor here
74 Taunton	64 *burgenses*. Also a manor here

Staffordshire

75 Stafford (*civitas, burgus, villa*)	36 *burgenses*; 110 *mansiones hospitatae*; 13 *canonici*; unspecified number of *presbyteri*; 51 *mansiones vastae*; 1 *vasta mansura*
76 Tamworth	22 *burgenses*
77 Tutbury (*burgus*)	*In Burgo circa castellum sunt xlii homines de mercato*

Suffolk

78 Beccles	26 *burgenses*. Also a manor here
79 Bury St Edmunds (*villa*)	310 *homines* etc. in 1066, to which had been added 342 *domus*. The following may be in addition: 207 priests, bakers, tailors etc.
80 Clare	43 *burgenses*. Also a manor here
81 Dunwich	316 *burgenses*; 80 *homines*; 24 *franci homines*; 178 *pauperes homines*. Also a manor here
82 Eye	25 *burgenses*. Also a manor here
83 Ipswich (*burgus, villa*)	112 *burgenses*; 100 *pauperes burgenses*; unspecified number of *monetarii*; 328 *mansiones vastatae*. The following may be in addition: 52 *burgenses*; 3 *mansurae*; 6 *domus*; 10 *mansurae vacuae*; 6 *mansurae vastatae*. Also a manor here
84 Sudbury	138 *burgenses*; unspecified number of *monetarii*. Also a manor here

Surrey

| 85 Guildford (*villa*) | 75 *hagae* (*in quibus manent* 175 *homines*); 2 *hagae*; 4 *domus* |
| 86 Southwark | 42 *mansurae*; 4 *hagae*; 1 *domus*; 1 *bordarius* |

Sussex

87 Arundel (*burgus*)	4 *burgenses*; 13 *hagae*
88 Chichester (*civitas*)	9 *burgenses*; 135 *hagae*; 97½ *hagae; in eisdem mansuris* (*sic*) there are 60 *domus* more than formerly; 3 *croftae*
89 Hastings	24 *burgenses*; 14 *bordarii*
90 Lewes (*burgus*)	180 *burgenses*; unspecified number of *monetarii*; 46 *mansurae hospitatae*; 11 other *mansurae*; 195½ *hagae*; 25 *mansurae inhospitatae*
91 Pevensey (*burgus*)	110 *burgenses*; 1 *domus*; unspecified number of *custodes castelli*
92 Rye (*novus burgus*)	64 *burgenses*. Part of manor of *Rameslie*
93 Steyning (*burgus*)	123 *mansurae*. Also a manor here

Warwickshire

| Warwick (*burgus*) | 19 *burgenses qui habent xix mansuras*; 113 *domus*; 112 *domus* (entered as 111 *mansurae* and 1 *domus* in a list); 4 *mansurae vastae* on account of the castle |

Wiltshire

95	Bedwyn (*villa*)	25 *burgenses*. Also a manor here
96	Bradford on Avon	33 *burgenses*. Also a manor here
97	Calne (*villa*)	73 *burgenses*; 1 *domus*. Also a manor here
98	Cricklade	*plures burgenses*; 33 *burgenses*; 2 *domus*
99	Malmesbury (*burgus*)	11 *burgenses*; 26 *hospitatae mansurae*; 24¼ other *mansurae*; 5½ *domus*; *foris burgum ix coscez qui geldant cum burgensibus*; 25 *mansurae in quibus sunt domus quae non reddunt geldum*; 8½ *vastae mansurae*
100	Malborough	No information but paid third penny
101	Salisbury	No information but paid third penny. Also a manor here
102	Tilshead	66 *burgenses*. Also a manor here
103	Warminster	30 *burgenses*. Also a manor here
104	Wilton (*burgus*)	25 *burgenses*; 5 *domus*

Worcestershire

105	Droitwich	116 *burgenses*; 35 *domus*; 4 *salinarii*
106	Pershore	28 *burgenses*. Also a manor here
107	Worcester (*civitas, burgus*)	7 *burgenses*; 28 *mansurae*; 100 *domus*; 25 *domus in foro*; 5 *mansurae wastae*

Yorkshire

108	Bridlington	4 *burgenses*. Also a manor here
109	Dadsley	31 *burgenses*. Also a manor here
110	Pocklington	15 *burgenses*. Also a manor here
111	Tanshelf	60 *burgenses minuti*. Also a manor here
112	York (*civitas*)	Unspecified number of *burgenses*; 84½ *mansiones*; 491 *mansiones hospitatae*; 145 *mansiones tenent francigenae*; 7 *minutae mansiones*; 20 *mansiones ad hospitia*; 29 *minuta hospitia*; 1 *hospitium*; 1 *domus*; *curia Archiepiscopi et domus canonicorum*; 400 *mansiones non hospitatae* (nevertheless paying geld); *quidam monetarius*; 540 *mansiones vacuae*; one of the seven wards of the city was *vastata in castellis*

APPENDIX 17

RFFERENCES TO MARKETS

An asterisk indicates a borough

Bedfordshire
Arlesey (212)   *Mercatum est ibi de x solidis*
Leighton Buzzard (209)   *Theloneum de mercato reddit vii libras*
Luton (209)   *De theloneo et mercato c solidi*
Berkshire
Abingdon (58b)   *x mercatores ante portam ecclesiae manentes reddit xl denarios* (entered under Barton)
Cookham (56b)   *De novo mercato quod ibi est modo xx solidi*
*Wallingford (56b)   *mercatum* (held on *Sabbata*)
Cornwall
*Bodmin (202, 120b)   *i mercatum*
Liskeard (228, 121b)   *i mercatum quod reddit iiii solidos*
St Germans (200, 120b)   *In ea mansione erat i mercatum ea die qua Rex E. fuit vivus et mortuus, in dominica die, et modo adnichilatur per mercatum quod ibi prope constituit Comes de Moritonio in quodam suo castro in eadem die.* (Virtually repeated under *Terrae Occupatae* 507)
St Stephens by Launceston (206b, 120b)   *i mercatum quod ibi iacebat ea die qua rex E. fuit vivus et mortuus, quod abstulit inde comes de Moritonio et posuit in castro suo, et reddit per annum xx solidos.* (Also mentioned under *Dunhevet* or Launceston, 264b, 121b)
Trematon (256, 122)   *i mercatum quod reddit per annum iii solidos*
Devonshire
*Okehampton (288, 105b)   *i mercatum qui reddit iiii solidos per annum*
Otterton (194b)   *ibi est i mercatum in dominica die*
Gloucestershire
Berkeley (163)   *Ibi unum forum in quo manent xvii homines*
Cirencester (162b)   *De novo foro xx solidi*
*Tewkesbury (163b)   *Mercatum quod regina constituit. ibi reddit xi solidos et viii denarios*
Thornbury (163b)   *Ibi forum de xx solidis*
Hampshire
Basingstoke (39)   *Ibi mercatum de xxx solidis*
Neatham (38)   *Mercatum de viii libris*
Titchfield (39)   *Mercatum et theloneum (de) xl solidis*
Herefordshire
*Hereford (181b)   *mercatum est modo* (entered under Eaton Bishop)
Hertfordshire
Cheshunt (137)   *Ibi x mercatores reddunt x solidos de consuetudinibus*
Kent
Faversham (2b)   *Mercatum de iiii libras*
Lewisham (12b)   *De exitu portus xl solidos*
Newenden (4)   *Ibi est mercatum de xl solidis v denariis minus*
Leicestershire
Melton Mowbray (235b)   *Mercatum reddit xx solidos*
Lincolnshire
Barton upon Humber (354b)   *i mercatum*
Bolingbroke (351)   *mercatum novum*
*Louth (345)   *i mercatum de xxix solidis*
Partney (355)   *Ibi est mercatum (de) x solidis*

Lincolnshire (*cont.*)
 Spalding (351b)   *Ibi mercatum (xl solid'* interlined above)
 Thealby, Darby and Burton upon Stather (338b)   *dimidium mercatum ad Chirchetone pertinens*
 Threekingham (356)   *Ibi est forum reddens xl solidos*
Norfolk
 Dunham (137)   *semper dimidium mercatum*
 Holt (111b)   *i mercatum*
 Litcham (207b)   *quarta pars unius mercati*
Northamptonshire
 Higham Ferrers (225b)   *Ibi est mercatum reddens xx solidos per annum*
 King's Sutton (219b)   *De foro xx solidi*
 Oundle (221)   *De mercato xxv solidi*
Oxfordshire
 Bampton (154b)   *De mercato l solidi*
Somerset
 Crewkerne (*105b*, 86b)   *i mercatum quod reddit per annum iiii libras*
 *Frome (*90b*, 86b)   *i mercatum quod reddit per annum xlvi solidos et viii denarios*
 *Ilchester (*91b*, 86b)   *i mercatum in Guilecestra quod cum suis appenditiis reddit in firma regis xi libras*
 Ilminster (*188*, 91)   *mercatum quod reddit xx solidos per annum*
 *Milborne Port (*91*, 86b)   *lvi burgenses et i mercatum et inter burgenses et mercatum reddunt per annum lx solidos in firma regis*
 *Milverton (*113*, 87)   *i mercatum quod reddit x solidos per annum*
 *Taunton (*174*, 87b)   *i mercatum quod reddit l solidos*
Staffordshire
 *Tutbury (248b)   *In Burgo circa castellum sunt xlii homines de mercato suo tantum viventes et reddunt cum foro iv libras et x solidos*
Suffolk
 *Beccles (283b, 369b)   *mercatum* (¼ with king; ¾ with abbey of Bury St Edmunds)
 Blythburgh (282)   *i mercatum*
 Caramhalla (?Kelsale, 330b)   *modo unum mercatum de dono regis*
 *Clare (389b)   *Semper unum mercatum*
 *Eye (319b)   *modo i mercatum . . . et in mercato manent xxv burgenses*
 Haverhill (428)   *Tercia pars mercati in eo . . . mercatum (de) xiii solidis et iiii denariis*
 Hoxne (379)   *In hoc manerio erat unum mercatum T.R.E. et post quam Willelmus rex advenit; et sedebat in Sabbato; et W. Malet fecit suum castellum ad Eiam et eadem die qua erat mercatum in Manerio episcopi W. Malet fecit aliud mercatum in suo castello et ex hoc ita peioratum est mercatum episcopi ut parvum valent; et modo sedet die veneris. Mercatum antem de Heia sedet die sabbati*
 *Sudbury (286b)   *i mercatum*
 Thorney (281b)   *Ibi est etiam unum mercatum*
Wiltshire
 *Bradford on Avon (67b)   *Mercatum reddit xlv solidos*
Worcestershire
 *Worcester (173b)   *In foro de Wirecestre tenet Urso de episcopo xxv domus et reddunt per annum c solidos* (entered under Northwick and Tibberton)
Yorkshire
 *York (298)   *ii banci in macello*

In addition to the above, there is a curious entry for Hill (192) in Cambridgeshire: *Pastura ad pecuniam villae et de portu iii socos.* The word *portu* may be an error for *pastura*, a possibility suggested by its context. Hill has not been included among the 60 places with markets.

APPENDIX 18

REFERENCES TO MINTS

Annual renders T.R.W.

Lincoln (336b)   a mint   £75
Thetford (119)   a mint   £40
Colchester ⎫
Maldon ⎭ (107b)   a mint   £40
Gloucester (162)   a mint   £20
Ipswich (290b)   a mint with moneyers   £20
Leicester (230)   moneyers   £20
Oxford (154b)   a mint   £20
Nottingham (280)   a mint   £10
Lewes (26)   a new mint   £5 12s;   a mint with moneyers   £1
Bath (114b, 87)   a mint   £5
Malmesbury (64b)   a mint   £5
Taunton (173b, 87b)   a mint   £2 10s
Pevensey (20b)   a mint   £1

Other references T.R.W.

Rhuddlan (269)   a mint
Wallingford (56)   a mint with moneyer
Sudbury (286b)   moneyers
Norwich (117b)   one moneyer
York (298)   a certain moneyer

References T.R.E.

Worcester (172)   a mint with moneyers
Chester (262b)   7 moneyers
Hereford (179, 181b)   7 moneyers
Huntingdon (203)   3 moneyers
Shaftesbury (11, 75)   3 moneyers
Shrewsbury (252)   3 moneyers
Dorchester (75)   2 moneyers
Nottingham (280)   2 moneyers
Wareham (12b, 75)   2 moneyers
Colchester (107b)   moneyers
Bridport (12, 75)   one moneyer

APPENDIX 19

EXTENSION AND TRANSLATION OF FRONTISPIECE

(Part of folio 190 of Domesday Book)

EXTENSION

In Basingborne tenet isdem episcopus i hidam et ii virgatas et dimidiam. Terra est iii carucis. In dominio i hida, et ibi est i caruca. Ibi unus villanus et iiii bordarii cum i caruca et altera potest fieri. Ibi ii molini de xx solidis. Pratum i carucae. Valet lx solidos. Quando recepit xl solidos. Tempore Regis Edwardi lx solidos. Haec terra iacuit et iacet in ecclesia Sancti Petri Wintoniensis, et ibi fuit i sochemmanus homo Stigandi archiepiscopi dimidiam virgatam tenuit et dare et vendere potuit.

iii. TERRA EPISCOPI LINCOLNIENSIS

In Witelesford hundredo. Episcopus Lincolniensis tenet in histetone ii hidas et Robertus de eo. Terra est ii carucis. Una est ibi et alia potest fieri. Ibi ii villani et ii bordarii. Pratum ii carucis et i molinum de viii solidis. Valet xl solidos. Quando recepit xx solidos. Tempore Regis Edwardi iiii libras. Hanc terram tenuit Siuuardus de comite Heraldo, et potuit dare cui voluit.

In Norestou hundredo. In Madinglei tenet Picot de episcopo Remigio i virgatam terrae et dimidiam. Valet et valuit v solidos. Tempore Regis Edwardi x solidos. Hanc terram tenuit Blacuin homo regis Edwardi et recedere potuit, sed soca Wluuio episcopo remansit.

In Cestretone hundredo. Manerium Histone pro xxvi hidis et dimidia se defendit. Hoc manerium est unum de duodecim maneriis dominicis episcopatus Lincolniensis. Ibi tenet Remigius episcopus xvii hidas i virgatam minus. Terra est xiii carucis. In dominio viii hidae et ibi sunt ii carucae et tercia potest fieri. Ibi xviii villani et xviii bordarii cum ix carucis.

TRANSLATION

In Bassingbourn the same Bishop holds 1 hide and 2½ virgates. There is land for 3 ploughs. In demesne 1 hide, and 1 plough is there. There, one villein and 4 bordars with 1 plough and there could be another. There, 2 mills yielding 20 shillings. Meadow for 1 plough. It is worth 60 shillings. When he received [it], 40 shillings. In the time of King Edward, 60 shillings. This land pertained and pertains to the church of St Peter of Winchester, and there was 1 sokeman, the man of Archbishop Stigand, who held half a virgate and he could give and sell [it].

III. THE LAND OF THE BISHOP OF LINCOLN

In Whittlesford hundred. The Bishop of Lincoln holds 2 hides in Hinxton, and Robert [holds] from him. There is land for 2 ploughs. One is there and there could be another. There, 2 villeins and 2 bordars. Meadow for 2 ploughs and 1 mill yielding 8 shillings. It is worth 40 shillings. When he received [it], 20 shillings. In the time of King Edward, 4 pounds. Siward held this land from Earl Harold, and he could give [it] to whom he would.

In Northstow hundred. In Madingley Picot holds 1½ virgates of land from Bishop Remigius. It is and was worth 5 shillings. In the time of King Edward, 10 shillings. Blacuin, the man of King Edward, held this land, and could depart, but the soke remained with Bishop Wlwius.

In Chesterton hundred. The manor of Histon is assessed at 26½ hides. This manor is one of the 12 demesne manors of the bishopric of Lincoln. There, Bishop Remigius holds 17 hides less 1 virgate. There is land for 13 ploughs. In demesne 8 hides and 2 ploughs are there and there could be a third. There, 18 villeins and 18 bordars with 9 ploughs.

APPENDIX 20

THE DOMESDAY GEOGRAPHY OF ENGLAND: EDITORS AND CONTRIBUTORS

APPENDIX 21

ON THE WRITING OF DOMESDAY GEOGRAPHY

I became interested in Domesday Book while working on the medieval Fenland in the early 1930s. The Domesday entries for the fenland villages yielded a harvest of information about such items as fisheries, salt-pans, ploughteams and population. I soon realised, however, that the individuality of fenland economy could only be appreciated by contrasting this information with that for the upland around. And this led to an examination of the complete Domesday texts for the surrounding counties. The first paper (on 'Domesday woodland in East Anglia') appeared in 1934 and others followed in the next few years. In the meantime, some of my pupils at Cambridge became interested; they also began to compile Domesday maps on a county basis, and a number of these were likewise published in the 1930s.[1] We were much concerned with the best way in which to present the information. Some of our early work was very unsophisticated as may be seen from a map of Wiltshire woodland which appeared in 1935 and which showed the formula 'm leagues by n leagues' as so many rectangles.

It was an exciting time, and the picture was changing from week to week. Much of the excitement arose from the fitting together of maps of adjacent counties and so seeing how the distributions carried over from one county to another. Working with me at this time was Mr F. W. Morgan, and he set out to plot the meadow entries for the Thames basin. I well remember calling at his rooms night after night, after dinner in Hall, to see how the pattern was developing and how best to devise the symbols. At this time (it was towards the end of 1935) the proofs of the 'Historical geography of England before A.D. 1800' were arriving, and I resolved even at that late stage to include Fred Morgan's map if it could be finished in time. It is a map for which I have always had particular affection.[2] The 'Historical geography' appeared in 1936 and it included a chapter on 'The economic geography of England, A.D. 1000–1250' in which the

[1] For a list of these early papers see *D.G.E.E.*, 24–5.
[2] H. C. Darby (ed.), *An historical geography of England before A.D. 1800* (Cambridge, 1936), Fig. 24 (p. 199).

following sentence appeared: 'much statistical work will have to be done before the full contribution of the Survey has been extracted'.

Following upon these experiments in the presentation of Domesday information, and with the completion of my work upon the Fenland, the stage was set for the great assault. I envisaged a 'Domesday Geography' in two volumes, and invited 15 contributors to take part. In order to keep ourselves working along uniform lines, I circulated detailed instructions in a paper dated 27 April 1937. It seemed as if this was the end of the beginning. The work thus started, however, was not to continue for long; rumours of war, and the outbreak of war itself, found many of us engaged upon other tasks, and the Domesday project went into abeyance.

After the war I did not return to the University of Cambridge, but went to the University of Liverpool in 1945. There, in the course of the next few years, I came back to the project with fresh thoughts. A number of points were clear. There would need to be six volumes, five on a regional basis followed by a general summary; this total later became seven when a Gazetteer was added. The maps needed to be more proficient, and the Leverhulme Trust most generously gave a grant to maintain a draughtsman for two years to undertake further experiments in mapping and to begin the drawing of maps for the early volumes. In the light of these new thoughts a fresh set of detailed instructions (dated September 1947) was compiled. In preparing these I sought the advice of Sir Frank Stenton, and, across the years, comes the pleasant memory of a day spent at his home in Reading, at Whitley Park Farm, that centre of pilgrimage for medievalists over many years. I also formally approached the Cambridge University Press whose Syndics and staff were most helpful.

In the meantime, not unnaturally over a span of ten years which included a war, there had been shifts in the interests of some members of the original team. Moreover, we suffered a grievous loss when Fred Morgan died in 1952 at the early age of 42. As a result of these various changes the project emerged with a number of new contributors. We all felt the fascination of the Domesday text. It seemed as if F. W. Maitland's words of 1897 had come true: many men from over all England had come within King William's spell, had bowed themselves to him, and, in the language of the feudal lawyers, had become that man's men. The names of the contributors are set out in Appendix 20 (pp. 373–4). It would be invidious to mention any of these colleagues by name, but I am sure that the rest of us would wish to make one exception. When I moved to University College

London in 1949 I met Mr G. R. Versey, who soon came to play a great part in the enterprise. His skill as a designer and maker of maps, great as it is, has been only a part of his contribution. He has given each one of us much general assistance at all stages of the work, and his knowledge of the Domesday vills of each county made him an ideal collaborator in the production of the *Domesday Gazetteer*.

The first volume, dealing with Eastern England, was completed before I left Liverpool in 1949, but, owing to the publishing complications of post-war years, it did not appear until 1952. It is with wry amusement that I recall how the statistical work for it was done laboriously without a calculator, and how my wife and I spent many hours checking each other's arithmetic. Subsequent regional volumes followed the same plan, but each had its own interest. With the second volume, 'Midland England', the project as a whole began to take more solid shape; moreover, the inclusion of counties along the 'March of Wales' brought to the fore a fresh set of themes. The third volume, the largest, covered a wide variety of counties in South-East England, and discussed the problems raised by the New Forest and the Weald. The fourth volume, on Northern England, was characterised by its massive evidence for 'the harrying of the north'. We encountered great difficulty over this volume because the very numerous linked entries for these northern counties made it impossible to include the full range of standard maps. Finally, the volume for the South-West took the series again into Celtic lands and also provided the opportunity to compare the text of the Exchequer Domesday Book with that of the Exeter Domesday Book.

The succession of reviews brought varied comments. Looking at these as a whole, six points of enquiry or criticism emerge, and I would like now to say something about each of them.

The most frequent comment sprang from the fact that each chapter was constructed on the same basic plan and that, as a result, there was 'a lot of repetition' even of phrases and sentences.[1] One reviewer called this 'irritating and uneconomical',[2] and another described it as 'increasingly irksome.'[3] I was comforted by a reviewer of the fifth volume who said that the editors were 'to be congratulated on the consistency with which

[1] *Antiquaries Jour.*, XLIII (1963), 315. *Medieval Archaeology* XIII (1969), 296; *Geog. Mag.*, XL (1967–8), 1483.

[2] *Derbys. Archaeol. Jour.*, LXXXI (1961), 115.

[3] *Eng. Hist. Rev.*, LXXXIV (1969), 790; *Irish Historical Studies*, XIII (1962–3), 277.

they have followed the pattern laid down in the first';[1] and by another who thought the method was 'brilliantly designed to reduce to order a mass of information';[2] and by yet a third reviewer who believed that the repetition was 'a small price to pay for the prevention of misunderstanding'.[3] One reviewer thought that the individuality of the authors had been 'rigorously, and on the whole necessarily, repressed'.[4] Others thought that the contributors had been able to follow a uniform plan 'without losing their alertness or their individuality'.[5] While having much sympathy with the reviewer who found the method 'wearisome'.[6] I must strongly defend it on two counts.

In the first place, the method meant, as one reviewer said, that the description of each county could be read or consulted without reference to the others.[7] Some reviewers found merit in this, and wrote of 'a wise insistence' upon uniformity,[8] and of the value of submitting 'to a common discipline'.[9] It was also pointed out that here was 'a method designed to bring out divergencies as well as similarities' between the different counties.[10] When writing the first volume I spent a lot of time experimenting to see if the repetition could be avoided, or, at any rate, reduced. I wrote out one chapter 'in full' and then compiled another by making allusion to the explanatory and expository matter of the first. This venture involved practical difficulties of presentation which will be apparent to anyone who attempts such an exercise, and even more to anyone who is faced with the prospect of another thirty-five such exercises. Maybe I lacked the skill or the resolution in attack. Looking back I can only agree with one reviewer, obviously as kind as he was sensible, who said that, although the method involved repetition, 'there can be little doubt that it was the best way to handle the subject, both for historians and geographers'.[11]

But there was a second, and even more cogent, reason for making both maps and chapters follow a uniform plan. From the beginning I had the

[1] *Antiquaries Jour.*, XLIX (1969), 172.
[2] *Times Literary Supplement* No. 2794 (29 April, 1955), 200.
[3] *Eng. Hist. Rev.*, LXVIII (1953), 602.
[4] *Irish Historical Studies*, XVI (1968–9), 371.
[5] *Geog. Jour.*, CXXIX (1963), 199; *Library Review*, XXI (1968) 322.
[6] *History*, LIII (1968), 396.   [7] *Medieval Archaeology*, VIII (1964), 305.
[8] *Antiquity*, XXIX (1955), 12.   [9] *Geog. Jour.*, CXXI (1955), 87.
[10] *The Listener*, XLIX (2 April, 1953), 573.
[11] *Oxford Magazine*, LXXII (1953), 22.

final volume in mind. In order to make sure that the treatment for all thirty-seven counties was comparable, some standard pattern had to be imposed. Anyone who has had the experience of running a team of contributors well knows how difficult it is, with the best will in the world, to secure a uniform treatment, and how easy it is for any member of a team to depart along an interesting by-way. When writing some of my own chapters I occasionally found myself unconsciously deviating from the agreed plan, and had to bring myself firmly back to it. The thirty-seven chapters are not thirty-seven articles written from different points of view and appearing in a variety of journals. They are, and were intended to be, thirty-seven contributions directed towards a final result. This was the very problem faced by the makers of Domesday Book itself. As an orderly description, it is only partially successful. Its uniformity often breaks down as between one circuit and another, or between one county and another. All its variety of phrase as well as of method makes the task of interpreting it even more difficult than it otherwise would be.

The second general point that emerges from the reviews is that the volumes too often ignore other late eleventh-century sources.[1] This is a substantial point of which I am very conscious. But to have attempted a complete examination of other sources would have greatly prolonged the work; and, moreover, the incidence of such evidence is very uneven as between one district and another. Rightly or wrongly, I saw certain advantages in restricting the scope of the study to the evidence of Domesday Book itself. This method, moreover, enables its massive contents to be more easily seen. The use of all sources from the period would perhaps be more appropriate in detailed local studies where Domesday evidence would take its place alongside other evidence, documentary and archaeological.

While, however, there is no systematic examination of non-Domesday sources the absence of reference to them must not be exaggerated. They are often used where they are manifestly important, as in the account of the settlements of Kent in general and of the Weald in particular. I believe that so far as most countrysides are concerned, the inclusion of all the available non-Domesday evidence would not greatly alter the general picture. It might, on the other hand, enable us to form clearer ideas of the size and

---

[1] *Oxford Magazine*, LXXIII (1955), 258; *Antiquaries Jour.*, XXX (1955), 109; *Geography*, LIII (1968), 437; *Times Educational Supplement*, No 2747 (12 January 1968), 106; *Medieval Archaeology*, XIII (1969), 296.

economic activities of a number of towns, e.g. Bristol. Looking back to the first volume I do not think I would greatly alter the method initiated there, but I might well include more frequent reference to those features, such as castles, churches and mints, that often go unmentioned in the Domesday text. At any rate one reviewer thought that the exclusion of non-Domesday evidence was 'perfectly reasonable, for the task is vast enough without any enlargement of its scope'.[1]

In the third place, a few reviewers regretted that place-names only rarely appeared on the maps.[2] This was simply the result of the limitations imposed by the scale of the maps. More important was the fact, as one reviewer put it, that there was 'no means of knowing how the Domesday place-names have been identified, since no concordance with present-day place-names is included in the text'.[3] I fully accept the force of this comment. Another reviewer hoped that the identifications would 'be preserved and published elsewhere'.[4] Before this hope was expressed, we had already arranged (with the forbearance of the Cambridge University Press) to add a seventh volume to the series. The *Domesday Gazetteer* shows the location of all Domesday place-names and, probably more important, it also shows how each Domesday place-name has been identified and allocated to a modern place-name.

The fourth general point concerns the treatment of annual values. They were discussed in each county chapter, but because of the uncertainties associated with them, maps of values were never included. Perhaps I should add that we had already experimented with quite a number of maps of values, some of which had appeared in print;[5] but we deliberately excluded such maps from the series. One reviewer expressed disappointment.[6] Another thought that values 'deserve more attention than they have been given in this series'.[7] Yet another reviewer took a stronger line

---

[1] *Econ. Hist. Rev.* 2nd series, XVI (1963–1964), 155; *Medieval Archaeology*, VIII (1964), 306.

[2] *Geog. Jour.*, CXXI (1955), 88–9.

[3] *Wilts. Archaeol. Mag.* LXIII (1968), 129.

[4] *Medieval Archaeology*, VIII (1964), 307; *Geog. Jour.*, CXXI (1955), 88–9.

[5] E.g. F. W. Morgan: (1) 'The Domesday geography of Berkshire', *Scot. Geog. Mag.*, LI (1935), 353; (2) 'The Domesday geography of Somerset', *Proc. Som. Archaeol. and Nat. Hist. Soc.*, LXXXIV (1938), 145; (3) 'The Domesday Geography of Devon', *Trans. Devon Assoc. for the Advancement of Science, Literature and Art*, LXXII (1940), 319.

[6] *Speculum*, XXX (1955), 99; *Speculum*, XXXIX (1964), 515.

[7] *Eng. Hist. Rev.*, LXXXIV (1969), 791.

and saw their neglect as 'a critical weakness' in the enterprise, and went so far as to say: 'If the Domesday values continue to be neglected, the Domesday Geography of England will remain unfinished'.[1] He expressed the hope that room for them would be found in the 'concluding volume'. Prompted in this way, I took a very close look indeed at the values for each county. The result may be seen in chapter seven. I still have doubts about values for the reasons set out in that chapter. They certainly cannot be satisfactorily plotted for some counties. But it may be that, while not without uncertainties, they reflect something of the economic realities of other counties. Anyway, these maps are placed on record for some future worker, and I am most grateful to Professor P. H. Sawyer for prodding me to produce them.

In the fifth place, another general point was raised by one reviewer who asked: 'Might not the county boundaries of 1066 fit the data better than those of 1966?'[2] The use of the counties of 1066 would have raised a crop of problems in the devising of density units for the mapping of population and ploughteams (these units incidentally number 715). In the first place, many Domesday counties had outliers within, and sometimes well within, other counties. Thus portions of the counties of Gloucester, Warwick and Worcester were intermingled in a strange manner that reflected the scattered holdings of the bishop of Worcester. Then again, there were outlying portions of Hertfordshire in Bedfordshire, and similar complications for other groups. In the second place, some vills were described partly in one county and partly in another, as, for example, in the folios for Derbyshire and Leicestershire, or in those for Huntingdonshire and Northamptonshire, or, again, in those for Bedfordshire and Huntingdonshire. There were also those villages in Oxfordshire described in the folios for other counties apparently because of some confusion in the returns.[3] Extreme examples are provided by Mollington, now wholly in Oxfordshire, with holdings in the three Domesday counties of Northampton, Oxford and Warwick, or of Sibford Gower, also now in the county of Oxford, but with holdings in the Domesday counties of Northampton, Oxford and Stafford.[4] Finally, there were those counties along the Welsh border to which it is difficult to assign western limits.

[1] *Econ. Hist. Rev.*, 2nd series, XVI (1963–4), 155–7.
[2] *Geography*, LIII (1968), 437.
[3] F. M. Stenton in *V.C.H. Oxfordshire*, I (1939), 392.
[4] *D.G.S–E.E.*, 186–8.

In view of these practical difficulties, we decided to base our chapters on the traditional counties (i.e. those prior to 1974), and to give a statement of what this involved at the beginning of each chapter. We may, too, have been influenced by the traditional pattern of the *Victoria County Histories* and of the volumes of the English Place-Name Society. I do not think the point is of great importance as far as the maps showing detailed distributions of population and teams are concerned, e.g. Figs. 34 and 41. Density units based on Domesday counties or on pre-1974 counties would be very similar, if not exactly the same. Furthermore, the distributions on those maps where symbols are plotted for individual places are exactly the same whichever county boundaries are shown, e.g. on the maps of meadow (Figs. 47–50) and of wood (Figs. 61–4).

When, on the other hand, types of formulae are discussed, as they frequently are in the present volume, it is better to do so in terms of Domesday counties and their respective folios; and the maps that now accompany these discussions have therefore been compiled on the basis of Domesday counties, e.g. those showing types of entry for meadow (Fig. 46), pasture (Fig. 51) or wood (Fig. 60). In the same way, any discussion of the idiosyncrasies of information as between one county and another can only be in terms of Domesday counties. Thus there were coscets in the area within the traditional boundary of Hampshire, but none is mentioned in the Hampshire folios because they appear in the folios for the adjacent counties of Dorset and Wiltshire (Fig. 24). In the same way there were cottars in the areas covered by the traditional counties of Bedford, Gloucester, Hampshire and Warwick, but none appears in the Domesday folios for those counties (Fig. 23). Maps showing other categories of population have likewise been compiled in terms of Domesday counties. Idiosyncrasy also enters into the information about ploughlands and their relation to teams (Figs. 38–9), and about churches (Fig. 17) and mills (Figs. 93–5). The fact that all such maps have now been compiled on the basis of Domesday counties is clearly indicated on each.

Given the idiosyncrasies, it follows that the statistical tables in each of the regional volumes would have been more happily presented in terms of Domesday counties. Assessment, for example, rooted as it was in the past, would have been more significant had it been calculated on the basis of the counties of 1066. So far as I am aware, only one reviewer made this specific point.[1] The same applies to ploughlands and so to teams if we are

[1] *Speculum*, XXXIX (1964), 514.

to consider the relation between them. The summary tables that appear as appendices in the present volume are therefore set out in terms of the Domesday counties. The figures do not differ greatly from those based upon modern counties but, clearly, it is more satisfactory to have them on a Domesday basis.

Were we to start all over again, we would probably do so on the basis of Domesday counties. There would certainly be no need for some of those tiresome introductory paragraphs to each county chapter. In suggesting a Domesday basis for treatment, I am thinking of the logic of Domesday Book itself. It is true that a Domesday basis, as we have seen, would not have made much difference either to the maps or text of the regional volumes; but it would have resulted in more appropriate summary tables such as appear in the present volume. It is conceivable that we might have taken these ideas further and attempted a treatment based not on five regional volumes but on seven volumes, each dealing with a separate circuit.

In the sixth, and last, place, a number of reviewers have made reference to the minor changes in presentation that have taken place as volume succeeded volume or reprint succeeded reprint.[1] There certainly have been minor changes en route. The third volume, that for the South-East, treated the statistics for the boroughs somewhat differently from the first two volumes in that the rural element was detached and included within the surrounding density units. A footnote said that 'in the summary volume the density maps for all counties will be calculated on the same basis',[2] but subsequent editions of the first two volumes made it possible to incorporate the changes before waiting until the end of the series. Furthermore, the treatment of 'waste' along the Welsh border in the first edition of 'Midland England' (1954) was altered in the second edition (1971), and has been altered again in this present volume. Moreover, the attempt to estimate the number of places with mills in all five regional volumes was very clumsy, and the method adopted in the present volume is much more sensible.

The appearance of new editions and new reprints has also provided an opportunity for minor rewriting and small alterations, some deriving from the comments of reviewers, but most from our own continual revision and

---

[1] *Geog. Jour.*, CXXIX (1963), 199; *Eng. Hist. Rev.*, LXXXIV (1969), 791–2; *Midland History*, vol. 1, no. 4 (1972), 38; *Geog. Jour.*, CXXXVIII (1972), 366.
[2] *D.G.S–E.E.*, 586.

recalculation. The reidentification of one holding, for example, sometimes involved the making of new blocks for over a dozen maps. Furthermore, as the preface to one new edition said, 'some facts and ideas would probably be presented a little differently today'.[1] Such rewriting had to be kept to a minimum for obvious financial reasons, but, even so, the minor alterations to the second edition of 'Midland England' were such that the text had to be reset and a new index made.

Finally, one reviewer complained that the series was 'unfolding so slowly'.[2] How right he was. It might have unfolded less slowly but for other activities and other books. Had someone told me in 1934 (or even at the fresh start in 1945) that the final volume would not appear until 1977, my heart might well have failed me.

H.C.D.

[1] *D.G.M.E.* (1971), xi.
[2] *Irish Historical Studies*, XIII (1962–3), 277.

INDEX

In the index the county to which a place-name is assigned is the traditional one (i.e. prior to 1974) even though it may appear in the Domesday folios for another county.